MARILYN, HITLER AND ME

MARILYN, HITLER AND ME

THE MEMOIRS OF MILTON SHULMAN

André Deutsch

First published in Great Britain in 1998
This paperback edition first published 1999
André Deutsch Limited
76 Dean Street
W1V 5HA
www.vci.co.uk

A catalogue record for this book is available from the British Library.

ISBN 0 233 99428 9

Typeset by Derek Doyle & Associates, Mold, Flintshire
Printed by WBC Book Manufacturers Limited,
Bridgend, Mid-Glamorgan

1 3 5 7 9 10 8 6 4 2

Front cover photos:
Marilyn © Kobal
Hitler © Popperfoto
Milton Shulman as a child, author's own

For Drusilla, Alexandra, Nicola and Jason

LIST OF ILLUSTRATIONS

CONTENTS

ACKNOWLEDGEMENTS

First of all, I want to thank John Ainsworth-Davis (Christopher Creighton) for having brought me into the world of espionage, intrigue and courage detailed in his book, *OpJB*, and having given his generous support to my version of events, as contained in my chapter about Martin Bormann and Nazi Gold. I also want to express my gratitude to Bridget Winter for her unstinting help in getting things right on the intricate negotiations and machinations that took place over the publication of *OpJB*.

Hannah MacDonald, as my editor, has provided valuable and imaginative advice about the manner in which these memoirs should be presented. A word of thanks, too, to Sir Robin Day who never ceased to encourage me, even though at times my resolve was slacking. Teresa Stokes, who typed and re-typed this book many times, always did so with smiling patience and often corrected grammatical errors and inconsistencies that had escaped me.

Finally a word of repentance to my family who, over the years, have been obliged to listen to many of these anecdotes being told over and over again without ever encouraging me to shut up

A BEGINNING: MARILYN

Bus Stop in Phoenix, Arizona...Marilyn, invalids and cowboys...Lettuce for Princess Grace...Monroe brings out the uncle in me...Applies her lipstick and misses the plane...Keeps Olivier waiting...Marries Miller and unites the Great American Brain with the Great American Body

(i) The icon

If I were asked to choose the icons most likely to be commemorated by posterity as representative of the 20th century my list would be Churchill, Hitler, Freud, John Kennedy, Einstein, Charles Chaplin, Bernard Shaw, Stalin, Lenin, Elvis Presley, the Beatles, Diana, Princess of Wales and Marilyn Monroe. When I interviewed her and wrote a long profile about her in April, 1956, she had just been elevated by the media from a sniggering joke to a national sex symbol. Since then hundreds, perhaps thousands, of books have concerned themselves with her appeal as an eternal image of the American libido.

'So we think of Marilyn who was everyman's love affair with America, Marilyn Monroe who was blonde and beautiful and had a sweet little rinky-dink of a voice and all the cleanliness of all the clean American backyards,' wrote Norman Mailer in his biography *Marilyn*, seven years after I had seen her. 'She was our angel, the sweet angel of sex, and the sugar of sex came up from her like a resonance of sound in the clearest grain of a violin.'

I had something of that impression when I talked to her in Phoenix, Arizona, where they were shooting *Bus Stop*. But that hygienic image has been considerably revised after her death with the torrent of revelations, true and false, about her bizarre marriage to Arthur Miller, America's most intellectual playwright, her reported affairs with Clark Gable, John Kennedy and Robert Kennedy, her connections with the Mafia and her mysterious death from barbiturate poisoning in Los Angeles.

1

The gilt on the portrait of her attractive vulnerability was already beginning to scrape off as the fear of losing her beauty began to plague her and her limited personal resources became clear to those who had to work with her. In Maurice Zolotow's biography there is an anecdote which has made every book of quotations about Hollywood.

> One evening, some of the cast of *Some Like It Hot* – though not Monroe – were watching the rushes of the yacht sequence in that film. Tony Curtis is posing as a rich man's son who suffers from a frigid libido. Girls cannot excite him. Monroe decides to cure him of his ailment by kissing him and making love to him. On the fifth kiss, the treatment succeeds admirably.
>
> In the darkness of the viewing theatre, someone said to Curtis, 'You seemed to enjoy kissing Marilyn.' And he said loudly 'It's like kissing Hitler.'

Had she lived on to middle or old age, it is likely that she would have been remembered only as a once-adored sex symbol, joining that pantheon of beauties like Pola Negri, Jean Harlow, Jane Russell, Ava Gardner, Betty Grable, Audrey Hepburn and Ginger Rogers whose faces made little or no dent on social history. But Marilyn's fame has been different. Death has lifted her from the mundane to the monumental. Tragedy has enhanced her popularity. She has become the material of fable and the essence of myth. It may well be that mine was one of the earliest attempts at providing an in-depth assessment of this surprising phenomenon. I had taken on the job of film critic of the *Sunday Express* in 1955, two years after I had given it up on the *Standard*. It was for the *Sunday Express*, which ran the profile in four consecutive weeks, that I produced this very early portrait of Marilyn Monroe's career to date. In 1956 I spent six weeks trailing around after her, trying to understand the impact she made before she became truly famous. This is the account, marginally edited, as I wrote it.

★ ★ ★

It was a hot day in Phoenix. The publicity man for Twentieth Century Fox, Roy Craft, stripped to the waist, bent confidentially over the telephone he was cuddling in both hands. He nodded to me to sit down.

'We'd be plumb delighted to have Marilyn photographed with the governor and the little girl,' he was saying. 'If he could come round before the parade – either on or off his horse – we could take them in front of the cameras. I know Marilyn would just love to have her picture taken with that sick child – so long as it doesn't interfere with the shooting – understand. And, honey, we're only too happy to do anything for the Governor of Arizona.' Roy Craft hung up, shook my hand and introduced me to three cowboys, two photographers, an assistant press agent, and a man in a blue suit. The small hotel room was rather crowded.

I had just flown into Phoenix where the first day's shooting of her new picture, *Bus Stop*, was to take place against a background of a mammoth parade and a 'world championship' rodeo organized by the city's Chamber of Commerce. It would be the first time she had appeared in front of the cameras since her walkout from Twentieth Century Fox almost a year and a half ago. The atmosphere was anxious.

'That was the governor's secretary,' said Craft, the press agent, letting us all in on the telephone conversation. 'There's one of Marilyn's fans – a little girl – who has just had a serious operation. She is still in a state of deep depression and her doctor thinks that meeting Marilyn might snap her out of it. The girl's father is a friend of the Governor of Arizona and the governor's office wants to know if we can take a picture of the governor and the girl with Marilyn. He's leading the parade on a horse tomorrow so I'm trying to arrange it before we start moving. The little girl is driving up specially from Louisiana just for this. Amazing the effect Marilyn has on people! Ought to be good for the picture, too.'

The telephone rang again. It was a reporter on a local newspaper. The three cowboys stood up, mumbled some thanks for the drinks and slouched out. 'Not real cowboys,' said the assistant press agent when they'd gone. 'Just Chamber of Commerce boys dressed up to give the town some colour.'

'Yes, we've spoken to Marilyn about that matter,' said Craft on the telephone, 'and she assured us that the police escort seemed to be going at a normal, safe speed. She doesn't think they could have been travelling at fifty-five miles an hour and she didn't see them go through any red lights. And she hopes no one gets into any trouble over it.'

The press agent hung up with a wry smile and shrugged his shoulders. 'That girl doesn't need anybody to get her publicity. It just happens to her,' he said.

'Now I don't know much about what's been going on around here,' said the tall man in the blue suit, standing up and looming over Craft's desk. He had been silently nursing a Bourbon and soda in a corner, 'but do you think there's any chance of getting Marilyn's cooperation for my proposition?'

'Well, I'm sorry, Mr Anderson,' began the press agent.

'*Morrison*,' said the man in the blue suit.

'Mr Morrison,' said the press agent, 'but as you see we've been in a kind of hassle around here today and it's slipped my mind. Now could you brief me on it again?'

'It's an idea for publicizing lettuce,' said Morrison. 'I represent the lettuce growers of Arizona and that's pretty big business. You ought to meet some of these lettuce kings. Why, Texas oil millionaires and film magnates have got nothing on them. Now I admit I don't know much about film stars and how you can tie lettuce up with them, but I thought it would be a good stunt if we could have Marilyn Monroe sponsor a crate of lettuce to be sent to Grace Kelly on her coming wedding day. All Marilyn would have to do is have her photograph taken with the crate of lettuce and two important lettuce growers. We'd look after sending the lettuce and everything else. I frankly don't know what Grace Kelly would do with the lettuce. Probably dump it into the Mediterranean. But we just want the public to realize the size and importance of the lettuce business.'

The press agent looked doubtful.

'Well, it may be alright for the lettuce growers and Grace Kelly, but what good will it do Marilyn?' he said. 'You see we can't have the public thinking Marilyn sent Grace a crate of lettuce for a wedding present. That's a pretty small gift for a girl in her position.'

'Oh, we can fix that all right,' replied Mr Morrison, eagerly. 'We can fly a whole airplane like a DC9 full of lettuce to Monaco, if you like. No one's worrying about the cost.'

The press agent still looked doubtful. When I left the room some fifteen minutes later they were still discussing it. The lettuce man seemed to be losing.

Why, then, is there this urge on the part of governors and lettuce growers and teenage fans to bask in the reflected aura of Marilyn Monroe's personality? What had made her the actress most likely to bring joy to cinema box-offices?

The most obvious explanation is that each generation must have its Dream Girl with measurements – 37-23-34 – that are more an incantation than statistics. In this particular artistic category Hollywood abhors a vacuum. Whenever a reigning Venus shows signs of losing her crown to Time, there is always a fresh, well-upholstered, built-in model with the latest gadgets, to take her place.

But Monroe has been around for a relatively long time. She has been America's most popular daydream for over four years. And on 1 June of this year, she will be thirty years old. At my first of several interviews with Marilyn, I reminded her of this fact. To reach her it had required negotiations lasting seven days with no less than nine intermediaries who claimed some responsibility for her press relations. She greeted me as if she were surprised I hadn't turned up sooner.

'I am really looking forward to my thirtieth birthday,' she said, sitting on her knees in a blue dressing gown beside me on a sofa. To my astonishment my only reaction to her proximity was a paternal desire to pat her on the head. I decided she must bring out the uncle in me.

'I would love to play old women,' she continued. 'Not just middle-aged women, but really old ones.'

It would be easy to discount a statement like this as one shrewdly designed to shock some easy copy out of a gullible journalist. But there is a guileless sincerity about everything she says which makes you believe she means it.

I have interviewed almost forty people who have known Marilyn Monroe more or less intimately. They have agreed on only two facts about her. None of them has ever really understood her, and none of them has ever known her to tell a deliberate lie. If she is asked a question that is either too difficult or too embarrassing for her to answer, she will skilfully evade it or tell you politely that she prefers not to answer it.

Her enthusiasm, then, for advancing age is less baffling when one fits it into the pattern of her recent behaviour. She rebelled against Hollywood because she refused to be typed as an erotic symbol. 'They wanted to put me in a picture called *Pink Tights*. After that why not *Green Tights, Blue Tights, Red Tights*?' she said. 'I'd rather work in a factory than go on doing that.'

Her flight from Hollywood to New York ended in her doing exactly what she said she would do and what no one expected she would do. She began to study acting seriously. Her partnership with Sir Laurence Olivier in *The Sleeping Prince* is a direct result of that decision. Yet Monroe was already one of the few fixed and firm stars in the nebulous Hollywood firmament before she developed more serious aspirations.

What had put her there? In my opinion Marilyn has brought something individual and unique to the imposing matter of sex. Mary Pickford made sex innocent. Theda Bara made it exotic. Dietrich made it remote. Garbo made it ethereal. Crawford made it agonizing, and Marilyn made it wholesome and fun.

There is something about that cherubic personality with a soul that looks as if it must be hygienically wrapped, that is at constant war with the suggestions of her metronome hips. The incongruity is hilarious. Watching Monroe, a man is forced to grin at his own imagination. 'She has taken the guilt out of sex and made it delicious,' said George Axelrod, who wrote *The Seven Year Itch*. Pondering the problem of Marilyn's appeal, Billy Wilder, the director of *The Seven Year Itch*, described her as 'the last of the surviving magnets'.

'She has never made a good picture, including mine,' said Wilder, 'yet she is this phenomenal success. She walks about wiggling this Taj Mahal of a body, oblivious to anyone watching her. Even women don't resent her. Perhaps her secret is that when the common man looks at Monroe he thinks he'd have a chance.'

Yet beneath the façade of fresh naivety there is in Marilyn Monroe a hard core of determination and calculation. Knowing what the public wants of her she tries not to let them down. To every journalist she presents a stare of disarming, wide-eyed charm. She will cuddle up close on a sofa dressed in a dressing gown or a tight sweater that does nothing to obscure her reputation. She is particularly sure of herself when facing photographers. She is meticulously aware of every disciplined eyelash, every strand of blonde hair waiting for orders.

'It's true that you can't take a bad picture of her,' said a photographer who had worked with her often. 'But it's quite difficult to take a good one. And Marilyn knows it. She has a bump on the end of her nose which discourages profile shots. When she is unhappy she tends to get fat. When her marriage to Joe di Maggio was breaking up she got so fat I felt that if we stuck an apple in her mouth she could be served up on a platter.'

I saw Marilyn being photographed with Buddy Adler, who had just been appointed executive producer of Twentieth Century Fox in place of Darryl Zanuck. In a way they were peace-pipe smoking with photographs marking the end of their long, contractual feud. As the camera clicked, Marilyn glided in and out of studied poses with the rhythm of a ballet dancer. Almost instinctively her mouth opened like a surprised goldfish, her lips softened with moisture, her body tensed gracefully, exactly as the shutters snapped. Once she noticed out of the corner of her eye that one of the photographers had his camera at an unsatisfactory angle. She abandoned her pose, moved up to him and pulled his camera down. 'Jim,' she said, 'you'll have us both looking like monsters.'

But this assurance deserts her in most other realms of her life. She is fundamentally insecure and frightened. She is forever seeking self-justification. Trying to seek out these fears is like going down a dark tunnel at the end of which is a locked door without a keyhole.

There could be few American children who began life as unfortunately and unhappily as Marilyn Monroe. Born Norma Jean Mortenson in Los Angeles in 1926, she never knew her father, a baker called Edward Mortenson. Her mother, a film cutter, was placed in a State institution when she was an infant. These facts of her early life had been covered up by a press agent, who felt that it would be wise for a promising starlet to have a more respectable background.

Nothing was said about her real name and she continued to use the name of Norma Jean Baker – her mother's name by a previous marriage – which she had used since childhood. It was agreed to have the father reported as killed in a motor car accident – no one seems to know what actually happened to him – and to describe Marilyn's childhood as having been spent in foster homes and an orphanage. Early accounts of Marilyn's life naturally drew the deduction that her mother was dead. But a few years ago a journalist revealed that Marilyn's mother was still alive. Marilyn's subsequent admission that this was true was a most humbling and humiliating experience for her.

'My motive was one of consideration for a person who had suffered much, and for whom I feel a great obligation,' she said.

Today she is far less reticent about discussing her family beginnings. We had been talking about some possible role she might do on the stage when I mentioned the name of Suzanne Valodon, a fascinating and beautiful artist and model who was the mother of the famous artist, Utrillo.

'He was her illegitimate son, you know,' I said.

'Oh, that's very interesting,' said Marilyn. 'I'm illegitimate, too. They're very narrow-minded about that kind of thing in America, but I know they won't mind so much in England.'

Getting to Phoenix, Arizona, from Los Angeles involved the sort of erratic adventure that almost always took place whenever she travelled anywhere. 'Marilyn insists on doing the packing herself,' her personal publicity girl told me. 'It's the only way she knows where everything is. She'll have to be up at five in the morning to catch a plane at seven. And you know how Marilyn is about time. But tomorrow she just must get that plane because there's a band and city officials and hundreds of cowboys and Indians from the rodeo waiting to meet her.'

Yet in spite of an evening of packing – she was only to be away a week – and in spite of the waiting reception committee and the band and the hundreds of expectant fans at the Phoenix airport, Marilyn missed the plane. The manner in which she missed it provides a revealing clue to the basic Monroe.

When the studio chauffeur arrived at 8.30 in the morning, Marilyn was still in her dressing gown. Most of the bags were not yet packed. Eventually, but with not much time to spare, the luggage was placed in a station wagon which was also to carry some of Marilyn's retinue. These days she is attended by enough people to make up a small-size gypsy camp. They include the vice-president of Monroe Incorporated, Mr Milton Greene, his wife, a personal publicity girl, Mr Greene's assistant, a dramatic coach, a hairdresser, a make-up man, a body make-up girl (for things below the neck) and two maids.

The minutes ticked by but no Monroe. Suddenly out came the maid in a flurry. A pair of slippers had to be found. The bags were hastily unpacked and re-packed. A few minutes later the maid came out again. This time it was some jewellery. Bags unpacked and packed again. A third time the maid came out. Now it was dark glasses she was after. Again the bags were opened, ransacked and closed.

'When Monroe was finally ready to leave,' the chauffeur said to me, 'we had fifteen minutes to reach the airport about ten miles away. I really hit it and when we got there the plane was still waiting to take off. Everyone leaped out. But not Monroe. She calmly opened her handbag, took out a mirror and began putting on lipstick. By the time she'd finished the plane had left. I have driven them all – big ones and little ones – but I have never seen anything like it in fifteen years.'

And while Twentieth Century Fox representatives made frenzied efforts to book a passage on another plane, Marilyn surveyed the panic with a calm, baby-like incomprehension. To anyone who has known Marilyn there is nothing untoward about this incident. For her time does not merely stand still, it is paralytic. Her life is cluttered with the debris of broken appointments. She has been late for everyone from Darryl Zanuck to Laurence Olivier.

Norma Jean Baker

Nor is this the temperamental gimmick of someone who now feels important enough to keep the world waiting. She is too aware of her own limitations to be a prima donna. Being late has become an unconscious response to almost every crisis or turning point in her career. 'She acted like a star when she was a nobody,' said an early friend, trying to explain it. As an ambitious and relatively unknown starlet, America's most important picture magazine sent along their best photographer to take her picture for their cover. She kept him waiting three hours. 'Most girls would have been there at dawn,' said the studio press agent.

Sir Laurence Olivier had a taste of Monroe tardiness when he arranged to meet her for the first time in New York to conclude negotiations for the filming of Terence Rattigan's play, *The Sleeping Prince*★. Monroe and Olivier were its co-producers. The fact that Olivier had come all the way from London just to meet her did not stimulate her into being on time. There was an appointment for noon and it was postponed by Marilyn until six in the evening.

At six sharp Sir Laurence, Terence Rattigan, Milton Greene and Jay Kanter, her agent, assembled in her flat and began to wait for Marilyn. She was in her bedroom getting ready. Sir Laurence was anxious that the meeting be prompt since he had put through a call to Vivien Leigh which was scheduled to reach him at six-thirty. At six-thirty Marilyn had still not emerged and arrangements had to be made to have Olivier's call transferred.

In spite of numerous anxious comings and goings on the part of Messrs Greene and Kanter, who kept issuing periodic bulletins on the state of her sartorial progress, it was not until seven o'clock that she finally appeared. She was wearing the simplest of dresses and apparently no make-up.

'I didn't know what to wear,' explained Marilyn when I asked her why she had been so late. 'Should I be casual or formal? Everything I put on wasn't kinda right. But Larry was very gracious about it. He kissed my hand and said: "You can keep me waiting as long as you like but don't do it to the British Press."'

But it is obvious that this concern about her clothes is merely an excuse for something deeper and more complicated in her personality. 'She knows about clothes and feels secure thinking about them,' said a costume designer. 'She uses them to put off facing things she is less sure about.'

★ The name of the film was changed to *The Prince and the Showgirl*

Marilyn herself supports this explanation. 'My social and personal life is still sort of a mess,' she said, puckering up her brow in an effort to work it all out. 'In my professional life being late is a desire not to be there and it's a desire that has something to do with my fears. But it's a habit pattern I'm determined to overcome.' Words like 'habit pattern' always sound strange coming from Monroe.

Another symptom of her uncertainty is the frequency with which she is attacked by viruses, has headaches, runs a high temperature. 'If anything went wrong on the set,' said the director Billy Wilder, 'she would go off and be ill for fifteen minutes.'

Yet coupled with a natural shyness is a real desire to be noticed and admired. She will wear clinging and obvious clothes that provoke every camera lens within miles into action and yet be genuinely annoyed when surrounded by amateur photographers. 'She is the shy exhibitionist,' said Terence Rattigan. 'The Garbo who likes to be photographed.'

(ii) The calendar

Monroe's contradictions and hidden fears have been troublesome enough to cause her to seek psychiatric advice. Her course of treatment has had an erratic history because she was usually *too late for the psychiatrist*. But to a well-known psychiatrist with whom I discussed Marilyn, her problems were quite straightforward. 'She would seem to be a typical hysteroid personality,' he said. 'Hysteroids crave to be loved, but, unfortunately, there is never enough love in the world to satisfy them.'

If lack of love and affection creates hysteroids then Marilyn's early youth was certainly an ideal incubator for her personality. Her childhood was spent in a series of private homes as a ward of Los Angeles county. The foster parents were paid $5 a month to keep her. Between 1925 and 1935 she lived in eleven of these homes. Not until she was sixteen did she know that her mother was still alive.

Shifted from environment to environment, Marilyn grew into a frightened, stammering, fantasy-ridden child. One family would be extremely religious warning her that dancing and films were the 'work of the devil'; another was a family of British actors – the father was a stand-in for George Arliss – who gave her lessons in juggling Indian clubs and doing a hula dance; another gave her whisky bottles to play with as dolls.

At nine she was sent to a Los Angeles orphanage for a year and a half, where her reports described her as 'normal, bright, sunshiny'. Not until she was eleven and sent to the home of a Mrs Anna Lower did Marilyn meet anyone she felt had ever loved her. Only then did she begin to emerge from the tight shell of daydreams into which she had withdrawn. But Mrs Lower was ill and there were two more homes that she was to live in before she was fifteen. It was then that the family with which she was living announced that they were going East and could not take her with them.

At the time she was seeing a good deal of a young aircraft worker called Jim Dougherty. The prospect of moving into another strange home terrified her. Impulsively, although she was only fifteen, she married him when he asked her.

'I wasn't in love with him,' Marilyn explained to me. 'That was the last thing I had in mind. But he was very kind and I didn't want to go into another home. And I was astonished and flattered at being asked.'

It was 1942 and Dougherty soon went off to join the Merchant Marine. Marilyn went to work for an airplane company as a waterproof-paint sprayer. Their immaturity and separation soon killed their marriage. But it was not until 1946 that they were finally divorced. Dougherty married again, became a father and joined the Los Angeles Vice Squad after the war.

To get pictures boosting the war effort in 1944, an army photographer had taken some photographs of Marilyn in a sweater operating a spray-gun. One look at the results and he was enthusiastically encouraging her to take up modelling.

She turned up at the Blue Angel modelling school in 1945. The vital statistics on her application card recorded the fact that she was then 5 foot 6 inches tall, weighed 118 lb, bust 36 inches, waist 24 inches, hips 34 inches, eyes blue, hair medium blonde.

'She hadn't enough money to pay for the course,' said the owner of the school, 'so I paid for it and she paid me back later. The first thing we tried to change was the horrible wiggle. It wasn't good for fashion models but it was Marilyn and we couldn't change it. She suffered from hyper-extension of the knee – in other words she was double-jointed – which made it impossible for us to teach her a graceful fashion model's walk. She also had unmanageable hair and her legs weren't very good. We advised her to give up fashion modelling and concentrate on photo modelling.'

Her picture on a number of magazine covers soon attracted the attention of talent scouts. She was taken the round of the studios. At

Paramount they decided she was not photogenic. Howard Hughes of RKO wanted to give her a screen test but before it could be arranged she had been introduced to Ben Lyon, then the talent scout at Twentieth Century Fox. 'She impressed me with her youth, beauty, charm and ambition,' recalls Lyon. 'I signed her even before we took a test of her. She was given a seven-year option contract, starting at 75 dollars a week.'

It was Lyon who decided that her maiden name, Norma Jean Baker, not her married name Dougherty, would do for an aspiring starlet. But later when he discovered that her mother's maiden name was Monroe, and thinking that she had some of the qualities of the movie star, Marilyn Miller, he proceeded to christen her Marilyn Monroe. Marilyn has never been particularly pleased with the name.

A year and a half later her contract was dropped. She had been given a tiny part in a film *Scudda Hoo, Scudda Hay* and it ended up on the cutting-room floor. Columbia then signed her for the part of a burlesque queen and she was again dropped. Now life had become grim. Determined to become an actress she had started to take dramatic lessons which were costing her ten dollars a time. At the Studio Club where she was living in a small room, she was behind in her rent. By eating only two meals a day, she tried to eke out a livelihood by her modelling.

But finally the pinch became too tight. Her car had been seized for back payments and she was four weeks behind in her rent and threatened with eviction. The day she got her eviction order, she phoned the wife of a photographer, Tom Kelly, who had once before asked her to pose in the nude for a calendar.

'They assured me no one would know my name or recognize me,' she said. 'I was told I would get 50 dollars for the pose. With Natalie Kelly in the room I let her husband take the pictures. I also signed a release giving him all rights to them.'

It is not easy to recognize Monroe in these pictures. With her face half-sheltered behind her arm and her long hair falling to her shoulders, the photographs might have remained in decent obscurity had it not been for the sharp eye of the secretary of a Chicago business man. Mr John Baumgarth then produced some 25,000,000 calendars a year – usually displaying cosy landscapes and cuddly children.

'I had paid Kelly 500 dollars to use the photograph as I saw fit and to use the name of the model,' said Baumgarth. 'I'd only printed a few of those calendars and had even forgotten the girl's name when one day my secretary shoved the calendar under my nose and said, "Know who that is? It's Marilyn Monroe." "You're crazy," I answered, but it was.'

The discovery was made three years after the photograph had been taken and just when Marilyn had achieved her first important success in *The Asphalt Jungle*. Over 8,000,000 calendars were sold in the early 1950s and the photograph has been reproduced on everything from ashtrays to playing cards. Mr Baumgarth realized about half a million dollars on his investment.

The lowest ebb in her career had been when poverty had forced her to pose in the nude. There had been bit parts which saw her on and off the screen like a mirage, but occasionally talent scouts would see them and offer her some work. In 1949 she could be glimpsed in the Marx Brothers' worst film, *Love Happy*, when she provocatively saunters in the office of Groucho Marx, playing a private detective. She is wearing a skin-tight silver lamé evening gown that converts every curve into a promise.

'I need your help,' she whispers, apprehensively.

'What can I do?' asks Groucho.

Marilyn turns on her heel and, lusciously hip-wiggling herself out of the door, replies: 'Men keep following me.'

The scene lasted about a minute and it was her most important role after almost three years of frustrating efforts to break into films. It was in 1949, she was twenty-three, and she had been shown the door more often than an ugly vacuum cleaner salesman. 'In those days everybody turned her down,' said her first agent, Harry Lipton. 'They wouldn't even have her as a dumb blonde stooge in an Abbott and Costello comedy. Her most important break came when a talent scout at MGM recommended her to John Huston for the part of a gangster's moll in *The Asphalt Jungle*.'

When she loomed up on the screen in clinging one-piece lounging pyjamas, preview audiences were reduced to long low whistles. Joseph Mankiewicz decided she was just what he wanted for a vacant blonde in *All About Eve*. As soon as Darryl Zanuck, head of Twentieth Century Fox, saw her in *All About Eve*, he ordered his henchmen to put her under contract. 'But, boss,' they protested. 'We had her under contract for eighteen months and dropped her.' 'I don't care,' said Zanuck. 'Bring her back.' She was given a seven-year contract at 500 dollars a week with options up to 3,500 dollars.

About all that can be said for the films she was called upon to make under her new contract – *As Young As You Feel*, *Let's Make It Legal*, and *Love Nest* – was that they kept her from being hungry. But if her studio showed no particular enthusiasm for her acting ability, they certainly had no qualms about exploiting her more obvious talents. She was photographed with everything from chimpanzees to flame-throwers. Millions of GIs from Berlin to Korea pinned her on their walls. She was voted Miss Cheesecake of 1951, The Woman Most Sailors Dream About, The Girl Most Likely To Thaw Out Alaska. But her career was stuck fast in the quicksand of bit parts and bad pictures.

Then one day in 1952 the news broke that propelled Marilyn Monroe from relative obscurity to stardom. It was reported she had posed for a nude calendar. Conscious of the Morality Codes and the Legions of Decency, her employers at first urged her to deny it. But Marilyn insisted on being honest about it.

'The calendar is hanging in garages and barber shops all over town,' she told the press. 'Why deny it? And, anyway, I'm not ashamed of it. I've done nothing wrong. I posed for it three years ago when I was broke and needed the money.'

To everyone's astonishment, the nation was delighted by her explanation. Americans can never get self-righteous about hunger. Her fan mail shot up to 3,000 and then to 5,000 letters a week. Not since Lady Godiva has nudity produced such a heroine. Twentieth Century Fox were quick to recognize the potency of the new interest in Monroe. They hustled her into lavish productions like *Niagara* and *Gentlemen Prefer Blondes* with all publicity sirens screaming. By the end of 1953, only a year later, she was drawing more money into cinemas than any actress in Hollywood – more than Doris Day, Ava Gardner or Rita Hayworth.

The studio press agents soon learned that the best way to get Marilyn into the papers was to stand aside and let her be herself. She was constantly baffling and delighting journalists with such pointedly witty comments that it was assumed they were manufactured for her by some sharp publicity man.

Asked what she wore in bed, she answered: 'Chanel No. 5.' Asked on a radio programme what she thought of sex, she said: 'I never give it a second thought.' Asked by a Japanese journalist – it was a Transpacific long distance call conducted through an interpreter – who taught her that walk, she replied: 'I learned it when I was eleven months and I have never had a lesson since.'

Marilyn herself is not sure just how seriously she wants these remarks to be taken when she makes them. 'There is always a stupid sincerity about them,' she told me, 'even when they sound ridiculous.'

Roy Craft, who looked after her publicity for six years at Twentieth Century Fox, is often credited with the authorship of many of these *bon mots*. He vehemently denies responsibility and can describe in great detail the accidental circumstances under which most of them were made.

When interviewing Marilyn we were periodically interrupted in her hotel suite in Phoenix by a telephone call from New York. She would leave me, sometimes for almost an hour. I was genuinely taken aback when I learnt that this dedicated caller was Arthur Miller, America's most distinguished playwright. What in the world did this badly educated, not particularly articulate sex symbol have to talk about for so long so often with America's most intellectual liberal dramatist? Yet at that time Marilyn's image was being converted from that of the girl-there-was-no-reason-to-talk-to, to that of the intellectual's crumpet. The media transformation was taking place because Marilyn herself was in awe of well-read personalities with a reputation for cleverness and because of the influence of Lee Strasberg, the New York guru of the Stanislavski Method school of acting, whose theories were being treated by actors like John Garfield and Marlon Brando with the reverence accorded the Ten Commandments.

During the filming of *Bus Stop* her every histrionic action was coached and monitored by Paula, a former actress who was Lee Strasberg's wife. Every line of dialogue was rehearsed and analyzed by Paula and Marilyn together as if they were uncovering the secrets of the Dead Sea Scrolls. A number of times my appointment with Marilyn was cancelled because she was having difficulty coping with her next day's lines. When I turned up to watch her, I found she had only one or two lines of dialogue to manage and needed an inordinate number of takes to get them right.

Yet the Strasbergs were pushing Marilyn to go on the stage when her memory for lines was as porous as a colander and it would be a miracle if she could ever get fifteen minutes of consecutive words in order in a role. It was true that Marilyn had done a short scene from Eugene O'Neill's *Anna Christie* before an audience of actors at Strasberg's studio. The Strasbergs went into the stratosphere of hyperboles about these bitty exercises with Lee actually saying, 'after Marlon Brando she has the greatest talent I have ever come across.'

A more objective assessment of her abilities came from a man who worked with her who told me: 'You can't get an idea across to her. Talking to her is like talking to someone underwater. She reminds me of a sloth. You stick a pin into a sloth's belly and eight days later it says "Ouch!"' Nothing I saw of Marilyn in the days I saw her performing in *Bus Stop* came remotely close to justifying the rapturous predictions that one day she would make a triumphant Lady Macbeth.

As a film critic I later reviewed her performance for the *Sunday Express*: 'Keeping her lips constantly open like a goldfish with a stutter, Marilyn's only new histrionic feat in this picture is the acquisition of a molasses-thick Southern accent. No other serious demands are made on her talent.'

But Marilyn's reverence for the intellectual aura surrounding Arthur Miller, and her eventual marriage to him, have roots that were dug in her psyche long before the Strasbergs came into her life. Their motivations were probably two-fold: to prove her body was not just a titter machine and to attract interesting and important men.

For some perverse reason, culture has always been one of Hollywood's favourite publicity gimmicks. Every starlet's career is launched on waves of cheesecake and Chekhov; every luscious lap must be photographed decorated with a copy of Proust or Schopenhauer.

Probably to compensate for a body that so obviously makes a fool of the mind, this highbrow aura has been particularly thick in the vicinity of Marilyn Monroe. She has been variously reported as being a passionate disciple of Albert Schweitzer, Tolstoy and Emerson; having a schoolgirl crush on Abraham Lincoln; brushing her teeth to the demanding chords of Bela Bartok; possessing well-thumbed volumes of Whitman, Rilke and Dostoyevsky, and reading no fewer than four books a week.

There is, however, a school of opinion that hoots with derision at these extravagant claims. An important executive producer revealed this scepticism when he told me, 'some of the local intellectuals had her around for laughs. I guarantee she's never finished a book in her life.'

The truth seems to be that Monroe is neither a highbrow nor a dumb blonde. In her desperate groping for self-justification she has recognized culture as a badge of achievement. She picks up names and ideas indiscriminately, like some amateur collector, and stores them away into some mental rag-bag for her own future wonder. They pop out unexpectedly and sometimes with hilarious results. In her early twenties she suddenly became aware of her limitations. 'I was terribly dumb,' she said to me. 'I didn't know anything about painting, music, books, history.' In 1950 she started to take night classes in English Literature at the University of Southern California. 'Marilyn was so modest, so humble that she could have just come from a convent,' was the assessment of her teacher.

Her cultural passion is likely to express itself in diverting ways. In her New York flat she proudly displayed two contrasting pictures – one of Albert Einstein and one of herself. They were both rear-view photographs showing the backs of Einstein and Monroe walking towards some distant horizon and, in an odd sort of way, they both possessed that same distinctive wiggle of a walk.

She is not particularly articulate about her cultural experiences and her critical assessments are hardly orthodox. Dostoyevsky's tortured metaphysical classic *The Brothers Karamazov* she describes as a 'sex story'. Her interest in art takes the form of periodic 'crushes' on great painters. 'I was in love with Michelangelo,' she told me, 'but then everybody is.' Then there was an El Greco phase. At the moment she has a passion for Goya. 'I know just the monsters he paints,' she explained. 'I see them all the time. And if Goya sees them too, I know I'm not out of my mind.'

To trace back the sources of her intellectual interests is to almost chart a complete inventory of the people who have influenced her life. Shy and unsure of herself, she has clutched with desperate devotion to anyone she could respect and who offered her friendship. She has had more Svengalis than an entire season of Trilbys.

Marilyn's attitude to men has been a blend of naivety and calculation. She is an Ophelia who knows that everyone thinks she's Cleopatra. And she encourages the illusion. She seems to be oblivious to the effect produced by a plunging neckline or a skin-tight dress, but she will spend hours organizing it. 'Sex is part of nature,' she once said. 'I'd rather go along with nature.'

When she first began to make pictures she would often ask a friend of hers for advice about how to handle men. 'She would phone me about how to rebuff some man who had just made some advances to her,' said the friend, 'and the man would be sitting in the next room while she was talking to me.'

The men who have been associated with Monroe – some romantically, most paternally – have little in common. They include, among others, a pianist, an actor's agent, a politician, a famous film executive, a film director, a journalist, a playwright and a baseball player. Most of these men have been much older than Marilyn and she seems to have needed them to compensate for the father she never had.

At the very nadir of her career – she had been told by every major studio that she was not needed – she fell deeply in love with a musician. To him can be traced her first interest in serious music. She became aware of her passion for him when she saw him put on glasses to look at some music. 'I don't know why, but I have always been attracted to men who wore glasses,' she said. 'When he put them on, I was overwhelmed.'

Her next romance was with Johnny Hyde, one of the most important agents in Hollywood. He was a tiny figure of a man – hardly more than five feet – who was in his late fifties. Monroe makes no secret about her feelings for Hyde.

'He really believed in me at a time when, I swear, not one living soul in the world did,' she told me. But she would not marry Hyde even though he desperately wanted her to. He was suffering from a serious heart condition and he knew he had little time to live. He was a millionaire, he used to argue with her, and she would have his money when he died.

'Although I love you very dearly, I'm not in love with you,' she told Hyde. 'Tomorrow I might meet somebody else, and it wouldn't be fair to you.' They broke up, and Hyde died shortly afterwards.

With so much exposure to the surface of culture but not very much in depth, Marilyn seems to have acquired the qualities of a good listener. That is why those telephone conversations could last for almost an hour. Arthur Miller at that time needed a sympathetic listener. He was the most prominent scapegoat of the un-American Congressional Committee, his plays were being picketed by the America Legion and for refusing to testify about his left-wing connections he had become, in some sections of the press, a media pariah. And, no doubt a topic of absorbing mutual interest, was the fact that Miller was then going through the arrangements for divorcing his wife in Reno.

(ii) The final years
What happened to Monroe after my portrait of her appeared in the *Sunday Express* converted her into the most written-about entertainment personality in the world. The fears and anxieties I witnessed

haunted her all her life. The details of her final years are easily summarized.

Arthur Miller got his divorce; nevertheless I was certainly taken aback when I learnt a few months later that he and Marilyn had actually married. The Great American Brain united with the Great American Body was the news event of the year. To prove her sincerity for her new role Marilyn took instructions in the Jewish faith and adopted that religion. It was reported that she was even learning how to be a Jewess in the kitchen, and was becoming adept at preparing such kosher dishes as gefilte fish, borscht, chopped liver and chicken soup with matzo balls.

It was, of course, a doomed enterprise from the start. When a sex symbol of this stature weds a political scapegoat of this prominence, the resultant hail of red herrings was inevitable. Monroe photographed reading Spinoza in a bubble-bath was the kind of intellectual activity expected of dumb blondes. It was good for laughs and helped sell pictures. But Monroe marrying a man who can actually quote Spinoza was carrying the joke too far.

The subsequent events that ended the marriage were predictable and inevitable. An uneasy relationship developed between Arthur Miller and Milton Greene, a thirty-four-year-old photographer who ran her business affairs and was vice-president of Marilyn Monroe Productions Incorporated. On a set, he could be found crouched by the cameras taking his own photographs; on the telephone, his was likely to be the voice telling you that Marilyn was too busy to see you; at interviews, he was the figure in the corner listening to it all and pouring drinks. He had surrounded Marilyn with minions as if she were the centre of a dark conspiracy. Getting an interview was recognized as one of the most difficult feats in journalism. I asked Greene which of his talents he felt equipped him for being the Napoleon of the Monroe Empire. 'I got intelligence and taste,' he said to me, 'and you can't buy that in a candy store.'

Miller's efforts to penetrate this protected Monroe world with his own taste and business acumen resulted in much aggravation and dissention. Her disastrous relationship with Laurence Olivier and Terence Rattigan while making *The Prince and the Showgirl*, the crumbling of the marriage during *Some Like It Hot* and its final disintegration while *The Misfits* was being made, was the fodder of gossip columns throughout the Western world. Her liaison with the President of the United States and his brother, Robert Kennedy, culminating in her sordid death through deliberately taking an overdose or accidentally taking one, or by being murdered by the Mafia have kept publishing houses busy ever since 1962. What you believe depends on which one of these many books have convinced you of their truth.

Back in 1956 as I waited in her hotel suite in Phoenix while she chatted away out of earshot to Arthur Miller, I often reflected on the bizarre accidents that propelled an insignificant lawyer from Toronto in a few short years to a position where he was sitting on a sofa close to, and being treated as a confidant, by America's most popular and enticing sex object. I realize, in retrospect, that all this sounds star-struck. If so, I accept that I must have been hypnotized, as so many millions still are, by such close proximity to her. But, I kept asking myself, what was I really doing there?

1

OH CANADA

In which I laugh as I grow... Have a narrow escape in an electric car... Name a good many famous Canadians... See my name in print... Have my first encounter with girls... Write short stories, spy on window cleaners and croon Sweet Sue... Am called to the Bar

(i) Me

The only thing I can clearly remember about being young is laughing. I have a photograph of myself at four dressed from puttees to bandolier to cap at a jaunty angle, carrying a wooden rifle like a Canadian infantryman. I am grinning, I hope, at the sight of myself. Every school photograph of thirty to forty children has me standing out like a lighthouse because of the flashing smile on my face. I still recall my ecstatic delight seeing Charlie Chaplin in *Shoulder Arms* as a floating candle passes him in a water-filled trench. The Marx Brothers in *Animal Crackers* plunged me into such apoplectic laughter that I literally toppled over into the aisle. As an adolescent in Toronto I swapped jokes and gags with Johnnie Wayne and Frank Shuster at Moscowitz's delicatessen until midnight, stretching out a corned beef sandwich on rye and a Coke to last until the tolerant boss turfed us out. Wayne and Shuster eventually became Canada's most popular comic team, with TV shows transmitted in America and Britain. At the University of Toronto my most distinguished contribution to the daily college paper, the *Varsity*, was a fortnightly column in which I dragged famous people like President Roosevelt and Eugene O'Neill through imaginary interviews stuffed with atrocious puns.

I realize that the dominance in my memory bank of these facetious moments over the more significant events in my life is in keeping with a career that has moved in a zig-zag course to nowhere in particular. Of course there have been times of bitterness and sadness. When I was six

My brother and I (aged 4 and 6).

I recall lying in bed with flu in the flat over our millinery store in Toronto, hearing my mother crying because my father, aged twenty-six, had just died. 'Why do these Jews have to wail so loud?' complained the hired nurse looking after me. It was my first recollected experience of anti-Semitism.

There were other moments, I know, when I was in no mood for laughter. The fight in the schoolyard when I was eight which I lost, and the entire audience went off with the winner while I was left to pick up my jacket and trudge my lonely way home. The Christmas Eve when I found a note on my pillow telling me that the girl I had loved for over a year had gone off with a famous film director. The times when I was fired – three or four. The guilt, when my mother died in Los Angeles, because I had hardly seen her at all in her final days.

Memoirs are like footstones of memory, taking you back to where you may or may not want to go. They are slippery conveniences that need careful treading. With advancing age, names, places, dates, whole sequential events, have sunk into that physiological bourne from which no reminiscence can ever return. I sometimes feel like Goldberg, who saw his doctor about his loss of memory. 'I can't remember what happened a month ago. Or even two weeks ago. Or even yesterday. What should I do, doctor?' 'Pay now!' said the doctor.

Fortunately I have written about the happenings in my life in various columns in various newspapers over the decades. Those articles, together with erratically kept diaries and a number of letters, provide me with some factual backing for these pages. Whether one should undertake this exercise at all is a moot point. I once asked the late Benn Levy, playwright, Labour MP and husband of the beautiful Constance Cummings, if he had ever thought of writing his memoirs. 'Indeed I did,' he said. 'I wrote twelve thousand words and then I gave it up because I found I wasn't in them.'

Well. I'll certainly be in these pages. To what end I know not. Call it false modesty or unconscious egotism, but I cannot imagine how, with my humble beginnings and my propensity to find life rather risible, I could have expected society to take my so-called achievements more seriously than they have. Journalists sneer at official honours but they accept them readily enough. I have accepted such second rank accolades as an entry in *Who's Who,* one appearance on the BBC *Brains Trust* and the DID, more fondly known as *Desert Island Discs*. Every significant development in my life has come about by accident. Or luck. I've covered the media front having written columns on social, political and cultural affairs; been a theatre, film, TV and book critic; worked six years producing TV programmes; chattered regularly on the radio and written a military history, three novels, two books on TV, a collection of profiles and three children's books. There is something arrogant about anyone who has written the millions of words I have and expected anyone to continue to pay me for them.

I abandoned a career as a lawyer to become a journalist and if I ever indulge myself in the business of regrets about what-else-I-could-have-done, I mildly flagellate myself for not having tried to be a full-time author of novels and biographies. Nothing more ambitious than Frederick Forsyth or Antonia Fraser. I realize I couldn't aspire to anything more significant because I lack the essential tool of a novelist's trade.

I have no deep curiosity about who I am. I have never sought Freudian or Jungian analysis because I'm afraid that if I began to discover who I really was I'd be trading relative tranquillity for nagging anxiety. As a critic of the arts I have, rather, suffered through and been enlightened by the inner journeys of others. I sympathize with Goldberg – my generic victim in all my Jewish jokes – who on his first visit to his analyst was told to lie down on the couch, say anything he wanted to, but reminded there was no compulsion upon him to speak a word. During the forty-five minute session Goldberg said not a word. 'That'll be 70 pounds, please,' said the analyst. 'I'll see you in a week's time.' At the second session, Goldberg was given the same instructions. Lie on the couch. Only speak if you have anything to say. 'Of course, you are not required to speak at all.' At the end of forty-five minutes Goldberg again had not opened his mouth. 'That'll be 70 pounds, please,' said the analyst. 'I'll expect you again next week.' At the third session Goldberg was again told that he was not forced to speak but only to talk if he wished to. After forty-five minutes of silence, as Goldberg was getting off the couch, the analyst again asked if he was sure he had nothing to say. 'Yes, doctor, I have something to say,' said Goldberg. 'Do you need a partner?'

★ ★ ★

In the late 1970s I was invited to attend a reunion of my 1937 law class which was being held in Toronto. Because the organizing committee did not have my address, they had sent my invitation to an ex-class member living in Dublin, presumably on the theory that since we were both in

Europe he might have some idea about where I was. He happened to be a reader of the London *Evening Standard* and having seen my name there as a theatre critic he forwarded the invitation to me at the paper.

The literature about the affair included a list of all the old boys and what posts they had held or positions achieved in their careers. There were 123 of us in the original class revealing how little the problem of overcrowding concerned the educational authorities in those days. I noted on the list – the names may be inaccurate – J. D. Cromerty, a judge of the Supreme Court of Ontario; John Parker, a judge in Yellowknife, North West Territories; H. Freshman Q.C. of Hamilton, Ontario; D. E. Calvert, deceased; M. Shulman, unknown since 1945.

Those words 'unknown since 1945' confirmed for me my suspicion that if you leave Canada for good, to your former countrymen you might as well be dead. But in Britain you are never allowed to forget where you were born. Although I have lived in England for over fifty years, taxi drivers, because of my stubborn accent, ask me if I am here for a visit, acquaintances brand me as a semi-foreigner and friends acknowledge that I am not just right.

For some inscrutable reason Canadians are taken as an amiable joke. Not as risible as Belgians, but almost. I take with equanimity a recent cartoon showing a man and a woman in an English garden. He is reading an account of an airline crash and says, 'No one we know, dear. They're all Canadians.' Americans are more aware of a Canadian identity, probably because there are some big league hockey and baseball teams whose successes make the headlines. But I don't have to be reminded that Al Capone, planning a speedy exit, said, 'Canada! I don't even know which street it's on.' And I've heard of parlour games in which the task is to name ten internationally famous Canadians, and whose winner could only name six.

Conscious of my homeland I can, of course, easily rattle off the names of a dozen famous Canadians: Banting, the discoverer of insulin, Lord Beaverbrook, Saul Bellow, Mary Pickford, J. K. Galbraith, the photographer Karsh, Stephen Leacock, Marshall McLuan, Bonar Law, the abstract painter Riopelle, the film director Robert Altman, Margaret Atwood. Distinguished as these figures are, they do not deter a journalist like Stephen Glover in 1995 writing in the London *Evening Standard*, 'Canada is one of the most uninspiring countries on God's earth. I am sure there are Canadian novelists and painters but I have never heard of them and I don't suppose anyone else has.'

That narrow idiosyncratic view is trumped by another journalist writing in the same paper, the brilliant TV critic Victor Lewis-Smith, saying, 'I fell in love at once with Montreal, a city that achieves an ideal synthesis of all that's best in America and France. It's what hyperactive, violent New York might become if it reduced its caffeine intake and succumbed to some laid-back Parisian sophistication.'

The mystery then remains as to why Canada, with a population of 29 million, twice the size of Holland or Belgium, seven times that of Norway, a major contributor to two World Wars, with an economy growing at a phenomenal pace and still subject to the same Queen as Britain, is treated with a shrug or a yawn or a hoot of laughter in British media or social circles. The conventional explanation is that its geographical proximity to the United States and its historical and traditional connections with Britain have made it difficult to develop a distinctive character of its own. But the British influence is receding at a rapid rate, particularly with the growing demands of French Canada for independence. Could it be that the accident of speaking the same English language as Britain and America has made it difficult for excellent novelists like Margaret Atwood, Robertson Davies, Mordecai Richler or Morley Callaghan to receive enthusiastic exposure in competition with the hype accorded to writers like Graham Greene or John Updike admired by critics and readers in their native lands?

Canada's culture, I'm afraid, is still treated as a poor cousin in the very markets where it would be expected to flourish. Probably because of its relatively ordered and law-abiding reputation, Canada rarely makes the front pages of British newspapers. What it needs to excite British editors is juicy political scandals, acts of terrorism and kidnapping, huge financial swindles, titillating tales of sexual aberration, riots by violent teenagers, serial killers or ecological disasters. Those are the kind of stories that might elbow Canada into the consciousness of the British public.

Although I left Canada over fifty years ago, I owe it an incalculable debt of gratitude for enabling me, an offspring of a poor immigrant family, to acquire the best education it had to offer even though, I must admit, I should have taken more advantage of its generosity.

* * *

My parents were born in Zhitomir in the Ukraine and were driven out of Russia by poverty and the pogroms against the Jews, usually carried

My father and I on Beatrice Street, Toronto

out by mounted Cossacks. Of their hardships I know very little. My uncle Norman, the eldest of two sons and two daughters in the Raisberg family, was the first to arrive in Toronto. He was in his early twenties and managed to earn enough money to pay the fare across Europe and the Atlantic to bring the family, in instalments, to Canada. My brother, Alexander, was born two years after me.

I have hardly any recollections at all of my father, Samuel, who died when he was twenty-six in the 'flu epidemic that killed millions after the war. Whether it was because he was not yet a Canadian citizen or his poor health that prevented him from being conscripted, I do not know. He must have been a shrewd businessman because, with little English at his command, he managed to acquire three millinery shops, with women's hats being made in the back rooms, as well as a men's haberdashery by the time he died. Photographs show him to be a pale, slight, dapper man with a cane and a thin moustache. We must have been fairly well off, because we owned a house on Beatrice Street, which was in a part of Toronto with middle-class pretensions.

We also possessed the first, perhaps only electric car, in the district. This was a narrow, tall, hearse-like vehicle that ran on batteries at a modest speed, like a present-day milk float. I assume it was bought because my father's health prevented him from driving anything more robust. It could be started by merely pulling a horizontal lever towards the driver. I remember one day playing with my three-year-old brother in the front seat of that lugubrious car, and the little tyke managed to pull the starting lever towards him. Slowly it began to make its majestic way down Beatrice Street. Not knowing how to stop it, this five-year-old leapt out of the car, raced into our house shouting to my father, who was having an early dinner, that Alex was driving the car away. By the time we had all bolted out of the house and into the street, the car was about 200 yards away with two men in front of it, holding back its progress until my father arrived to push the lever back to a halt position. My brother seemed to be enjoying it all. Although I was told much about my father's curiosity and acumen by relatives, it is sad that the only first-hand incident lodged in my memory about him is this episode about the electric car.

I was six when my mother, Ethel, took me to my first primary school on Spadina Avenue. Like most children faced with that awesome prospect, I clung screaming to my mother's skirt until a sympathetic woman teacher took me by the hand, dried my tears and separated me from my agonized mother. It was a mixed lower middle-class and working-class area, and there were about sixty children seated behind their own simple wooden desks in that classroom. I have no idea what technique was used to iron out my Yiddishness and replace it with an indomitable, strong English Canadian accent.

When I was nine my mother got married again, to a man who superficially had everything she needed to help her manage four shops and two wilful boys. He was handsome, over six feet tall, born in America and came from a successful American-Jewish family called the Gottliebs. Unfortunately beneath the façade there was a very stupid man, always opening his mouth in the wrong place with crass and tactless remarks that drove my mother hysterical with humiliation. She had the dark, generous looks and ample bosom that might have marked her out as an Italian madonna had she not been a Jewess. She was ever conscious of the name she was making in her tight Jewish circle and I often found her in tearful paroxysms of rage at some leaden-footed decision or comment Murray, her husband, had made in the company of friends or business associates.

Not being able to read or write English, she had believed that an impressive-looking, native-born American would have the qualities needed to help her with the merchandising, accounting and taxation problems associated with a business that specialized in women's hats sporting bird-of-paradise feathers retailing for over 100 dollars in the early 1920s. With the 1930s depression, everything was gone and my mother was in penury, helped to maintain a reasonably dignified lifestyle by the generosity of relatives. My brother and I, not shy about revealing our dislike of Murray, did our best to avoid any intimate contact with him. The few occasions when he tried to beat us resulted in such infuriated tantrums and such grovelling apologies on his part that we were never really afraid of him. Astonishingly enough they stayed married for another forty years, when they both died in Los Angeles.

My maternal grandfather and his third wife had a flat on the top floor of our house. With his trim beard and erect, square-cut body, he always gave me the impression that he had a personal hot-line to Jehovah. Having retired from being a butcher, he walked to his synagogue every morning to engage in prayer and study of the Torah. The only time I felt comfortable with him was when I beat him at dominoes – the only game he ever played.

Because my mother had taken on the responsibility of housing her father, she felt obliged to abide by his orthodox demands: the holy days like Passover, Yom Kippur and Chanukah were faithfully observed and the traditional ceremonies carried out. My mother kept two sets of cutlery and dishes, so that meat and dairy products should not be contaminated by being eaten off the same plates or with the same utensils. Every Friday evening a small Gentile lad would be paid a few cents for turning on our electric lights, which could not then be switched off until sundown on Saturday. Frightened as I was of the wrath of Jehovah, I thought, even in those days, that paying a non-Jewish boy to commit a sin was a fairly hypocritical way of ensuring one's path to Heaven. Talking about this practice recently with an acquaintance, he assured me that it still goes on in orthodox homes in London, only now it is the TV as well as the lights that are switched on.

Like all Jewish boys I had to prepare for my Bar-Mitzvah at the age of thirteen. When school ended each day at 3.30 p.m. I trudged to the local synagogue for Hebrew lessons which began at 4 p.m. On my thirteenth birthday I read a Hebrew passage in the Torah before the full congregation, my mother sitting proudly in the gallery. I did it faultlessly, which was not surprising since I had been trained to do it for months. And at a large banquet that evening, I made a speech with the expected opening words 'Today I am a man'.

In those days I never was quite sure in which synagogue I was expected to do my Bar-Mitzvah turn. This was because my grandfather was a very argumentative fellow – a characteristic he has passed on to his grandson – who seemed to be shifting allegiance arbitrarily from one structure to another. My mother had to sit patiently while he harangued her about the dreadful shenanigans about finance or protocol his fanatical co-religionists were up to. He was constantly threatening to take his prayers elsewhere. I suspect he would have behaved much like the Welshman who had been shipwrecked on an uninhabited Pacific island for fifteen years. A British destroyer finally found him and sent a landing party to take him off. The officer in charge of the rescue craft asked the Welshman how he had kept himself sane and busy for so long entirely on his own. 'It was very difficult at first,' said the Welshman. 'But then I found God and helped by my faith I survived.' He led the officer through a clearing and pointed out a large wooden structure. 'That's my chapel,' he said. 'I built it with my own hands and it has comforted me.' But a few hundred yards further on, the officer saw a similarly shaped structure. 'But isn't that another chapel over there?' asked the officer.

'Did you build that one too?' 'Oh, yes,' came the Welshman's reply. 'But that's the one I don't go to.'

(ii) A little learning

Harbord Collegiate was about twenty minutes' walking distance from my home. It had the same social mix as my primary school but the classes were smaller – about thirty-five teenagers in each. The male teachers were nearly all veterans of the Great War. Miss Saunders – probably not her name – awakened my interest in English and books. It was *Gulliver's Travels*, *Treasure Island*, *Robinson Crusoe* – properly expurgated where necessary – that had me glued to the page each night, long after lights were supposed to be turned off. I became adept at reading under the blankets with a small torch I had smuggled into my bed.

These classics were supplemented by a regular diet of boys' comics and magazines which were published in England. Every Friday I took an hour's walk to the only store in my neighbourhood that stocked them, so that I could get my weekly fix of *Film Fun*, *Chums* or the *Boy's Own Annual*.

It was at Harbord Collegiate that I first experienced the joy of seeing one's name in print. I wrote a letter to the *Toronto Star* when I was about thirteen complaining about the fact that thin flakes of plaster were falling from the roof in our classroom and adding, provocatively, that it gave the impression that we were all suffering from dandruff. This brought about a re-painting of the roof and made me a celebrity for a few days.

This was heady stuff and it encouraged me to try my hand at writing an adventure novel along the lines of the stories that filled the English magazines. It was called *In Quest of Inca's Treasure* and the first line read 'All was hustle and bustle at St Stephen's.' The place was packing up for the summer hols and my characters somehow managed to get to the wilds of Peru, where they skimmed hitherto unknown rapids, encountered deadly snakes and hungry crocodiles, fought off primitive pygmies armed with poison-tipped arrows until they returned for the next term of St Stephen's.

It was about 50,000 words and I carried the manuscript, written in longhand, in a brown haversack to the offices of a boys' magazine published in Toronto. I was met with a certain amount of amused tolerance by the secretary who saw me in the outer office. She was very sympathetic but told me that they did not read manuscripts in longhand, and that I would have to get it typed if I intended to submit it to them again. Without a typewriter or enough money to pay someone to type it out, the great work languished unseen in a bottom drawer in my bedroom. When about a year later a friend of my mother's did type it, the magazine had folded and I realized that it was too unoriginal and derivative. But during this exercise I certainly got bitten by the writing bacillus. From then on, I knew what I wanted to do.

To an athletic boy, Canada was bliss. There was snow up to your waist in winter, offering hours of ice hockey and tobogganing. In the summer there was baseball and swimming. We had a cottage at Long Branch, a suburb of Toronto, which was perched on a coast line about thirty feet above the lake. A rickety staircase to the stony beach made swimming a far less attractive sport to baseball, at which I acquired a small reputation as a pitcher.

At Long Branch I acquired my first taste of sex. I must have been fourteen when I cuddled up with a local thirteen-year-old girl at night, in the park bandstand, which used to be occupied by a brass band which gave concerts on Saturday and Sunday. The romantic evening took an unpleasant turn when the girl's father caught us in the act and threatened me with devious violent reprisals should I tempt his daughter to come out with me after dark again. From then on my adolescent gropings were always performed with an ear cocked for an angry father descending upon me with flailing fists.

Sex, too, provoked the most serious confrontation I had as a boy with my mother. I had passed my matriculation examinations with no particular distinction – mostly Bs and a couple of As – mainly because I did little work during the year, but by some intense swotting before the finals and a good memory achieved enough for entrance to the University of Toronto. But I had fallen in love at fifteen with Sonia who lived not far from us on Beatrice Street. She was my age and entered for a stenographic course at a local business school. Wanting to be near her, I argued passionately that learning about business was far more useful to someone of our background than an Arts degree leading nowhere. After all, I ranted on, nobody else in my class was going to a university. Why me? My mother was adamant. She had scrimped and saved to have the entrance fee available and unless I wanted to leave home, I would do as she wished. I told her nothing about Sonia and when I discovered that she was hanging around the corner with other boys, I decided then there was no future with Sonia and I gave in to my mother.

I spent four years at University College at Toronto University, which turned out to be the most enjoyable part of my life up to then. Each year I passed the required exams using my tested formula of intense swotting a month before they were held, and answering questions usually by remembering pictorially where the answers existed on the pages in the relevant text books. It was a mixed hors *d'œuvre of* an education with lectures and tutorials demanded in subjects as diverse as economics, philosophy, English, biology, French, psychology, Latin and mathematics. The list sounds impressive but we just skimmed the disciplines, leaving me with little more than a vocabulary of ideas with which I could impress listeners in an argument.

Most of my hours at university were spent, I'm afraid, not in acquiring knowledge but in what is euphemistically called extra-curricular activities. When I was not kicking or catching a ball to make some team or other, I was developing my skills at snooker and bridge. My financial resources did not allow me to take the regular crap games that were available out of sight of the authorities, but I fancied myself at rolling the dice. Much of my social life was spent in the purlieus of a fraternity called Beta Sigma Rho. It mimicked the initiation ceremonies and customs of the fraternities that had a grip on American universities, but its brothers were confined to Jewish students. This was because the Gentile fraternities wouldn't let us in. My generation took for granted religious discrimination against Jews and, instead of moaning about it, Toronto Jews organized their own societies, their own tennis and golf clubs, their own fraternities. Only the threat of anti-Semitic fascism inspired by Hitler forced this benign approach into something more defensive and aggressive.

It was the presence of Johnnie Weingarten (later Wayne) and Frankie Shuster that got me involved in the theatre. Shuster attracted our special respect because he was the cousin of Joe Shuster, the cartoonist who invented Superman, which was then becoming one of the most popular comic strips of the time. Little were we to know that Joe Shuster and his partner, Jerry Siegel, were early on deprived of all their rights to this treasure trove through litigation over contracts, and Shuster ended his days blind and in poverty.

I was obviously intrigued by the theatre at that time because I would attend night classes twice a week devoted to the teaching of Stanislavski, the Russian producer of the Method school of acting. Our teacher had been trained at Lee Strasberg's studio in New York where such famous stars as Marlon Brando and Marilyn Monroe tried to master the techniques of this dedicated system. As a dilettante who did not take it all very seriously, I did such exercises as trying to behave like a lost child or a forlorn tree, using the disciplines of improvization and sense perception to put myself wholly into the character. Since I never remotely thought of myself becoming an actor, I suspect I was there more for the girls than the art. Surprisingly, it all turned out to be very useful when, much later on, I had to make judgements about acting performances as a critic of the English theatre for almost forty years.

But far and away the most important interest of my university days was writing for and helping to produce the *Varsity*, the undergraduate newspaper which appeared five times a week and was financed by a dollar contribution a year from six thousand students. It reported all the news and activities on the campus with a special emphasis on humorous articles, sport and pompous editorials. In my four years on the staff I moved up the masthead from Night Editor to Special Writer to Assistant News Editor to Associate Editor.

At Christmas the *Varsity* held a competition for the Best Humorous and Serious Short Stories. There was a five dollar prize for the winning entries. The judges were an English professor, two lecturers in English and the Editor-in-Chief of the *Varsity*. I modestly re-print an extract from the Judges' Report.

> After some hesitation the judges awarded the first prize in the two prose divisions to the same competitor, Milton Shulman. His story 'A Sense of Humour' so clearly surpassed the other humorous prose in substance and workmanship that it merited first prize in that section. At the same time his story 'They're Going to Hang a Coward' far surpassed the quality of the other serious prose, and made no other choice possible, in view of the imaginative power and skilful arrangement of the story, and the sustained competence of the style. We take the opportunity of offering Mr Shulman our warmest congratulations.

If there were ever any compelling guidelines in my life pointing to the obvious direction my future had to take, it was the recognition by those two prizes that I had some skill as a teller of tales and a competent writer. I was only nineteen and in my third year at university, and I hadn't the faintest idea of what I was going to do with myself when I graduated the following year. Now I knew that I was destined to be a novelist or journalist or historian or foreign correspondent or show-biz columnist – or anything to do with words. The idea of being a critic never occurred to me. Although I had scribbled some puffs masquerading as criticism – free passes to a down-town cinema were only given if we said something kind – I had never read or been interested in any serious criticism of any art form. With my record on the *Varsity* I thought I would be able to get some sort of journalist job on the *Toronto Star* or on the *Globe and Mail*. My last year sharpened my knowledge of how a newspaper works by showing me how to compress news into four or five paragraphs, write headlines, avoid libel, meet deadlines and edit someone else's copy.

(iii) Called to the Bar

I have a love-hate relationship with money. Sometimes I have been contemptuous about the business of acquiring it. At other times it has ranked up there with such other major interests as work, women, play and health. After my graduation it played a decisive part in determining my future. In 1934 Canada was still in deep depression, not having yet recovered from the effects of the great financial crash of 1929. My mother had lost all her stores and in 1931 she, her husband and my brother Alex moved to the neighbouring city of Hamilton, where my stepfather eked out a sparse living driving a jitney, which was our private car used as a kind of mini-cab offering rides for five cents each. I stayed in Toronto with my Uncle Louis who housed me for most of my university days.

By making determined financial sacrifices my mother succeeded in finding the small sums needed for my tuition fees at university. When, three years later, she had to find one hundred dollars to pay for my brother Alex's second year at medical college, she had to beg, with tear-filled eyes, the medical bursar to permit her to pay the hundred dollars in four instalments of twenty-five dollars each. Her plea was accepted.

To contribute something to the cost of my tuition, I took on a series of jobs at week-ends and through the summer holidays. My most regular employment was being a salesman on Saturdays in my Uncle Norman's haberdashery store on Yonge Street. It stayed open from 9 a.m. to midnight which, of course, was an invitation on lonely winter nights for thieves to beat up my uncle two or three times a year and rob the till of the proceeds from the sale of shirts, ties, socks, handkerchiefs, hats and underwear. Fortunately for me, they left the shop alone on Saturday nights.

One of my weirdest jobs began when a friend of my family told me to report to a window-cleaning firm at 6.30 the next morning where there would be work for me at two dollars a day. Acting very mysteriously, the proprietor, a tall man who looked like a llama in a blue serge suit, tiptoed me round to an outside shed with a finger to his lips signalling silence. He handed me a small pad of writing paper, a pencil and six street car tickets for the Toronto trams.

'You see that man there,' he whispered, pointing to a man carrying a small ladder on his shoulder and carrying a bucket. 'Follow him so that he doesn't see you and write down every place he goes to clean windows. He will be going to places that need the street car tickets.' My subject was already fifty yards down the street when I was pushed off to do my job as a secret investigator of window-cleaners.

Since the streets were totally empty so early in the morning, I had to duck behind parked cars as he went into places like May's Hairdressing Salon or MacGregor and Son Grocers where his job of washing their shop window would take about twenty minutes. As the streets filled up with people bustling to work, I had to walk about ten yards behind him to avoid losing him in the crowds. Occasionally he would pop into one of Toronto's skyscrapers and I would have to wait for him to emerge on the eleventh floor, perched on the window sill of some solicitor's office with his feet dangling inside.

By the next time I arrived for the same job following the same man, I had learnt what the job was about. The window cleaners were mostly Polish or Ukrainian emigrants only recently arrived in Canada and could speak little English. While covering the list of jobs they had to do on their daily rounds, some of the more enterprising individuals would do an odd moon-lighting job, using the firm's equipment, and pocket the money received without reporting it. Over a period of time they would acquire enough of these free-lancing jobs to set up on their own and usually taking some of the firm's customers with them. To discourage this activity, the boss had warned them they would not only lose their jobs if they were caught but would also have to pay him a relatively large penalty in compensation when they left. I was hired to keep the suspects in line by reporting any deviance from their customer list. The boss trusted me no more than he did them because I never knew where they were supposed to go, thus preventing me from writing all the names down on my report and taking the day off.

At that time I was acquiring a left-wing bias against bosses and it struck me that the task was recruiting me as a capitalist stooge. The next day I decided to follow the suspect at such a close distance that it would be obvious to him he was being followed. He would therefore do nothing to deviate from his instructions, even if he had intended to, the boss would be reassured and the new Canadian would keep his job. I had also decided to resign from this short-lived employment.

That morning at about seven while he was busy hosing down the large window of a jeweller's shop, I sat opposite him on the pavement twiddling my thumbs. Since the street at that hour was virtually deserted except for us, I assumed that I had given obvious notice that he was under surveillance. For the next two hours, I followed my usual routine of observation, keeping track of him in crowded places by the top of the ladder he was carrying, but that day walking so close to him because I had lost interest in this form of employment. I then noticed that he seemed to be taking a very devious journey, turning right and left into criss-crossing streets for no particular purpose. I had lost sight of him turning a corner when he suddenly popped up to confront me, brandishing his pail and anger spitting from his mouth. 'Stool-agent!' he shouted. 'Stool-agent!' Caught aback, I said nothing. 'You been following me for one hour. Why? Why?' Recovering my composure, I said, 'One hour? I've been trailing you for two days. I'm working for your boss.'

From splenetic fury, his mood changed to apologetic cringing. 'I know. You want me I lose my job. I no cheat. I go only places here.' He thrust forward the notebook containing his engagements. 'I no cheat. You no tell the boss I cheat.' I assured him I had no intention of doing him any harm and that I was quitting my job as a window-cleaner detective that very moment. I waved him good-bye and went home. The next day I handed in my resignation and received four dollars for my efforts. 'I understand,' said my llama-like employer, nodding his large head in agreement. 'It's not a good job for a college boy.'

Another venture to raise money was almost as bizarre as my window-cleaning exploit. Facing the summer of 1934 with no paid employment, I talked two friends of mine into backing a dance hall as a financial proposition. I had seen an advertisement offering a building for rent near the town of Muskoka in the Northern lakes of Ontario. It had been the sole spot for large parties and dances held in the area and was now empty. I had two aims in mind for becoming a business entrepreneur at the age of twenty. I would test my theory that it was not difficult to become rich if only one dedicated oneself to the effort. And I would try out my abilities as a crooner and see if there was any chance of me cutting a record and becoming a professional songster. I had often been complimented on my melodic, low-register singing voice, which had been modelled on such popular radio stars as Russ Columbo and Whispering Jack Smith. Bing Crosby had just started to make a name for himself by perfecting a similar technique.

We managed to raise 500 dollars between us and found four musicians who were prepared to act as a band for a free holiday in the North and a percentage of the profits, if there were any. We got credit for a concession to sell sandwiches, soft drinks and chocolates in the building and we were in business.

The location turned out to be just the kind of wooded romantic spot with a sparkling, isolated lake and massive pine trees that might act as a backdrop for red-coated singing Mounties in musicals like *Rose Marie*. To our dismay we discovered that the previous occupant had had to close up his dance hall because there had been a murder committed on the grounds and local parents wouldn't let their daughters go there. We had to combat this image and did so by presenting ourselves as young, good-looking, trustworthy lads trying to work our way through university through this enterprising venture. We invited parents to come and have tea or coffee with us. We organized a baseball team with the band and the backers and played some friendly games with teams in the area.

The dance hall was lit by a revolving chandelier casting traditional spots of fairy lights over the dancers. I crooned with the band, holding a megaphone for amplification. My usual repertoire was 'It's Only a Shanty in Old Shanty Town', 'Sweet Sue' and a jazzed up version of 'The Sheik of Araby'. But nothing could beat the recent murder voodoo that was associated with the place. After three months we had no money to pay off the suppliers of the confectionery and soft drinks. We had to close, having lost our investment, as well as amassing a few hundred dollars in debts which we managed to pay off in due time.

The experience put a severe dent in my vague ambitions to become a professional singer. Another drawback to my crooning plans was the fact that, from mid-September to the end of October, I suffered from acute hay fever. Being allergic to ragweed pollen which blossomed in those weeks my nose became completely blocked, my eyes reddened with severe itching, my head ached and my voice was reduced to a frightening croak. So severe were some of these attacks that I often had

to wear a metal filter over my nose whenever I was outdoors, giving rise
to much ribaldry amongst my friends about the Man in the Iron Mask
in their midst. I took anti-pollen injections for many years and it was
only when I was over fifty that I ceased to be affected by some form of
hay fever allergy from either tree pollen or house dust. I have always
considered being free of this affliction as one of the compensations of
reaching middle-age.

My diversions at this time into making money never dimmed my
passion for writing. Encouraged by the prizes I had won on the *Varsity*,
I decided to try my hand at fiction. In those days when television was
only a gleam in a mad inventor's eye the most popular magazines – the
Saturday Evening Post, Liberty, the *Strand* – had a ravenous appetite for
the short story. I had a natural aptitude for plots with a beginning, a
middle and an end and I modelled myself on the imaginative tales of
De Maupassant and O. Henry. The trick was to produce a surprising
twist at the denouement of 1200 to 1500 words.

My chief target was Today's Prize Story which ran for a column in
the *Toronto Star* every day. I submitted my early efforts in a self-
addressed, stamped envelope and became philosophical at the sight of
my own handwriting lying inside our front door as my submissions
were returned to me with a polite rejection slip. Six or seven failures had
not dampened my ardour for the elusive prize. Coming down for breakfast one morning in April, 1934, I noticed an unfamiliar envelope at the
door. It had the words *Toronto Star* printed on its face and I hardly dared
breathe as I tore it open. Sure enough, it was an acceptance of my short
story, 'Heat Wave', and a note saying I would be sent a cheque for three
dollars.

Basking in the congratulations of my family and friends, I was determined to prove that this was not just a one-time accident. Two months
later they accepted another piece of mine called 'A Sense of Humour'.
It was actually the same story that had won the Humour Prose prize in
the *Varsity*. Again the fee was three dollars. My third story, accepted two
months later, 'The Gas Stove', had a pleasant surprise in the envelope. It
told me my fee had now been raised to five dollars. When I took the
five dollar cheque for my fourth story a few weeks later, called 'No
Refunds Allowed', to a local bank to have it cashed, the teller studied it
and then said to me, 'Are you *the* Milton Shulman?' That was my first
moment of glory as a writer.

These curious, quirky jobs gave me some glimmerings about life outside of a university which had dominated and cocooned my goals and values for four years. But there was no substantial future for me from a financial standpoint in any trade, craft or profession that I could envisage. I wrote several letters to government agencies, insurance companies and retail chains offering my services but in most cases my qualifications did not even warrant an interview or a polite rejection. There was still high unemployment in Canada and any work going was not likely to be offered to someone with the name of Shulman. The incipient anti-Semitism in establishment quarters was acquiring an ugly momentum at the time, due to the access of Hitler to power in Germany and the burgeoning of fascist, ultra right-wing forces in Europe and North America.

My mother, being a typically Jewish matriarch, had ambitious dreams of her two sons being a lawyer and a doctor. My brother, Alex, had already indicated that if we could afford it, he wanted to go to medical college. My mother's arguments for me taking up law were logical as well as selfish. Unable to write English or read it adequately herself, she had no serious conception of what being a writer actually meant. She thought it was a frivolous activity for a boy which I would eventually grow out of. Why not spend the next three years studying law? By that time economic conditions might improve and, if I didn't want to practise law, I would have qualifications that would equip me for a respectable job. Another important consideration was that training for law with the Ontario Bar Society required me to be articled to a law firm, where I would be expected to attend every afternoon and during the holidays. All lectures were in the imposing Victorian edifice of Osgoode Hall and were confined to the mornings. I would be paid a small salary, which would cover my tuition fees and enable my mother to acquire some savings to send my brother to the medical faculty at Toronto University.

I realize that I am giving the impression that my mother played an imperative role in every important decision of my life. Although Freudians might disagree, I don't think that was so. Having been beset by financial problems she could not handle as a young widow, and burdened with a stupid husband, she built a mental fortress around herself to protect her from the many concerns that assailed her. She probably communicated some of that anxiety complex to me. I was rather like that Jewish son who received a telegram from his mother which read 'Letter following. Start worrying.'

My mother in the 1920s, wearing one of her gorgeous hats

If I had had the courage or the will to pursue a writing career at this stage, I might have emigrated to America and tried my luck in New York. But the depression south of the border appeared even more ugly and onerous than it was in Canada. I was still young. I would be twenty-three when I had been called to the Bar. So, even if in a sense I was pushed rather than called to the Bar, I decided to take that course of action.

★ ★ ★

I have never regretted the three years I spent studying law. Indeed, I am very grateful for them. It made me realize that without law, humanity would be at the mercy of its most violent and selfish instincts. What distinguishes us from the beasts is our ability to reason and, in the words of the 16th century English jurist, Sir Edward Coke, reason is the life of the law. I have much sympathy with the playwright Arthur Miller's generalization that the law is only a word for what has a right to happen. It is popular to deride the law as an ass, but more often in its manifestations it is a wise old owl. The base motivations that we are born with and that give us the illusion that we are something special need curbing and restraint if any society is to exist. To end this burst of unaccustomed profundity, I believe that this constraint is exercised by religion through fear of superstition, and by law through fear of reason.

At Osgoode Hall I went through the entire repertoire of subjects needed to qualify as a barrister and solicitor. In Canada, as in the United States, there is no splitting of these two functions in the practice of law. Criminal, contract, property, constitutional, company law as well as tort and ethics were examinations that had to be passed. I was most intrigued by criminal law and torts. The question of what evidence was available to convict or acquit someone charged with a crime was, I realized, the mark of a successful barrister. The famous O. J. Simpson case in Los Angeles revealed how the proliferation of facts, non-facts and innuendoes could squeeze through the barriers of inadmissible evidence to provide a smokescreen about the truth and provide a jury with no means of penetrating it.

I was articled to the firm, if memory serves me right, of Levinson and Levinter. After morning lectures at Osgoode Hall I would turn up at their offices just after noon and stay until about four o'clock. I had a desk amongst the secretaries in the outer lobby, where I waited for somebody to ask me to do something. There were four partners and the senior one was Mr Levinson, a balding, imposing man who always talked to you as if you were in the witness box. He was a specialist in accident cases and I was often sent out to interview a witness who may have seen a woman fall off a bus because it accelerated too quickly, or a car crash because one driver tried to beat a red light. Mr Levinson was very expensive and only the most affluent citizens could afford to talk to him. The cost has of course grown so that Goldberg passing his solicitor in the street said, 'Nice, day, isn't it.' On reflection he retraced his steps to the lawyer and said, 'I'm telling you. Not asking you.'

I satisfied my yearning for writing by editing Osgoode Hall's month-ly law journal, *Obiter Dicta*, which paid me a few dollars and enabled me to practise my propensity for earnest, pompous editorials. The certificate I received after three years at Osgoode Hall proclaims me to be a bar-rister, solicitor and notary public of the Ontario Bar.

I had already made arrangements to join a lawyer named Louis Herman who carried out property transactions for an uncle of mine who owned a lot of unprofitable slum houses. He had achieved the remarkable feat of convincing other relatives to invest in fourth and fifth mortgages in order to save him from losing the lot. I was given an office rent free and shared a secretary for helping Herman prepare cases for lit-igation, and for generally handling the less important matters that came his way.

A few car accidents, some divorce cases and the setting up of a small company gave me some reasonable hope that a lucrative career as a lawyer was on the way. Although I still penned the occasional story for Canadian publications, only a few of which were accepted, I was beginning to con-centrate my mind on acquiring contacts that might give me work.

My writing was receding in my mind as a major priority and was being relegated to the status of an occasional hobby. I probably would have gone on to cultivate a respectable practice, perhaps have drifted into provincial politics and ended up as a County Court judge or even a trifle higher. Something, however, intervened. On 3 September 1939, Neville Chamberlain announced that a state of war with Germany existed from 11 a.m. that day. A week later on 10 September, Canada followed the Mother Country into battle against the Germans.

2

THE WAR AND MI 14(b)

Socialism becomes my new religion... Turn right for the army... Singing saves my life... The gardens of England... Secret Agents, resistance fighters and pigeons with parachutes... The battlefields of Normandy

(i) From Socialism to the Armoured Corps

I cannot recall any turbulent personal struggle but it was in these years that I tussled with and resolved the religious and political dilemmas of my life. I became an atheist and a socialist. It has been said, and the Nazi decrees reinforced the generalization, that you are always a Jew if others say you are. Although Disraeli was baptised as a child, he is permanently recognized by the British as a Jewish Prime Minister. My decision, therefore, to reject and abandon the religious practices and tenets of the Jewish faith did not mean that I no longer considered myself a Jew. I will always be proud of my birth and my upbringing but I found its orthodox demands, its exclusivity, its ominous threat of perdition for sinning, both stultifying and hypocritical.

My increasing orientation towards socialism, with Karl Marx's dictum that religion was the opium of the people establishing the church as a bulwark of capitalism, hastened my progress towards atheism. I recall being in mental crisis over all this for many months. I realized the inherent resistance to making such a spiritual leap when Professor A. J. Ayer, the logical positivist and professed atheist, known to his intimates as Freddy, many decades later told us about his effort to talk Graham Greene, the novelist, out of becoming a Roman Catholic. There were eight of us engaging in stimulating conversation in front of a blazing fire after a garrulous dinner party when someone asked Freddy to give us his views about an afterlife. He was reluctant to talk about it, he said, because he recognized how much pain could be caused by the awakening of doubts about the existence of God.

45

As I recall his talk, he said that Greene, a personal friend, had asked for a meeting because he was about to convert to Catholicism and wanted to hear the arguments against it. They talked for a whole day and Freddy claimed that as he took Greene step by step through the intellectual fallacies inherent in every religion, the novelist agreed with every one of his contentions. But when it came to the final crunch, Greene balked at taking the ultimate intellectual leap. 'I realized I could not break through Graham's insurmountable barrier to reason, which was faith,' said Freddy. 'Nothing I had said had undermined his faith. A few weeks later he became a Catholic.'

I had no such rigorous examination to guide me on my Road to Damascus. Intellectually I would never have been up to the arcane justifications that lie at the heart of faith. I know only that one morning I arose with a firm conviction that Jehovah did not exist, and that there was no other God that I could find more credible. Instead of a feeling of fear at my heretical audacity, I was overwhelmed with the gratifying sensation that I had shed, that morning, all my pent-up anxieties about sin and guilt. Jehovah had planted them in my psyche and with His obliteration I have never seriously been troubled by either of these spiritual sensations ever since.

When I realize the formidable wisdom of the great philosophers and scientists who like Einstein believed that He exists and does not play dice with the universe, I must humbly admit that there are times I would gratifyingly accept the evidence that I was wrong. I can understand why W. C. Fields, when asked why he was reading the Bible, replied that he was looking for loopholes.

In moments of deep pain and sorrow, like the deaths of my mother and brother, I whisper the opening words of a Hebrew prayer. I realize this is a cowardly attempt to ingratiate myself with the Bookkeeper in the Hereafter who records our heresies in His ledger. I am consoled by the words of the poet, Heinrich Heine, who when asked on his deathbed if he thought God would forgive his sins, said, 'Of course, He will. It's His business.'

Believing that socialism was the political panacea that would eventually cleanse the world of all its gross inequalities was the natural stance of the young in the late 1930s. It took neither moral nor intellectual courage to take up that position. Being a young Jew from a poor immigrant background who was increasingly aware of Nazi and fascist parties proliferating throughout the Western world professing anti-Semitic policies, I recognized that only the Left was ready to oppose these racist ideologies. The conventional parties, Conservative and Liberal in Canada, appeared to be in sympathy with movements that could be counted upon to combat communism. The British government of Chamberlain and Halifax was ready to make outrageous concessions, such as the Munich Pact, to Hitler. Right-wing influences like the German-American Bund, the ranting radio rabble-rouser, Father Coughlin, and the American hero, Charles Lindbergh, were spreading their extreme right-wing views to their neighbour to the North.

There were already marches of Nazi supporters in Toronto, precipitating violent clashes with the Left. In addition to my natural disposition to ally myself with movements that denounced anti-Semitism, my reading convinced me that capitalism was a doomed, inefficient and unfair system that would inevitably be crushed by either the dictatorships of the Right or the people's and workers' parties of the Left.

I had dipped into *Das Kapital* but, like Labour's Prime Minister, Harold Wilson, I had never managed to get past 100 pages. I had read John Strachey's *Coming Struggle for Power* and the left-wing tracts like *Guilty Men* published by the Left Book Club of Victor Gollancz. I was tempted to join the Communist Party but I found their jargon too anti-patriotic for my taste and I was wary of any card-carrying commitments to a party. Nor did I ever join any socialist party, although strange to say, as I will recount later, I did become the representative of the CCF in Britain, the Canadian Socialist Party, for three years after the war.

The war relegated all my long-term plans about writing and the law to a never-never land of future expectations. Anti-war propaganda, peace ships and books like *All Quiet on the Western Front* had warned our generation that the Armageddon of the First World War, with tens of millions of dead, was bound to be repeated in another war against Germany. I knew that I would have to be in it sometime and I was reconciled to the fact that I probably would not survive it.

The phoney war was just what Canada needed. For a small country of less than nine million people, the First World War had been a costly and bloody affair. No less than 628,000 Canadians had served in it and 60,000 had given their lives. The aftermath was a country whose people were imbued with a sense of pacifism and whose politicians spent as little as possible on defence and promised the electorate it need never fear being involved in a European war again. The expenditure of Britain and France per head of population on defence was almost twenty times greater than Canada's appropriation. In 1939 the land forces of Canada had an authorized establishment of 86,308 men (barely enough for three divisions) and 4,844 horses.

When war broke out there was hardly enough military equipment for training let alone fighting. Under the circumstances there was no particular urgency voiced by the government for men to join up. When they did, many of them were told to go home for three to six months. My own enquiries convinced me that I was not then wanted. Nevertheless, I knew that if the war dragged on, it was inevitable that some day I would be in uniform. In the evenings and at week-ends I would attend army classes to gain the necessary qualifications to be enrolled as an officer cadet. When I had received my certificate of training as an infantry officer, the nation still didn't need me. I did another course and ended up with the qualifications for an artillery officer. By that time France had fallen, Britain had survived the Blitz and Russia had been invaded.

I remember standing on a street corner, having just passed a shop where army recruitment took place, and wondering if my mother would have an hysterical fit if I signed up. That was the most important decision of my life. I can trace everything that has happened to me back to the timing of that thought process and its consequences. If I had turned left and gone on, the accidents that shaped my future would have been different. I turned right and volunteered for the Armoured Corps, because no more officer material was needed for the infantry or artillery.

My mother wept for days but since it would be some time before I actually went overseas, she got over it. She had to face the prospect of losing both her sons for my brother, Alex, had qualified as a doctor in 1939 and immediately took up an internship at the Cedars of Lebanon hospital in Los Angeles. He served as a neurosurgeon with the American Medical Corps in France and Germany. My mother was now left alone with a husband she had only just learned to tolerate.

I cannot remember a great deal about my induction period into the army but I never found it congenial. I always felt uncomfortable sleeping in a large barracks with dozens of other men. It was much too cold in winter. And I loathed being wakened at six in the morning. I was very clumsy at the domestic aspects of soldiering, finding it impossible to get the proper shining gleam on my army boots no matter how earnestly I polished them; nor could I make up the blankets on my bed in the neat authorized manner everybody else seemed to manage. However, being weighed down with educational qualifications – a BA, a law degree and artillery and infantry officer certificates – I was given the status of an officer cadet and sent to a training school at Brockville, Ontario, from which I would emerge as a second lieutenant in the Canadian Armoured Corps.

Our first contact with tanks was with the ones that had been the surprise weapon of the First World War, and being in one was what a kipper in a can must have felt like before it was smoked. The fumes and the smell of petrol were so overwhelming that, after five minutes, one had to emerge from the cramped turret gasping for air. We knew that better tanks were on the way or most of us would have been begging for a transfer to submarines. We took intense courses in gunnery, map reading, wireless and the driving and maintenance of tanks, lorries and motorcycles. There were about a dozen cadets on the course and when the final results were announced, I was the only one who had failed.

I was, of course, surprised and shattered. I had no inkling that I was doing anything worse than the others except for my inability to adjust the blankets and sheets on my bed as impeccably as them. Fortunately I had made some close friends during the three-month course. They were indignant about my treatment and in their enquiries they let me know that the major in charge of the course had been irritated by my habit of singing when I shaved in the morning. He thought such conduct unbecoming a tank officer and refused to qualify me. I naturally suspected this was a thin disguise for his real reason for wanting to send me back to the ranks. There were not many, if any, Jewish officers in the Armoured Corps and my singing in the early hours may have reinforced his prejudice that Jews did not have the correct martial character for combat.

My friends sent a petition to the colonel of the training camp expressing their unease about what had happened to me. Such a protest was most unusual, but after interviewing me the colonel decided that I would not pass out with my class, but that he would take me under his personal supervision during the duration of the next class. We got along well and, three months later, I was made a second lieutenant.

Had I not been initially rejected I would have arrived with my class in England in 1942 and probably have taken part in the Dieppe raid on 19 August 1942. In nine hours out of a total force of about 5,000, 840 were killed in action or as prisoners of war, 586 were wounded and about 1,800 taken into captivity. In other words over 3,000 Canadians were either killed, wounded or made prisoners-of-war in what was up to then the bloodiest defeat the Allies had suffered in the war.

A large proportion of the men in my class acted as beach officers at Dieppe, and their job was to land first on the French mainland and lead in the landing craft and armoured vehicles. They were sitting ducks for the Germans in their well-entrenched positions high on the cliffs, and most of them were killed or wounded. My friends were numbered amongst them. So would I probably have been but for my custom of singing while I shaved. The disaster at Dieppe put back the chances of Canadian troops being involved in any other action for some time. I continued to make myself useful as an aide to the colonel of the training camp.

I had a vague idea that I might end up in Intelligence because of my time spent with anti-defamation groups before the war, and I read as many manuals as I could about the strength and formations of the Wehrmacht. I spent most evenings with Hugh's *German Grammar* and listened to the full course on German on Linguaphone records. I also gave lectures to incoming classes of officer cadets on the identification of German tanks and planes.

When it was decided to form the 2nd Army Tank Brigade in Canada for eventual dispatch overseas, I was probably as qualified as anyone else around to become its intelligence officer. At least I could speak tolerable military German and knew how German infantry and armoured units were organized and equipped. The job carried with it the rank of captain and by the time our brigade left for England in June, 1943, I had become an acting captain. How ironic that the accident of my being rejected by one prejudiced major resulted in those who passed out above me and supported me probably being killed or captured at Dieppe, while I was promoted from second lieutenant to captain in an unseemly period of time. Of all the twists and turns that have marked my life, this was probably the most fortuitous and bizarre.

With so many of our officers decimated at Dieppe, the command of our formation was given to an English brigadier. He was a congenial, sensitive looking man named Gianelli – which struck us an odd name for an Englishman, but he immediately demonstrated his Anglo-Saxon credentials by insisting that all officers in his mess drop the Canadian way of eating food by switching from a knife to a fork only and synchronizing knife and fork simultaneously.

The 2nd Army Tank Brigade was formed in January, 1942, but it didn't get to England until June, 1943. It consisted of 3,500 men organised into a Headquarters staff and three tank regiments. For over a year we trained and trained and trained. My thoughts at the time are recorded in the opening pages of a diary I started in 1943. 'I hope it will be a record of the things that may have made me laugh or cry or, most importantly, think,' I wrote. 'During this next year I have little doubt that important and strange things will happen to this small-town lawyer who has seen little of life beyond the printed page and the animated screen. War will dominate my thinking, since most of my days will be spent in an atmosphere of preparation for killing. Yet the most characteristic aspect of my past year and a half in the army is the fact that in spite of the grimness of it all, I have found it very easy to laugh – and the Lord knows there has been plenty to laugh at.'

As a brigade we could hardly get ourselves into proper fighting shape because it wasn't until well into 1942 when we got our first Canadian 'Ram' tanks which we were expected to use in combat. I had become a very proficient organizer of courses and a lecturer on map reading, enemy organization and tactics, enemy identification, security and propaganda. My pupils, junior officers in the brigade, would start with a resentful feeling that their time was being wasted and generally end up having found part of the course interesting.

Inevitably, ludicrous orders were issued, administrative matters were bungled, inefficiency ran rampant and time was monumentally wasted. War is no place for curing stupidity. The American magazine, *Time*, devoted an article to what it called the SNAFUs and TARFUs of military life: 'Situation Normal All Fucked Up' and 'Things Are Really Fucked Up' but the magazine used 'Fouled' for 'Fucked'.

SNAFUs abounded at 2nd Army Tank Brigade in those days at Camp Borden when we were waiting for action. A letter was sent to the Ordnance Corps requesting four gum erasers. A reply was received saying that the used gum erasers would have to be returned before new ones could be issued. Our adjutant snipped off four blobs of gum from his existing erasers and returned them with a note 'Enclosed your four used gum erasers. Ordinarily we use them until they are completely gone but henceforth we will save a little for Quartermaster Stores.' He got his erasers. This SNAFU was capped by another one when permission was asked from a higher authority to destroy a number of useless documents. A letter was received authorizing their destruction 'as long as copies are made'.

I was responsible for security in the brigade, which meant every suspicious event had to be reported to me – such as the leakage of any times or dates of sailings across the Atlantic. U-boats were still a menace and troopships were obviously major targets for them. Pamphlets warning about careless talk constantly had to be issued.

One morning a tall, well-built man wearing the black beret of a tank trooper was marched into my office, saluted and sat down at my desk. He appeared extremely agitated and kept clasping and unclasping his hands between his knees. He gave his name as Thomas Kula, a tank driver in our Saskatchewan regiment. He claimed he was being pressurized by German agents to reveal the movement and destination of his regiment when we were ordered overseas. If he didn't co-operate they had threatened to kill him. Why had they contacted him, I asked? He had worked on German-American ships on the Atlantic route before the war and the man making the demands was now a member of the German-American Bund and had been a dedicated Nazi when employed as a steward on Kula's ship.

I thought this was a very serious case of attempted espionage and asked him to give me the name of his contact. Kula refused. He thought he had done his duty by reporting the matter. He saw no reason why he should place his life in jeopardy by naming his tormentors. I said I could not send such a report to higher authority without names. They would either dismiss him as a fantasist or send someone much senior to me to winkle out the names eventually. He could be in real trouble if he persisted in keeping quiet. His voice had sunk to a mumble and he began to sweat profusely. I was frightened by the mad look that had come into his eyes. However I pressed on, calling on his patriotism and his loyalty to his comrades. Sandwiches were brought in. Long silences took place. I refused to dismiss him. Finally, after four hours of pressure, he gave me the name of Erhart. He didn't know his first name and the only address he had for him was the ship he used to work on for the German-American line. I knew that was the most I could get out of him and, apparently extremely relieved, he went back to his unit. I wrote out my report and sent it that day to the brigade major. No one got back to me about it.

About three months later I was summoned by the brigade major, who informed me that a body had been found in the Niagara River on the American side of the border, which they thought was Thomas Kula. Since I had spent some time with him and knew what he looked like, would I go to Buffalo and identify the body. I was given his file, which included his medical and dental documents, to help in the examination of the body. I was overwhelmed with a sense of guilt. Had I pushed him too far and had his enemies murdered him as he said they might if he revealed Erhart's name? Or had he committed suicide because the fear of what he had done had engulfed him?

The burly American cop, looking exactly as if he had stepped out of a police thriller, explained that they calculated the body had been in the river for almost two months and was therefore extremely bloated. He would hardly resemble the man I had interviewed. Why did they think he was Thomas Kula? He was wearing a Canadian battle-dress and the jacket revealed three numbers on its inside pocket which had not been obliterated by the water. Those three numbers were the last numbers of Kula's army registration number. The first three letters were undecipherable. There were also two faint initials on the jacket which might be T. K., but they weren't sure. He had probably committed suicide by jumping near the Falls. Why did he think it was suicide rather than his being pushed or thrown over the cliff, I asked? His army boots were found at the spot he apparently leapt from. The cop informed me that most suicides take their shoes or boots off before plunging into the rapids. He wasn't prepared to speculate as to why humans committed this bizarre ritual before drowning themselves in the raging torrent.

The body that was shown to me on the slab that had been pulled out at the mortuary was completely unrecognizable. The thin man I remembered was now swollen to grotesque proportions and the face resembled Lon Chaney in one of his horror films. I shook my head. I was afraid, I told the American, I could not make a positive identification. However I had his dental chart and perhaps if we examined his mouth we might get some clue from that. The chart showed that there were at least six teeth missing in the lower and upper jaws. I was invited to run my fingers through the mouth which had been prised apart for my inspection. To my relief, no teeth seemed to be missing. He had a full set of teeth and I was not keen on discovering whether or not they were dentures. On the train back to Canada, I felt that the load of guilt I had carried about Kula's death had now lifted. Kula was undoubtedly missing from his regiment, but I was relieved that the pressure I had exerted on him could not have resulted in his murder or suicide. I reported all this to the brigade major. Alas, he had some bad news for me. The dental chart I had taken with me was out-of-date. Kula had recently had treatment which had filled in all the gaps in his mouth. I had to write to the Buffalo police revising my opinion. How Kula actually did meet his death I never found out.

* * *

I love women. Not all of them, but most of them. Ever since the girls who made hats in the back room of my mother's millinery shops made a fuss of this eight-year-old and admired his dimples, I have metaphorically pirouetted in front of them all my life preferring their approval to that of men. But I have never been sure, whenever I have bedded them, whether I was the victor or the vanquished.

I have every sympathy with Sir John Betjeman, the Poet Laureate who, when asked in a BBC documentary towards the end of his days what was his chief regret, answered, 'Not having enough sex.' I didn't really get on the sexual turntable until my early twenties. As a teenager I had some intense petting sessions with girls whose names and faces I've completely forgotten, but in those days in Toronto finding a place where copulation could take place was very difficult. The girls lived at home and there was never any chance of being alone in our small flat or my uncle's house, where I lived for most of my university days.

I was desperately frightened of women in my teens and early twenties. I can still remember the terror I felt when I had to contemplate crossing a dance floor to ask some isolated, apparently unaccompanied female for a dance. Being relatively short-sighted and too vain to wear my spectacles, I would wonder why she had been left as such a wallflower. But as I approached her, I became aware that distance had lent enchantment and the attractive creature fifty yards away emerged as extraordinarily plain the nearer I came. Having obviously committed myself, I managed to disguise my disappointment as I did a round on the dance floor, no doubt boring her with my line of chat which usually began with the line, 'Have you read any good books lately?' I suspect that as an opening conversational gambit for the young these days, that sentence is about as obsolete as 'I arrived late because my hansom cab was struck by lightning.'

I was nineteen when I became involved with Joyce. She was sixteen. Her Jewish family lived not very far from us in Beatrice Street. She had a slim, athletic figure and a face, not beautiful, but sparkling with vitality and fun. When we finally made physical love on the living-room sofa, we had been stroking each other for months and were both virgins. I suspect it was many weeks before we really knew enough about what we were doing to really enjoy it.

She took an Arts degree at Toronto University and, I believe, was working in advertising when I joined the army in 1941. Although we had been inseparably linked for a number of years, I am not sure that we would have married had the war not come. Once in uniform I could only see her on my monthly week-end leaves, and with those separations our appetite for each other grew more intense. Marriage was something I refused to contemplate at that time. The more I was encouraged by my friends to settle down – meaning giving up bachelorhood – the more I resisted. Yet I knew that I would soon be going overseas and I had a fatalistic conviction that I would not be alive at the war's end. Joyce, determined to have a ring on her finger, hinted that she might be pregnant. My diary entry of Sunday, 28 March, 1943 indicates my frame of mind when I eventually caved in. 'Tonight Joyce and I decided to marry,' I wrote. 'I'm a little dazed, frightened and upset by the prospect, but I guess I'll get used to it in time. It shouldn't be too bad – a lot of other people have done it.'

We married three weeks later in a Toronto hotel on 18 April. The ceremony took place under a small canopy and I smashed a glass with my foot in true orthodox fashion. There were about 150 guests including my brother, Alex, who had come up from Washington in his American officer's uniform. He was doing a course in neurosurgery since he was to specialize in brain damage when his unit went into action. I had been given a week's leave because, according to my diary, 'I had been a good boy.' The gifts included $400 in cash and the usual domestic bric-à-brac – glassware, cutlery, linen, blankets, coffee pots and toasters. 'Joyce is saving a lot of this junk,' I wrote, 'for the day when we open a home of our own. Which I don't feel is any too soon.' Our honeymoon was in Montreal. Two months later I was on a troopship headed for England. I never saw her again.

* * *

On 16 June 1943 we were marched from our train in Halifax to the troopship *Andes* which was moored at the port. Eight officers were allocated to what used to be a single cabin on the *Andes* in peacetime. Six could have bunks and two had to sleep on the floor. We tossed for it and I won a bunk.

The *Andes* was a luxury liner that had been commissioned in 1939 but had never carried a civilian passenger. In addition to our entire Army Brigade on this trip it carried a large contingent of Air Force personnel, 300 reinforcement personnel and about 100 Red Cross transport women who, my diary notes, 'were getting a run around by the many wolves aboard.' If the officers thought eight in a small cabin were cramped conditions, they realized they were much more comfortable than the other ranks who had to sleep in hammocks so close to each other that not an inch was wasted.

The officers were given a briefing by the American general who was in command of the troops aboard, and we did not feel particularly honoured when he assured us that German U-boats were especially anxious to sink the *Andes* and that we were, in his words, Number One on their Hit Parade. I thought back to my experience with Thomas Kula and wondered if his claim that he had been harassed for sailing information was true and not a fantasy.

We were not made particularly happy by the news that we would be travelling alone, with no accompanying escort of destroyers and submarines. We knew that the only other ships that sailed the Atlantic alone carrying troops were the Queens *Mary* and *Elizabeth* and that was because they had too much speed for any U-boat prowler. However the *Andes* was a veteran at this job, having taken three convoys of Americans to Oran and Casablanca. It, too, had a formidable speed of 22 knots with U-boats being able to travel at only 10 to 15 knots. The ship took a zig-zag course, veering to the opposite direction every eight minutes. Since torpedoes had a speed of only 4 knots, it would be a lucky shot that would hit us.

The voyage turned out to be uneventful except for a few days when rough seas had us tumbling about like rolling pins. Life-boat drill twice a day, deck tennis, bridge and the organization of a concert from the talent in the brigade filled the time rather pleasantly until we serenely floated into the docks at Liverpool.

I fell in love with England the minute I saw it. 'And what is so rare as a day in June? Then, if ever, come perfect days,' sang the poet James Russell Lowell. And this was 24 June 1943. The weather had that glorious serenity that sinks into the soul and makes it glow. As we gawped out of our train window taking us to the south of England we were enchanted by the well-kept gardens and green parks that were evidence of the tender care and pride that had been lavished on the land. Victory gardens blossomed everywhere, even between the railway tracks. At the doors and windows of the neat houses, the symmetry of which was occasionally broken by bombed-out buildings, stood housewives, farmers and children waving their arms at our troop train, holding thumbs up and flashing the 'V' sign. We reached Haslemere in Surrey in the blackout and were welcomed by the sight of thin needles of light from the anti-aircraft searchlights that had caught a silver moth-like plane in its tentacles and were pursuing it across a black sky.

An elegant, twenty-room country house had been requisitioned to act as the Army Brigade's Headquarters. We were particularly impressed by the bathrooms with walls of pink, blue and yellow tiles, chromium-framed looking-glasses, showers with glass doors and bidets. This latter piece of plumbing was the object of much ribaldry and bad jokes because most Canadians had never seen its like and didn't know precisely what it was for. The house had been stripped of most of its furniture, which included the beds so that, although only two officers shared each bedroom, we had to bed down in sleeping bags on the floor.

The next few months were packed with days of exploration, stagnation, frustration and desperation. The country roads that had no road signs and twisted and turned inexplicably through meadows and hedgerows made map-reading a job for clairvoyants. Finding streets in London was just as confusing since they mysteriously changed their nomenclature so that the Mall at Trafalgar Square changes into the Strand as you go east, which converts to the Temple and then becomes Fleet Street where it very soon metamorphoses into Ludgate Hill, and past St Paul's Cathedral it inexplicably calls itself Cannon Street.

The food was also an experience that ought to have pleased a socialist like myself since rationing brought equal misery to all stomachs, high or low. In the army one was resigned to unappetizing margarine for butter, but the bread was not only monotonous but had a dirty grey look that was hard to swallow. The sausages might have been made of sawdust and clung to the roof of the mouth like tasteless glue. Dehydrated eggs instead of the real thing smelt almost sickeningly bad to newcomers to such a delicacy, and suggestions in our mess as to the best way to enjoy them included wearing a clothes-peg on one's nose.

A meal in a first-class hotel hardly offered anything much better. At the Old Ship Hotel in Brighton the dinner was only sumptuous in the profusion of cutlery that surrounded the plates. The soup did little more than skim the bottom of the plate and tasted like hot water that had some ingredient like onion or chicken wafted over it – but not too close. The main course could be a thin edge of beef or an unpalatable piece of fish. The so-called sweet was an unsweet trifle or a sliver of cheese. With a glass of port, the bill came to twelve shillings – twice as expensive as the five shilling limit charged in most restaurants in London. Coffee, if you can honestly call it that, was extra.

It was clear in the very first days of our settling in to our quarters that the future of our armoured brigade was dubious and clouded. Our units had no central location and were spread in a higgledy-piggledy fashion over a twenty-five mile area. We had no tanks or armoured vehicles to train on and rumour had it that there was no place for us in the Establishment that was to go into action in Europe. Because as the Brigade Intelligence Officer I was singularly unemployed, I was sent on a four-day course to a school in Highgate which was located in a mansion formerly owned by the Earl of Mansfield. I had digs not far away in a pleasing house and shared a room with two American captains. Since I had not been told what the course was about, I was surprised to discover it was a priority hush-hush affair about escaping from prison camps. It was designed primarily for RAF personnel who might be shot down over Europe.

On our course, in addition to seven RAF Intelligence officers, we had four naval officers, an artillery captain, twelve Americans and myself as the sole Canadian. Lectures began at 9.30 a.m. and with periodic breaks for tea and meals went on until late in the evening. We had lectures about famous escapes of the First World War, the techniques of tunnelling, routes to take to get one out of France and the Lowlands and the location of native helpers who would give us shelter. Spain was the best route out and the Channel crossings were considered far too dangerous.

The most intriguing and difficult exercises we took part in were learning the complicated codes that would be used to communicate with us should we ever land up in a prisoner-of-war camp. These codes would be contained in the routine letters sent to us by our girl friends or wives or parents, and would contain vital information that was needed for any escape plans by the inmates. Through having taken the course, we were automatically designated as having a special leading role in anything contemplated by the men, from assassination to forged passports and travel documents. Because all this was so obviously secret we were not allowed to take down any notes and had to commit the complicated sequences of numbers involved to memory. I managed this memory feat well enough for a few weeks after I returned to the brigade. I did put some key sequences on a slip of paper which I sewed into the inner lining of my jacket. However, if I ever had been captured, it would have been hopelessly inadequate, assuming I hadn't lost it, to help me decipher any messages I might be getting from Joyce or my mother. This fear that I might be placed in such a predicament with a body of men waiting for me to tell them about secret instructions, and authorities in England reading my domestic letters for return messages, haunted me all through the Normandy and German campaigns. I had nightmares about the humiliation of forgetting the codes. It was one Intelligence course I could have well done without.

The night the course broke up I decided to stay in London, celebrating with an American whose name was something like, but not, Temple. Temple was the randiest man I had ever met and he went after women like a ravenous dog sniffing for meat. I should have known better because I had already spent one evening with him when he picked up a prostitute and wanted me to go with them to the Berkeley Hotel for dinner and whatever else. Being newly married and boringly worthy about sex, I declined.

I had no high hopes that a popsie trawl through London's West End would give me any memorably titillating experience. My one disappointment about England to date was the plainness of its women. Those that I had come close to had weak eyes, mottled complexions and bad teeth. They were supported by fat legs which I attributed to the prodigious amount of walking and bicycling they had to do in the war years.

'They don't seem to care how they look,' I wrote bluntly in my diary. 'With clothes rationing this conspires to give most of them the appearance of a charlady on a busy day. They can converse at a terrific rate and are probably a bit more educated than Canadian girls. But without girdles to keep them in, dresses to flatter them and high heels to give them pretty legs, they don't appeal to me enough to get started in a conversation. Maybe I'll get used to it.'

Indeed I did. I married an English girl and am now the besotted father of two daughters who have each been suggested in the Press as being amongst the most beautiful women in England. Without the constraints of a war-torn society and with the advantages of a proper diet, the

English woman in her teens and early twenties has a lithe freshness and piquant vivacity that in its naturalness puts the artificial comeliness of most American and Continental women in the shade. It also has the quality, if properly tended, of defying the depredations of age, leaving behind features whose bone structure makes possible an aura of haunting, confident radiance.

I never ceased to wonder at the obsession Americans had with women. They collected lays like so many notches on a belt. Being locked away in barracks seemed to stimulate their libidoes to a dangerous pitch whenever they were given leave. Lieutenant Temple was not typical because his need for women, any women, was almost psychotic. My diary about my last night with him reads like an introduction to a low-level Bacchanalia.

Although Temple was only twenty-four, he looked much younger. This was because he had fair hair which was so light it seemed to be no more than peach fuzz on top of his head. His features were small, almost cherubic, but they disguised an uncontrollable temper. We all knew he had a rich father who generously supplemented his service salary and that in civilian life he had had a reputation as a playboy. Rumour had it that he had spent $3,500 in his first six months in the army. In today's currency that would amount to almost ten times that much.

Why he picked on me, a most reluctant sybarite for his companion that evening, I shall never know. He had booked two adjoining rooms with one bathroom at the Grosvenor House. Usually one needed to reserve rooms at least two weeks in advance, and hotels did their best to discourage men in uniform from taking them, but Temple seemed to have no difficulty finding rooms in an overcrowded London. I suspect it was his reputation as a big spender that won him his priorities.

Our first hunting site was the Grosvenor House tea dance where Temple drank 14 shillings worth of Scotch without seeing anyone he fancied. We then did a frantic exploration of the Piccadilly Hotel, Queen's Hotel, Oddenino's, the Trocadero and the Café Royal. His tactics were to dash into the bar, order a double Scotch, survey the joint for possible interest and after a few minutes, frustrated, leave. Getting desperate at his lack of success, he decided to contact an American girl who had organized dates for him before. Unsure of her address, we went around to two wrong places in a taxi and then drove to the Rainbow Club, which was a respectable meeting place and dance hall for Americans to be introduced to English girls. They were not the kind of female companionship Temple was looking for and we left.

The more elusive his prey, the more frantic Temple became. It was not the drink that inflamed his frustration because he rarely downed the whiskies he ordered, but merely bought them as an initiation fee at the bar he was investigating. Nor was it lust, because at this stage he still appeared to have some discrimination about the women that appealed to him. I suspect he was now motivated by pure vanity and a determination to prove to me that he was not a sexual failure. Our next stop was back again to the Berkeley Hotel for dinner where he ordered four double Scotches and two crème de menthes which I helped him consume. He also had a terrible squabble with a waiter who had accused us of using the wrong forks.

It was now about eight in the evening and we staggered on to the Café Royal where Temple picked up a woman who claimed she was a Polish countess. She boasted about her lineage and the grand parties she gave in Turkey and Italy. I noted her dirty fingernails and cheap clothes and even Temple was put off by her obvious lying attempt to impress a pair of naive North Americans. It was now ten o'clock and Temple was getting desperate. Back again we went to the Café Royal, Oddenino's and the Trocadero. He hailed a taxi to take us to the Casablanca Club, but the driver didn't know where it was and didn't want to look. After another altercation we got out of the taxi and had to pay the cabbie three shillings.

I was becoming more and more disgusted with him and myself but felt that, out of loyalty, I would have to stick the evening out with him. To my chagrin I found myself walking around Piccadilly with him, surveying the available prostitutes. He began bargaining with two tarts, one of whom had no teeth, and when I took a stand and said I would not be seen in public with either of them, he put them in a taxi and dismissed them.

I was totally fed up and decided to leave him on his own. I had just received instructions from a passer-by about how to get to Grosvenor House in the blackout. Temple implored me to walk with him until the next turning. He promised to come back with me if he had no luck. That did it. Hardly had we moved fifty yards when he was in conversation with two blondes. They assured him he could buy drinks at the Regent Palace Hotel where we arrived at about a quarter to midnight. I dragged along with the plump one while he linked arms with the more striking blonde. Hardly had we sat down when the band played the National Anthem, indicating the bar was shut. However since he had ordered ten double Scotches, they served us and everyone but me proceeded to get plastered.

I left Temple with his find while mine insisted I take her home. It was now close to one o'clock. In the taxi she asked me how much money I had. That would determine her price. I told her I had none for her. Indignant at the rebuff she complained that I was 'just a gigolo', started to abuse me with maudlin conversation and, realizing that I was adamant about not paying her anything, she left me outside Grosvenor House and wandered off into the blackout.

'I had just entered the hotel lobby,' reads my diary, 'when Temple arrived with his blonde. He took her up to our adjoining rooms and gave the lift boy a pound at her insistence. When we arrived she made a play for me but I managed to drive her back to Temple and retreated to my room where I barricaded the door between us. All night long I could hear her shouting "Stop it! I'm a married woman!" and was scared stiff that the hotel detective would come up. At about four in the morning it all died down.'

The next morning Temple told me the night had cost him £15 and he had got nothing out of it but a headache. That would be over £150 in today's money. He wanted me to contribute something substantial to defray that profligacy but I only gave him £3 to help pay for the hotel bill. 'He believes his shaving kit was stolen by the plump blonde,' reads my diary, 'because it was nowhere to be found. He told me his pick-up had asked for £5, whereupon he socked her a couple of times and it was quite a mess. I hope it taught him a lesson but I doubt it. But it taught me to leave Americans of that kind alone from here on in.'

When I arrived back at Brigade Headquarters at Haslemere, the expected news had just come. The brigade was to be broken up and its personnel dispersed to other units or held in barracks as reinforcements. It was a depressing denouement to all the sincerity, loyalty and friendship that had been built up in the brigade. For us at Headquarters it was a particularly chilling event because there was no longer any use for us since we had no regiments to command. I realized that my acting captaincy would be withdrawn and that I would have to revert to being a lieutenant, with a serious loss in seniority as well as a drop of $80 a month in pay. From an army career standpoint I would be back to where I was when I first qualified as an armoured officer in 1942.

With almost indecent haste the administrative details of winding up the brigade were undertaken and postings made to units in Sicily and to reinforcement camps in England. Being an Intelligence Officer, it seemed no one knew what to do with me since all active formations already had their IOs. Having been turfed out of our comfortable head-quarters in Haslemere, myself and two officers were given rooms in Victoria Barracks in London. These buildings had formed married quarters for Other Ranks before the war but they hadn't been occupied for six years. The cubby holes called rooms that we were given were cheer-less, damp, gloomy and dirty. The walls were painted a greenish yellow colour that made one bilious. The springs on the beds were covered with three square burlap bags laid end to end which were supposed to act as both a sheet and a blanket. There was no hot water. No batman. Just dirt. In the two days I was there I acquired large red bumps and welts on my legs and arms. The barracks were infested with lice and bedbugs. This was the closest I ever came to having a war wound. If I had been in the American Army I might have been invested with a Purple Heart.

My next move was to a slightly more salubrious barracks where the rooms and corridors were almost as dreary and to get water for my wash basin I had to cross over to the bathroom across the hall. I groaned about having to pack a sheepskin coat, two battle dress, four pairs of shoes, assorted shirts and laundry as well as a large number of pamphlets into my bed roll. It took me from 9.30 in the morning to 2.30 in the after-noon to visit all the officials who had to sign the eleven releases to let me go: Medical Officer, Dental Officer, Quartermaster, Library, Pay Officer, Meals Secretary, Records, Post Office, Personnel Selection Officer, Barracks Officer and Wing Two Quartermaster.

My new home was a dumping ground for Medical, Dental, Provost and Intelligence personnel awaiting postings. I was fretting about the possibility that I would lose my captaincy and, worse, that I might have to sit out the rest of the war at a desk job. There were hints that a sig-nificant job was in the offing for me but, knowing the army, I pinned no hopes on it. Then the Big Accident syndrome that had shaped my career to date happened again. The fate that enabled me to write *Defeat in the West*, and through it follow a career as a journalist and critic, inter-vened once again with its arbitrary and enigmatic hand. Had the brigade not been broken up, I would probably have gone into battle in a Sherman tank in Normandy and maybe not have come out again. And had I not made friends with a Major Felix Walter, who was responsible for finding suitable employment for officers who had lost their positions through re-organization of units, the next Big Accident that changed the shape of my life would not have taken place.

Felix had known about my interest in the Wehrmacht because we had talked about it many times. He was at the Headquarters of the Canadian Army, saw my name on the redundant list of officers and thought I ideally fitted a temporary job that had just become vacant. I went to see him at Canadian HQ and he told me that I had been posted to MI14(b) at the War Office in Whitehall for at least six weeks. I was to start immediately, would live in London and get $4 (about £2) extra as subsistence money.

(ii) Not MI5 or MI6 but MI 14(b)

Everyone of modest intelligence in Britain has heard about MI5 and MI6, but MI14(b)? Whenever I mention the fact that I was in it, I get an incredulous laugh. I did not realize it at the time but this was the best and most important job in Operational Intelligence that one of my limited experience could have been given. In those hush-hush days, it was a relatively high level secret that MI14 dealt with Germany. Other numbers concentrated on Italy, the Middle East, the Balkans, Russia. There was 14(a), (b), (c), (d). There may have been an (e) but if so I didn't know what it did. Each specialized in aspects of the German war potential such as transport, oil, food. My section, b, dealt with the Order of Battle of the Wehrmacht's formations, and it was our task to compile a card index report of every senior German commander, his record, his personality and his whereabouts; to estimate the strength in arms and personnel of German formations the Allies were likely to face in battle; to locate their movements and positions and to predict their likely destinations and aims. No longer would I have only a worm's-eye view of the war but here I would have the panoramic view of an eagle of man's military follies. I realized that the division – 15,000 to 20,000 men – would be the smallest unit I'd be dealing with and it made my head swim.

It was a very large room in Whitehall in which we worked from 9.30 a.m. to 7 in the evening. It was compartmentalized into geographical sections, so that a large map of Russia proliferating with coloured pins indicating the German positions would be separated by a few yards from

As a Canadian Armoured Corps Officer, 1942.

similar large maps of Finland and Norway which indicated where the
experts on the Scandinavian war situation were at work. I was attached
to the most exciting area of the lot – France and the Lowlands – because
we all knew an invasion of the Continent and a Second Front must soon
take place.

When I arrived at MI14(b) on Sunday, 22 August 1943 – there were
no week-ends off in that work – the head of all the MI14s was the
Honourable Peter Acton. He was a blond, aesthetic-looking, charming
Englishman in his early thirties who had been involved with German
Order of Battle since the beginning of the war. He was the complete
master of his job, with a phenomenal memory that retained more details
about the Wehrmacht than probably anyone on the Allied side. When he
was visited by brigadiers and generals to discuss German strength in
France, the Balkans or Russia, they would leave with their heads brim-
ming with divisional numbers and the probable gun power of enemy
corps and armies. Their gratitude at the surprisingly detailed information indicated a new respect for what Acton and his department were
up to.

Major Eric Birley, who had been studying Order of Battle for as long
as Acton, was the top man in MI14(b). Wearing horn-rimmed glasses
and talking with the precision of a philosophy professor, Birley could
rattle off the regimental numbers in German divisions destroyed in 1941
and then tell you the strength of Landschutz battalions in Sarajevo in
1942. When he died in November, 1995, the obituaries recognized him
as Britain's leading authority on studies of Hadrian's Wall, the Roman
army and Roman frontiers in Britain. For fifteen years he had been
Professor of Romano-British history and Archaeology at Durham
University. He had become almost a legendary figure in Intelligence circles because his study of the Roman legions had enabled him to guess
the details of new and old German formations, since they numbered
their units in almost the same way as the Romans.

My immediate boss was a Canadian, Reg Unwin, and it was probably because I shared his nationality that I was selected to assist him. I
soon recognized that this trio of Acton, Birley and Unwin was the
exceptional brain-power behind the accurate information about the
Wehrmacht that was regularly being fed to 21 Army Group under
Montgomery and SHAEF under Eisenhower. There were officers senior
to them in MI14 who knew precious little about the complex details of
intelligence gathering, who were unable to check or collate what they

were given and merely had the assessments of Acton and Birley re-typed and handed up to higher authority. The system, inevitable because of the amount of hours spent in detecting and collating facts, resulted in no one in the top echelons having the time or facilities to do anything about what MI14 sent them. In other words, the War Cabinet had to rely upon the judgement and knowledge of rather junior officers.

My first task under Unwin, who treated me sympathetically since as a novice I could have been more of a nuisance than a help, was to study in great detail the map of France. On it were about sixty-two pegs – round for infantry and square for armoured – indicating the locations of the German divisions. Each division and its map locations which were designated in squared numbers (Nîmes – 200; Paris – 213) had to be recorded on geographical cards. Should a division move, the pin would also move and the details would be noted on the cards. The flood of information which came into us, mostly in French, was the fount of our knowledge.

My French was elementary, in spite of studying it at high school and two years at university, but the vocabulary used was mostly military so I could manage and, if in difficulties, I looked up any unfamiliar word in an Anglo-French dictionary. The amount of information was voluminous. The bulk of it came from agents throughout the world, mostly in English, but there were many reports in French, German, Dutch, Russian, and Spanish which were distributed to the several MI14 sections. Then there were captured or stolen enemy documents, prisoner-of-war interrogations, military attachés' reports from Spain, Portugal, Sweden, Switzerland. These latter were sketchy and, we thought, usually not very reliable. Then there were the operational Intelligence reports from Wavell's or Eisenhower's HQs in Italy or Africa. A vital wealth of data was plumbed by Unwin from microfilm of French train schedules, as well as the reports from Frenchmen working on the railways who sent us in secret bundles the movement of all trains in every direction. Seventy trains emerging on the tracks in a certain destination meant that an infantry division was on the move. For an armoured division 120 trains would be filled. The positioning of the Wehrmacht was, of course, imperative to Eisenhower's plans. Where was the armoured reserve located to be launched as a counter-attack against our beachhead and were there only weak infantry divisions on the Atlantic Wall to meet our first onslaught? This train material came in such abundance, it seemed that almost every French railway worker was chipping in his knowledge.

There was information, too, from French residents who would let us know if the Germans were requisitioning billets in their town. What was the colour of the braid on their uniforms, the numbers, the emblems? Even the churchyards could offer up clues about what unit had arrived. The tombstone setting out the battalion or regiment to which a man belonged would inform us about his division. Occasionally a bizarre rumour would be sent to us indicating no specific source. I realize now that some of these unattributed data probably came from our triumph in breaking the ultra-secret German Enigma code, but in our work we were rarely told the names of informants where MI6 or other clandestine agencies were involved. The one I remember said that a Japanese Kamikaze pilot was in Le Havre, where he was preparing himself for a suicide assault on London. He would be flying a German bomber which would be dive-bombed on St Paul's Cathedral. I don't know how seriously this story was taken, but I was reassured that a couple of our own agents would be dropped in the area to check out the report. I never heard any more about it.

Another unique, and sometimes productive, channel of information were the carrier pigeons which were strategically dropped in Occupied France. The pigeons were tumbled out of planes and each had a small parachute strapped to its body so it landed safely. They had on them questionnaires which asked the locals who found the birds to fill in such queries as when did any fresh Germans appear in their area, what were the results of the recent Allied bombings, what industrial or military targets could they suggest, details of the tanks or guns they had seen. The co-operative French peasants detached the parachutes after filling in the forms and released the birds to fly back to the roosts in England from which they had come.

The hatred of the Germans and the realization of the French that they were soon to be defeated was evidenced by the enthusiasm with which hundreds of these pigeon notes came back, always signed by false names. The return of the pigeons was regularly acknowledged on the BBC in broadcasts to which most Frenchmen were clandestine listeners. Each note was a story in itself. One woman cursed 'the dirty dogs with whom we shall get even'. Another pleaded for an immediate invasion of France. One young man described with great glee how German soldiers could be seen frantically running about trying to catch these parachuting pigeons before the locals snatched them. One cautious farmer reported that there were no military targets near him, but there were some a little farther on. Some became very fond of these feathered couriers and gave them pet names and cursed the Italian who had killed one and ate it – 'the dirty canard'.

> 'The information is only fairly informative,' I wrote in my diary 'from an Order of Battle standpoint because the peasants are not sufficiently military-wise to send correct or pertinent data. And there is always the danger that the Germans could fill in the notes themselves with false information and send them back to us. But on the whole they are probably more useful as a morale booster to these enchained people by making them aware of the fact that there are free peoples outside fighting on their behalf.'

For over forty years I kept my involvement with MI14(b) totally secret. But after the publication of *The Spycatcher*, with the subsequent loosening up of bans on Intelligence history, I saw no harm in amusing my friends with a hint that such a curious numbered unit did exist and I had been in it. As a regular panellist on Robert Robinson's quirky chat show, *Stop The Week* on Radio 4, in a moment of irrelevant badinage I mentioned MI14(b). I got a welcome, surprise letter from Professor Eric Birley. 'I used to be in charge of it,' he wrote in 1986. 'I had heard you mention it in passing on the show quite a while ago, and I had wondered; but German Order of Battle is a clinching reference.' In subsequent correspondence with Birley, it was clear why he knew little about me, since he was promoted to higher things just a few weeks after I had joined Unwin. I was just a temporary attachment and not expected to stay at MI14(b) very long. In the event my six-week posting was stretched to about three months. 'I expect you worked with Reg Unwin,' wrote Birley. 'He had been the IO of the Canadian Corps involved in the Dieppe raid and before the raid he gave his general his reading of the German plans for dealing with an invasion there. The general refused to accept Unwin's views (which in the event proved to have been very near the mark indeed) and the upshot was that he was disposed of – and I fancy the general was decorated. We picked him up when Canadian HQ told us he was jobless. I believe he played a major part in studying German defence plans before D-Day.'

When I joined Canadian Army HQ about three months before the invasion of Normandy, the last map Unwin had drawn then was almost a copy in detail of the Invasion map used by Eisenhower for Overlord.

The Germans, pressed by the Russians in the East, had no ability to transfer additional divisions to the sixty-odd they kept in France, nor did they move them much about while awaiting our assault. The Allies had almost perfect intelligence on 6 June 1944 about where the enemy was positioned and it gave me quiet satisfaction as a tiny cog in MI14(b) to have played a small part in that success. At Canadian Army HQ, as their Order of Battle expert, I helped prepare a daily record of the German forces and armoury facing the Canadians in the fighting from Normandy to the end of the war. We regularly received information from an outfit called MIRS (Military Intelligence Research Section) which would warn us about new divisions the Germans were sending into battle.

We would be told, for instance, that a hitherto unknown division numbered 543 had turned up on the Italian front, and that we could therefore soon expect to find nine more divisions numbered between 540 and 549 turning up between Russia and France. Soon enough, they would all emerge. These mysterious predictions were the achievement of Birley, who had been promoted to head MIRS a few weeks after I went to MI14(b). He had realized, long before others, that the Wehrmacht had used the same system that had been used by the Roman legions in the days of Caesar as a model for the identification of their units . 'My main help was that I had been used to reading German views on the Roman Army,' he wrote me in one of his letters. 'And that, I suppose, put me on the right wavelength. I came across sufficient captured German army documents to make me realize that they were far more valuable than MI6 reports, most of which were nonsense or works of fiction.'

One of the main reasons the Germans lost the war was their inefficient Intelligence service, which was wrong about Russia, Normandy and America. When they got things right, Hitler, who had total contempt for his intelligence officers, relied on his intuition rather than their reports. The British, on the other hand, were punctilious in their efforts to recruit into Intelligence the best academic and creative brains they could find. Field Marshall Montgomery was a fanatic about demanding efficient Intelligence. His chief IO was Bill Williams, later Sir Edgar Williams, and was described by Monty as 'intellectually far superior to me'. When the war began Williams had already achieved a considerable reputation as a historian of 18th century politics. He died in 1995.

Other bright young men assigned to Military Intelligence, to analyzing German strategic plans, to producing wicked, ingenious black propaganda included Isaiah Berlin, Malcolm Muggeridge, Richard Crossman and Sefton Delmer to mention but a few. Eric Birley, who also died in 1995, was pre-eminent among those who gave our commanders the information needed to defeat Hitler.

(iii) War-time London and D-Day

Not being attached to any specific Canadian unit while I was seconded to MI14(b), I was expected to find accommodation and feed myself in London on my acting captain's pay of $6.50 Canadian dollars plus a small subsistence allowance. Because London was so over-crowded no hotel or club would allow a man in uniform to rent a room for more than a couple of weeks; more usually only three or four days. My first lucky break was finding a room at the Dominion Officers' Club which was located in Grosvenor Street, near the American Embassy. It was a gracious, Romanesque house with hand-worked panelled walls in its lounge and library and a gracious Italian garden. It was closed when the war broke out but some authoritative persuasion had convinced the owners to re-open it as a Dominion Officers' Club. They held dances every Tuesday and Friday night which gave lonely Canadians a chance to meet middle-class English girls usually in Wren or Waaf uniforms. My room cost only five shillings a night, but my maximum tenure was three weeks. After that I lived a hotel gypsy's life, booking rooms three or four weeks in advance for two or three days each. During that spell in London I became familiar with almost every splendid hotel in the capital, having lived a few days in the Berkeley, the Savoy, Grosvenor House, Mount Royal, and the Overseas League who took me in for four days.

The blackout, however, made social life a dull and limited event. My normal routine was to leave the War Office at seven in the evening, eat an austerity meal at some place like the Dominion Club or the Overseas League, by which time it was impossible to wander outside because of the dense blackout. Buses stopped running at 10 o'clock, and without transport, and with my limited knowledge of London streets, most evenings I spent reading a book or improving my German.

Food packages arrived regularly from Joyce and my mother. They contained, in addition to cans of fruit and soup, such precious items, useful for bribes to get hotel rooms, as soap, shaving cream and razor blades. The chocolates came off rather badly in these tightly packed boxes since they absorbed the smell of the soap around them and I felt I would be blowing soap bubbles every time I took a bite out of a Nealson's Jersey Milk bar. Restaurant meals were paralyzingly monotonous. Whether you paid sixteen shillings at the Savoy, or two bob in Soho, the menu, sometimes adorned with French names, would be a depleted hors d'oeuvre, watery soup, bully beef or minuscule meat patties or tired fish as the main course, with a sweet of pears and custard or apples and custard or just plain custard.

There were a few restaurants that tried to be individual and tasty with their limited resources and my diary provides an inventory of these relatively exotic eateries. There was the Hellenic Restaurant in Greek Street which specialized in moussaka, which I discovered was a combination of chopped cheese arranged in tempting layers that always arrived hot and appetizing. The Comedy Restaurant in Panton Street, near Piccadilly Circus, concentrated on rabbit and pigeon dishes which needed some getting used to. It had a rococo atmosphere aspiring to grander Victorian times and its glass and cutlery was far too opulent for the pathetic food they contained. The waiters all wore dinner-jackets and although six of them would bow you out on leaving, a meal seldom cost more than five shillings. Albert's Restaurant in Soho was French and had a select, civil service clientele who appreciated the natural culinary skills of its proprietor who managed to give an aromatic Gallic flavour to ingredients that other cafes had given up on.

Then there was Lyons Corner House in Marble Arch which was reached by a long escalator into a vast space which seemed to be occupied by hundreds of customers being served by darting waitresses dressed in the traditional white cap and apron of domestics in grand country houses. It specialized in brunch, which was cold salad and sausage followed by a chocolate trifle rather overpowered by some accompanying vanilla. The relentless comings and goings, up and down the escalators, of thousands of people a day filling themselves automatically like so many internal combustion engines with enough energy to get the same substance the next day, gave me visions of those robot-like characters in German Expressionist films.

On my daily walk from the War Office in Whitehall to the Dominion Officers' Club in Grosvenor Street, I would run the gauntlet of invitations from the ladies of Maddox Street who had made this particular area their chief centre of operations. Maddox Street, running off Regent Street, was during daylight a typical office neighbourhood in the West

End. About six o'clock the madames would take up their posts on both sides of the street looking like so many predatory sentries. Flamboyantly, but for the most part tastefully dressed, from a distance they looked like the more chic women who worked as secretaries and telephonists in these offices. But the closer one got, the more disillusionment set in. Their faces were hard-lined, their make-up too elaborately plastered on, their smiles too mechanical. Most of them had a plush, over-long silver fox fur wrapped around their shoulders and many of them held a leash to which was attached a small fox terrier which rarely barked. They would parade majestically up and down their little patch of this nondescript street and if you looked interested, their lips would open into a broad smile as they intoned 'Hello, darling.' A man who stopped was immediately engaged in a conversation about terms, which were quickly agreed, and taking hold of his arm she would direct him to some flat she had in the neighbourhood. The ladies appeared to be on friendly terms with each other and there was no spirit of competitiveness as they chatted animatedly to each other in groups before the evening trade arrived.

Most of the girls were French and glamorously dark. The English prostitutes weren't nearly as attractive because of their yellow teeth and unimaginative clothes. When it rained they carried dainty little cellophane umbrellas, indicating business as usual. In the blackout when visibility was seldom more than five yards, they would flash a light at you and try to stop a man with words like 'What's your hurry, darling?' or 'Hello, sweetheart.' If a constable appeared they would scurry away like anxious rabbits and hide in the nearest vestibule until he had made a routine appearance obviously intending to arrest no one. Because I passed by them about three times a day, they stopped accosting me when early on I had told them I had a wife and three children in Canada who demanded my fidelity. They greeted me with either a half-smile or a disinterested look of recognition. As a group they considered themselves the élite of their profession, and as high-ranking artists they charged between three to five pounds for their talents, which was expensive for what a soldier or sailor usually got.

It was at one of those dances at the Overseas League organized for American and Dominion officers that I met Nita. She was a Wren with the job of conducting intelligence tests for the navy so that sailors with requisite aptitudes could be allotted a proper place in the senior service. She looked delicious in her blue naval uniform, was a compulsive chatterer, had blue eyes a painter would die for and the spun-gold blonde hair that seems to be the exclusive preserve of English and Scandinavian women. The relationship that began that day at an afternoon tea dance lasted for almost a year, platonic at first but more intimate later. When the music had stopped, I asked her to have dinner with me at the Berkeley Hotel. Our introductory conversation was distracted by the surprising appearance of Clark Gable, in an American captain's uniform, taking the table next to ours. His party consisted of two other American officers and three girls. With my knowledge of London femininity I guessed that the girls had probably been picked up in Maddox Street. Gable's companion was the prettiest but she had the hard-bitten, peroxide blonde look of a woman who had been trampled over many times since the war began. The other two had the same brassy, semi-frightened look of girls ill-at-ease at finding themselves stared at because of Gable. 'From snatches of the conversation we could overhear,' reports my diary, 'Gable gave me the impression of being both crude and stupid. Without the magic of the camera to help him, I'm afraid he is a most disillusioning character. Why he should choose to be seen in such company is beyond me. The attractive diners at other tables looked crestfallen as they could see the clay feet of their idol melting before them. Nita was particularly crumpled and pained by this revelation of the true Hollywood.'

Being a dedicated socialist at the time, I was always uneasy about the relations of MI14 with the Russians. In 1941 it was expected the Russians would collapse in six or eight weeks against the triumphant might of the Wehrmacht. But two years later they were driving the Germans back to the Ukraine, having fought over 250 German divisions, while the combined Allied armies of America and Britain, up to the invasion of Sicily, had only confronted in combat the two or three German divisions of Rommel's Afrika Korps. Yet in spite of their sacrifices and the tactical efficiency with which they were destroying Hitler's armies, there was an atmosphere of deep distrust whenever we had to meet them to exchange information. Colonel Acton had regular weekly conferences with the Americans – usually generals – to compare Order of Battle data. Even with the Americans, we had to decide that certain items should not be divulged to them, probably because it came from MI6 or code-breaking activities which we did not want the Americans to know about.

Evidence of the disdain in which the Russians were held could be measured by the fact that the huge ten feet by ten feet map on which

Captain Redpath, who ran the Eastern section, kept track of the tremendous battles taking place on the Russo-German front had been printed in czarist times before the Communist revolution. It was part of my job to help him bring the battle lines up to date by reading the dispatches that flowed into MI14. I would call out the almost unpronounceable names that had been fought over and Redpath would find them and make the necessary pin adjustments. His task was not made too easy by the geographical locations on the map still being named by their czarist appellations which the Russians had changed to more proletarian labels. It was a sad reflection on War Office mentality that after almost three years of war the Russians were still thought of in terms of twenty-five years earlier.

While the Russians kept demanding information about the German divisions in France, our weekly meetings with them were efforts at evasion and even duplicity. Both sides negotiated with each other with delicately balanced chips on their shoulders. We had to contend no German divisions were being withdrawn from France to strengthen the Germans in the East because that would reinforce the Russian claims for a Second Front. We were not yet keen on a cross-Channel invasion that the Russians should know about. We kept our cards very close to our chests about our sources of information and the Russians did the same. 'I often think we distrust them more than they distrust us,' I was told by one of our negotiating team. At the time I was dismayed by this suspicion between Allies, but with hindsight and knowing about the dangerous days of the Cold War, I must admit that we were right to protect our intelligence secrets and I was naively wrong.

Late in October I said my good-byes to Acton, Unwin, Redpath, Henderson and the others at MI14(b) and spent about a month at Matlock reinforcing my knowledge of German identification, tactics, weaponry, map-reading and propaganda. In the area of Order of Battle I knew much more than my instructors. It was obvious that I had been fully prepared for the position I was to take up at Canadian Army HQ as their expert on the formations and weaponry that would be faced by the Canadians when they finally met them in combat in France. In the months of planning for Overlord, the Canadians were settled in the Portsmouth area, where we lived in local houses or under camouflaged netting. Head of Intelligence at our HQ was Colonel Peter Wright, a pre-war lawyer who had the sharpest and quickest mind I had experienced in uniform. Under the severest pressure, he always exuded confidence and reliability. Under him was an Englishman, Major Leslie Chater, who had probably been seconded to us because of his knowledge of German, with which the rest of us were only fleetingly acquainted. He was a mercurial personality determined to make the war as comfortable as possible for himself, and in our command vehicle, which housed maps and documents, he had installed a plush armchair and added vases of flowers whenever possible.

Because of the limited area designated for the beachhead in Normandy, Montgomery's 21st Army Group would make the initial assault with the 1st US Army and the 2nd British Army attacking side by side. Patton's Third US Army and Crerar's Canadian Army would come in later when there was sufficient room. This meant that on D-Day the Canadian division was under the command of the British, while our own HQ twiddled its thumbs in Southern England until General Crerar could have complete operational control of his own army.

It was gratifying to me that the map of the location of German divisions in France sent down from 21st Army Group was virtually unchanged from the map that Unwin and I had drawn up about five months earlier (see map on page 77). There were the same sixty divisions identified by their circles for infantry and squares for armoured, with three Panzer divisions relatively close to the Channel while a reserve force of another three crack armoured divisions – 12 Panzer Division 'Hitler Jugend', 21 Panzer Division and Panzer Lehr Division called the Panzer Group West – were stationed north of the Loire to act as a counter attack force against the early Allied bridgehead.

About a few weeks before D-Day, set for 6 June, Montgomery addressed the HQ staff and officers above the rank of colonel in the Canadian army. He outlined the plan and goals of Overlord with informative maps and with his precise, clipped language that was intimidating but at the same time, confidence building. Before he began his talk he told us that he would be speaking for twenty minutes. 'There will be no coughing while I am addressing you,' he said, looking at his wrist watch. 'You now have one minute to cough. After that there will be no coughing.' In the embarrassed silence a few brave souls cleared their throats. But after that, there was no coughing.

'Last night I was frantically trying to set up a tent to house a large secret radio set for Colonel Wright,' I noted in my diary. 'I was being helped by Wally (I've forgotten who he was) and pointing to the dull sky I said 'It looks like tonight.' He nodded in agreement. In the morning, having heard nothing more, I assumed we'd been wrong. That afternoon, however, Major Chater announced that the invasion had begun last night. We worked like hell getting all our stuff out of the houses we were in. In twenty-four hours we were all living and working under tents because we were now operational.'

And although we operated as an Army Command Headquarters writing daily Intelligence reports based on information sent down to us from 21 Army Group and up to us from the British and American Corps in the beachhead, it was not until 21 July, six weeks after the invasion had begun, that room had finally been found for Crerar's Canadian army to function in Normandy in the reinforcing role that had always been planned for it. In the meantime the only physical danger we faced in England was the appearance of Hitler's trumpeted secret weapon, the V1 flying bomb. They started to come over in frightening numbers – four to six at a time – and were clearly targeted at the troop formations in our area. Looking like avenging black arrows with fire shooting out of their tails, they were more terrifying to see than the fear of actually being hit by one. My diary notes that on 16 June, a V1 landed a few hundred yards away but I was more satisfied on that day with the news that twenty German divisions were now engaged in the bridgehead and we had predicted that by that date – D-Day plus ten – there would be twenty-five divisions fighting us. This meant our aerial bombardment of the roads and hesitancy on the part of the Führer were giving us a better chance of holding on to the beachhead.

On 21 July, the day after the plot that almost assassinated Hitler, we were at last ordered to France. There were six of us with our luggage, packed like sardines in a large lorry that rumbled towards Southampton. I lay, with two others, with my feet towards the tailboard while the other three were stretched sideways in the remaining space. We were fed by Americans when we reached Southampton and I mistook the reddish liquid I was given to drink for soup when it was tomato juice. 'Gee, you're the second guy who said that,' said the American cook, not realizing that tomato juice was a luxury we had not consumed in England for years. The landing ship, the *Empire Rapier*, was very large and took 2,000 across the Channel. We were all issued with two packs of rationed food, vomit bags and lifebelts for the journey which took place stealthily through the night.

The Canadians were on the left flank of the Allied advance and, as an army, fought their way along the Channel coast. From the capture of Caen, they took part in the carnage of the Falais gap, the encirclement and surrender of the Channel ports – Boulogne, Dunkirk and Le Havre – the advance through Walcheren Island, towards Brussels and Amsterdam, and ended up, when peace came, in Holland.

As far as I can remember, there were six to seven officers at Canadian Army HQ with some Other Ranks to look after meals and transport. In addition to Colonel Wright and Major Chater, myself and Robinson who reported on details of German units confronting us, were Gray, Webster, Philips and Rhiele who interpreted and translated the vast amount of German documents that poured into our HQ. Each day we produced an intelligence report between six to ten foolscap pages long, depending on the importance of the data we had to report. The report was divided into three parts. Part One, written by Wright and Chater, summarized the overall tactical position, then the enemy on the Canadian, British and American front, then air operations and finally a section predicting immediate enemy intentions. Part Two, the responsibility of myself and Robbie, handled character and background of senior officers opposing us, prisoner-of-war interrogations, German propaganda and enemy morale, while Part Three was filled with technical details of the weaponry in newly identified units and the capabilities of German armoured ammunition carriers or anti-flail tank mines or even a five-barrelled projector on a two wheel and 12 cwt mounting.

There was always someone on duty and we averaged a ten-to twelve-hour day. Since there was always activity on either our front or adjacent fronts, meals and sleep were our only requirements when we were not putting together information for our commanders. The Germans had been in such headlong retreat towards the German border and had suffered such heavy losses in Russia during the months of October and November, 1944, that a certain complacency had set in about a reasonably quick ending to the war. Four American divisions were stretched thin in the Eifel–Ardennes sector on 16 December 1944 when the cold stillness of the wooded Ardennes was broken by the rumble of guns, the clatter of tanks and the roar of battle. Out of the heavy mist crept hundreds of tanks and thousands of men. Westwards they moved with such unprecedented power that they quickly shattered the cohesive front line of the astounded American forces. This was Hitler's last great offensive.

The Canadians were on the sidelines of this last great battle of the war, but Colonel Wright and Leslie Chater were detecting something ominous in Holland opposite our front. While Montgomery was brought in over the American General Bradley – much to the fury of the Americans – to contain the advance of von Rundstedt's tanks, there was a growing suspicion that another offensive was planned in the north. On 21 December 1944 we reported, 'The evidence is reasonably conclusive that the enemy is preparing a large paratroop operation to take place very shortly to disrupt the communications of the armies dependent on Antwerp and Brussels. It is abundantly clear that there are paratroops in German Holland and that their movements tie into this design. It is equally clear that were the Ardennes plans to succeed to the extent that the enemy crossed Meuse between Liège and Given in force, a para landing behind our forces would assist him immeasurably and might, in the longer view, disorganize our offensive plans.'

On the 23 December, as the main battle still was draining the life blood out of the Wehrmacht, evidence of a major diversion in our direction seemed almost conclusive. Our intelligence report that day was acutely alarmist. 'Further unmistakable evidence of the enemy's offensive intentions in Holland came today from our friend "the reliable source". Undoubtedly there has been an influx of enemy recently into the area between the Maas and the Wall. Sources put their strength as high as 10,000; they are crowded into all the villages and are said to be very optimistic. There had been greatly increased activity on the Maas ferries … Engineers and their material are being assembled: rubber boats, bridging material and amphibious cars; charges are being removed from bridges and obstacles from roads. Twenty armoured cars and fifteen medium tanks have been seen and a divisional staff has arrived. The troops talk quite freely of an impending crossing of the Maas and a drive to recapture Antwerp.'

That was enough to take the semi-alert stand in which the Canadian forces had been, to a full alert. This meant that the Christmas festivities had to be cancelled and instead of turkey and crackers, which had all been sent from home to be enjoyed, the Canadians had to spend their Yuletide crouched in their tanks or over their guns peering into the dark for the oncoming Wehrmacht. But the Germans never came. They never reached the Meuse River which would have triggered a supporting assault from the north. A week later the Canadian army was stood down to normal readiness and the intelligence, which was us, was roundly abused and ridiculed for advice that spoilt their Christmas. Not being able to divulge the sources of our information, we had to accept our humiliation in silence and with as much dignity as we could muster.

To substantiate our intelligence, we were from time to time expected to contact forward divisional or brigade HQs to find out if the information we were sending them was useful and if they had anything significant or unusual to report. Since battle-lines were fluid and in France and the Low Countries fixed positions were not held for very long, it was exciting for us at HQ to occasionally feel we were actually in the front line. I always carried a loaded revolver in a holster on these expeditions and only once can I recall ever firing it in what might laughingly be called action. It was in the bocage country when the Germans were on the retreat and I spied someone suspicious behind a tree. I called out for him to come out and when he didn't I fired a bullet at the tree. Out came a quivering French farmer, with his hands up, who had not understood my English. I was almost as frightened as he was. Having checked his credentials I sent him back to where he had come from.

The battle of Falaise was a defeat for the Wehrmacht of the magnitude of Stalingrad, Moscow and El Alamein. Between 19 and 22 August 1944 the Canadians swooping towards Falaise from the north and General Bradley's American forces coming up towards Argentan had managed an encircling movement which trapped the remnants of fourteen German divisions estimated at about 80,000 men. As usual Hitler had delayed giving them permission to retreat and now there was only a narrow five mile gap for them to use to escape to the Seine. The killing was ominous as the once-mighty conquerors fled through the wooded and hilly country of the Dives valley. The actual number of dead and wounded in that massacre can never be known, but it is estimated that in those few days between 10,000 and 15,000 Germans lost their lives. The battle yielded up about 45,000 Germans to swell the bursting Allied prison cages.

At the height of this battle Major Chater and I were ordered to take a Jeep and find out what was going on in the gap through which the Germans were streaming. The messages we were getting were a chaotic flood of triumphant news of surrendering troops. Over the scene of smashed vehicles, abandoned tanks, unmanned guns hung the heavy, sickly-sweet smell of death. Bodies were lying in the ditches and one unnerving sight was a lone hand, palm outstretched, which had been severed from its owner. The supplicating fingers of that image have lived with me ever since. But amid all this horror I saw a small boy, about six, walking towards a nearby farmhouse in an adjacent field. I approached him and asked him what he was doing there. He pointed to the farmhouse, indicating that was where he lived. I noticed he was immaculately dressed. His white shirt was sparkling clean, his short blue trousers neatly pressed and his small shoes shiningly polished. I asked him in French why he was so beautifully clothed. 'Ah,' he replied, 'mais c'est Dimanche.' The Sabbath, it seemed, still commanded respect even in the most ungodly of places.

A supplementary intelligence duty that I was responsible for was checking the security arrangements for General Crerar and the rest of his HQ staff. Military police organized the details but we were expected to keep an eye on any weaknesses that could be dangerous. With my sensitivity about everything worn by Germans, I suspected that in Normandy the average soldier at our HQ was not particularly conversant with what a German officer looked like as compared to the many other national officers – American, French, Polish – who made visits from time to time. I decided to test my theory. Sir Peregrine Worsthorne, then a young lieutenant attached to Montgomery's personal Phantom unit and later to become one of England's most distinguished and provocative columnists, has described the occasion in his memoirs, *Tricks of Memory*.

My arrival at B squadron coincided with a long lull in the advance as plans were drawn up for the crossing of the Rhine. My first task was to keep the maps up to date – a task greatly simplified by there being so little need to move the flags. B Squadron was attached to General Crerar's Canadian Army HQ where discipline was pleasantly relaxed, as was security to a fault. Sitting at my desk on my first morning I noticed an officer enter. He went straight to the maps on the wall and started to study them intently, without any of the other officers looking up. That was unsurprising enough. Less unsurprising was the fact that the officer studying the maps, with his back to the rest of us, was in the full field uniform of a captain in the Wehrmacht. After a few minutes, unable to contain my curiosity, I tapped him on the shoulder and this was how I first met Milton Shulman. At that time he was an intelligence officer in the Canadian army and had decided to dramatize the deficiencies of

GHQ security arrangements by seeing how long it would take before anybody noticed that they had a German officer in their midst. Apparently he had passed through all the checkpoints without a single challenge until my tap on the shoulder, which hardly counted as a challenge. Milton was absolutely delighted with the success of his coup, news of which caused a great sensation and was talked about for weeks, without leading to many improvements in security – perhaps the first recorded evidence of that journalistic talent which in later life so impressed Lord Beaverbrook.

In the final days of the war, I was billeted with a Dutch family in the town of Apeldoorn. The owner of the house was an author who had written many books in Dutch but none of them had been translated into English. He was currently engaged on a book that would contend that Shakespeare was not one individual but many. He could not believe that any one human being could have acquired the vast knowledge of royal affairs, constitutional matters, military tactics, legal procedures, aristocratic manners, French, Welsh and Scots customs, metaphysical philosophy, proletarian jargon, romantic and tragic emotions and then managed to display it all in the most ennobling prose and poetry of all time. At the time, knowing little of the Bard, I thought he was a rather eccentric Dutchman. But having been constantly amazed and mystified as a theatre critic for over forty years by the wonder and magnificence of the Bard's talent, I am not so sure he was entirely wrong. That particular argument will probably never be settled.

When the war in Europe was over, although the Japanese conflict was still raging, I was promoted to an acting major and was Mentioned in Despatches for my work in Normandy. This entitles me to a bronze leaf to be attached to the ribbon of one of the medals I have never yet worn. Canadians had to wait several months for shipping to take them back and there was still some uncertainty as to what role we would be expected to play in the continuing war against Japan. Eventually, I was posted back to London.

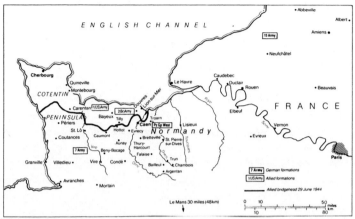

The Normandy Bridgehead

3

HITLER'S GENERALS

Interrogating the defeated, the bitter and the unrepentant . . . Defeat in the West –
a publishers punt . . . Overcoming the Official Secrets Act with a liquid
lunch . . . falling in love . . . The Reuters bluff

(i) Hitler allows the British to escape at Dunkirk
It was Major Chater's idea that we should interrogate the captured generals who had been in command of the forces opposing the Canadian army. From July 1944 to May 1945 we had been trying to guess what the enemy intentions were and how they hoped to carry them out. Wouldn't it be invaluable, from a historical point of view, to catch these beaten commanders shortly after they had been defeated when they might be amenable, even anxious, to justify and excuse their failures? Weren't they likely to be honest about what happened to them immediately after the crushing experience of defeat, rather than wait until some time later when they might build up contrived explanations for their downfall from invincible conquerors to crumpled prisoners in an Allied cage?

The head of the Canadian Historical Section, Colonel C. P. Stacey, saw the value of such first-hand evidence for the Official History of Canada's war on which he and his staff were working. Since there would be a long delay in getting shipping to take many Canadians across the Atlantic, it seemed to be a useful way of employing the knowledge about the Germans I had acquired before discharging me from the army and sending me home. The Historical Section was stationed in small top-floor rooms at the Canadian Embassy in Trafalgar Square. I shared an office with Captain Robert Mackenzie who was assembling material for Stacey's history. Bob later wrote a classic account of British political parties and taught at the London School of Economics under

Professor Harold Laski. He acquired national fame as the originator of the Swingometer which he displayed with great aplomb at every general election on the BBC, to demonstrate the percentage swings required by an Opposition to unseat a Government. Like me, he was a socialist and represented Canada's closest political party to the non-communist Left, the CCF. Our lunches were filled with idealistic dreams about how to set the world aright and when Bob left to become an academic he asked me to take over the representation of that party. It meant writing long reports about Attlee's Labour government which we both thought was selling out to liberal pressures. For three years I attended International Labour conferences and become aware of the compromises and cynicism that the Left had to adopt to retain power against a virulent anti-Left press that had no compunctions about manoeuvring to bring the Tories back into power.

In September 1945 Colonel Wright sent us the piece of paper we needed to gain entry to the prison camps in England and Europe where the Wehrmacht commanders were being held. 'The bearers of this authority,' it read, 'Lt. Col. L.V. Chater, GSO1 Int. HQ CFN and Capt. M. Shulman, GSO3 Int. HQ, CFN, are engaged in the Interrogation of high ranking German personalities. For this purpose they have been granted permission to travel through the countries of Germany, Austria, France and Belgium. May every assistance be provided them to enable them to carry out this mission.' This was supported by a similar authorization from Colonel Stacey and a high-ranking American Intelligence general. Wielding these papers at Allied prison camp commanders from Bridgend in Wales to Frankfurt in Germany, we were provided with meals and sleeping accommodation, as well as jovial hospitality, wherever we went. Carrying out the interrogations and writing the reports, all of which were couched in my words, took about nine months. Since my German was still not good enough to engage in deep tactical and strategic conversations with men like Field Marshal von Rundstedt and Colonel General Kurt Student, Commander of Germany's Airborne Troops, the questioning was handled by Chater but when he left his posting with the Canadians before we had finished, two other fluent German speakers, Webster and Phillips, helped finish off our planned quota.

One field marshal (von Rundstedt), three colonel generals, eleven generals, seven lieutenant generals, two major generals, one colonel (the Commandant of Fortress Le Havre) and one lieutenant colonel (the

Commandant of Fortress Calais) – twenty-eight senior officers in all – agreed to tell us their accounts and excuses about their war. Most of them unequivocally blamed Hitler for bringing about their catastrophic defeat; a few remained defiantly loyal to their Führer. The Americans showed little respect for their captives, locking them up in single cells at night and keeping them under constant, unsympathetic surveillance. The British were more gentlemanly, allowing them to congregate in common rooms, to take classes in Western democracy and generally to commiserate with each other over their fate. It was the British sense of humour that usually prevented too fierce an approach being taken to their enemies. This was illustrated when, after the surrender of the Afrika Korps in North Africa, Churchill was asked by a Labour MP in the Commons what steps he was going to take against Montgomery for fraternizing with his defeated opponent, General von Thoma, by inviting him to lunch. 'Poor von Thoma,' answered Churchill, rising to his feet. 'I, too, have had lunch with Field Marshal Montgomery.'

The only striking feature of German generals as a group was their normality. They looked like anyone else. The monocled, scarred, bullet-headed prototype of a Prussian officer belongs to Hollywood and the popular magazines. In reality these men, who represented the final stage in the evolution of a caste, looked and acted like any other representative group of middle-aged bankers, brokers, clerks, teachers and businessmen that one might find in England, the United States, Russia or France. They were blond and swarthy, tall and small, thin and fat, stupid and clever, stolid and energetic, eager and listless, polite and rude, good and bad. They were loyal, treacherous, vain, petty, humble, courageous, officious, domineering, weak, strong and any other adjective that might be used to describe the average man.

It was these interrogations, coupled with my experience in MI14(b) and at Canadian Army HQ that provided me with the material for my book on the collapse of the German war machine as mostly seen through the eyes of those who had led the Wehrmacht and lost. It was published in 1947 and called *Defeat in the West*. Its impact on my life was formidable. In their drab prison uniforms, stripped of the glamour of their many medals and decorations, they poured out, with a mixture of bitterness and resignation, the mistakes they had made and those they had been forced to make.

The military personality that dominated both the first year of the war and the last year of the war was undoubtedly that of Field Marshal Gerd

von Rundstedt. To him was given the task of leading the German soldier to his most glorious victory and to his most abysmal defeat. He per-
sonified the traditional, conservative, exclusive, aristocratic career soldier
upon which the German General Staff liked to believe its members
were modelled.

Von Rundstedt had a face that was ageless. A straight firm nose, long
thin lips and determined blunt jaw gave the impression of a sculptured
bust, immutable and relentless. The tiny wrinkles and serried lines that
striated his skin helped to create this effect of chiselled rock. The eyes,
however, bright and restless, revealed the presence of warm blood. The
occasional limited smile coupled with a dry, restrained wit confirmed
the fact that this man was human after all. If stone predominated in the
field marshal's physical appearance, it probably betrayed what had taken
place in the spirit as well. This transformation to granite can hardly be
wondered at, for only ossification could have withstood the buffeting
storm of howling events that had assailed him from all directions.

In May 1940 von Rundstedt's Army Group poised on the edge of
the Ardennes broke the Maginot Line with a classic example of the use
of armour and infantry in the offensive. The French, caught completely
unawares in the good tank country west of the Meuse, could do nothing to halt the drive of the panzer formations to the Channel coast. The
Allied left wing, comprising the bulk of the British army, was caught
against the Channel and could not break through the tightly-held
salient carved out by von Rundstedt. The Allied position thus having
been cut in two and all attempts to pry open the trap having failed, there
remained only one course open – the evacuation of the British from
Dunkirk. Hitler suffered his first defeat at Dunkirk. The authority for
that statement was von Rundstedt himself. His account in our interrogation was the first explanation after the war of what the British always
had claimed was 'the miracle of Dunkirk'.

'To me,' remarked the field marshal, rather ruefully, 'Dunkirk was one of the
greatest turning points of the war. If I had had my way the English would
not have got off so lightly at Dunkirk. But my hands were tied by direct
orders from Hitler himself. While the English were clambering into the
ships off the beaches, I was kept uselessly outside the port unable to move.
I recommended to the Supreme Command that my five panzer divisions
be immediately sent into the town and thereby completely destroy the
retreating English. But I received definite orders from the Führer that under

The ageless face of von Rundstedt.

no circumstances was I to attack, and I was expressly forbidden to send any
of my troops closer than ten kilometres from Dunkirk.'

With the fall of France on 22 June 1940, the obvious next target for
Hitler's ambition was Britain. The French when they surrendered
thought Britain would only be able to survive another three weeks.
Churchill obviously thought differently. It was clear the British would
not capitulate without an invasion of their shores. Reluctantly, because
the German general staff had no experience of a sea-borne operation
and were apprehensive about the might of the British Navy, a tentative
invasion date was set for 21 September 1940. Hitler had received assurances that by that date the Luftwaffe would have blown the Royal Air
Force out of the skies.

In spite of the definite characters of these activities there seemed to
be no enthusiasm for the operation. Hitler himself appeared particularly hesitant. A great part of the blame for the lukewarm atmosphere can
be traced to the vast over-estimates of English strength prepared by
German military intelligence. They guessed they would encounter thirty-nine reasonably-armed British divisions, when in truth there were
only about three properly equipped for battle after the debâcle of
Dunkirk. Von Rundstedt admitted that England at this time was a
'Sphinx'. Although ordered to command Operation Sea Lion, the ageing Field Marshal was most unenthusiastic about its prospects.

'The proposed invasion of England was nonsense,' he told us, 'because
adequate ships were not available. They were chiefly barges which had to
be brought from Germany and the Netherlands. Then they had to be
reconstructed so that tanks and other equipment could be driven out of
the bows. Then the troops had to learn how to embark and disembark.
We looked upon the whole thing as a sort of game because it was obvious that no invasion was possible when our navy was not in a position to
cover a crossing of the Channel or carry reinforcements. Nor was the
German air force capable of taking on these functions if the navy failed.

'I was always very sceptical about the whole affair. I have a feeling that
the Führer never really wanted to invade England. He never had sufficient courage. He used to say: "On land I am a hero, but on water I am a
coward." Hitler definitely hoped that the English would make peace over-
tures to him. It was useless to attempt an invasion later on since by then
the English had become much too strong.'

With Goering having failed to fulfil his promise to destroy the British air force and with Hitler's conviction that Britain would eventually seek peace terms, he turned to the major prize he had always coveted: the conquest of Soviet Russia. By the middle of December 1940 plans were already being made for the invasion of Russia. Soon after 22 June 1941 the Wehrmacht had two hundred divisions marching towards Leningrad, Moscow and the Caucasus.

It was the young and fanatical disciples of Hitler that fought for him as some sort of God and whose faith in his beliefs burnt fiercely in their breasts even after Germany's humiliating defeat. No one better represented the fanatics than Major General Kurt Meyer. Meyer spent nine years in prison for war crimes. He had been sentenced to life imprisonment for having incited his men to shoot Canadian prisoners-of-war. A devoted disciple of Nazism and all that it stood for, his mind was so distorted by pseudo-philosophy, military jingoism and bald lies that not even the traumatic experience he had been through could diminish the fervour of his faith.

We visited this thirty-four-year-old ex-commander of the 12 SS Hitler Jugend Division about three months after the war had ended. It was a time when most older officers were ready to tell all about the treatment and degradation they had undergone as a Wehrmacht commander and the disillusionment they now felt about National Socialism. But Meyer's first words to us were: 'You will hear a lot against Adolf Hitler in this camp but you will never hear it from me. As far as I am concerned he was and still is the greatest thing that ever happened to Germany.'

During the two-day discussion with Meyer about the operations of his division in Normandy, I had an opportunity of seeing what went on in the mind of this representative product of Hitlerism. At first Meyer scrupulously refrained from talking about anything other than the military problems of his formation. But once he felt assured that our visit was concerned only with historical facts and had nothing to do with the war crimes with which he was charged, he became more expansive and intense in his speech. When he began to wander into the political and philosophical fields, his virile, handsome features lit up with enthusiasm and it might have been the reincarnation of Hitler or Goebbels voicing their cant.

'Germany fought this war for the preservation of Western culture and civilization,' Meyer assured us. 'The menace of the East was always appreciated by the Führer and his one object was to save Europe from the evil

of Bolshevism. We had no quarrel with the English or French but these
countries, unfortunately, had no idea of the Russian system of life and its
people. The leaders of the East want to sweep away all Western culture as
we know it, and set up in its place their own half-developed, animal-like
existence. This Germany tried unsuccessfully to prevent.'

According to Meyer this Eastern threat was not confined to Russia
alone. It was a question of the European peoples attempting to stem the
advance of the barbaric Asiatic peoples. 'So seriously do I believe in this
menace,' continued Meyer, 'that I have spoken to many of my young SS
officers in this camp with me.' (The camp was classified as a 'black' camp
containing the most unregenerate and dangerous Nazis amongst
German prisoners-of-war.) 'They have all agreed with me that this
Eastern danger must be dealt with first and this in my opinion includes
Japan as well as Russia. I am therefore prepared to offer to the Allied
authorities my services, and those of the other SS officers in Allied
hands, in helping them fight the Japanese.' (The war with Japan was not
yet over when this discussion took place.) 'My proposition is that I be
given permission to recruit one SS division of about 23,000 men from
amongst the German prisoners-of-war. This formation will be named
the "SS Division Europa" and it is to be equipped with German
weapons and equipment. I will have no difficulty in raising the men for
such a unit to take part in the struggle against the East. We will then
show you how Germans can fight.'

It seemed incomprehensible to us that Nazi propaganda had bitten
so deep into the psyche of young Germans like Meyer that it seemed
perfectly logical to him that the British and American troops would
welcome as allies so soon after the war's end an SS division which represented everything they had been fighting against for so long. Perhaps
better than hundreds of books that have been written on the subject,
this one speech of Meyer's revealed how difficult was going to be the
task of totally eradicating the virus of Nazism from this breed of young
Germans. Kurt Meyer died in 1961 without ever uttering a single word
of regret for the deeds he had done in loyalty to his Führer.

(ii)   Becoming a journalist
Although I could understand German, particularly military German,
very well, I was not grammatically fluent enough to enter into any
serious conversation with the Wehrmacht and SS commanders who

were interrogated. My job was to take notes while Chater, Webster or Phillips pressed on with digging out as much information we could get from our subjects. I was present at all the interrogations and had the job of writing them into reports which were delivered to the Canadian Historical section. Several weeks would often elapse between one interrogation and another, so between the actual trips to prisoner-of-war cages I would concentrate on writing up the interviews that had just been done. It was a congenial job since I was stationed in London and was able to afford a tiny one-room flat, kitchen and bathroom, at a large, pleasant block called Kensington Close in Kensington. For £3 a week it provided me with just the facilities I needed. Until the task of seeing all our quarry was completed, there was no pressure on me to go back to Canada. Meanwhile the prospect of going back to law where my name was still on the door and letterhead of Louis Herman KC – Milton Shulman (On active service) – filled me with gloom.

There were three reasons for my resistance to taking advantage of the free passenger ticket which serving Canadians were entitled to until the end of 1946. The first was that I thought that my last chance of becoming a writer or journalist would be in England and not in Canada. Second was the blissful anonymity that enabled me to be seen anywhere, restaurant or nightclub, without the news spreading instantly to my family or friends. The third reason was that I'd fallen in love. By this time my relationship with Nita had become a victim to the long absences that we experienced because of my service in France. When I had been in London waiting to go to Normandy, we had managed to synchronize our leaves so that we could spend an occasional week-end together. My most romantic memories of those rendezvous was sitting on the steps of the Haymarket theatre with a seductive silvery moon casting a glow over the blacked-out metropolis while an elderly man trundled a piano on wheels slowly up the muffled avenue. When he stopped he would play the *Warsaw Concerto* with fingers that protruded from mittens that had been cut so that the tops of his hands could be kept warm while his fingers could manipulate the keyboard. With anti-aircraft searchlights sweeping across the sky and the drone of planes, usually ours, on the way to some mission in Europe, it managed to align romance with danger to a sensuous effect. Our sex life was limited to the few times when we managed to meet in her home, I think in Croydon, from where I would have to walk to a hotel I had booked in

London starting at six in the morning because females, particularly in a Wren's uniform, were strictly forbidden.

By the time the Germans had surrendered, Nita and I had stopped seeing each other. She, I believe, had taken up with some officer who was much more available, while after at a dance at the Overseas League I became enchanted with a piquant, smiling face belonging to a nurse who introduced herself as Jackie. She had ambitions to become an actress and soon she had become my constant companion, visiting me at Kensington Close whenever I was not away interrogating generals.

Although Joyce was still expecting me to return to Toronto it was clear to me that any renewal of married life, after almost four years' separation, in view of my feelings about Jackie and my ambitions to become a writer rather than a lawyer, could eventually lead only to frustration and unhappiness. I at first prevaricated, claiming that my work delayed me taking a passage home, but early in 1946 I asked her for a divorce. To my relief she seemed to bear no ill-will at the news. My excuses for not trying to secure a quick return to Canada must have prepared her for the inevitable. I soon learnt that she had become involved with, but not committed to, someone else. After all, three year's separation was a long time.

Since adultery was the only acceptable cause for divorce in Ontario at the time, the farce of producing evidence with a person unknown had to be undertaken. I was not keen on naming Jackie in these proceedings, but she agreed to spend a prominently displayed night with me at the Grand Hotel in Brighton. The porter who brought up our baggage had to be given an extraordinarily large tip so that he would remember us and we engaged in animated conversation about the delights of Brighton with the boy who brought up our breakfast while we were still in a double bed together so that he, too, lubricated by another large tip, would be sure to recall the occasion when Joyce's London solicitors approached them for evidence of our illegal liaison. Complications about legal costs and tardiness on my part dragged the proceedings on until the early part of 1948, almost a year after they had begun, when a final decree was issued.

With divorce proceedings on the way, I had cleared the path for taking the biggest gamble of my life. Should I risk being discharged in England and try my luck at getting a job as a journalist? My chief concern was that I would have no money to keep myself other than the rehabilitation grant I would get from the Canadian Government after five years of service, from 26 September 1941 to 20 December 1946. This would be about eight hundred pounds. How long would I be able to survive on that without some paid work? While still in uniform and writing reports at the Historical Section, I applied for any kind of writing job that was going.

Applications to the Appointments Officer of the BBC, the *New Statesman and Nation* and other publications received polite but negative replies. As the day of my impending discharge loomed ever closer, I began to fear that shortage of money would drive me back to Canada with my aspirations shattered for good and all.

One of the closest friends I acquired at Kensington Close, who also occupied one of the cubicles we called flats, was Charles Gibb-Smith. He handled the press and public relations of the Victoria and Albert Museum and through that job had contacts with editors and journalists who worked in Fleet Street. His short-sightedness had prevented him doing military service but he was a very keen activist in the Home Guard Fire Service. His mind was stocked with the most formidable amount of intellectual bric-à-brac I had ever encountered in any individual. Not only could he wax lyrical about the multitude of historical treasures in the museum but he was also a keen student of aviation and, as a member of the Inter-planetary Society, assured anyone who cared to listen how one day soon a man would land on the moon. We were amused by his scientific jargon but dismissed him in this regard as a science fiction crank. I believe it was more his infatuation with Jackie rather than with me that brought him almost nightly into our company.

When I wrote an article called 'Do We Care What Canadians Think?' and hadn't the faintest idea of how to get it published, it was Gibb-Smith who suggested I might try it on Harold Keeble, the Feature Editor of the *Daily Express*, a paper with over four million circulation. He told me that the *Daily Express* was owned by the pro-Empire, Canadian publisher and statesman, Lord Beaverbrook, and that his employees, recognizing these connections, might be prepared to give me an interview. And so it turned out.

Harold Keeble's secretary, hearing that I was a Canadian major, gave me a morning on which I could see him. I met Harold Keeble, not in his office, but in one of the busy corridors of the shiny, ebony-black, unique building with a surface of black glass and chromium, facetiously dubbed the 'Black Lubianka' by its journalists after the notorious prison in Moscow. Keeble was a fair-haired, chunky, dynamic man with a reputation as an innovative lay-out artist who could make the most uninspiring articles look interesting.

When I told him I wanted to submit an article, his face dropped like a failed souffle. 'I'm afraid, Major Shulman, we do not accept contributions from outside writers,' he said. 'We only have a twelve-page paper and we have difficulty printing pieces from our own staff. We have a man in India who sends us regular copy and I doubt if we printed a word of his stuff in the last two years.'

'Would you look at it?' I pleaded. 'Perhaps you could tell me where else I could try.'

Reluctantly, he took hold of the five type-written pages and held them in front of him as if they were some sort of police summons. I watched him read page one, then two, and to my gratification he went on until the last page.

'Just a minute,' he said, disappearing down the corridor. It was obvious he thought Beaverbrook might be interested in such a pro-Canadian, anti-American article. He returned in about ten minutes. I don't know whom he had consulted. Probably one of the leader writers. 'Leave this with me. I'll be in touch.'

Two weeks later I received a cheque for £21 and an invoice indicating that the article was 'in stock'. It was by far the largest sum I had ever received for anything I had written. It was never published but it marked the start of my career in journalism.

Encouraged by this surprising largesse I again sought the advice of Gibb-Smith, who was as astonished as I was about my success. He thought if I was going to write any more articles I ought to get an agent to help me sell them and suggested Curtis Brown in Henrietta Street might be interested. He didn't tell me that Curtis Brown, at that time, was probably the most respected and important literary agency in Britain. Again I got an appointment to see one of their representatives by brandishing my military rank and trusting that curiosity would get me past the barrier of secretaries.

The agent at Curtis Brown, whose name my memory has lost, tried to be as courteous as he could when I told him I hoped his firm might take me on as a client. He told me that unknown writers were not part of their stable. He cited Noel Coward and Somerset Maugham as the kind of authors that monopolized their efforts and said that I should try and find myself some smaller agency that might be interested.

'You tell me that you sold articles to magazines and newspapers in Canada, but have you done anything in this country?' he asked.

'Well, I just sold an article to the *Daily Express* for which they paid me twenty-one pounds,' I replied.

'You sold an article to the *Daily Express*!' he said, very astonished. 'That's a remarkable achievement. What was it about?'

I told him and it became clear that I had only succeeded because of the specific interest of Lord Beaverbrook. He was about to usher me out when he asked me what I was still doing in uniform because this was April, 1946, almost a full year after the war's end. I told him I had been interrogating German commanders like von Rundstedt, Student, Blumentritt. They were trying to explain why they had been defeated and were bitterly blaming Hitler for most of their disaster.

He was fascinated. Could I write about it? I probably could when I was discharged, which I expected would be in a few months' time, but I had not yet made up my mind whether or not I would go back to Canada. That was why I was trying to get some assignments as a writer or journalist, and no doubt my experiences as an intelligence officer had given me some extraordinary material.

He took down my address and phone number and said he would keep his eyes open for something he thought I could sell. About three weeks later he phoned me and told me to get in touch immediately with George Malcolm Thomson at the *Daily Express*. Mr Thomson was writing a series of articles about the war and the agent had suggested that I might be able to help him with some background material.

Thomson was not only Lord Beaverbrook's chief leader writer but also an intimate interpreter of Beaverbrook's ideas and crusades for publication in any of his three newspapers – the *Daily* and *Sunday Express* and the London *Evening Standard*. Thomson was a slight, wiry, balding Scotsman with a brilliant pen and a wicked sense of humour. Whenever he was seen with Beaverbrook he had a note-book in his hands to take down the avalanche of instructions that never ceased to flow from the old man's mouth. Beaverbrook was then sixty-eight years old. Sharing the office with Thomson was David Farrer, who was Beaverbrook's personal private secretary. Between the two of them they knew more about their proprietor's tastes, fads, opinions, idiosyncrasies and private life than anyone else in the land.

I very soon gleaned that Thomson was following instructions in planning the four articles he was going to write for the *Daily Express*.

So well-known was Thomson as the echo of Beaverbrook's mind that even when they were out riding together, Thomson sat astride his horse with a note-book at the ready. 'There goes Napoleon and Marshal Yea,' said a Fleet Street wit, observing this unusual sight.

We went for lunch to Chez Victor, a small French restaurant off Shaftesbury Avenue. Thomson's task was to rebut and denounce a book called *Top Secret* by Ralph Ingersoll which was an uninhibited, vitriolic account of the manner in which Montgomery had conducted the British campaign in Normandy and France. It derided the British for their inability to break out of the Caen sector in Normandy. It was a particularly nasty piece of military journalism, coming soon after the public still believed all had been harmony and good-will between the Allies.

We talked for almost three hours and in that time I had provided Thomson with the German side of these battles, which enabled him to write the kind of pugnacious, pro-British articles that Beaverbrook wanted. I sent Thomson a summary of my views in writing and, to my delight, soon afterwards I received a cheque for £30. To be rewarded so generously after only a lunch impressed the agent, who urged me to write down my ideas for a series of six articles which I would take on as soon as I got out of uniform. He took me to the editor of the *Sunday Express* who indicated he was exceptionally pleased with my synopsis for that series and, although he could not make a positive financial commitment six months in advance, he assured us that the chances that the *Sunday Express* would buy them were very bright.

The sale of my last two efforts and the encouraging noises from the *Sunday Express* were the incentives I needed to make my mind up to take the big plunge and not go back to Canada. I sent Lou Herman a letter telling him he was now free to take my name off his letterhead and that my immediate future was to be in England. I did add a precautionary note that I was not planning to take up residence in England, and that it was possible that after a year or so I might go back to the law in Canada. With only £800 rehabilitation money and no source of income on the horizon, I felt it was prudent to keep a financial escape-hatch open should my hopes collapse into no more than wishful dreams.

Thinking about how I should present the series I eventually hoped to sell to the *Sunday Express*, I decided the most intelligent way of organizing the material was to write it as a book. Eventually a book could

be sliced into four or six sections as required. Finishing off my interrogation reports and working on the book which I had decided to call
Defeat in the West kept me writing almost eight hours a day. I had latched
on to my title because it seemed an ironic reversal of the film by Leni
Riefenstahl called *Sieg am Westen* (*Victory in the West*) which was a
grandiloquent, beautifully photographed triumphalist documentary,
recording the collapse and humiliation of the French army. It was also
one of Hitler's favourite films.

I was soon brought up sharp by the realization that a Fleet Street
promise was as dependable as a flying feather in a hurricane. Only a few
weeks later, although I had assumed the *Sunday Express* would wait for
my articles, which I indicated would be available in February 1947, the
paper was advertising and starting to publish extracts from a forthcoming book by General Bedell Smith, General Eisenhower's Chief-of-
Staff. Although he was more concerned with the Allied tribulations than
the German side of the conflict, his detailed reminiscences of the battles
of Normandy and the Ardennes inevitably covered much of the same
material I was intending to disclose exclusively in my book.

I telephoned my fears to the Curtis Brown agent that the *Express*
would not likely want to print another version of the same operations
told by an unknown Canadian major, when they had only a few months
previously presented their readers with an authoritative account from
Ike's Chief-of-Staff, one of the highest level officers on the Allied side.
He agreed that we should no longer pin much hope on a *Sunday Express*
purchase, but he urged me to go on with my book and said he would
try and sell it elsewhere. Whereas I had previously been flogging myself
to get something significant done by the year's end, I no longer considered it one of my priorities, and now occasionally did some work on the
book only when there was nothing more pressing to do.

It was at this stage in my life that another one of those Fickle Fingers
of Fate intervened in my affairs. The accident of my meeting George
Malcolm Thomson, who shared an office with David Farrer, had semi-
nal repercussions on everything that happened to me after that. For,
strange as it seems, it was a historical work like *Defeat in the West*, that
was the direct route by which I became a film, theatre, book and TV
critic for most of my later working life.

By a fortuitous coincidence my glancing introduction to David
Farrer, when I met George Malcolm Thomson, took place just when
Farrer had decided to give up his job as Private Secretary to Lord

Beaverbrook, a post which he had held since 1940. Farrer had been called to the Bar but practised for only a short time. He had gone to India to be private tutor to the heir presumptive of the Maharajah of Gwalior but poor health took him back to England where, in 1940, he was given a censorship job in the wartime Ministry of Information. Beaverbrook charmed him into becoming his private secretary with the task of keeping him in touch with what other newspapers were saying.

One of Churchill's first appointments as P.M. was to make Beaverbrook Minister of Aircraft Production. Thus six weeks after Farrer had reluctantly decided to link his fortunes with Beaverbrook, he found himself at the centre of events that were to determine the future of this nation and probably Western civilization as well. When the war ended, Farrer decided he had had enough of the excitement, the tension, the unpredictability, the tantrums, the crises of being a member of Beaverbrook's entourage.

He was in Bermuda with Beaverbrook when he heard of his mother's death. It was a deep emotional blow but it had one compensation. He had inherited enough money to become a partner in the firm of Secker and Warburg, a distinguished publisher who had Thomas Mann and George Orwell on their list but were short of capital for post-war expansion.

Farrer admits that by the time he had plucked up enough courage to tell Beaverbrook he was going to leave him (usually it was Beaverbrook who did the firing), he had developed a deep affection and admiration for his employer. Nevertheless Beaverbrook never allowed sentiment to become too obtrusive in his relations with those who took his largesse.

'A week before I was due to leave his employment Beaverbrook summoned me to his London flat,' writes Farrer in his autobiography, *G – for God Almighty*. 'There he cross-questioned me closely.

'"This firm of yours, is it making money?"

'"Yes, Sir, quite a lot."

'"Have your lawyers looked at its books?"

'"Yes, closely."

'"Have you put all your money into it?"

'"No, not all of it."

'"What would happen if the firm went broke? Would you be able to live?"

'"In reduced circumstances, yes."'

'"But you'd be hard up."

'"Yes, but I'd have enough to live on. I could get another job."

'"You're sure of that?"

'"Yes, quite sure."

'He picked up his dictaphone and rasped into it to his private secretary, "Mr Millar, you can cut Mr Farrar out of my will."'

(iii) Defeat in the West

Sometime in May, 1946, I got a surprise telephone call from the agent at Curtis Brown. How far had I got on that series of articles about the German generals? he asked. I said I had given up shaping it as articles and had decided to write a book. How much had I done? About ten thousand words, I replied. I was lying. I'd written no more than six thousand. Would I send them round to him, as well as an outline of what I intended to say in the rest of the book. I spent a frantic week-end fulfilling the claim I had made and produced a five-page synopsis setting out the nine long chapters envisaging the shape it might take. I called it *Defeat* which soon afterwards became *Defeat in the West*. I eventually divided the material into Book One – *The Road to Defeat* and Book Two – *Defeat in the West*. It was split into thirty-four chapters. The query about the book's progress had come from David Farrer.

> 'A few weeks before I was due to leave the Beaver,' writes Farrer in his autobiography, 'a literary agent came in to the *Daily Express* offices, bearing with him a synopsis of a book which he suggested would make a good serial. I happened to catch a glimpse of it. The book would be written by an unknown major in the Canadian Army, who had been given the task of interviewing German officers captured on the Western Front. It seemed to me a brilliant synopsis, and I alerted my future publishing partners, suggesting that they made a substantial offer for the book rights. They did so, and so surprised was the literary agent that they had even heard of it that he accepted the offer. The book was called *Defeat in the West*. It is still a reference book and has sold many thousand copies. The author has become famous in more than one field. His name is Milton Shulman.'

Fredric Warburg, the senior partner in Secker and Warburg, indicates that he had some misgivings about making Farrer a partner in his firm and particularly about his judgement over the first book he was recommending to his respectable and rather cautious publishing house.

'Farrer was something of a gambler,' reflects Fredric Warburg in his memoirs, *All Authors Are Equal*. 'Through the fifties he made many a call to his bookmaker and went often to race meetings. In becoming a publisher, it might be said that he had discovered a more respectable method of gambling, backing unpredictable books and authors, instead of unpredictable horses. It was with a gamble that Farrer started his publishing career. In the *Express* offices he had read the first four chapters and a synopsis of a full-length book by a thirty-year-old Canadian, Major Milton Shulman ...

The book was to be called *Defeat in the West*, and it was, as the *Evening Standard* said later in its review, "a panorama, complete and fascinating, of the war as seen from the other (German) side." Farrer recommended it strongly and rang me up. "Buy it," he said, "though it will cost rather a lot." I rang Curtis Brown, and read part of the MS, falling for it immediately. Terms were agreed involving an advance payment of £450, equivalent to an advance on about 7,500 copies. This was a lot of money for a book by an unknown Canadian major.

'*Defeat* was the first book to tell the story of the collapse of the German armies in the West, and the reasons for it. Published at 15s. on 17 April 1947, it sold rapidly and well. All 6,000 copes of the first printing were sold in four months, and a second impression of 3,500 copies was ready in September. Since then it has sold many more thousands of copies, and has been set as a textbook in military training courses. *Defeat* was well-written, readable and exciting, qualities in a book which Farrer recognized as those most likely to make a book saleable. So Farrer's first book had been a major success, it must have given his ego a boost, though it was some time before he found another as good. He had also encouraged me to take gambles myself.'

Once the contract had been signed I delivered the book in chunks of two and three chapters at a time, which Warburg himself read and commented upon. I was also bombarded with readers' reports which kept picking up incorrect or doubtful dates that I had in the first part of the volume which dealt with the historical account of how the Wehrmacht was reborn, the Phoney War, the invasion of Russia and El Alamein. If I could get it written by the end of October, Warburg hoped to publish it in April 1947. This gave me less than six months to write it. By 2 October I delivered the final pages. The printers were urged to give it top priority and on 17 April 1947 *Defeat in the West* made its appearance. It proved to me that if I was not a particularly gifted writer, I was certainly quick.

There was one more significant snag to be overcome. Because most of the documents I was relying upon were classified as Confidential or Secret – including my own interviews – I had to get clearance from the War Office for permission to use them. None of the intelligence information could in any way be categorized as data which might involve a breach of security likely to endanger the nation, but I was still restricted by the Official Secrets Act because of the work in which I was occupied. I found out which branch of the War Office I had to send the book to and met an amiable major who was about to leave the army in a few weeks and did not think historical facts about the war were any longer of much interest or concern.

I took him out to a liquid lunch, assured him that anything vital about how the Germans were defeated had already been published in books by Ralph Ingersoll, General Bedell Smith and others, and that as a lowly major I would not have been privy to any very vital intelligence secrets. He took away my manuscript and whether or not he did very much more than skim through the pages, I received in mid-September the permission to publish that I required. As far as my future career was concerned, it was probably the most valuable document I had ever received.

When the last pages of *Defeat in the West* were completed, I was still in uniform and there were three months to go before I would be formally discharged. With the £450 advance from Seckers and the £800 rehabilitation from the Canadian government for my six years' military service, I calculated that I was financially secure for all of 1947. But I realized, from all the rejection letters I had received, that the prospects for permanent employment when I became a civilian were, to put it optimistically, very dubious. I thought I had reasonable qualifications for a job as a foreign correspondent, and believing that Russia was the country that would be of interest to British papers, I decided to enrol as an advanced student leading to a Bachelor's degree at the School of Slavonic Studies at the University of London.

Lectures for advanced students were given in the evenings and although I was excused the entrance requirement of Latin, I was expected to pass the intermediate examination in Russian in six months' time. Aside from the Russian language my main courses were in Russian history and Russian economic studies. Andrew Rothstein, with a stocky build, heavy glasses and no humour, gave dour, fact-encrusted lectures on The Civil War, The Struggle for Industrialization, the First and Second Five Year Plans and the Stalin Constitution.

I suspected that they were all heavily loaded with praise for the achievements of the victorious Russians, but I did not realize until later that he played a significant role in the activities of the British Communist Party, defending intellectually every twist and turn of Soviet policy from the pact with Germany in 1939 to the crushing of the Hungarian and Czechoslovakian uprisings. His rigid, doctrinaire mind, supporting every form of Stalinist brutality, had him dubbed as 'the most evil man of our time' by the journalist Bernard Levin, when Rothstein died in the 1990s.

Although my rent at Kensington Close was only £3 a week and Jackie and I could eat at chic Chelsea restaurants for about £2 including wine, I was beginning to fret about my future livelihood. There was no guarantee that my book would bring me any more money and if the notices dismissed it as a far-fetched, unconvincing analysis of why the Germans lost the war, and if there was no entry for me into British journalism, I could envisage myself returning to Canada in 1948 with my tail between my legs.

It was Charles Gibb-Smith who again came to my rescue. He made an appointment for me to meet a Mr Fisher at United Press, an international news agency. Fisher turned out to be a large, amiable man ready to help a former journalist coming out of the army. I, of course, carried on with my deception that before the war began I had been a reporter on the *Toronto Star*. There were no jobs available at United Press, but I was free to spend the day at their offices and see how the very complex machinery of feeding red-hot news to Fleet Street worked. I spent the morning on the domestic desk and the afternoon on the foreign desk.

There were something like six or seven men seated around a large table, to which cables from United Press reporters would be handed by the chief sub-editor. To save money because the wireless stories were charged by the word, Latin prefixes were attached to nouns so that adParis would mean 'to Paris' or cumRepublicans would do for 'with Republicans'. Again to save money, the correspondents only put in their cables the essential topical facts of the story, and the task of the sub-editors in London was to dig out from the agency library the background material which provoked or surrounded the news. The story that an assassination attempt had been made on a Swaziland foreign minister would be re-written with a short biography of the minister – his age, reputation and previous assassination attempts – and the political rivals who wanted to get rid of him.

The subscribers to United Press – most of the important papers like *The Times*, the *Express*, the *Manchester Guardian* – would add their own introductory paragraphs and individual flourishes to the body of the story, so that readers would not be faced with exactly the same account if they happened to buy two or more papers. By the end of the day a few of the helpful journalists gave me some unimportant stories to handle and I found I had caught on to the technique quite quickly. My years on the *Varsity* as well as the editing of the law journal, *Obiter Dicta*, had acclimatized me to the thinking process by which news events were transmuted into the fodder of newspapers.

Fisher agreed that I seemed to have caught on quite rapidly to the art of the foreign sub-editor and assumed that this was because of my professional experience on the *Toronto Star*. Although United Press had no immediate vacancies why didn't I try the American agency, Associated Press? He would phone the Agency's Director, a Mr Lindsay, and arrange an appointment.

Mr Lindsay turned out at first to be as discouraging as everyone else had been about work prospects. When he heard I had handled Agency stories in Toronto, he said he would give me a three-day trial on Associated Press's foreign desk. 'I have two men down with flu because of this winter's epidemic,' he said, 'so I might be able to fit you in if you can do the job. But I must warn you that every man on that desk is an experienced American sub-editor with many years' background. And at Associated Press we expect only the best.'

My first day was rather tentative. The few hours I'd spent at United Press certainly familiarized me with the skeleton of the job, but I was baffled by certain idiosyncratic abbreviations to save word costs that AP indulged in. Fortunately my co-workers on the desk were only too ready to translate some of the jargon as I apologetically mumbled that I had not been doing this kind of work for six years. The second day offered few problems. I had no difficulty supplementing the information from the library material to the incoming story. My training in law and intelligence equipped me for collating data and my university journalism had taught me how to shape a newspaper story. In the middle of my third day, the chief-sub after reading one of my edited stories said, approvingly, 'It's clear that you were at this kind of thing for a long time.' I didn't dare whisper to anyone that my career as a foreign agency sub-editor had to date amounted to only four days.

Since both of the flu victims had recovered and my three-day trial period was up, there was no longer any need for me at Associated Press. Lindsay, however, still seemed keen on hiring me. Would I wait? He'd be in touch with his New York office about taking me on. After a month I contacted them again and Lindsay said his problem was that I was a Canadian and that special authority had to be obtained to hire a non-American.

It was now the middle of March 1947, and no regular money was coming in. Gibb-Smith suggested I try Geoffrey Imeson, News Manager at Reuters in Fleet Street. On the telephone, I gave him a brief outline of my qualifications and followed it up with a letter. Again I lied about my previous experience but told the truth about what had happened to me recently. The letter was persuasive enough for Imeson to offer me a three-day trial on the foreign desk. After coming through the four day learning process at United Press and Associated Press, another test held no terrors for me. I was hired at a salary of £11 a week.

I found the job congenial and within my capabilities. It entailed an eight-hour shift which could vary from day to night work. Its chief advantage from my standpoint – I was taking Russian night classes and organizing publicity for my book which was to be published in a month – was that there was only a minimum of responsibility associated with the job. Some event might take place in Denmark – a parliamentary election, for example – which I would report, but by the time I returned to the desk two shifts later, the story had been transformed in such a way that what I had written had become stale news. I could only follow up what two other sub-editors had said about it. The keenest competition amongst the Agencies was speed. And each day we heard how we had beaten Associated Press by two minutes thirty-five seconds over some riot in Korea or student protest in Paris.

The critical reception for *Defeat in the West* when it appeared on 17 April 1947, was more favourable than anything either myself or my publishers could have prayed for. As an unknown Canadian major my authority for writing such a sweeping historical analysis before anyone more respected had yet attempted it, was certainly dubious. Seckers, however, had managed to get Major General Sir Ian Jacob, Assistant Military Secretary to the War Cabinet and one of Churchill's closest war-time advisers, to write a three-page Introduction to its pages. His support gave it just the credentials it needed. 'There is no doubt about the essential accuracy of the picture that emerges,' he said. 'Further research may lead to modification of the details, but the main facts and conclusions that can be drawn from them are likely to remain unchallenged.'

The fanfare of approval stretched from the *Observer* ('Very rarely of late has historical fact been so carefully checked and sifted, so engagingly recorded, and so skilfully disposed in what deserves to be a thoroughly popular book') to the *Times Literary Supplement* ('There are few major events of the whole war that are not turned by Mr Shulman into a startling light from this new angle. It is a fascinating study') to the *News Chronicle* ('It has some claims to be the *All Quiet on the Western Front* of World War II').

Naturally, with the wealth of expertise available to the reviewers of the book, faults were found with some of the historical details, reservations were voiced about some of my strategic generalizations, suspicions raised about my credentials for taking on such a huge task and superior comments dropped about my writing style. I was not as upset as I should have been about these dismissive complaints. I was honestly surprised there were not more of them. After all, I was not a professional soldier nor trained to be an historian of any kind. Yet my basic thesis for the downfall of the Wehrmacht was generally accepted by almost all critics and by senior Allied figures like Major General Sir Ian Jacob. I asserted that there were at least three major weaknesses that existed in the framework of the Wehrmacht which combined to produce a defeated, rather than a victorious, Germany. 'These weaknesses might be summed up in three words: Hitler, discipline and ignorance,' I wrote in Chapter One.

It was gratifying to me that instead of being derided for these massive generalizations, Captain Liddell Hart in his review in the *Listener* wrote, 'The introductory part is perhaps the best part of the book. Major Shulman considers that three basic factors underlay and explain Germany's defeat: "Hitler, discipline and ignorance". He discusses them with much shrewdness and a gift of vivid phrasing in successive chapters under those titles.'

Amongst the complimentary letters received by my publisher supporting the general thrust of the book was one from Sir John Slessor,

Commander-in-Chief of the British Air Force, and another from Lieutenant General Sir Leslie Hollis, a military secretary to Churchill's War Cabinet. But I felt my ultimate seal of approval came when in August, 1947, in a speech to mark the anniversary of the Battle of Falaise, Field Marshal Montgomery listed the reasons for the defeat of the Wehrmacht as discipline, ignorance and Hitler. And in his speech credit was given to *Defeat in the West*.

The 6,000 copes printed were sold out in about six weeks. Because of their limited paper quota, Seckers were not able to bring out another edition of 3,500 copies until September. Although it, too, sold reasonably well, the momentum for sales of the original reviews was largely lost. It remained in print for the next fifty years but it never actually attained the status of a best-seller.

Foreign rights were quickly sold to French, Dutch and German publishers. A Czech publisher could not complete his contract because of currency difficulties and Polish rights were sold, only to have them rescinded because the government decided it was not pro-Russian enough for the communist authorities. The book was never translated into Spanish because the publisher that displayed an interest wanted me to delete certain passages referring to Franco's close association with the Nazis before and during the war. I refused.

My major disappointment was the delay in finding an American publisher. There was already beginning to be a surfeit of books about the war and the danger was that American readers would soon become weary of the subject. About four months before the British publication date I met Alfred Knopf who was head of one of the most prestigious publishing houses in America. He had the massive presence of an arrogant Jewish patriarch and I was suitably overawed when he talked to me in his room at Brown's hotel.

'I have not read the book but I have seen the readers' reports provided by Seckers and they are very impressed,' he said. 'I gather your book will explain how and why the Germans lost the war. What authority have you got to write such a book?'

I explained that my work in Intelligence and my interviewing of major German generals had given me the facts upon which the book was based.

'But you claim to know all about Hitler's mistakes, Rommel's suicide, the differences between von Rundstedt and Hitler, the weaknesses of the German General Staff,' he said, leafing contemptuously through the typed reader's reports in his hands. 'And you are only a major! Surely you'd have to be at least a general to take on such a huge subject.'

I was now beginning to lose my temper.

'Mr Knopf, I have convinced just as sceptical people as yourself as to the reliability of my book. I did not come here to beg you to believe me. The book speaks for itself and when you've read it perhaps you'll know what I'm talking about.'

He never read it and he never published it.

It was clear that when E. P. Dutton eventually bought the rights, we could hardly have made a worse choice of publishers. The critical reception in America was even more enthusiastic than the one in Britain. William M. Shirer, author of the classic, *The Rise and Fall of the Third Reich*, in a full page review in the *New York Herald Tribune* called it an 'absorbing history of the war in the West with much that is fascinating in this rewarding book'. The *New York Times* book review section gave it a full page with its reviewer, Shepard Stone, saying 'Mr Shulman's book is a first rate contribution to our literature of the war. And it is good reading.'

The critical notices poured in from almost every newspaper in America. It was claimed that it could have out-sold *Forever Amber*, if published three years earlier. But my American publisher, Dutton, made sure it outsold nobody. They published it on 22 January 1948, which is the kind of date, missing the Christmas market, reserved for dud books they have no intention of promoting, and indeed they did nothing in the way of publicity. Dutton gambled on a miserly print order of 2,500 copies and three days after publication the major book shops in New York had already sold their tiny stock.

When the enthusiastic reviews started to appear, Dutton's publicity director tried to put a gloss on their extraordinary judgement by assuring me that, at a very high level, it had been decided *Defeat in the West* would not make popular reading because the public was fed up with war books but that it would be kept in print for academic and military outlets. Meanwhile I was to know they had considered it a privilege to be able to publish it. To which my agent, Spencer Curtis Brown, replied, 'I am glad it has been a privilege to publish the book but I cannot help being more interested in profit than privilege.'

Eventually the continued demand for the book (in the top ten Most-Asked-For-Books in New York libraries) and the reviews in magazines and radio forced someone in the higher echelons at Dutton to spend some money on advertising it. On 22 February 1948 the first word of its existence turned up in a half-page advertisement in the *New York Times*.

4

MARTIN BORMANN AND
NAZI GOLD

Am instructed to find Martin Bormann or go to the Palladium ... 40 years on, Creighton's mysterious claims unfold ... Nazi gold and Ian Fleming's plot ... Bormann dead or a double? ... Convincing publishers ... Doubt and death threats ... The conspiracy theory

(i) Involved in the mystery of Nazi Gold

The Führer and his cohorts re-entered my life over 40 years later when I received a mysterious letter in response to an article I had written about my first day at the *Evening Standard,* back in 1947. On that day, the *Standard's* editor, Herbert Gunn, told me that my initial assignment, because I was a German army expert and had just written *Defeat in the West*, was to go to Berlin and find Martin Bormann. Startled by such a task, I protested, 'But Bormann is dead. I don't think it would be much of a story.'

'Are you sure he's dead?' persisted Gunn. 'I thought there was considerable doubt about that.'

'Yes,' I said. 'Some historians don't believe the evidence, but it would take some time to discover anything fresh.'

'How long?'

'About three or four weeks at least. And it would be rather expensive, with probably nothing new to show for it.'

Gunn pondered my reply for a few minutes.

'Alright,' he said. 'If you don't think you can find Martin Bormann, will you go the Palladium and interview Chico Marx?'

Like a barrister who one day will sue a tabloid for libel and soon after defend another tabloid for a similar sort of libel, the journalist's briefs are the idiosyncratic demands of his editor. News, the lifeblood of a newspaper, has no orderly agenda. The dominant criterion of a journalist's work is readability; chronology is far less important.

110

In August 1989, complying with the imperative of topicality that is expected to dominate every weekly newspaper column, I used the peg of the anniversary of the defeat of Japan to write about the last days of Hitler. I retold my first day's experience on the *Evening Standard* when I was told to go to Berlin and find Martin Bormann. The headline read 'Find Bormann? But he's dead ...'

My life has had many curious twists but none so strange as the consequences of that innocuous headline on the next eight years of my career. The following day I received a letter from Christopher Creighton. The name meant nothing to me, although he assured me we had met some years before because of my friendship with his sister, a very attractive girl who was studying to become an opera singer. She gave up those aspirations when she married the owner of a small country inn and helped him run it. I had not seen her for many years when I heard that she had unexpectedly died after a brief illness.

Creighton, knowing my background in Intelligence, thought I might be more interested in Bormann than was indicated in my column. Did I want to know how he and Ian Fleming got him out? To establish his credentials as someone knowledgeable about Intelligence and Security matters, he told me he was the author of *The Paladin*, a novel written with Brian Garfield, which was based upon his true operations as a boy spy in 1940 and '41. The book was a great success, having made the bestseller lists in Britain and America, sold over 100,000 copies and been serialized in the *Daily Express*.

My first inclination was to treat the letter as one of those crank missives, usually written in red or purple ink, that often plague journalists and are dealt with by a quick toss into the nearest wastepaper basket. But because I had been extremely fond of his sister – and I was convinced that his introductory credentials were genuine – I felt I ought to put him off with a courteous reply. I asked Angus McGill, the paper's most experienced feature writer, for some advice about how to handle this strange note and, to my surprise, he was intrigued by its contents. He urged me not to dismiss Creighton and to find out more about him. I decided to give him a call. It was a decision that was to involve me in an intriguing international mystery whose ramifications – after having been investigated by intelligence experts, historians, academics and journalists – are still bewilderingly unresolved eight years after I first spoke to Christopher Creighton.

I listened with increasing fascination to the startling story Creighton summarized for me on the phone. I was, of course, well aware of the atmosphere of disbelief that existed in Fleet Street about any purported account of yet untold secrets about the final days of Germany's defeat. There had been a gullible market for such tales in the years immediately after the Armistice, but two intricate stories that turned out to be elaborate hoaxes had converted this area of historical speculation into a mendacious minefield that no editor was likely to put a toe into.

The editor of the *Daily Express*, Stewart Steven, was forced to admit that he had been conned into believing Martin Bormann had been discovered alive in the Argentine. An even more notorious hoax was the forging of documents purporting to be Hitler's War Diaries, which had taken in the *Sunday Times* as well as other respectable European papers. When Creighton had divulged what appeared to be another incredible Bormann story I told him I was intrigued by his tale but I had a small reputation as a military historian and did not want it to suffer the fate of Hugh Trevor-Roper, the author of *The Last Days of Hitler*, who supported the authenticity of Hitler's Diaries only to have to make a humiliating confession that he had been thoroughly duped.

After the collapse of the Ardennes offensive, the failure of Hitler's V-1 and V-2 secret weapons to wreak any significant havoc against England and the speedy advance of the Russian armies in the East, it was obvious to anyone other than an ardent Nazi fanatic that Germany had lost the war. By the beginning of 1945, senior Nazi officials and functionaries were already making plans to get as much money as they could out of Germany, and trying to arrange some bolt-hole for themselves and their families in some neutral land, either disguised or not.

Vast amounts of gold, foreign currency and art treasures were being lodged in foreign banks, chiefly in Switzerland. Some of those closest to Hitler – Ribbentrop, Goering, Himmler – were making clandestine approaches to contacts in Sweden, Portugal, Switzerland, Paraguay and the Argentine for a safe haven after the surrender and Hitler's expected assassination or suicide.

They assumed that, even if they were arrested after the war, they might have to face a term in prison after which they could live out their days with the hidden resources they had stashed away. The concept of War Crimes trials and the execution of the defeated leaders was a novel and unthinkable prospect. After Germany's defeat in the First World War political and military leaders like the Kaiser, Hindenburg and Ludendorff had been allowed to become prominent and powerful figures in a vanquished Germany. It was a tradition that the Nazi establishment expected the Allied victors to respect.

Aware of the avalanche of German resources and pillaged treasures leaving the Reich, Churchill was determined to do something about it. One of the many steps taken was to put Naval Commander Ian Lancaster Fleming in charge of an exercise to discover where some of this gold and currency was being hidden and how it could be returned to the Allies when the war was over. He had been the personal assistant to the Director of Naval Intelligence, Rear-Admiral John Godfrey. In Room 60 in the Admiralty on the 4 January 1945, Fleming met Major Desmond Morton, Churchill's personal security chief and a personal friend since World War I.

Creighton told me that Morton was his godfather. Morton, born in 1891, had served in the First World War and received a bullet in his heart which no operation could remove and remained with him all his life. His bravery was recognized by his awards of a Military Cross, a *Croix de Guerre* and a mention in despatches. After the war he was seconded to the Foreign Office and in 1930 he set up a body known as the Industrial Intelligence Centre, a front for a super-secret organization which was privately financed by successive monarchs – George V, Edward VIII and George VI. Although Creighton referred to it as the M Section, he told me that there was no official intelligence operation with that title. One of its earliest activities was to supply Winston Churchill, then out of office, with information about German rearmament, which helped alert the Baldwin and Chamberlain governments about Hitler's aggressive intentions.

Creighton described Morton as a tall, athletic man with an authoritative manner and an upper-class accent. He was a friend of Creighton's father, Jack Ainsworth-Davis, who had qualified as a doctor at Cambridge and was a member of the British 4 x 400 metre relay team which won a gold medal at the Antwerp Olympics in 1920. Involved with supporting that team were three undergraduates: Sub-Lieutenant Lord Louis Mountbatten and two of his cousins, the Duke of York (later George VI) and his younger brother, the Duke of Gloucester. These contacts with his father brought the young Creighton, as a boy, to the attention of both Desmond Morton, Churchill and Lord Louis Mountbatten.

As a surgeon, Jack Ainsworth-Davis had operated on Joachim von Ribbentrop when he was Germany's ambassador to Britain. They were also on social terms. Their friendship had begun when they were at

school together in Metz before the First World War. It was there that
Creighton's father spent a year studying German. Convinced that war
was on the way, Morton could see in the young Creighton's social contacts with Ribbentrop prospects of using him in some clandestine activity when hostilities began. After Creighton's parents divorced, Morton
had him enrolled at Ampleforth for a short period and then sent him to
the Royal Naval College at Dartmouth in September, 1939, at the age
of fifteen and a half, where he was instructed to call himself by a pseudonym and never be known as John Davis nor John Ainsworth-Davis
again.

I learned about this background information many months after I
agreed to offer him some advice about the book he was planning to
write about Martin Bormann. His first letters were so startling, giving
me a general outline of what he had done, that I could not resist finding out much more about it.

The task Fleming was given when he met both Morton and
Churchill early in 1945 was to discover what means the German government and the Nazi Party were using to remove from their territory
the billions of pounds of cash, gold, jewellery and art treasures and hide
it away in foreign banks and secret caves where it could be recovered
when the war was over. Using intelligence resources that had been nurtured before the war, Fleming discovered the names of two Swiss banks
where this plundered loot was held in secret numbered accounts. In the
course of acquiring this information and transmitting it by wireless to
England, a young woman secret agent, very close to Creighton, had
been tortured and murdered.

When I first discussed with Creighton how he planned to write this
story, he believed it could only be done, even as late as 1989, as faction
– a combination of fiction and the truth. Because Creighton was almost
paranoic about security, my initial contacts with him were almost com-
ical in their remoteness. I did not meet him personally until well after
he had started sending me the first sections of his book which was then
called *Project X-2*.

At first I never wrote to him but telephoned him with any comments
I had to make. He has been to my flat a number of times but I have
never been to his home, although I have spoken to his wife on many
occasions on the phone. At the beginning he stressed that because
Operation James Bond – which was later the real code name of Project
X-2 – was under the M Section, its existence was never to be made

public. In his book *OpJB* Creighton writes: 'Even at the highest level, only a handful of people outside the M Section should know of the project's existence. It had never been mentioned in any document, except under its naval party assignation, or code number. It never would be mentioned. It had simply never existed, and never would.'

It would be an understatement to say that the details of Creighton's adventure with Ian Fleming and Bormann, if true, provide one of the most daring and amazing stories of the last Great War. Perhaps Otto Skorzeny's rescue of Mussolini from Allied hands, with German parachutists, comes close to the venture in magnitude of audacity.

As Creighton's story unfolded to me in batches of about 2,000 words every fortnight under the pseudonymous title, *Project X-2*, I learnt that Ian Fleming's first task was to read through the file of the young man whom Morton had recommended to him as a particul-arly qualified deputy. So weird and secret were the contents of those papers disclosing Creighton's war-time career to date, that the room in which Fleming read them had to have its doors and windows firmly bolted and two of M Section's security officers stationed outside it while Fleming perused the official documents.

'Fleming read my record with astonishment,' comments Creighton in *OpJB*. 'If he himself had not been on the periphery of some of the events described, he would have doubted the account's veracity; but because he had often been involved he knew that the narratives were genuine.'

Fleming's second task after agreeing to have Creighton as his operational commander was to fly to Basle in Switzerland where on 11 January 1945, a pre-arranged meeting had been organized with the Swiss Foreign Minister, Ernest Nobs, and two of his colleagues. He carried with him a diplomatic passport, wore civilian clothes and bore a personal letter from Winston Churchill. The letter asked the Swiss minister for help in returning to the Allies the vast wealth that had been deposited in Swiss vaults by the murderers and tyrants of the Nazi hierarchy. The minister's first reaction was to deny any knowledge of any illegal accounts held in Swiss banks by Hitler's despoiling minions.

When Fleming revealed that he knew the names of the banks in which most of this exported money was held, as well as the numbers of the suspected accounts, the Foreign Minister's answer was that it would be a criminal offence for him to disclose such information. Even if he knew it. Swiss banking regulations prevented him from naming the holders of such accounts and their identification could only be revealed if the proper signatories were obtained. But, Fleming pressed on, surely if it were proven that such funds had been illegally expropriated from conquered territories, the Swiss government would agree to have them frozen and investigated as soon as the war was over. The Foreign Minister agreed that if proof could be found that individuals or even explicit companies had been robbed by the Nazis, the banks would be ready to look into their claims; but as far as funds belonging to independent foreign states like Germany were concerned, they had absolute immunity unless the proper signatories for release were produced. They had reached stalemate when Nobs asked what would happen to these monies if they were handed over to the Allies. Fleming had a prepared answer. They would ask the Swiss government to act as trustee of these funds until an international committee had studied the claims made upon them and decided who were the rightful owners. Any money that could not be traced to its original source would be distributed to peoples most damaged by the war – even Germans and Italians – as a form of reparations.

Although the discussion appeared to have hit a dead-end the minister was strangely insistent that Fleming stay for a few minutes for sandwiches and coffee. Sipping his coffee in a large empty room, Fleming was joined by a young, smartly dressed woman wearing a raincoat and carrying a briefcase. She indicated that she was a member of the Swiss Intelligence Service and that she had something of interest to show him.

An hour's drive away, they arrived at a small village in a high valley in the Alps. Fleming's observant eye noticed small gun emplacements deployed unobtrusively in the area and innocent-looking chalets hiding large steel doors opening into a side of the mountain.

Fleming was told by his guide that this was a secure vault of the National Bank of Basle carved out of pure rock, and once inside his eyes feasted on an incredible Aladdin's Cave of gold nuggets, diamonds, emeralds and other precious stones including Crown jewels from the Hohenzollerns and other royal dynasties of Europe. In huge wooden crates were stacked masterpieces that had been looted from museums and galleries in France, Belgium, Holland, Denmark, Norway, the Ukraine and Luxembourg.

The means by which these art treasures were seized or bought with unstated threats at ludicrously low prices has been meticulously documented in a scholarly work, *The Rape of Europa*, by Lynn H. Nicholas, in which Martin Bormann, Hitler's private secretary, is pinpointed as the individual who decided which of this growing art treasure should be seized or purchased after being shown to the Führer. Hitler personally selected the ones to be sent to the town of Linz where he was amassing what he hoped would be the greatest art museum the world had ever seen. These masterpieces were probably destined for Linz.

Fleming, amazed at the vastness of this cornucopia, asked what part of it belonged to Germany. All of it, he was told. On the military airstrip outside Basle, a white envelope was handed over to Fleming by his Swiss companion. He was told the Finance Minister had asked her to give it to him before he flew off. Inside was a single sheet of white paper, bearing one typed line: '*Nationalsozialistische Deutsche Arbeiterpartei 60508.*'

★ ★ ★

It was at Birdham, a cover name for a Commando training establishment for the Royal Navy and Royal Marines near Portsmouth, that Creighton assured me the M Section had its operational headquarters. Even before Fleming returned from Switzerland, personnel were already being assembled for the prospective expedition that would be needed to stem the flow of Nazi resources out of the country. It did not take long to learn that number 60508 of the German National Socialist Workers' Party was Martin Bormann.

But how important was he? Amongst the well-known figures that constituted Hitler's inner circle – Goering, Goebbels, Himmler, Kaltenbrunner, Ribbentrop, Hess, Keitel – the name of Bormann never made any headlines in the Western press. He was known to be head of the Nazi Party Chancellery and Hitler's personal secretary but in photographs he was always a shadowy figure, listening to or putting documents in front of his Führer to read or sign. A chunky man with a hook nose and a bully-like appearance he exercised his influence with the unobtrusive, unrelenting persistence of a mole. When history's curtain was dropped, Bormann was revealed as probably, next to Hitler, the Nazi Party's most powerful figure.

Reichsleiter Bormann was born on 17 June, 1900, in Saxony, the son of a regimental trumpet player. He saw front line duty in the First World War and became an early member of the anti-Semitic Freikorps, spending a year in prison for complicity in the murder of one of his comrades suspected of being a police spy. Through dedication and diligence he had risen to the rank of Reichsleiter and SS general when Hitler came to power in 1933. He became involved with the responsibility of handling the financial affairs of the Nazi Party when he was made Chief of Staff of Hitler's Deputy, Rudolf Hess. He was also in control of Hitler's personal funds which were immense, largely because of the royalties he was receiving for the publication of *Mein Kampf*.

When in May, 1941, Hess made his curious and sensational flight to Scotland in a futile attempt to reach a peace settlement with Churchill, Bormann stepped into Hess's shoes and the post closest to the Führer's ear. Although almost universally detested by power-seeking rivals in Hitler's court – Goering, Goebbels, Ribbentrop, Himmler – Bormann rose relentlessly to a position that almost made him indispensable to the Führer. Hitler was not prepared to hear a word against him.

According to Walter Schellenberg, Head of Germany's Secret Service, Hitler had this to say about Bormann: 'I know he is brutal, but what he undertakes he finishes. I can rely absolutely on that. With his ruthlessness and brutality he always sees that my orders are carried out.'

According to Professor H. R. Trevor-Roper, Martin Bormann was 'the Brown Eminence behind the Führer's throne, the most powerful, the least public, and the most mysterious of all the Nazi leaders.' He deliberately avoided publicity and his features were unknown to the German people. In Hitler's last year Bormann reigned undisputed over the court. He built around the Führer a Chinese wall impenetrable except by his favour. He exercised complete control over the whole structure of the Third Reich.

'As Party Chancellor,' continued Trevor-Roper, 'he controlled the entire Party machine throughout Germany. All the Gaulieters were appointed by him and under his order, all careers within the Party were dependent on his favour. His power was enormous and could be compared to the power exercised by Stalin in the last days of Lenin.'

It was therefore not surprising that Bormann's presence dominated the last few days and hours of Hitler's life. His name is on Hitler's wedding certificate to Eva Braun and in the Führer's personal testament – written a few hours before his suicide – Bormann, 'my most loyal Party comrade', is appointed as sole executor of Hitler's will 'with full legal authority to make all decisions'. Both the will and the political testament were witnessed by Bormann.

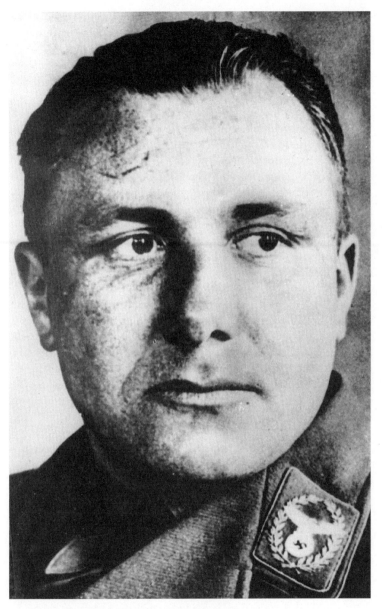

Hitler's ubiquitous and powerful Deputy – Martin Bormann.

With the knowledge of Bormann's powerful position verified by British Intelligence, Ian Fleming identified his task as a relatively uncomplicated one. Find Bormann, kidnap him, bring him to Britain and have him sign the necessary documents the Swiss banking authorities were demanding to release the German funds in their banks. It was at this stage that Creighton's early association with Ribbentrop as well as his activities in the first three years of the war which had established him as a double spy in the eyes of the Gestapo and Admiral Canaris, the Wehrmacht's head of Intelligence, made him an indispensable part of the plan to bring Bormann to England.

Through Desmond Morton's contacts, there were intimations that Ribbentrop wanted to meet Christopher Creighton. It was at first suspected that the Foreign Minister's aims were part of a German peace feeler. Trying to organize an armistice deal and some security for themselves was already occupying the minds of the top Nazi establishment. It all had to be done without Hitler's knowledge, for the Führer was ready to execute any of his close comrades should he learn of such treasonable activity.

Creighton, untrained in the diplomatic manoeuvring that might be necessary if Ribbentrop was contemplating using him as a negotiating instrument, thought that Ian Fleming should accompany him, not only for his experience in such matters but because he spoke fluent German while Creighton would have relied on Ribbentrop's English for communication. Fleming had already chosen OpJP as the code name for the operation: looking for an innocuous name that would give no hint of what it was covering up he recalled the author of a classic ornithological work about birds in the West Indies. After the war when he wrote his popular series of thrillers, he recalled the Bormann operation and thought James Bond an appropriate name for his hero because it was a thoroughly neutral and nondescript title to disguise the startling adventures of Agent 007.

Other code names for OpJB were picked from A. A. Milne's children's classic, *Winnie the Pooh*. Churchill was Tigger; Ian Fleming, Pooh; Desmond Morton, Owl; Bormann, Piglet; Ribbentrop, Roo; Hitler, Rabbit; the SS, Rabbit's friends; Susan Kemp (third in command), Miss Kanga. Admiral Mountbatten alone was not an A. A. Milne character and was named Charlemagne.

At Birdham personnel were being assembled and trained for what was increasingly being recognized as a vital and dangerous expedition.

Morton did the recruiting and only accepted young men and women capable of undergoing the most strenuous commando training which would leave them with superior skills in jujitsu, unarmed combat, expertise in the use of knives and hand guns, silent killing and the handling of kayaks and parachute drops. They also had to be able to sustain great pain and physical hardship.

Almost 400 took part in Operation James Bond including highly trained commandos from the navy and marines, a contingent of highly trained Wrens and nearly one hundred German Freedom Fighters, mainly young Jewish men and women who had found asylum in England and were determined to contribute to the destruction of Hitler's Germany.

A large part of *OpJB* describes in great detail the clandestine and almost bizarre negotiations that had to take place before Martin Bormann would agree to sign the necessary documents that would release the millions of German government and Nazi Party assets in Swiss banks. The first meeting with Ribbentrop entailed Fleming and Creighton flying from Lisbon to Basle to Zurich on 8 February 1945, wearing civilian clothes and carrying diplomatic passports. One of Ribbentrop's emissaries took them to a castle overlooking Lake Constance where they were grandly wined and dined for four days until the German Foreign Secretary finally turned up. To seal the understanding that Creighton was a double spy, he was driven back into Zurich where a large sum of money – Creighton claims it was about £100,000 – was placed in his Swiss bank account – he also claims he never drew a penny of it – for his services in getting Ribbentrop to England.

Another exceptional feature of the enterprise was the ingenious method that had been devised to keep Desmond Morton and Bletchley in touch with Fleming and Creighton. Creighton, during his naval career, had trained as a pianist and after the war in 1955 was good enough to be part of a jazz group entertaining professionally in a popular jazz club in New York's Greenwich Village. The coded message he transmitted was in music. Winding transmitter wire round the leg of the piano in the German castle and running it out of the window to a small transceiver radio in their bedroom Creighton, by playing three notes, could use them as Morse signal keys. Within ten minutes their messages were received and decoded at Bletchley.

At that first meeting Ribbentrop admitted Germany had lost the war. He was relying on Creighton to allow him to disappear in the chaos that would follow the Führer's death. He hoped to get to South America but there was one obstacle that still had to be overcome. He told Creighton that his ambition was to seize for himself some of the vast assets the Nazis had accumulated abroad so that he could live out the rest of his days anonymously and financially secure.

'But there is one man I need to suborn,' Creighton reports Ribbentrop as saying in *OpJB*. 'Martin Bormann! The Führer's secretary! He is head of the Party Chancellery and personally controls all the assets outside the Reich.'

Creighton said he had never heard of him. 'It doesn't matter,' said Ribbentrop. 'Through you I intend to offer Bormann a means of escape. I have demanded a large payment of money from him but as soon as we get out, I shall hand him over to you British or liquidate him – whatever you suggest.' Creighton then brought in Ian Fleming, who told Ribbentrop that he was the leader of a gang of unscrupulous British deserters ready to do anything for money.

A fortnight later on 4 March, word was received through a British agent in Zurich that Bormann had shown some positive interest in the proposition and Creighton and Fleming should fly to Berlin to meet both him and Ribbentrop. On hearing this news Morton decided to activate the scheme by dropping a small parachute group called Operation James Bond Vanguard (JBV) into the Müggelsee Lake.

It was now evident that the Bormann escapade was on. Returning to Birdham, Creighton and Fleming decided that the most effective way of bringing Bormann out of Berlin was through the profusion of waterways that run through and around the German capital. A large model of these waterways was built with every island, stream and bridge pinpointed for all those taking part to memorize in every detail. Although only Fleming, Creighton and Susan Kemp knew the exact purpose of the operation, the others merely knew a very important figure was being lifted, they all realized they had to become adept at the assembling, dissembling and manoeuvring of the kayaks which were to be their main means of transportation.

On the second trip to see Ribbentrop, in Berlin, Fleming and Creighton flew to Zurich from where they were driven by car to Vaduz, the capital of Liechtenstein. Here they changed into Waffen-SS uniforms and from a military airstrip they were flown in monoplanes with open cockpits to a bomb-cratered airstrip some three miles south of the shattered city. A large Mercedes drove them to what at first they thought was the German Foreign Office, but which turned out to be the Party Chancellery which housed not only the Foreign Secretary but Bormann, Hitler and his entire remaining entourage.

They were taken to a concrete cubicle which contained a couple of bunks and a single tap above a hand-basin and a hole in the floor for a lavatory. A short wait and they were escorted by two SS men to Ribbentrop's office which had obviously once been grand and luxurious but now its windows were cracked, furniture was dust-covered and the meal offered them was some cold sausage, black bread and ersatz coffee.

Ribbentrop assured them that the previous arrangements about money were in place, with substantial sums for both of them in Swiss francs. Having convinced the Foreign Secretary that they had personnel close by to get both Bormann and Ribbentrop out of Berlin when required, they were locked in their tiny quarters until a square, bull-necked man with a prominent scar over his left eye came to see them. It was Martin Bormann. With him was a girl interpreter. Fleming pretended he knew no German. Bormann acknowledged that the war was lost and that Ribbentrop's agreement with their English rescuers should be undertaken.

He accepted the use of kayaks, but he had to make sure that after the war there would be no international hunt for him because he had disappeared. A double must be found whose body would be the same height and weight as his, with plastic surgery to his features which would stand up to a post-mortem examination even if the PW's face was blown away, because of the means by which he was murdered.

At the same time he handed over a bulky file containing his official medical and dental records. These were subsequently doctored in London to match the German PW they had found in a camp in Canada, a man who was willing to act as a double for a promise of a prosperous future after the war. Little did he know that he was destined to be murdered. It was Susan Kemp who was given the task of finding the victim who is code-named Günther in Creighton's book. Creighton told me that Günther was put in the hands of the renowned plastic surgeon, Archibald McIndoe, and a dentist named A. B. Aldred of Mayfair for the necessary physical adjustments to his body which could be forged on to Bormann's official records.

While all these preparations were taking place, Creighton and

Fleming received a signal to come to Rheims, temporary home of Eisenhower's Headquarters for the Allied Expeditionary Force. At SHAEF* HQ they were civilly met by the Supreme Commander, given a cup of coffee and then asked bluntly by Ike what they were up to. He revealed in no uncertain terms that his own Intelligence sources had told him all about the M Section, Operation James Bond and Churchill and Morton's plan to recover plundered Nazi assets hidden outside Germany. Although he did not explicitly say that he thought Churchill was trying to pull a fast one on the Americans by retaining such gold and art treasures, he wanted to ensure that every last gold ingot or art treasure regained through Bormann's cooperation was to be reported to him, so that their final disposition would be under joint British and American supervision and not Churchill's alone. To that end he insisted that one of his most efficient liaison intelligence officer, a Lieutenant B. W. Brabenov (a pseudonym) should be attached to Operation James Bond for its entire duration. Brabenov could speak Russian and German fluently and could obviously be very useful. Churchill complained bitterly to Desmond Morton about this leak of a vital British secret to Eisenhower but was not told that Morton himself had privately briefed his opposite American number, General W. J. 'Big Bill' Donovan, chief of the Office of Strategic Services (OSS) who, duty-bound, had passed on the details to Eisenhower and Roosevelt. Whether Churchill would ever have told the Americans about OpJB had the British succeeded without their intervention is a matter of conjecture.

While further commandos and marines were sent to join the advance party around Berlin – the advancing Russians had to be considered as much a threat to OpJB as the retreating Germans – on 6 April 1945, Eisenhower's emissary, Lieutenant Brabenov, turned up at Birdham.

Creighton and apparently everyone else involved with OpJB were overwhelmed by Lieutenant Brabenov. Eisenhower's representative was a woman. She was, says Creighton, an attractive, well-formed woman with strikingly blonde hair wearing on the khaki jacket of her US uniform a most impressive galaxy of service medals. For the past six months she had been working in the UK under the direct orders of General Donovan, chief of the OSS. Although she was strictly speaking only a liaison officer, she interpreted her assignment of reporting everything to

* Supreme Headquarters Allied Expeditionary Force

Eisenhower by conscientiously taking part in operational exercises in which she demonstrated her speed at drawing a .38 Smith & Wesson and firing at twenty paces bullet after bullet, as she put it, 'up a gnat's asshole'. She was an adept horsewoman and quickly learnt the technique of mastering a kayak. It must have been someone like Brabenov, if not that agent herself, who was the inspiration for all those long-legged, glamorous, sharp-shooting, karate expert women who made millions for the many James Bond films based on Ian Fleming's adventure novels.

A Russian speaker like Brabenov would be an invaluable aid if confronted with hostile Soviet troops barring their way. She immediately volunteered to take part and, at a meeting between Donovan and Morton on 9 April at Birdham, permission for her involvement was granted and she was given the pseudonym of Alice, another name borrowed from A. A. Milne's children's books.

The details for Operation James Bond were meticulously organized and rehearsed over and over again by all those involved. The main command group would land in the Müggelsee by a parachute drop and be picked up by the advance party. After lying up for a day in organized safe houses, they would proceed by kayak north-west down the Spree taking Günther – Bormann's double – with them and protected by German Freedom Fighters and Royal Marine commandos. They would disembark some twelve miles downstream just before the Weidendamm Bridge, leave their kayaks with their escort and proceed by foot to a rendezvous organized by Ribbentrop or Bormann near or in the Party Chancellery.

It is not my intention in this chapter to do more than provide a brief outline of what was done in the Chancellery just before and after Hitler's death. Graphic details are contained in Creighton's book, *OpJB*, which in their excitement, tension and suspense read like the most daring adventure stories produced about the last Great War. Even those who refuse to believe a word of Creighton's yarn concede that its readability matches the most pulsating fiction produced in the books of Jack Higgins or Alistair MacLean.

As the concluding chapters of Creighton's story reached me at about 2,000 words a time, my incredulity about it all was modified by the staggering detail Creighton was able to produce about every facet of the operation. A typical example was his description of the gear they were to wear in Berlin and in the kayaks. There were two changes of underwear, oiled long-johns, boat shoes, trousers and Ursula jackets specially water-proofed in the manner used by Waffen SS patrols. His cap had an SS badge on the outside and when reversed it became a Russian fur cap with the badge of a special Intelligence Group. Under this top layer, they wore thin British uniforms to which they would strip off if captured to prevent them being shot as spies. They all carried a fighting knife, a Smith & Wesson .38 revolver, two 36 grenades, waterproof watches, underwater writing tablets and life jackets.

Whatever Creighton described – whether it was a travelling route, a conversation, an intricate intelligence device, a piece of complex technical equipment like infra-red instruments to enable night-time vision, the aircraft in which they travelled, the experience of falling in a tree after a parachute drop – minute facts were provided to justify authenticity. In seven years of monitoring his accounts, I found an astonishing consistency about these myriad details, and under questioning by numerous experts and investigators he rarely wavered.

After their parachute drop, the command group stayed in one of their safe houses until they were carried by kayaks to the Chancellery where, after being challenged a number of times, the safeguards arranged by Ribbentrop enabled them to reach a cell-like room in one of the air-raid shelters. Creighton, Fleming, Brabenov and Günther (Bormann's double) had the task of managing the exodus of Ribbentrop and Bormann. But a surprise awaited them on their arrival. Fleming and Creighton were ushered into Ribbentrop's office, where they were told by a slightly embarrassed Foreign Minister that he had changed his mind about going with them. He had privately arranged a passage out of Berlin through Count Bernadotte and the Swedish Embassy. But Bormann would keep to all the arrangements.

Ribbentrop's escape plans turned out to be abortive and he was arrested by British troops in Hamburg on 14 June 1945. He was sentenced to death at Nuremburg in October 1946.

Bormann's doctored medical and dental charts, which now matched Günther, were handed back to him. After two of his guards had to be disarmed they received assurances from him that he would cooperate fully in signing all documents needed to hand over all the gold, jewellery, bank deposits and other assets in his control. After waiting three days in their confined quarters, Bormann arrived on 30 April to tell them that Hitler was dead and that the break-out would take place the next evening. The pick-up kayaks, headed by Susan Kemp, were contacted by wireless and told to be ready. They were informed that four of the rear-guard group had been killed in a shooting exchange with the Russians. This disaster had no serious effect on the operation because such casualties were accommodated in the contingency plans.

During the final search of Bormann for secret documents and suicide pills, they discovered a large buff envelope which Bormann was trying to hide and which turned out to be a copy of Hitler's will. Six copies of this document had been made and distributed amongst important emissaries, to be delivered to figures like Doenitz and others. Fleming stowed the will in a waterproof case and it was eventually handed over to the M Section when Bormann himself was delivered.

As the OpJB personnel joined a group of about twenty German freedom-fighters crouching in the shelter of two tanks, with their instructions to break off and meet Susan Kemp's kayaks 300 yards short of the Weidendamm Bridge, a Russian shell made a direct hit on the leading German tank killing Bormann's double and Hitler's doctor, Stumpfegger, instantly. Although the real Bormann, Fleming, Brabenov and Creighton were knocked over by the blast, they only suffered superficial cuts and bruises and were able to make their way to the pick-up kayaks. Creighton told me that he was grateful that, in the event, he did not have to carry out the task of killing Günther and leaving his body where it would be likely to be picked up and identified as Bormann's. Fate had saved him from one more repellent, murderous task.

There were six kayaks, led by Susan Kemp, occupied by a party of twelve including Bormann that proceeded down the Spree and down the Havel towards the Elbe to deposit their valuable German prisoner. Just before they set off, an urgent message was received from London that Fleming was to return immediately to the rear party on the Müggelsee, where a Lysander would pick him up and fly him back to London. No explanation was given for this sudden need for Fleming, but intelligence revealed after the war was that it was King George VI who had asked for a commando group to go to Tambach Castle near Frankfurt belonging to the Hesse family. He believed there were embarrassing letters in the Castle written by members of his family to their relatives in the German royal family revealing a too intimate connection between Queen Victoria and her eldest daughter, who became mother of the Kaiser, as well as correspondence between the King's own mother, Queen Mary, and her German relations. Of even greater concern was the possibility that amongst these letters would be found some showing the pro-Nazi leanings of the Duke of Windsor. Fleming, along with

Roger Hollis, future Director General of MI5, and Anthony Blunt, the art historian later to be revealed as a Russian spy, was sent to snatch these documents. This extraordinary expedition was authenticated and revealed in the British press many years after I had first read about it in Creighton's chronicle of OpJB.

As the flotilla of kayaks paddled their way to the Elbe, they were challenged and assaulted by German and Russian troops. It was Brabenov's ability to pass herself off as a senior Russian commander that saved them on numerous occasions from being arrested by Russian troops. Bormann cooperated all the time in the manning of the kayaks on water and land. On 8 May they got a signal that Germany had surrendered but drunken, rapacious, victorious Russian soldiers still provided a deadly hazard. Four lives were lost before the objective of Operation James Bond had been carried out and Hitler's Deputy, Martin Bormann, was handed over to a commando escort, accompanied by Desmond Morton in civilian clothes, at a designated rendezvous on the banks of the Elbe.

(ii) Who will believe OpJB?

This brief outline of Operation James Bond was in essence what Creighton had been posting to me in large brown envelopes almost every fortnight from August 1989 to June 1990. Telling me that he had finished his book, he also sent me the actual maps of the Müggelsee, Spree and Havel that they had used for the operation. It was another nail in the coffin of my scepticism about the entire affair.

Admittedly, like almost everyone else who first heard about Bormann's connivance with the British to escape to England, I dismissed it as the vivid imagination of either a fantasist or a liar. I went along with it at first, expecting at any time to hear about something that was demonstrably untrue. Then I found myself talking to him on the phone or sending him memos more about the style and extraneous matters in it than about the truth of the facts he was recounting.

I soon began to realize that I was not dealing with an amateur scribbler but with a professional writer whose style may at times have been over-heated and clumsy, but who had a disciplined ability to present complex facts so that they were not only readily digestible but were credible as well. Since the potential financial aspects of the story – if true – were enormous, I agreed with Creighton that we should acquire a literary agent.

What I had not paid much attention to before was that Creighton had already been involved with two books about his intelligence activities which had been commercially successful. Both had been written by well-known thriller writers but, whether fiction or faction, they both emphasized the fact that essentially Creighton had been at the centre of all these events, and that the demands of security had prevented the publisher from claiming they had actually happened.

The Paladin, written with Brian Garfield, was mainly concerned with Creighton's assignment by Morton as a sixteen-year-old boy on a bicycle to report on the whereabouts of any U-boat pens that were hidden on the west coast of Ireland, from which they sailed forth to create havoc amongst Allied shipping in the Atlantic. At that young age he guided in a Combined Operations attack on a U-boat base near Donegal. It was the first time he had ever killed anyone, murdering four men – three, he claims, with his bare hands. He was subsequently decorated secretly for his courage.

The other book, *The Kruschev Objective*, was published in 1988 and tells how in 1956 Creighton, then earning a living as a jazz pianist in New York's Greenwich Village was recalled by the M Section to take part in a complex security operation in England involving the protection of the Soviet leaders, Kruschev and Bulganin, from being assassinated by anti-communist White Russian terrorists. This meeting with Anthony Eden was the first time that the Soviet leaders were in touch on English soil with a British Prime Minister since the revolution. The plan was to blow up the warship on which they were at dock in Portsmouth. The mutilated corpse of the British frogman, Commander Lionel Crabb, was found near the docking site of the Soviet ships after they had departed. Creighton's book claims to unravel the mystery.

It would be disingenuous of me to claim that Creighton's explanation of all the highly secretive activities in which he was engaged, in OpJB, never altered. He admits that he cannot verify that every date and happening he recorded was absolutely accurate (no one's memory about events almost fifty years ago wouldn't occasionally be vague). Furthermore, because he relies on records he kept himself, as well as other operational reports which colleagues like Susan Kemp leaked to him from time to time, which bolstered his recollections, it is hardly surprising that in the many versions he wrote some discrepancies would appear. His critics have tried to discredit his book by attempting to catch him out about details of his acting and scholastic career, his description of security procedures at places like Bletchley, his activities as a double spy at Dieppe and Normandy; but astonishingly little, indeed not a single significant fact have they produced that would hold up as acceptable evidence in a court of law. Scepticism, hearsay, gossip, dubious factual claims, fear of another hoax like Hitler's Diaries were the basis of most rejections of Creighton's story.

At this early stage in our relationship, my own involvement in the book was initiated more by amused curiosity about where Creighton's imagination would eventually take him rather than by any serious faith in this incredible tale. But I was soon impressed by the staggering detail Creighton was providing to justify his book, as well as dozens of memoranda he was posting and faxing to me whenever I queried some inconsistency or doubt about a conversation which I suspected he had invented.

When he had written six chapters or about 25,000 words, as well as a detailed synopsis of the rest of the book, he agreed that I should approach Ed Victor, an American with an impressive reputation as a literary agent, to represent him over this volume. Victor had been his agent over *The Paladin* and therefore was obviously the first person to contact. After reading the summary, he phoned to tell me that he was reluctantly turning down the offer. He admitted that he had made a great deal of money out of *The Paladin* and had also been personally present when another of Creighton's exploits, the sinking of a Dutch submarine, was accepted by Queen Wilhelmina of Holland. However, he always felt uneasy about the bizarre events in Creighton's career and was not very keen on having to go through the arduous effort of convincing publishers that most of what Creighton said was true. In any case he was now spending most of his time in Los Angeles, where he was involved in conjuring up mega deals for adapting novels into films and would not be in London often enough to take on another enterprise like *The Paladin*. He recommended Andrew Nurnberg, who had worked with him, and who had achieved prominence as the representative of major political biographies written by European statesmen, and was soon to be handling the memoirs of Russia's President, Boris Yeltsin.

Although Nurnberg had serious reservations about the book's authenticity, he still thought that it was one of the most exciting and intriguing stories of the last war and would probably have no difficulty finding a publisher. Although neither of us knew Nurnberg, Creighton agreed to accept Ed Victor's recommendation. Even more curious was the fact that although I had been involved with Creighton for almost four months, sometimes almost daily by letter or phone, I had never actually met him. I had no idea what he looked like. Now that an agent was playing a role, it was obvious that all three of us would have to meet soon.

Early in January 1990 Nurnberg told me that Grafton Books, a subsidiary of HarperCollins, wanted to have a meeting with me based upon the synopsis they had read. At their offices in Old Burlington Street, Nurnberg and I faced four of their senior executives with a tale we knew they were unlikely to believe. What proof, aside from Creighton's word, did we have to back up what they agreed was potentially one of the most compelling tales of the last war? They were not interested in fiction or faction, exciting as the story was. It had to be true, and convincingly true, if they were to go ahead. I told them that there were letters from Churchill, Mountbatten, Ian Fleming and others that Creighton could produce backing up *OpJB* but there were still security problems about the originals of these documents. At our next meeting I would show them what we had. In the meantime Creighton would carry on finishing the book which he estimated would take him another five or six months.

Nurnberg and I met Creighton for the first time on 30 January 1990, at Scott's Restaurant. Born in 1924, he was a surprisingly lithe, athletic-looking sixty-six when he shook my hand, confirming an intimacy we had enjoyed after many months of discussing his project. Although he trusted my judgement, it was clear he was often irritated by the role of 'devil's advocate' into which I had been cast. If I pressed too hard for facts he had deliberately not sent me, his memos took on an acerbic note of disapproval. For example, he did not see why I should know his real name and thought that the pseudonym of Creighton was enough for me at that stage. His blond features were unlined and revealed little of the clandestine, violent, tortured, double-dealing war he had been through. He was over six feet tall, with disconcerting blue eyes and the slightly hooked nose that has been associated with martial Englishmen ever since Wellington. The only evidence of a traumatic life was a restless, jittery energy which he seemed unable to subdue.

At that lunch he produced the supporting documentation he had told me about, but which I had never seen. There were letters marked Most Secret from Churchill and Mountbatten which both indirectly and directly confirmed that a high level secret operation involving

Bormann had taken place. In October, 1954, Creighton had written to General 'Pug' Ismay, the Prime Minster's Chief of Staff, for permission to write this book about his war-time experiences. Ismay passed the request on to Churchill who, in a letter dated October, 1954, on 10 Downing Street notepaper replied:

> Dear John,
>   Lord Ismay has told me of your wishes but I am afraid that it is still impossible for anything to be done and you must not now speak of these matters. When I die, then, if your conscience so allows, tell your story for you have given and suffered much for England. If you do speak, then speak nothing but the truth, omitting of course those matters which you know can never be revealed. Do not seek to protect me for I am content to be judged by history. But do, I pray you, seek to protect those who did their duty honestly in the hope of a future world with freedom and justice for all.
>   Yours sincerely,
>   Winston Churchill

There was another letter from Lord Mountbatten dated 16 December 1976 on notepaper from Mountbatten's home, Broadlands, Romsey, Hampshire. It read:

> Dear John,
>   As you know, I am most concerned that the vast amount of cover established to guard against any possible verification of the very gallant part you played in secret intelligence operations both during and after the war, may well result in your never receiving proper recognition.
>   However, since you already have Churchill's permission, and indeed mine, to 'tell your story', subject to security clearance, I am going to let you have memoranda setting out in precis your main operations and your part in them. If you decide to publish your story, then you also have my consent to publish this letter and any relevant memoranda to confirm the truth of your incredible career.
>   As always, my very best wishes,
>   Yours sincerely,
>   Mountbatten of Burma

Accompanying this letter was a memorandum from Mountbatten, dated 9 January 1977. It concerned 'Operation James Bond' and confirmed in precise detail the fact that the 'Morton Section had established that the vast Nazi wealth plundered from occupied Europe had been transferred to the security of the Swiss Banking System.' It then repeated the information that the accounts and safety deposits were controlled by Bormann, and that through Creighton's 'private relationship' with Ribbentrop an agreement was made for Bormann to hand over all Nazi external assets 'in exchange for Bormann's safe conduct to England and absolute protection for his future life here in comfort and security as a British immigrant.'

The memorandum listed the personnel engaged in Operation James Bond who carried out 'an incursion into the Berlin lakes, unobserved by the enemy'. The memorandum then went on: 'On May 2nd, you escorted Martin Bormann out of the bunker and made your escape downstream on the Rivers Spree and Havel, arriving on the West Bank of the Elbe to the safety of Allied forces there on May 11th...I wish to record once more, my great admiration for Commander Fleming and yourself, and the men and women of your command for the great skill, courage and enterprise which you all exhibited during this extremely hazardous and difficult operation...' The memorandum is signed in Mountbatten's own hand. According to Creighton, Susan Kemp became head of the M Section after Morton retired.

The only flaw in this apparently convincing evidence that OpJB did take place was that all of the letters were photostats. Creighton explained that the originals were lodged in the archives of the M Section and would never be released. The M Section was, according to him, split about what documents should be released to Creighton, since some felt that this amazing expedition should be made known to the public while others insisted they should never be released. It was probably through Susan Kemp – who for a short time after the war was Bormann's Intelligence Control – that Creighton was given these photostats. He insisted that he'd had them studied by graphology experts who assured him they were copies of originals.

Impressive as these documents were as corroborative support of the Bormann operation, they were surpassed in significance by the contents of a leather case he opened for us. They were medals and decorations he claimed to have been given by the nations for whom he had done his various military and espionage exploits. He rattled off what they were without revealing what he had done to win them. I recall one was the Soviet Order of the Red Star. There was an Orange Order from Holland

and two French decorations as well as one from the United States. The medal that caught my eye was a piece of rather dull bronze which I recognized as the Victoria Cross. Creighton allowed me to pick it up, and engraved on the back were the words 'Secret Award', the date June, 1945, and the recipient 'Christopher Robin'.

After lunch Nurnberg and I discussed this cornucopia of evidence. The documents, since they were all photostats, could be forgeries. Some of the medals could be fakes, but was it likely that anyone would have a false Victoria Cross counterfeited and attempt to pass it off on experts? Although it might be a genuine VC, how could one find out whether Creighton had been given it because the Secret List – confined to honours for the heroic deeds of anonymous espionage and intelligence agents – officially did not exist. True identities could not be attached to such decorations. Yet it was obvious that there was somewhere in the nation's secret archives some such roll of honour for some of the bravest individuals in the land. And a Victoria Cross could fetch at auction anywhere between £30,000 to £70,000. Hardly a bauble Creighton was likely to purchase on his own to help sell a book that might never earn that much. Although Creighton was willing to display his medals, he never allowed anyone to take them away for verification or physical examination. He had evidence of attempts to snatch them from him and was suspicious that out of his control, they could be 'accidentally' damaged or tampered with.

The material we were shown was always preceded by warnings about Confidentiality, Secrecy and Most Secrecy. Indicative of Creighton's obsession with security was the fact that seven months after we had begun to work together he had still not told me his real name and I knew nothing about his family. Although I had by then guessed what his real name was, I did not tell him I knew. It was a long time since he had been involved in any mayhem associated with security, yet he always lived as if any day someone out of the past might seek revenge for the terrible deeds he had perpetrated on behalf of his country.

He warned me that since I was involved with OpJB and the millions of pounds that were still hidden and undetected, I ought to take some elementary precautions to discover if I was being watched or followed. He had extra chain locks on his windows. A string of hair would be left each day a foot from the floor pressed against the doorway, so that it would be unknowingly disturbed by any intruder. He stacked his shirts in a precise order in their drawer so that anyone rifling through his cupboards would probably leave a tell-tale shift in their position. Items on his desk like scissors or paperclips would be left in a complicated geometric pattern difficult to reproduce. He warned me to keep a look-out for any unfamiliar cars that parked near my home too often whose licence plates I had not memorized and to be particularly wary of any van or lorry that seemed to be carrying too much aerial. Up to a point, I found all this rather comic but I did find myself looking over my shoulder and checking mysterious telephone calls more often than I used to.

While Nurnberg continued to negotiate with Grafton, as their executives kept asking for more and more facts to back up the book, I set about checking the authenticity of the Churchill and Mountbatten letters and the bona fides of the Victoria Cross. I met Dr Peter Beale of Sotheby's, who was the senior man in their Books and Manuscripts Department, and asked him if the Churchill and Mountbatten photocopies were based upon forged documents. He studied them very carefully with a magnifying glass and then told me he had examined many attempts to forge both Churchill and Mountbatten signatures, but on a rather cursory examination they looked perfectly genuine to him.

He also knew the many methods that were used with a photocopying machine to piece together items like signatures of counterfeit documents to produce a very realistic-looking forgery. But he did not believe any such methods had been used on the two letters I'd shown him. He admitted that an ingenious forger might be able to deceive him but he thought – always qualifying his judgement by the fact that he only had photostats before him – that these letters were genuine.

I next set about finding out what I could about the Victoria Cross. Although he had not received it for his involvement in OpJB, the mere fact that he had won such an illustrious award would have established his credentials as a man of courage, and a man who had been integrally involved in key operations. Creighton, indeed, played a puzzling game about this VC, for although he revealed it from time to time when he felt his integrity was being questioned, he never actually claimed he had won it until he appeared on a controversial TV programme in late 1996.

Having learnt that the Victoria Cross was exclusively produced by Hancocks, a jewellers near the Burlington Arcade in London, I asked their chief authority on the subject, David Callaghan, if Creighton's wording on the back of his medal was the usual form. Without seeing the medal, he agreed they sounded authentic enough except for the words 'Secret Award'. When I queried him further about the existence of a Secret List, he said he had never known of any VC recipient who had been on it but he was neutral about whether such a List did or did not exist. 'Even if I knew there was one,' he said, mischievously, 'you wouldn't expect me to tell you, would you?'

The whole question of these Secret Awards has bedeviled efforts to test Creighton's claims, because it has been an oath of silence to the Sovereign or the Official Secrets Act that has prevented such a disclosure being made. Yet that such a List exists is confirmed by logic, because it would be intolerable that deeds of the greatest heroism in clandestine activities could never be honoured by the nation, and because I have been told of two other men who have admitted that they have received such never-to-be-revealed medals.

Another remarkable letter produced by Creighton, which I did not take to Sotheby's, was a personal letter to Creighton from Ian Fleming, written in October 1963, ten years after his first James Bond novel, *Casino Royale,* made him a very rich man. It was addressed to Creighton in his true name, John Ainsworth-Davis. It spoke warmly of their joint venture in bringing 'Piglet' – Martin Bormann – to England and the recovery of most of the Nazi assets plundered from Europe and deposited in Switzerland. 'You and your operation were my secret inspiration for all that followed,' ends his letter, 'a secret I have never revealed to anyone else.' With the letter was £20,000 in crisp, white £5 notes which Creighton knew was meant to be distributed amongst survivors of the operation.

With all this impressive, confirming material, Nurnberg and I thought it would have much more chance of being published if Creighton were to come out and claim that the story was true, rather than a mixture of fact and fiction. It would mean Creighton having to re-write what he had already done in the first person. At first he did not find this a congenial task, because it meant him intruding many of his personal amorous and religious emotions into the story when he had preferred to have the book written as objectively and impersonally as possible. Since the book was re-written at least four times, this blend of cold fact and individual rhetoric was never completely resolved even in the final version.

On 12 February 1990 another meeting was arranged with four executives of Grafton books and Nurnberg and myself. But this time Creighton was present. They had certainly done their homework and put Creighton through an intense cross-examination of all his more incredible claims. Why were Ribbentrop and Canaris and others ready to believe he was a traitor prepared to betray his country for money? Would he demonstrate the means by which messages were sent to Bletchley through a piano? Why had he decided forty years after the war's end to tell his story? (His answer was that the ghost-writers of his earlier novels thought the Bormann story too long to tell at that time, saying it should be written later on its own; and he had promised both Churchill and Mountbatten not to divulge it while they were still alive. The publication of *Spycatcher* by Peter Wright had also done much to undermine the reasons for the tight security still maintained by British Intelligence.)

They also probed him about what happened to the two SS men shot by Brabenov when Bormann was being brought out and to explain the presence of Blunt and Hollis at Birdham. He showed them the letters from Mountbatten, Churchill and Fleming and I reported my conversation with Sotheby's about the likelihood of their being genuine. He also showed them his medals, and the Victoria Cross, I suspect, influenced any of the waverers to lean towards acceptance of OpJB.

I was queried about my role in the enterprise. I said that, if true, it was undoubtedly the greatest untold story of the last war and its implications, particularly about Nazi gold, were of great significance. I also said I assumed it would be a huge publishing success and I was not averse to acquiring a small share of the inevitable serial and film rights that would follow publication. I intended, too, to write a prologue to the book explaining Bormann's connection with Hitler, his importance and the reasons why I doubted the many accounts – particularly the findings of the 1972 Frankfurt Tribunal – that the missing Bormann had died in Berlin in May, 1945.

The publishers seemed duly impressed with Creighton's casual and disarming manner which never seemed remotely thrown by any question and the way he offered a plausible explanation for anything that appeared counter to logic or common sense. A contract was signed with Grafton on 13 June 1990 for an advance of £65,000, of which £5,000 was to be paid on signature and the balance in two instalments on acceptance and publication.

By the end of the year enough material of the new first person version had been sent to Grafton for them to ask two readers to assess its merits. They both damned it unreservedly, claiming it was obviously fiction and it was most unlikely that any of this was true. We asked if we

could see their actual reports but Grafton claimed that they were bound
by a promise of confidentiality not to show their views to Creighton.
This was naturally very frustrating for him, because without the specific details that had aroused the readers' scepticism, he had no way of discovering what case he had to answer. I have since been told by a Grafton
executive that neither reader had presented any facts negating
Creighton's claims. They merely could not believe the entire story –
facts or no facts – and Grafton had decided that similar unsubstantiated
negative attitudes would dominate most of the critical reviews of the
book and they were not prepared to face that kind of media hostility.
Although the contract had a clause stating that a new contract could be
negotiated on the basis of the book being fiction, they no longer
thought there was much future financially for it as fiction and therefore
wished to opt out of publishing *OpJB*.

After almost a year of negotiations, this was, indeed, a grievous blow.
No new facts or provable evidence had emerged to justify Grafton
dropping £5,000 and totally losing faith in the project. It was the curse
of the Hitler Diaries.

To complicate the problem of credibility, Creighton had won his
many medals being involved in operations before OpJB that were just
as hard to believe as the bringing of Bormann to England, such as the
aforementioned part he played, aged sixteen, in the destruction of the
U-boat base in Ireland.

Even more difficult to swallow was his account of having single-
handedly destroyed the Dutch submarine *K-XVII* just before the
Japanese attack on Pearl Harbor. The *K-XVII*, then under the command
of the British fleet in the Pacific, had sighted a large armada of Japanese
warships sailing in a zig-zag course which the Dutch captain rightly calculated was heading towards Pearl Harbor. He sent the message to
Bletchley, where Morton and Churchill were determined to destroy
everything in connection with it. Should the Americans know of this
Japanese threat, the enemy would probably turn around because their
whole enterprise depended on the element of surprise. Churchill knew
that unless the Americans could be persuaded to enter the war,
Germany would probably win it. A Japanese effort to cripple the US
Navy was the kind of provocation needed to galvanize the Americans
into action. The Dutch message and all who knew about it had to be
silenced. With the credentials of an engineer investigating the sub's
equipment, Creighton spent a few days aboard the submarine with

packages of cyanide gas and his explosives disguised as Christmas gifts. Leaving these behind to explode and destroy the entire crew of fifty-eight men, Creighton was taken off by a Berwick flying boat. The British signal operators at Bletchley who knew the contents of the Dutch warning also had to be silenced.

After the war Creighton reported this story on Dutch television with his face covered up and claiming to be an IRA terrorist. As already mentioned, he had also told it to Queen Wilhelmina when she was in exile in England and she fully accepted Creighton's version of these events. Confirming the fact that such a meeting with the Dutch Queen did take place is the American literary agent, Ed Victor, who was there in his capacity as Creighton's representative. I have seen the voluminous correspondence between the historical section of the Dutch navy and Creighton which took place when the Dutch publisher of *OpJB* sought authoritative support for the story. The controversy ended in a verbal stalemate because neither side could agree as to whether the *K-XVII* was at the bottom of the sea where Dutch naval records had placed it or where Creighton claimed he had sunk it. Until an expensive underwater expedition is undertaken to find out the location of the controversial submarine, this debate is unlikely to be resolved.

A third questionable exploit described in some detail by Creighton in *OpJB* was the role he was given by Desmond Morton to establish himself as a British traitor in the eyes of Admiral Canaris, Chief of the Abwehr, who was known to have anti-Hitler sentiments. The Russians and the Americans were pressing for a cross-Channel invasion of Northern France in 1942, but Churchill thought such an onslaught against the Atlantic Wall would be suicidal. He had plans for an attack on the under-belly of Europe in the Eastern Mediterranean in 1943. The Dieppe raid used Canadian troops as the sacrificial lambs to prove how futile such a cross-Channel invasion would be.

To make sure Dieppe was a failure – although it was assumed the losses would be relatively minimal – Creighton was sent to meet Canaris in Berlin and tell him of the coming raid. In the process he would establish himself as a useful British defector whom Canaris could trust because of the accuracy of his information about Dieppe. Creighton claims it authenticated him as a British traitor but he never knew whether the information he provided about Dieppe was passed on to the commander of the garrison at Dieppe. In proving the impregnability of the Atlantic Wall and postponing Overlord for almost two years,

Dieppe achieved its purpose. But at the cost of over 3,000 men – mostly Canadians – killed, wounded or captured in an action lasting just over nine hours.

His credentials as a spy for the Germans were particularly vital in his role in the invasion of Normandy and in Operation James Bond. The Allies had organized a huge and complicated deception plan to convince the Germans that Overlord would take place in the Pas de Calais. Wireless messages were full of coded orders which, when deciphered, indicated the Pas de Calais was the target. Bombing operations hit roads and railways leading to the Pas de Calais, as if designed to hinder reinforcements arriving there when the invasion began. Dummy ships were floated on the English coast nearest Calais, with troops being embarked on them in daylight when they could be seen and taken off at night when they could not.

Creighton was one of the agents used in this deception. As a British informer he was delivered to Rommel's HQ by E-Boat and at a high level staff meeting informed the German commander that the invasion would take place in the Bay of Seine in Normandy. He had been informed by Morton that the true landings would take place in the Pas de Calais and he had been given suicide pills to take before he revealed that fact. The Gestapo interrupted the meeting by disclosing that they knew he was a British agent, arrested him and tortured him to reveal the true location of the landings. Under the most extreme torture he swallowed his pills only to find they were innocuous. Morton had not intended to kill him but to make him withdraw his contention that Normandy was the Allied goal and confess that it was, indeed, the Pas de Calais. Before he could be executed, he was rescued by Allied commandos. Again his purpose had been fulfilled because when Ribbentrop and Bormann investigated his record as a German agent, they found he had done his best to tell them the truth about Normandy but had not been believed by Rommel or the Gestapo.

These four operations which Creighton insisted on revealing in *OpJB*, provided an armada of disbelief about the probability of anything like Operation James Bond ever having taken place. Could any one individual ever have been involved in so many bizarre incidents and lived to tell the tale? Anyone who seriously investigated this inventory of super-courageous deeds would have to conclude that Creighton was either one of the greatest unrecognized heroes of the last war or a remarkably shameless liar and fantasist. When *OpJB* was ultimately pub-

lished in September 1996, the Press unanimously opted for the latter
verdict. They managed to achieve this consensus of derision about the
book, less by any expert evidence of what happened to Bormann than
by their refusal to accept as credible his alleged activities as a double-spy
and British secret agent. In the thousands of words produced on the
subject I have yet to read anything uncovering a single, concrete, provable fact that establishes decisively that Creighton has been an ingenious
hoaxer.

My own role at this stage in this book was to write an 8,000 word
prologue in which I would introduce the reader to the significance of
Martin Bormann as Hitler's Private Secretary and sole executor of his
will, and then go on to summarize the efforts that had been made to
find him since he disappeared after Hitler's death. I began with the
account of Bormann's presence as a witness at the Führer's marriage to
Eva Braun and then moved to his giving the Nazi salute at the crema-
tion of Hitler's body in the Chancellery Garden.

I then reiterated the conventional accounts of his death – being
blown up as he was escaping from Hitler's bunker – and a body being
unearthed in a children's playground in Berlin in 1972 which was established by an official tribunal in Frankfurt as Bormann's skeleton. I cast
doubt on those findings in my prologue because the remains had been
suspiciously unearthed in the presence of invited journalists, whereas
only four years previously a similar press gathering organized by *Der
Stern* had found nothing in almost exactly the same place. Hugh
Thomas, in his intensively researched book, *Doppelganger*, dismisses the
manner of these findings as a 'forensic fraud'. His evidence in this area
is most convincing.

With the collapse of the Grafton deal, the book was sent to Secker
and Warburg who took the contents seriously enough to seek an opinion about its authenticity from Rupert Allason, who under the pseudonym Nigel West had a considerable reputation as the author of a number of books on British secret intelligence and espionage. In a brief
hand-written two page report West dismissed *OpJB* as a 'work of fiction'. To Creighton his reasons for such a peremptory conclusion were
far too flimsy and cursory. It was evident that he had used Creighton's
novels – which had been interlaced with deliberate fictional incidents –
to support his view that Creighton was a fantasizer. Nor did he place
any credence in Creighton's historical versions of D-Day or Dieppe. His
most damning conclusion was that Creighton demonstrated a familiar

psychiatric condition known as paraphrenia, in which individuals attempt to aggrandize themselves by putting themselves at the centre of heroic or sensational events dropping names of famous or important personalities to justify their own significance.

Having received such a report, it was natural that Dan Franklin, Secker's Editorial Director, turned *OpJB* down. He noted in passing that he had also heard something of the experience Grafton had had with the work, but if Creighton wished to challenge West's reasoning West would be happy to meet us about it. Because the book had now been rejected without any concrete facts to prove it was fiction, Nigel West was commissioned by Creighton and myself to expand upon his criticisms of the book and do a thoroughly investigative job on Creighton's story.

For this we paid him £1,000 in June 1991 and, three months later, we received thirty-three pages of typewritten foolscap, setting out his reasons for maintaining his position that *OpJB* was a work of fiction. In his opening paragraphs he added that he had used *The Paladin* as a basis for uncovering the inconsistencies and conflicts inherent in Creighton's book, but he added that in this research he had sought the assistance of Brian Garfield, the author of *The Paladin*, who had confirmed to West his continuing confidence in Creighton's account of these events. Another disclaimer from Nigel West – that his report would not detail any historical research which would be required in The Hague and Germany – meant that the final days of Bormann would, at best, undergo no serious textual revision based upon Third Reich or Nazi sources.

There followed a series of lengthy exchanges between Creighton and West. The thrust of West's analysis was that the totality of Creighton's exploits could not be believed by any responsible historian. To establish the justice of his finding, he set out to prove the impossibility of Creighton's story as told in *The Paladin*, although Garfield repeatedly said that what West picked up as untrue was what he himself had invented as the author of a book of pure fiction. Nevertheless West insisted that fiction or not, it provided – because it was said to be based on Creighton's career – sufficient evidence that Creighton was a liar.

In addition to this sweeping generalization that a novel could be used to discredit *OpJB*, he picked up a number of facts in *The Paladin* which, he said, established Creighton's ignorance and unreliability about places and people he wrote about. For instance West doubted that Creighton's father had ever been part of the British relay team that took part in the

1920 Olympic Games, yet the *Who's Who* entry under Jack Ainsworth-Davis (his true name) states clearly that he was on that winning team. West also discounted Creighton's accounts of U-boat destructions, Canadian training camps in clandestine killing and the sinking of the Dutch submarine *K-XVII*. To the last objection Creighton simply replied that if divers were employed he would be proved right.

West also noted that Churchill's letter was dated 'October, 1954' and claimed that the precise date was never omitted in the Prime Minister's personal letters. Creighton produced other Churchill letters dated exactly this way and put forward the name of one of Churchill's secretaries who said she had actually typed it. There were more picayune details about Creighton's childhood and schooling which were easily rebutted. The charge of paraphrenia was soon dropped because Creighton had overwhelming documentation to prove his family connections with Churchill, Morton and Mountbatten as well as undeniable proof that he worked with Olivier and Coward, Roger Moore, Donald Sinden and Martine Carol. West's contention that Creighton was a paranoic name-dropper turned out to be a preposterous allegation.

The most disappointing aspect of West's report was its paucity of information about OpJB. Only five pages of the thirty-three submitted dealt directly with attempting to rubbish Creighton's facts. There was a contemptuous dismissal of the claim that Blunt and Hollis were ever at Birdham. There was an assertion that Ian Fleming could not have been with Creighton on 20 March 1945 at Eisenhower's HQ in Rheims, because on that date Fleming was in Jamaica negotiating for the purchase of Goldeneye. Creighton asserts that the negotiations for the purchase by Fleming of Goldeneye actually took place a year earlier when he bought the property. To try and check which of these claims and counter-claims were correct would have taken months – probably a year – of expensive research, and as a bystander I could only assess this voluminous exchange of contradictory facts as ending in a stalemate. If a winner had to be chosen, Creighton's specific details were, in my opinion, more convincing than West's often vague or instinctive allegations.

To give him credit, West was frank about acknowledging the difficulty of assessing an operation which Creighton had originally dubbed 'The Operation That Never Was'. The secrecy surrounding it was total and any written documents about it had had to be shredded and destroyed. On Morton's instruction not a single hard fact was to be left behind from which future historians could garner that such an operation ever took place.

'Morton's orders from Churchill had been totally clear,' wrote West, reporting Creighton's account. 'Nothing, but nothing of the truth of this operation must ever leak out. The doctoring, the forging, the shredding and the manipulating had to be carried out in such a manner as to make it conclusively concrete that no such operation had ever been mounted, nor could it have been.'

West assesses this explanation of a massive conspiracy of breathtaking proportions as the reason for the total absence of any corroboration for any aspect of the story. Only three people who knew what was going on – Creighton, Susan Kemp and Barbara Brabenov – are still alive. MI5 and MI6 were excluded from the plan. 'Although Susan Kemp is supposedly willing to authenticate Creighton's story she has neither come forward nor revealed her true identity.' West's report was written in August 1992. In 1996 Susan Kemp did reveal her real identity to me in my flat, and also spoke to two associates of Simon & Schuster, who published *OpJP* in that year, asserting that her involvement in the Bormann affair as contained in Creighton's book was true.

Although Nigel West remained adamant in his view that the book was a work of fiction he nevertheless agreed, if asked, to write a foreword to it. This would present the pros and cons of Creighton's tale, as objectively as possible, as he had done for a book called *The Penkovsky Papers*. When in 1996 West asserted on a TV programme that he didn't believe a word of *OpJB*, I asked him why, in that case, he was ready to associate himself with it by contributing a foreword. 'Even though I think it's fiction,' he answered, 'I believe it should be published because it's such an exciting read.'

After Grafton's abandonment of their interest, Andrew Nurnberg tried other publishers with mixed success. Constable's letter of rejection was perhaps typical. 'The discussion about this book was animated and heated,' it began. 'There was a healthy degree of scepticism though everyone here agreed that on present evidence the book was impossible to refute.' Doubleday took it even more seriously. They examined all the letters and read Nigel West's report and decided to advance £5,000 while they conducted their own investigations. Their contractual letter said they intended to publish provided that 'No evidence acceptable in the Supreme Court arises which substantially refutes the story's authenticity.' It was dated 14 April 1992.

His closest confidante and collaborator was, at this time, Bridget Winter – a clever, imaginative, dedicated and industrious film producer who had a track record of involvement in major BBC documentaries about the Nazi period, which involved interviewing key figures such as Hjalmar Schacht, Putzi Hanfstaengl, Martin Niemoller and many others. Creighton got in touch with her when Doubleday began to have doubts. For the next year or two he and Bridget concentrated on writing a film script and acquiring financial backing for the project. Just when the film was about to be made, it was blocked on a very high level and the deal fell through.

With the collapse of the film, Doubleday's enthusiasm for publishing the book was seriously dampened and by the beginning of 1995, the chances of getting a book printed had reached a very low ebb, and without a book deal Bridget found US film and television companies difficult to convince. The major stumbling block was that almost all the evidence came from Creighton himself. The corroborative photocopied documents from Churchill, Mountbatten and Fleming could still have possibly been forgeries. His medals – particularly the VC – since they were on a Secret List, could not be investigated for authenticity.

None of the thirty-three other participants in OpJB whom Creighton said were still alive were prepared to vindicate the expedition, and Creighton argued it was not his job to force them to. According to him, there are many documents hidden in the secret files of the now defunct M Section, which are still bound by the Official Secrets Act. One of these is the 800-page transcript of the debriefing carried out on Bormann at Birdham when he came to England in May 1945. Each of these pages carries the initials of Martin Bormann. Since Bormann was Hitler's sole executor and aware of all the Nazi Party finances that went into Swiss banks before the war ended, the exposure of the contents of that debriefing would cast an extraordinary light on the whereabouts of the Holocaust money said to have entered and exited Swiss banks.

Nevertheless there was one person who was in OpJB from its very beginning, who was in one of the kayaks that brought Bormann out, who dealt with his early days in England, who played a senior role in the M Section and advised Creighton about almost every important action he took after the war and was probably the source of the reports of the Intelligence information leaked from time to time to Creighton. Sometimes the information she fed him was true; sometimes it was false.

The cover name by which she is known in the book is Susan Kemp. Her address has never been revealed. In 1992 she swore an affidavit confirming her involvement in the operation.

Susan Kemp was third in command on OpJB, after Ian Fleming and Christopher Creighton. When Creighton first met her at Birdham in January, 1945, she had the rank of a second officer in the Wrens and had striking looks, auburn hair, blue-grey eyes and a well-endowed figure. She had completed a commando and unarmed combat course and had reached the highest standards of training in jujitsu, the use of fighting knives, silent killing and endurance at sea and in the mountains.

What happened to Bormann in England was not known at first hand by Creighton. He has relied upon reports he has seen in the M Section, conversations with Ian Fleming and chiefly information provided by Susan Kemp. Soon after his arrival, Bormann was flown to Basle to sign the necessary papers to release the bulk of Nazi cash and gold in several banks. They remained in those banks for a few weeks but the initial transfers were completed by the end of June. If this story is correct then the recent release of names of deposit holders – probably Holocaust victims – which were extensively advertised on 23 July 1997, involves relatively minuscule sums that were left over after Bormann's hand-over of Party and government funds to the British and Americans. There have been various calculations about how much money was reaped by this deal with Bormann, and these range from seven million pounds at the time to seven billion pounds calculated at 1997 money values. The vast sums involved – with records about them shredded by the banks – explains why so much secrecy has surrounded OpJB.

Although the excuse for this clandestine expropriation could justifiably be that this sum was only part of the reparations Germany owed the Allies for the destruction Hitler's war had caused, the Russians could legitimately claim that some of it should have been shared with them. The answer to such a demand would be that the Russians had robbed or looted the German territories they had conquered, seizing for example invaluable art treasures which they have only just recently displayed to the world. At no time did they suggest that they might share these 'reparations' with their allies.

As soon as Bormann was debriefed at Birdham, Morton decided his looks would have to be changed and a makeshift operating theatre was set up for Archie McIndoe, the plastic surgeon, to work on him. Alterations were made to his ears, lips and nose. His fingerprints were changed and the scar on his forehead was extended because it was too deep to be eliminated. His English was now quite good and he spoke with a cultivated stammer.

Susan Kemp, who was now in charge of a sub-section set up by Morton to seek out prominent Nazis like the rockets expert Wernher von Braun whose knowledge would be of use to the West, was Bormann's personal control. Such Nazis, if they cooperated, would not be tried as war criminals, would be reasonably paid and offered a chance of becoming, with faked passports, American or British citizens. It was a similar deal to that accepted by Bormann.

What happened to Bormann in England has undergone several variations since I was first informed about it. A brief summary of the first version had it that after his face had recovered from McIndoe's attentions, he was housed in Highgate where he was looked after by two German girls from the unit of German Freedom Fighters who were briefed with enough information to ward off awkward questions about the pseudo-father he was now supposed to be.

Because foreign Intelligence agencies, particularly the French, suspected Bormann was in London, it was decided he should be transferred to a less conspicuous domicile. Susan Kemp knew an Austrian girl who had been a close friend of hers before the war. She had married a former naval captain – called Peter Grant in *OpJB* – and they ran a riding school in an English village. After elaborate and detailed planning, it was agreed that Bormann would be brought to the Grant household and introduced to the villagers as Martin Schuler, the father of Grant's wife, Marlene Schuler.

Since Bormann was an adroit horseman, he settled in quickly to the activities of a riding school. For months he had been briefed about the personality of Martin Schuler, who had been killed in Austria as a member of the Resistance. The Grants played along with this deception, only knowing that 'Schuler' was an important figure needing such anonymity for British intelligence purposes. They understood the imperative of secrecy, were never told the real identity of their house-guest and were well paid for their cooperation. The villagers were easily taken in by Bormann's cover story and he integrated himself into the life of the community for ten years. Then, Creighton was told by Susan Kemp, Martin Schuler (Bormann) had been taken ill and died and was buried in a village churchyard in 1956.

When *OpJB* was being offered to Grafton and Doubleday, this was what they were told when they asked Creighton about Bormann in England. It was a lie concocted by Morton's section. Creighton, too, was duped by it. 'Even I, who had been so intimately involved in snatching Bormann, was led to believe that his life had ended before the age of sixty,' he writes in the final chapter of *OpJB*.

★ ★ ★

By 1995 the likelihood of the Bormann story ever appearing in a British book had dwindled almost to vanishing point. The refusal or inability of Creighton to provide any supporting individual who would say he or she had been on the operation was the sticking point that deterred publishers from gambling on a tale that, properly and enthusiastically handled by them, would have excited many thousands of readers and made them a lot of money. At one stage the sum of a million dollars was temporarily put on the table by one publisher.

The fiftieth anniversary of VE Day on 8 May 1995, was the opportunity for an orgy of reminiscences about the war in TV documentaries, old and new books, films shot in action, interviews with much-decorated veterans. My own book, *Defeat in the West*, based upon my work as an Intelligence officer and my interrogations of senior German commanders like Field Marshal von Rundstedt, was re-issued as a paperback to mark the occasion.

When on 5 May 1995, I was invited to talk about my book on the Simon Bates show on a London radio station, I decided that somewhere in a short interview I would bring up the question of Martin Bormann. The whole issue of what had happened to him had sunk into a slough of silence. I thought it might be raised from the almost-dead, if it got some media airing.

I hinted to Geoffrey Goodman, the well known political journalist interviewing me, that if he asked me towards the end of our talk if I knew of any war secrets that had still not been revealed, he might hear something interesting from me. After our scheduled four-minute chat in which I confined myself to the mistakes that Hitler made which lost him the war, Goodman popped my suggested question. I said the untold mystery was how Ian Fleming, the author of the Bond novels, had led an expedition that brought Martin Bormann to England where he lived until his death in 1956. Goodman and his producer were so startled by this astonishing claim that they pressed me for another three minutes for more details, and I explained the motive for bringing him here and a short summary of how kayaks defied Russian and German fire-power to achieve the rescue.

The Press Association picked up my interview, and although the daily papers only thought it worth a short paragraph, the *Mail on Sunday* gave it about six inches on its front page after its reporter, Nick Fielding, spoke to me about it on the telephone. It was not news coverage, however, that brought *OpJB* to astonishing life again, but a message on my answering machine from a John Ffitch-Hayes who trained horses in his establishment in Lewes, East Sussex.

What Ffitch-Hayes and his wife, Anne, had to tell me in a long conversation on the phone was mind-boggling in the context of our search for the final days of Martin Bormann. Anne had been working on a book about Bormann in England which was in its final stages of preparation and research. It seems that John Ffitch-Hayes's son had been the close friend of the son of a woman, Hanne Nelson, who possessed formidable evidence that she had been Bormann's mistress in England and had borne him a daughter. The Ffitch-Hayes had photographs, letters, passports which Hanne had given them proving their relationship.

I immediately called Creighton with this startling development, and as a man who had for years been accused of inventing the OpJB fable he was extremely delighted with this corroboration of his story that Bormann had, indeed, been brought to England. For me this positive reaction on his part was heartening because if he had fantasized the whole thing would he not have produced a Hanne Nelson in his story in the first place?

John and Anne Ffitch-Hayes met Christopher and myself at my flat on 17 May 1995, and we were shown close-up photographs of a man with the same broad cheekbones and hairline as Hitler's secretary. Only later were we told that extensive plastic surgery had been done on this man's face to make him look enough like Bormann, who had undergone operational surgery on his features.

They produced a photo of a tweed-suited man posing leisurely in an English meadow who called himself Peter Broderick-Hartley. They also had British passports, issued in 1946 by the Foreign Office, showing that Broderick-Hartley had been making trips to South Africa and South America while living in England. A letter was produced written by Bormann in the bunker three days before Hitler died and compared to a letter written to Hanne in 1963, which a graphologist believed was

written by the same hand. Later we were shown a smiling photograph
of Broderick-Hartley with his arm cosily around the waist of a con-
tented-looking Hanne Nelson.

Hanne Nelson's relationship with Broderick-Hartley is briefly
chronicled in *OpJB*. Bridget Winter spent days meeting her, weeks on
the telephone talking to her and questioning the Ffitch-Hayes about the
evidence they had that Hanne's story was true. She was a Dane whose
British husband had died a year before she met Broderick-Hartley in
July 1960, when he leapt on to a moving bus and sat down beside her.
He said he was a civil engineer and an affair developed between them.
Not long afterwards he began speaking to her in German and 'revealed'
that he was Martin Bormann. By this time Hanne, although deeply disturbed by his pro-Nazi and anti-Semitic sentiments, was so deeply in
love with him that she decided to remain silent about his past. They
never co-habited together – although she bore him a daughter on 1
August 1961 – because he was sharing a house with his housekeeper,
Hilda or Amy Gant, who had a mysterious hold over him which Hanne
never fathomed.

According to Hanne, Broderick-Hartley had grandiose plans for a
new National Socialist Union in Europe, with its capital in Berlin,
which would first of all unite all European countries and then convince
the Americans to become part of a new world-empire in which
German would be the first language. His passport shows that he travelled extensively in the Argentine, Paraguay and South Africa, where his
cover as an engineer enabled him to contact émigré Nazis who shared
his feverish ambitions. Hanne says he asked her to marry him in 1984
but she declined because her family had Jewish antecedents and she
thought that Bormann's (Broderick-Hartley's) racist prejudices would
undermine such a marriage. When he died on 20 June 1989, he was
buried in an unmarked grave and Hanne did not attend the funeral.

Creighton was just as overwhelmed by this story as Bridget and
myself. What he had discovered, however, was that the M Section had
been aware of this liaison and when he told them that Hanne was
revealing all, they cooperated with him in discovering if Hanne was
really the same woman who had been Broderick-Hartley's lover six
years before. At a small hotel in Sussex, Bridget and Creighton had
lunch with her during which he expertly picked up by its base a glass
she had been using and passed it to a waitress who was in reality an
intelligence agent. Twenty-four hours later security control told him

that Hanne was undoubtedly the woman who had been consorting with Broderick-Hartley.

Creighton, although he was still uneasy about Hanne's claims since he thought that the photographs of Broderick-Hartley did not quite match the Bormann he remembered, even accounting for the effects of plastic surgery, had now come round to believing her assertions and those of the Ffitch-Hayes that they had unravelled the mystery of Bormann's last days.

Rather surprising at this stage in the saga was that Susan Kemp, his main source of information, was not discouraging him in that belief. It was she who on 18 April 1991 informed him that Morton's records had not all been destroyed – which he had ordered – but that she and the M Section's photographic experts had made copies of them all before Morton died. She insisted, however, that for the book she knew he was writing, none of the originals could be taken away and that he could only use handwritten notes of relevant material.

Shortly after the disclosure of Hanne's relationship with Bormann/Broderick-Hartley, Creighton and Susan Kemp had lunch in a pub in the Surrey countryside and then stopped outside a cemetery. Walking along one of the paths, they stopped by a patch of mown grass. With a mischievous deadpan voice, she informed him that he was standing on Piglet's grave and that her original story that Bormann had died in 1956 had not been true. She confirmed Hanne's tale that he had died in 1989 and this unmarked spot was his last resting place. 'For a moment I was so startled that I did not believe her,' wrote Creighton, now having acknowledged to the Press his real name of John Christopher Ainsworth-Davis. 'But then I looked at her and decided that she was not joking.'

All this fresh clinching evidence of the claim that Bormann had been brought to England by Creighton and Fleming roused Doubleday's interest once again, and since they had already paid £5,000 they were entitled to push ahead with publication plans. Their editorial director, Sally Gaminara, had seen all the Ffitch-Hayes material and thought that Creighton's book would be strengthened if a great deal of it could be incorporated in *OpJB*.

Bridget Winter was called back urgently from America where she was seeing a film company about a deal. After many meetings between Bridget and both Hanne and the Ffitch-Hayes, the terms of a contract with Doubleday were agreed. On 8 June 1995, Bridget Winter turned up at Doubleday's office in Ealing to finalize the deal but just before the contract was about to be signed, Hanne came through on the telephone and demanded to speak to Sally Gaminara and renounced her part in the book and everything she had told us.

Faced with this startling dramatic turn, the deal fell apart, with Doubleday accusing us of perpetrating a hoax on them. On 17 June 1995 Bridget wrote to Sally Gaminara, defending herself against innuendoes of dishonesty and justifying her position by informing Doubleday that since that unfortunate and acrimonious meeting Hanne had telephoned her three times 'and on each occasion has agreed that *what I said*, was true – I also have it on tape'.

With Doubleday out of the way, I phoned HarperCollins, who had now absorbed Grafton, and asked to speak to Jonathan Lloyd, one of the Grafton executives who had considered the book in the first place. I thought they might think again if they saw the Broderick-Hartley photographs and documents produced by Hanne. I learnt that he had left to join the literary agents, Curtis Brown, as their Managing Director. Andrew Nurnberg eventually decided to abandon his role as Creighton's agent, because his faith in the book had been undermined by Christopher's inability to produce any individual other than himself who had been on the operation, or any other 'hard evidence' that satisfied him of its authenticity.

When Jonathan Lloyd saw the additional material, he thought as a literary agent that publishers in an auction were likely to pay a high price for *OpJB*. His judgement was quite right. No less than four prominent publishers put in substantial bids for it with the winner being Simon & Schuster who offered £450,000, plus a supplementary £50,000 depending on certain complex film and paperback rights. Nick Webb, the Chief Executive, like everyone else, was so excited by the book that he thought it would be a best-seller even if it could not be proved to be true. Its readability had been considerably enhanced by a re-write job done by the respected historical writer and journalist, Duff Hart-Davis. At first sceptical about its authenticity, Hart-Davis – after spending many months with Creighton – became a whole-hearted supporter of the enterprise. Hart-Davis, having heard about the project, contacted an executive at Doubleday and asked if he could read the manuscript. He had lunch with Creighton and Bridget Winter, after which he agreed to re-write the book. To gather more information about it, he had Creighton stay a couple of nights at his home. He wrote two chapters and a new outline, and it was on the basis of this that Doubleday put in their bid.

Nick Webb could hardly have been more enthusiastic about what he felt was a great publishing coup for his firm. Writing to Jonathan Lloyd on 6 November 1995 he said, 'We are all so thrilled with this project that it is becoming quite a torment being so discreet.' However he had not become so starry-eyed that he had lost his perspective about the book's value. In that same letter, he asked for a fresh Clause Four to be added which read 'The Publishers shall have the right to withdraw from this Agreement if it shall be proved that the Work is not authentic and shall be promptly reimbursed by the Proprietor (John Ainsworth-Davis) for any monies paid by the Publishers to the Proprietor under the terms of this Agreement.' Around this paragraph there developed a whirlpool of controversy in the coming months.

The Press reacted with a mixture of envy and incredulity that anyone had paid £500,000 for such a book. After all, the name Bormann had become a music-hall joke after the *Daily Express* and the Hitler's Diaries fiascos, and anyone venturing a suggestion that he had not died in Berlin – as recognized by the Intelligence establishment – was regarded as a nut-case, not to be taken seriously. When I sent a copy of *OpJB* in manuscript form to a senior editor of a newspaper group, it was returned to me with a polite rejection very quickly. It was evident from the pristine quality of the 400 or so typewritten pages that not one of them had been lifted from their original position and read.

In December 1995 double-page features turned up in the *Daily Mail* and the *News of the World* with photographs of Peter Broderick-Hartley cosily snuggled against Hanne, now named Johanne Nelson. She had been found by two *Daily Mail* reporters and told them of her life with Borman who, she said, had also been known as William Hornegold. 'But I know in my soul that he was Martin Bormann.'

According to Hanne, Broderick-Hartley had told her he came to Britain after being forced out of Paraguay when that regime decided they no longer wanted to shelter war criminals. In that detail her story conflicts with Creighton's, but they unite in the conviction that Bormann did not die in Berlin and that at some time after the war he lived in England. She did not add much credence to her story by her belief that the housekeeper, Amy Gant, with whom she shared Broderick-Hartley's life, was really Eva Braun, Hitler's wife. She had no concrete evidence for such a bizarre speculation except that photographs of Gant revealed a woman who looked remarkably like Eva. Hanne's story about Bormann is still an enigma.

Having accepted the challenge of publishing *OpJB* with zest – a four-page colour advertisement in the trade journal, *The Bookseller*, enthused about the 'astonishing true story that will cause history to be rewritten' – Nick Webb became assailed by doubts. The fact that deals were quickly tied up with German, Dutch and Japanese publishers did not console him. He hired Gary Murray, said to be a former MI5 agent, to do a thorough investigation of the book and when Murray came up with a twenty-two-page denunciation, setting out details that branded Creighton as a forger and a liar, Nick Webb stated that unless the contract was revised he would seek legal redress to have publication stopped. He printed a disclaimer in the first pages stating that the publisher's independent research was unable to verify Creighton's account and that the 'documentary trail was often at odds with the author's narrative'. He also demanded that the advance be reduced to £150,000.

There followed months of acrimonious letters because Creighton insisted his story was true and that Gary Murray had dug up nothing more revealing than Nigel West's report for which we had paid £1000 three years ago. Two relatively piddling details, about Creighton's schooldays at Ampleforth and the date of his registration and arrival at the Royal Academy of Dramatic Art, apparently convinced Nick Webb that Creighton was a compulsive prevaricator.

Yet just as he had done with the West report, Creighton produced fact after fact supporting his version of the events which I, for one, found far more convincing than the vague accusations being made by Gary Murray. Creighton could bring in Cardinal Hume to verify his stay at Ampleforth. He insisted, with much justification, that the memory of a girl student who claimed that she saw him at RADA fifty years earlier on the first day of registration, when he had asserted that he was then on the Elbe and had been registered by friends who knew that his service duties would not allow him to be there until two weeks after the term began, was hardly damning evidence enough to demolish his credibility about OpJB.

Hoping to act as some sort of conciliatory liaison officer between Webb and Creighton, I invited Webb to lunch at a Chelsea restaurant. He confessed that his faith in *OpJB* had reached an abysmally low ebb. The reactions from colleagues and fellow publishers about his being taken in by a transparent hoax had put him in the most humiliating position of his professional career. He still wanted to publish, but he could get no help from Creighton about producing the concrete evidence he needed to persuasively vindicate his story.

Creighton became even more infuriated with Webb's lack of enthusiasm. However, claiming he was being mercilessly pressurized, he told me that he had persuaded Susan Kemp to come to my flat and answer searching questions about OpJB. She would also reveal herself to two employees of Simon & Schuster who were handling the publicity for the book. Creighton decided that it was not necessary to involve Nick Webb in such a meeting. This was by far the most heartening and supportive news anyone of us involved had received since becoming involved in the project. Not only had Susan Kemp been third in command in the kayaks bringing Bormann to Potsdam, but she was also Bormann's Intelligence Control when he arrived in England and eventually she took over Morton's position as head of the M Section. It was from her that all the truths and untruths had emanated about both Bormann and Broderick-Hartley. In every critical moment of the past eight years, Creighton had gone to her for advice, from handling ticklish queries by the press to resolving financial negotiations with publishers.

None of us knew her real name or address. We only knew that she had reached a relatively high position in the civil service and was now retired. In 1992, as already mentioned, she had sworn an affidavit in a solicitor's office in London in which she declared in its first paragraph that she fully understood 'the criminal penalties that may apply to any false statement knowingly made in this affidavit.'

She then goes on to swear that having seen the manuscript of three hundred and fifty eight pages called *OpJB*, she is the Operational Second Officer Woman's Royal Naval Service referred to in it by the *nom de guerre* Susan Kemp. She then confirms that she took part in the actual operation described in the book and in the subsequent cover-up operations to establish that OpJB never did take place nor that Ian Fleming had ever been in command of it.

If she was truly the Susan Kemp, whose name appeared regularly in the thousands of pages I had seen about OpJB, then surely she would satisfy Nick Webb's insistence that another single individual involved with the expedition should come forward before he would once more be convinced of its authenticity.

She turned out to be a rather ample, cheerful elderly woman with brown hair, of medium height who wore glasses. Christopher Creighton arrived with her at my flat and made very few interjections during the course of our forty-five minute conversation. I began my chat with her – I felt it would be inappropriate to press her as if she were undergoing some sort of cross-examination – by saying how pleased I was to see her at last since I had been living with her by proxy for seven years.

She explained that it was chiefly her training as a wireless operator that got her into Operation James Bond. Paddling a kayak had come easily to her because she had done a great deal of punting at school. Here Creighton interrupted that he was never keen on her paddling technique since she only paddled on one side of the kayak, rather than alternating sides as was the usual method. She never liked Bormann because he seemed rather grubby to her. I asked her about Fleming and if he ever made any flirtatious passes at her. She admitted there were other girls who received his advances but she wasn't one of them because she had a regular boyfriend at the time. She confirmed Creighton's statement that she had not destroyed all of the M Section documents, and that most of the originals were still in Security custody.

I had decided I would not press for details about her life at Birdham or how OpJB was organized technically because, if she was a phoney, these were the easiest details she could have mugged up on and repeated to me. Before seeing me she had spoken to two of Simon & Schuster's publicity people and it was their task to interrogate her about the technical secrets they wanted revealed. Before leaving, having seen some family photographs in my drawing room, she asked if one of them was a relative of mine she had gone to school with as a child. She jotted down a small friendly note indicating her delight at the coincidence that, by such a strange route, she had been reminded of someone she had known as a small girl. Having been involved with actresses on and off stage for forty years, I was thoroughly convinced that she was not putting on a performance for me and that she was the Susan Kemp revealed in Creighton's book.

Some months after that interview she told Creighton precisely what had happened to Bormann after he came to England. She also confessed that Creighton had been lied to about Broderick-Hartley, his activities and the place and date of his death. Creighton, like so many other people who had been used for intelligence purposes, had been fed a cover-story for M Section's purposes.

In *OpJB* Creighton sets out the details of this deception. In essence it concerned the nervousness in government circles about the chances that their harbouring of a convicted war criminal, in order to further a secret deal with America about German funds in Swiss banks, would be found out, with obvious serious and embarrassing consequences. The best way to sustain the cover-up was, on the one hand, to provide convincing supporting evidence that Bormann was killed in Berlin as reported by Hugh Trevor-Roper and others and, on the other hand, to encourage so many false stories about sightings of Bormann in every part of the world that the Press would do no more than suppress a yawn at any news about him. The *Daily Express* fiasco about his presence in the Argentine was exactly the kind of event British Intelligence cherished.

In furtherance of this all-important goal, the M Section did not refrain from using someone like Creighton, who had been in on the operation from its very beginning and thought he knew what was going on, as a victim of their disinformation strategy. He was thoroughly taken in by the Broderick-Hartley masquerade and proof of his innocence lies in the fact that he agreed to pay large sums of money to both Hanne Nelson and the Ffitch-Hayes for the exclusive right to their material, and to prevent them from selling it to other publishers interested in a Bormann story. It is extremely unlikely that such money out of his projected royalties – almost £50,000 – would have been promised for information which he knew was phoney if, as has been charged, he had made up the entire fictitious epic on his own. Surely this is corroboration of his persistent claim that he was not perpetrating an elaborate hoax.

In *OpJB* he writes, 'Although I did not know it, my own section was playing me along. For several months I was greatly excited by my belief that I had at last stumbled on the truth about Bormann's later years. I knew that during the early 1950s suspicion and rumour had been rife throughout Europe, with many fingers pointing at England. I also knew that after the end of the war several *doppelgangers* had performed well in Italy, Germany and other countries. What I did *not* know was that in 1952 the M Section had found a strikingly good replica of Bormann, in the form of Peter Broderick-Hartley, on their own doorstep, and had decided to make use of him also. The idea was that, if ever anyone seemed to be coming uncomfortably close to the truth, the British authorities could produce the resident double and say, "There you are. Of course he looks like Bormann, but in fact he's got nothing to do with him."'

The man selected to play the part of Bormann/Broderick-Hartley was a small-time confidence man named Hornegold with several children scattered in various countries, who enthusiastically took to his training and education in the ways of Martin Bormann, since he was well-paid and it enabled him to indulge in a very full sex life.

I must confess that even though Creighton went along with the Broderick-Hartley deception, I always felt, when we discussed it, that he had reservations which he would not reveal to me. In *OpJB* he confirms that he could never reconcile the photographs of Broderick-Hartley with the image of Bormann stamped on his mind fifty years earlier. Susan Kemp was, as usual, the person to reveal to him what the M Section's devious tricks were up to. In the spring of 1996, perhaps because the years were eroding the justification for secrecy, she told him that when he started work on his book in 1989, the Section had deliberately set out to discredit him by making him believe Bormann had died in Hampshire in April 1956, and that the grave Susan Kemp had shown him was authentic.

But what had upset the Section's disinformation plans was the accidental appearance of Hanne Nelson with her version of events. They were afraid she might publish her story independently, thus necessitating their involvement in some extremely tricky manoeuvres to rubbish her experience. At first they decided to support her claims to Creighton, but once they realized that Creighton was convinced that Broderick-Hartley was not Bormann, Susan Kemp was given permission to tell him the truth.

It seems that what had actually happened between 1945 and 1956 was that, from his base in England, Bormann made several trips to South America, under the control of the M Section and the American CIA where Barbara Brabenov – still in the intelligence service – supervised his activities, resulting in large sums of cash and jewellery being unearthed, as well as the undermining of several conspiracies by wanted high-level Nazis still engaged in plotting a return of a fascist regime to the newly democratic Germany.

Creighton and Fleming were, of course, not concerned with the ethical question of harbouring a convicted major war criminal in England after the war. They assumed the Intelligence authorities must have had valid state reasons for carrying out such a deception and they obeyed orders. Although Churchill authorized the original decision to use Bormann to save vast sums of money for a financially weakened Britain, it was ultimately a decision that must have been confirmed by Attlee, whose Labour administration came to power in July 1945.

Naturally there was a great deal of anxiety lest the news of Bormann's eleven year stay in Britain would be discovered. It was the visit of the Soviet leaders, Bulganin and Kruschev, to Britain in April 1956 at the height of the Cold War that increased the edginess of security circles about the presence of their controversial visitor. It is Susan Kemp's revelation that she was called into the office of Prime Minster Anthony Eden and screamed at by an hysterical Eden, who attacked her for allowing such a risky situation to continue.

Losing his temper in a string of obscenities, he banged the desk and shouted 'We're cossetting him like a fucking VIP. I want him out of the country before these bloody Russians get here. Why don't you just cut the bloody man's head off and throw him into the sea!' Calming down after this tantrum, he returned to his normal, polite self and in a courteous voice said, 'Be so good, my dear Miss Kemp, as to escort him out of the country by 25 April.'

Herr Schuler, the alias under which Bormann had been living in the riding school, conveniently 'died' and a coffin bearing his name was buried in the village graveyard that Creighton was first lied to about by Susan Kemp. Under escort, Bormann was flown to the Argentine, where he was put under the control of the section headed by Brabenov. Although he was only fifty-five, his health was failing and no more information-gathering activities were demanded of him. He was moved to Paraguay, where after a long illness he died in February 1959. What happened to the corpse after that has been the subject of much debate.

In order to maintain the secrecy of the deal by which Swiss banks released funds to Britain and America within a month of the war's end, it was imperative that Bormann be killed while escaping from the bunker. If his body was found in Paraguay many years later, it would provoke many embarrassing questions. According to Hugh Thomas, whose book *Doppelganger* convincingly documents what happened, a deal was made between the CIA, the pro-Nazi Paraguayan government and cooperative German intelligence sources, for Bormann's remains to be exhumed and returned to Berlin where they were buried in the Ulap Fairground, where some workers claimed they had dug a grave for the body in 1945. One must assume that this news was then conveyed to the magazine *Stern*, who four years earlier had failed to find a corpse in the Fairground; but this time, surprisingly enough, within a few yards of where they had last been digging, two skeletons were found which were declared to be those of Bormann and Stumpfegger by the 1972 Frankfurt Tribunal.

But Hugh Thomas has shown the many contradictions surrounding this explanation of the location of these skeletons, not the least of which is that the Bormann skull, which is in the possession of his family, reveals dental treatment that was done long after 1945, and was caked with red-brown clay that did not match the sand subsoil in which it was found. He describes the findings as a 'forensic fraud'.

The Bormann family is not united about their father's death in 1945 and his oldest son, the priest Martin Bormann, has recently given an interview to the *Frankfurter Rundschau* expressing doubts about the 1972 Tribunal's findings. When Creighton went to see the family in 1996 he asked them to allow a DNA test on the skull. They refused permission at that time, but in July 1997 a newspaper report said that they had changed their minds and that a DNA test would take place. In the meantime, confusion and uncertainty still exists about what the remains found in 1972 in the Ulap Fairground actually proved.

(iii) A hostile reception and a death threat from Germany

OpJB was published on 1 September 1996. The critical reception that it received can only be described as horrendous. Some of those who reviewed it reacted as if they had been personally insulted by having to read such a farrago of nonsense. A few days earlier, Andrew Roberts, the historian I had met a number of times at the Garrick, phoned to tell he me was reviewing the book for *The Times*. 'It's a lot of balls, isn't it?' he said. 'How many pages have you read so far?' I asked. 'Only fifty.' 'Well, you may change your mind when you've read a few more,' I said, summarizing my reasons for not dismissing it as a hoax. When the review appeared on 14 September it was headlined 'I spy some big fat lies.'

Admitting that facts to discredit Creighton's story were almost impossible to come by, he wrote 'It is truly extraordinary that a reputable publisher such as Simon & Schuster should produce such a childish fantasy as fact.'

This provoked a letter from me to *The Times* which said, amongst other comments, 'Andrew Roberts writes that I "have been taken in by the book's absurd claims" … In a long telephone conversation I had with him I told him that over six years a number of intelligence experts have been paid to investigate its claims; their doubts about details have been rebutted by Creighton to my satisfaction. I told him I had met "Susan Kemp" and that I am convinced she is who the book says she is ... None of this is contained in Mr Roberts's review. He does acknowledge that I and my colleagues have offered a reward of £20,000 to anyone who can, on factual evidence, prove that OpJB did not take place. Curiously enough, he does not believe that anyone will ever win it.'

The view that Churchill, let alone Attlee, Roosevelt and Truman – leaders who had not had their consciences troubled by the dropping of an atom bomb on Hiroshima – should have engaged in such a heinous act of duplicity troubled some historians as an outrageous accusation. 'Simply not British, old boy,' one of them told me.

Richard Overy, Professor of Modern History at King's College, London, articulated this objection in an interview in the *Independent*. 'The idea that Churchill should authorize such a preposterous operation simply beggars belief,' he said. 'I cannot believe Churchill would have risked alienating our allies by secretly protecting someone as senior as Bormann while every effort was being made to apprehend other war criminals.'

Perhaps the prize for the most self-righteous, vicious review should go to Robert Harris of the *Sunday Times* whose moral indignation was directed at Simon & Schuster – 'it boasts forty-eight Pulitzer prizewinners' – for publishing this 'unutterable tosh' while 'knowing it almost certainly to be false'. Mr Harris has been rightly praised for writing two brilliant novels – *Fatherland* and *Enigma* – on the peripheral edge of events associated with the Second World War. But there is no evidence anywhere that he has anything but a journalist's layman's view of how Intelligence functions or functioned. The only single fact he produces in a large piece of vituperation about the book's authenticity is that 'Bormann's body was dug up in Berlin and identified from dental records'. The findings of the Frankfurt Tribunal have been totally discredited, and it is surprising that Harris still has faith in them in 1996. And anyone reading this chapter can hardly accuse Simon & Schuster of being irresponsible when real experts have investigated every fact in the book and a reward of £20,000 was offered for proof that *OpJB* is either a hoax or a fantasy.

I wrote a letter to the *Sunday Times*, printed on 15 September 1996, which implicitly challenged Mr Harris to put up or shut up. He discreetly decided to do neither. 'One hardly knows where to begin in answering Robert Harris's attack on *OpJB*,' I said. 'The initial premise which Harris claims makes nonsense of the book is the dug-up bodies' dental records. Hugh Thomas's book *Doppelganger* calls the event a "forensic fraud" and those involved in cooking up that story have not dared to sue for libel. For a start the skull in question reveals dental work that was done long after 1945. Even the family are not united in believing he died in Berlin.

'Recently opened policy archives in Argentina and Paraguay reveal almost conclusively that Bormann was in the Argentine in the 1950s and probably died in Paraguay... The recent revelations from US archives in Washington, that Nazi gold and money deposited in Swiss banks before the war's end (officially identified as the Ribbentrop Gold Fund) was shared between the British and American governments, support the reasons why Bormann was brought to England in the first place... It is obvious that as Hitler's sole executor (in his will), Bormann, if he were still alive, would have played a vital role in the disposal of Nazi assets in Swiss banks. The shortfall disclosed by the Foreign Office this week between $500 million deposited in Swiss banks and the $58 million accepted by the Allies in 1947 is probably explained by the secret deal between Bormann and the British and American Intelligence agencies.'

But the critics who damned *OpJB* without, between them, providing a single fact to justify their scepticism managed to provide a fog of disbelief about Creighton's story that no missives tucked away in the letters pages could dissipate. Determined to try and arouse some individual who could prove the letters were forgeries or that Fleming was nowhere near Birdham between January and May 1945, or that operations elsewhere would show OpJB was impossible or that Creighton's many facts were ludicrous, two large advertisements – 8" by 3½" – were placed in *The Times* and the *Independent* in mid October 1996 which had the figure £20,000 prominently displayed. These advertisements cost almost £2,000. The text read:

> *OpJB* is an account of how Ian Fleming and Christopher Creighton, the book's author, led an expedition that brought Martin Bormann, Hitler's Secretary, to England at the war's end. The book has been the centre of sensational controversy. Bormann, as the sole executor of Hitler's will must have played an essential part in the disposal of Nazi assets. Bormann's authority to release such assets was the reason the Allies wanted him in England. This is a matter of supreme historical importance.

Simon & Schuster, in the interests of truth, is publicising the offer of a reward of £20,000 to anyone who can provide evidence that OpJB did not take place.

Conditions of the reward. Applicants must provide direct, first-hand, factual evidence, not based on rumour, gossip, hearsay or opinion, provable in a court of law, that Operation James Bond, as described in *OpJB*, did not take place. Applicants must also be prepared to rebut and negate the evidence produced by Creighton that OpJB did take place. The facts to be relevant must have occurred between Jan. 1 1945 and May 15 1945. This offer is open until Dec. 31 1996 and only the first person providing such conclusive evidence will receive the £20,000 reward. If legal costs are involved, each side will pay its own. Applications to be sent to Christopher Creighton, c/o Curtis Brown, Haymarket, London.

None of the reviewers or historians who asserted with such confidence their denunciation of the book as a fraud came forward with their knowledge to claim the reward. Neither did Nigel West or Gary Murray who had been paid substantial sums to investigate it. Indeed there were only four serious claims and their facts were so decisively rebutted by Creighton that they made no further efforts to acquire the £20,000. The closing date of the offer – 31 Dec 1996 – came and went without a single legally provable fact turning up to establish that OpJB did not take place. Nor has such a fact been revealed by the date of the publication of this book.

Each time the book turned up in translation the foreign publishers in Germany, Holland, France made intensive efforts to check the authenticity of its contents, and each time decided to publish even though Creighton's inability to provide them with every answer to every one of their questions left them uneasy about the inconclusive nature of some of the evidence.

Nick Webb was not impressed with the results of the advertisement nor with my report of my meeting with Susan Kemp who, he felt, was some actress Creighton had hired or was someone involved in Creighton's elaborate hoax. Indeed, Nick Webb still maintains serious doubts about the authenticity of Creighton's story. Such newspapers as retained any interest in the story continued to deride any effort made to reveal something positive about it. Snippets of information substantiating Creighton's story would turn up from time to time, but were never any longer taken seriously.

One of the frequent so-called 'facts' used to discredit *OpJB* was the assertion that Ian Fleming was only a 'chocolate' soldier, and would never have been involved in any such physically hazardous operation as the Bormann affair. But on 17 August 1996, the *Daily Telegraph* reported a plan 'released by the Public Record Office under the government's policy of greater openness'. Fleming, then the personal assistant to the Director of Naval Intelligence, had put forward a daring scheme to seize a German ship which would have enemy cryptograph material that would enable us to crack the Enigma ciphers.

This plan was advanced in September, 1940, at the height of the German blitz. 'Pick a tough crew of five, including a pilot, wireless operator and word perfect German speaker (which would be Fleming), dress them in German Air Force uniforms, add blood and bandages.' After the next German air raid on London, these men would occupy one of the captured German bombers in British possession and join the tail-end of the German bombers returning to the Continent. Once on the French side of the Channel, they would switch off one engine, lose height fast and, with smoke pouring from a candle in the tail, ditch into the sea. The men would then put to sea in a dinghy and after the bomber had sunk, radio German naval units of their plight and wait for a German ship to be sent to pick them up. Fleming's plan was then to kill the crew of the rescuing boat, dump their bodies overboard and sail the ship back to England with its valuable cryptograph code-books.

There was great enthusiasm for this scheme at Bletchley Park. When Operation Ruthless had to be cancelled because our reconnaissance plane could not spot a German vessel in the Channel that might be sent to rescue them, the head of Bletchley Park's Naval Section had to postpone and eventually cancel this 'very ingenious plot'. Before another suitable occasion came up, the British had already started to break the Enigma code.

According to Admiral Norman Denning, a post-war Director of Naval Intelligence, this scheme was typical of many of Fleming's planned missions. 'A lot of Ian's ideas were just plain crazy,' said the admiral. 'But a lot of his far-fetched ideas had just a glimmer of possibility in them that made you think twice before you threw them into the waste-paper basket.' Does Fleming's involvement in OpJB seem so far-fetched after one reads of his part in an officially acknowledged true expedition every bit as dangerous and bizarre as bringing Bormann to England?

While sales of *OpJB* reached 19th on the best-seller list in Britain, it was never taken up with any enthusiasm by the major book-sellers because they had been put off by the ridicule heaped on the book by the critics. It was not distributed with any enthusiasm by Simon & Schuster, who behaved as if they might catch leprosy through handling it. Nevertheless it is such a gripping and unputdownable read that it had more than earned its £150,000 advance by the end of 1997. Nearly one million copies were sold throughout the world. Despite all his negative instincts about the story, Nick Webb has printed a paperback version of *OpJB*.

The revelation, because of Jewish pressure from Holocaust victims in America, that Swiss banks had been collaborating with Hitler's minions in hiding away looted treasure in their vaults, made *OpJB* even more relevant than ever. Did not Creighton's book reveal, eight years earlier, what Swiss banking officials were now shame-facedly admitting? The list of names that have been publicized as owners of bank accounts untouched for fifty years is a startling development. What is surprising in all the disclosures about this scandal, is that no mention has been made of Martin Bormann. After all, as Hitler's sole executor and custodian of German funds outside of the Reich, his part in what happened would be crucial.

Even if he had died in 1945, someone would have had to take his bureaucratic place to enable looted money to be released. Who then was the adopted executor of Hitler's will – his *Mein Kampf* royalties were worth millions – if Bormann did not perform that function? Why has no government statement from Britain or America made any disclosure about this mystery?

When the book was published in Germany, Creighton was contacted by former Nazis determined to substantiate the story that Bormann died in 1945 so that they could claim he was not a war criminal when he was killed. On this legalistic basis, it is believed that there are still some valuable assets of Hitler's Deputy waiting for claimants under his will which have not been vitiated by his being a convicted war criminal.

At about seven in the evening of 14 October 1996 a large brown envelope with the word SHULMAN on it was dropped into my letter-box. The doorbell had not been rung to alert me to its presence. Badly typed on cheap paper it read:

Milton Shulman

You sensible experienced journalist and army intelligence man. You know we serious. You Creighton, Winter, Hart-Davit, Econ Verlag and

associates have not yet declared publicly that book Operation James Bond
is lie and that Martin Bormann did not die 1959 Paraguay but Berlin
May 1945.You have also not denied that Creighton M Section have complete records Swiss/Nazi gold and part control.

   Do not tell Police or newsmen except Operation James Bond false.

   We depend to you Shulman to get these done otherwise we shall take
serious violent action.

                                     Reichsleiter Friends.

It was clear from the pigeon English in which the note was written, and
the reference to the German publisher, Econ Verlag, and the misspelling
of Hart-Davis's name, that the writer was trying to give the impression
that it was the appearance of *OpJB* in Germany that he was trying to
stop. However, the well-phrased expressions 'not yet declared publicly'
and 'you have also not yet denied' seemed at odds with such basic foreign errors as 'you know me serious' and 'we depend to you'. My first
suspicion was that it was written by an English speaker and naturally one
felt it might be Creighton. But what for? When I phoned him he told
me he had received a similar death threat.We both agreed that it would
be useless telling the newspapers because they would accuse Creighton
of concocting a publicity stunt to help sell the book and no one would
print it. It placed me in a dilemma because if the threat was real, the
scepticism of the Press towards the book would ensure that all I would
get from them would be hoots of derision. I told Creighton I intended
to go to the police, and the next day a detective from Scotland Yard
heard from me all the details of the facts leading up to this ugly missive.
He took it seriously, came to see me a second time and about a week
later phoned to tell me that he had been in contact with the German
police, who knew all about it, and that I had nothing to worry about
because they were dealing with it.

   Creighton told Bridget and myself that he was going to Berlin to sort
out the Reichsleiter and his associates. Reichsleiter was the rank
Bormann had in the Nazi party as its National Organizer. The new
Reichsleiter was probably the head of some underground resurgent
Nazi movement and very likely the German security forces were well
aware of their activities.

   Creighton disappeared for eight days and because of queries from his
distraught wife, Bridget and I did our best to find out whether he had
been killed or not in Berlin.We managed to get hold of Susan Kemp

who denied any knowledge of Creighton's whereabouts, although we never believed her professed ignorance. But Creighton did return to England, apparently having satisfied the German police that his mission had been genuine. He was immediately admitted to a hospital suffering from two bullet wounds. As yet Creighton has maintained complete secrecy about what went on in Berlin, except that he has assured Bridget and myself that the Reichsleiter is unlikely to trouble us any further.

With the intrusion of the revelations of the money deposited in Swiss banks and the intense efforts of American and Jewish authorities to learn the truth, the evidence in *OpJB* has acquired a more significant dimension than mere history. All those involved in this search have commented on the lack of enthusiasm on the part of the British to release the secret documents in their archives that dealt with the activities of Desmond Morton and Ian Fleming. It took over fifty years to reveal Fleming's plan to acquire the Enigma code and one can be sure that many more such schemes are still officially buried, disclosing the fertile imagination of the author of the James Bond novels.

If Creighton's story is true and millions if not billions of German funds were creamed off by the Morton Section and the CIA, with very little left over for the looted victims in 1997, would it not be imperative that any cover-up operation be continued to discredit any suggestion of a deal between Bormann and Allied security forces? Trying to weigh the balance of evidence between a complete hoax and a complex cover-up needs much more investigation and analysis than the so-called experts in the media have given it so far.

Against OpJB being a true record of a daring intelligence coup are the following considerations:

(i)   Creighton's account of his part in discovering U-boats in Ireland, informing Admiral Canaris about the Dieppe raid, blowing up the Dutch submarine and his efforts as a double spy to deceive the Germans about the location of the Normandy landings, are of such a heroic, important nature that to achieve any one of them would have been a classic Intelligence achievement. To assert that one individual did them all has been too much for critics to swallow, even though no one has yet provided first-hand verbal or documentary proof that Creighton is little more than a Baron Munchausen, inventing fables of military derring-do.

(ii)   The letters from Churchill, Mountbatten, Fleming have only been seen in the form of photostats. Creighton claims that the M Section will not release the originals.

(iii)   The Victoria Cross which Creighton has shown to many people involved with this book remains a decoration of much mystery. The firm that has made all such decorations has no record of one given to any of the many names employed by Creighton. Creighton, with much logic on his side, insists it was awarded to him on a Secret List which the government maintains for all Intelligence and Security personnel, who would obviously need such protection if they were to continue to function as an Intelligence or Security agent. But Creighton will not hand over the medal for such expert scrutiny.

(iv)   Creighton claims that there are about thirty persons still alive who took part in OpJB. He has tried to get some of them to come forward, but either they feel bound by the Official Secrets Act or are not willing to face the media attention of such a disclosure, but no one – except Susan Kemp – has personally supported his story.

(v)   Although Susan Kemp did swear an affidavit and reveal to me that she was on OpJB, she has refused to come out again and meet either the media or Creighton's publishers. She is still adamant in that refusal. Barbara Brabenov, who was very active in organizing hiding places for Germans whose knowledge as scientists or informers would be of use to the Americans or the British, has often indicated her willingness to support Creighton's book but claims that CIA pressure has prevented her from doing so.

(vi)   There are many petty details about this operation that have been used by critics to destroy the book, but they are only of a peripheral nature due to loss of memory over the years or a conflict of evidence, such as the date when Creighton first turned up at RADA – either the first day of term, when he would have been on the Elbe, or two to three weeks after that because his active service was accepted by the RADA authorities as a credible excuse for his having been late starting the classes.

For the theory that there has been a cover-up by Desmond Morton and the security forces, there are events so strange and improbable that the most likely explanation for their having been done was to create an atmosphere of disinformation through which no one could ever pick a way to the truth.

(i)   One of the very remarkable aspects of Creighton's book is the mass of technical detail it enlists to describe the tactics, the weapons, the clothing, the orders involved in the various raids on land and water in which he was engaged. No one has yet faulted *OpJB* in its display of intricate military expertise.

(ii)   The fact that Creighton has never been loathe to face investigation or interrogation is shown by his financing of Nigel West to reveal the material's fallacies and improbabilities.

(iii) Creighton has been interrogated by many experts. Dozens of small improbabilities about travel routes, aircraft, units employed have been flung at him, but he has almost always bested these critics. A reading of the very lengthy rebuttals of the reports of Gary Murray and Nigel West would convince any objective observer that Creighton's defence of his position is far more convincing than the criticisms levelled at him.

(iv)   The sequence and shape of any operation in which he took part has always been described with amazing consistency over the years in which I have known him.

(v)   Other hoaxes in military affairs have always collapsed as soon as convincing evidence has been adduced. Hitler's Diaries were abandoned by their counterfeiters as soon as the evidence against them was produced. Similarly, the story offered by Farrago about Bormann being found in the Argentine collapsed as a commercial proposition immediately the photo of Bormann turned out to be a chef known to Farrago. *OpJB* has never deviated from its claim that – except for memory lapses – it is true. Dozens of opponents have made statements and produced photographs to demolish the book's foundations, but Creighton has never conceded their authenticity or been forced to shift his ground about this event.

(vi)   No one has proved that the letters of Churchill or Mountbatten are forgeries. Creighton has offered to show the original in a lawyer's office and in front of a handwriting specialist, but no one has yet asked him to do so.

(vii) My colleagues are aware of individuals who have received decorations registered on the Secret List. Common sense dictates that there must be such a List. The insistence of Creighton that his Victoria Cross is on a List of that kind should in no way undermine his claim that he was honoured with a VC.

(viii) When the Ffitch-Hayes turned up with Hanne Nelson and

Broderick-Hartley claiming he was Bormann, Creighton was convinced that the real Bormann had at last been found. So sure was he of the authenticity of their evidence that he paid them almost £50,000 to have their material incorporated in his book. If he knew then that the whole operation was just a hoax or a figment of his imagination, would he have handed over such a large sum of money to back up his deception?

(ix)   Throughout this operation, the M Section or the security authorities at MI5 have fed Creighton, through Susan Kemp, disinformation so that stories about Bormann would be contradicted so often no one would believe anything more about him. Without using the powers of the Official Secrets Act, they had made *OpJB* such a laughing stock that they did not have to worry about the truth being discovered through its pages.

(x)   It is strange that a book called *The Search for Martin Bormann*, proving Bormann died in 1945, was published only two weeks before *OpJB* and was described as a 'spoiling operation'. The book received hardly any reviews or attention. Who, one might ask, would finance such a spoiling operation?

(xi)   A reward of £20,000, for anyone providing facts that proved convincingly that *OpJB* never took place, has never been effectively claimed. Nigel West has since written to me saying that the fact that he did not make a claim for the £20,000 reward should not be interpreted as a sign of his confidence in any of Creighton's claims.

If *OpJB* is not an historical account of a true event, or it is true but been discredited through an elaborate cover-up plan, then we are left with only one other explanation. It is an amazing work of adventure fiction which can rank with the best of that genre about the last Great War, and Creighton deserved great acclaim for that achievement.

But while investigations are still taking place in official government circles about the deposition of Nazi gold in Swiss banks, surely Creighton should be subpoenaed or requested by one of these tribunals – the World Jewish Congress ought to be interested – to tell his story. Bormann's authority to handle all this money cannot just be hushed up while Creighton asserts that there is an 800-page debriefing of his role which would reveal where a great deal of this looted money went. If Creighton claims that the M Section will not release that evidence, then pressure should be brought to bear upon the British to release it before it is shredded, or to prove that such a debriefing never existed because Bormann was never in England. Creighton says he is willing to face the cross-examination of such a tribunal.

5

MONEY, LIQUOR AND WOMEN

A summons from Beaverbrook... The Big Clock at Cherkley... Pretty women and the Central Line challenge... Olivier is cautious about his lifestyle... Bertrand Russell rambles... Contemplate becoming an editor... A sad letter from Bing Crosby... Hollywood wants me fired

(i) What do you know about film?

While I was grateful that I was working at Reuters because the atmosphere, though hectic, was pleasant and my colleagues were very amiable, I never considered it to be my ultimate journalistic goal. There were on the desk some men who had grown into advanced middle-age on the job and I did not contemplate such a future for myself. I was still studying Russian and Russian history with a vague plan that one day I might put myself up for the post of Reuters' correspondent in Moscow.

With the publication of *Defeat in the West*, the BBC showed some interest and I did some political features on the North American service for them about Canada. But the British press displayed no eagerness in utilizing me. I saw an opportunity for writing a freelance article when Field Marshal Kesselring was rather belatedly tried for war crimes and condemned to death in May, 1947. My argument on the whole was for mercy and I sent it to the London *Evening Standard*. I received a letter by return from the *Standard*'s feature editor, Charles Curran, who described my piece as 'altogether admirable', but unfortunately there was no room for it in the next few days and he was returning it to me. He had, however, shown the article to the editor, Herbert Gunn, who would like to meet me. Would I make an appointment with his secretary?

Herbert Gunn was a tall, ambassadorial-looking man with a perpetual worried look. It is interesting that he should turn out to be the father of Thomas Gunn, one of Britain's most distinguished poets. I was asked about my qualifications, aside from writing *Defeat in the West*, and how firm was my contract with Reuters. The *Standard* had just received an additional quota of newsprint, enabling them to produce a sixteen rather than a twelve-page paper, and would I be willing to join them, on a two-month trial basis, as a feature writer?

On 29 May, 1947 I wrote accepting the offer. I had had considerable pangs of guilt deserting Reuters after only six months with them and the kindness that had been shown to me by Geoffrey Imeson – but it was an offer, as the cliché has it, that I couldn't refuse. My salary would go up from £11 to £15 a week and in the much respected *Evening Standard* I would be given a chance to have my own words written under my own name, rather than editing some other correspondent's words and thoughts in obscurity.

I have already described in my account of my involvement with Martin Bormann and Nazi gold the details of my first day on the *Evening Standard*. After I had told the editor about my doubts about finding Martin Bormann he paused for reflection and changed my first assignment from Hitler's Deputy to Chico Marx of the Marx Brothers, whom he wanted me to interview at the Palladium.

I left his office somewhat stunned. Was this then life in Fleet Street? Without the slightest shift in the inflection of his voice to indicate he recognized the ironic incongruity of the two tasks he had set me, he left me with the impression that I had a great deal to learn about the priorities of Fleet Street. Bormann or the Marx Brothers. In its way, I have always regarded my first day on the *Standard* as a prototype experience for any working journalist.

The feature editor, Charles Curran, had the craggy face of a man you wouldn't want to get into an argument with in a dark alley. He was assertive, garrulous and right-wing. He managed for some time to combine his job with being a Tory MP. There was no particular subject upon which, as a feature writer, I was expected to specialize. I was sent to Hopeman in Morayshire to ask the villagers what they thought of the young Philip Mountbatten – just engaged to Princess Elizabeth – who had spent four years amongst them when he was a pupil at Gordonstoun.

I interviewed a seventy-nine-year-old widow in Brighton who had written a letter to the *Standard* asking the editor to send a reporter to

her, so that she could give him £500 in one pound notes to be distributed to impoverished old-age pensioners in Croydon. I wrote a long
piece about the remarkable Hans von Meegeren, with the help of an
expert who had been a witness at van Meegeren's trial as a forger in
Holland, about how he had succeeded in painting Vermeers authentic
enough to convince museums to pay large sums of money for them.

The subjects were eclectic but the pieces were all printed. None
were spiked. I thought I was getting on reasonably well when on 17
September 1947 I received a letter from Gunn firing me.

> 'Your engagement was extended by a month while I was away,' he wrote.
> 'That month expires at the end of this week. In view of the restrictions
> on newsprint, and the lack of space in the paper, there is not enough
> opportunity to use you on features, and so, regretfully I shall have to bring
> your engagement with us to an end, as from Friday week, 26 September.'

Although I felt betrayed, I cannot say I suffered deep resentment about
this turn of events. I suppose I had become so accustomed to being buf-
feted about by the arbitrary winds of fate that nothing much could surprise me. But the reality was that I had given up a secure job at Reuters
and was now once again facing a perilous financial future. I could not
ask them for my job back. I had not been able to save any money on
my £15 a week – about £11 after tax – and royalties from *Defeat in the
West* would not keep me on their own.

I had contemplated writing a biography of Peter the Great and sent
David Farrer a synopsis about how I would treat it. I realized that my
Russian was not yet good enough to read the non-translated material
that existed in Moscow about this extravagant Czar, but Farrer indicated Seckers would give me an advance if I decided to take on that formidable task. Hunger would probably have turned me into a competent
Russian speaker. But again Accident or Chance or Luck diverted me
from the obvious.

Somewhat gracelessly Gunn insisted on my working out my last ten
days' notice. I was asked to cover two events in those last days: an international chess competition and a jitter-bugging contest. They were
items for the paper's gossip column, the Londoner's Diary – a daily
intrusive, informative and often cynical look at people and events in the
capital. I decided to treat them with flippancy and indifference. I expected my mocking descriptions, reminiscent of my undergraduate humour

days, would get them spiked. I didn't care. To my surprise the editor of the Diary cooed with delight at these juvenile efforts. He wanted more.

What happened after that is best reported in an exchange of letters between David Farrer and myself. As my publisher and a friend, Farrer wrote commiserating me about my unexpected misfortune.

'This is only a line to say I am so sorry about the *Evening Standard*,' were his words, 'and also to tell you that George Thomson had it from Gunn that your leaving had no connection with your competence at the job, which Gunn held highly. Let me know your plans. I feel sure you'll have no difficulty in finding another niche in Fleet Street. *Defeat* is selling steadily.'

'Thanks very much for your kind note,' I was able to reply the very next day. 'Strange things occur on Fleet Street but none more strange than those that take place within the Beaverbrook Empire. The day before I was scheduled to leave the *Standard*, Gunn called me into his office and told me he felt it would be a mistake to let me go and re-hired me.

'That means for the present I am giving Britons a fuller life by writing about beauty contests, Russian chess games and jitter-bug competitions for the Londoner's Diary. How long this essential work will continue only God and Gunn can tell. Such goings-on I accept rather philosophically as part of that journalistic neurosis brought about by inadequate newsprint, fear of what the Government will do next and a monotonous diet. My reprieve has made me plunge more energetically into my reading of Peter the Great ... Thanks again for your interest in my somewhat unpredictable affairs.'

I decided not to wax indignant or take umbrage about the manner in which I'd been treated. I needed the job and I needed the money. I naively assumed that it was my light-hearted Diary items, written on my way to the editorial chop, that had so intrigued Gunn he had changed his mind about my usefulness. I discovered from George Malcolm Thomson, many months later, the true explanation for the sudden volte-face. David Farrer had sent a copy of *Defeat in the West* to Lord Beaverbrook at his home in Bermuda, where he spent a good part of the year.

Beaverbrook was so impressed with it that he telephoned Farrer, his former private secretary now with Secker and Warburg, about where he could get hold of the author. The fact that I was a Canadian, like Beaverbrook, had sharpened his interest in me. Farrer told him that he should have no difficulty finding me for I had been working for him for the past three months. If he contacted Herbert Gunn, the editor of the *Standard* would tell him all about me. Within a few hours, Beaverbrook was in touch with Gunn. 'Do you realize you have a writer on your staff?' he barked down the phone to the perplexed editor. When Gunn admitted he was aware of me, Beaverbrook said, 'Well, why aren't you using more of him instead of hiding him away on the Diary?'

Beaverbrook editors had learned that to hold their positions they did not argue in cases like this. Dissemblance was wiser than candour. Gunn said not a word about having fired me and, in a strange coincidence of timing, was able to make amends by re-hiring me before he had to admit the embarrassing truth that he had thought me an expendable journalist. I was sent a new contract cancelling the one that had just dismissed me, but this time not specifying that I was on trial and giving me three months' notice should they decide to get rid of me again.

From then on, although I continued to work for the Diary, I was asked to interview well-known people, usually in show business, and my efforts were displayed in the paper's leading pages with a prominent by-line to accompany them. I shaped these pieces as part interview and part profile and amongst my early collection were Danny Kaye, Michael Redgrave, Hermione Gingold, Alfred Hitchcock, Joe Louis, Nijinsky – who most people had thought dead, and the newly appointed British Ambassador to Washington, Sir Oliver Franks.

My articles were never re-edited or cut and I realized how sacrosanct my words, having Beaverbrook's seal of approval, had become when I had an interview with Mae West published on the same day that Mahatma Gandhi was assassinated. To an Empire-oriented paper like the *Standard* this was a news event of overwhelming significance. The afternoon edition was cleared of every feature and news story to make way for analysis of the repercussions on the Empire, the prospect of civil war between Hindus and Moslems, and a massive obituary about Gandhi himself which took up every inch of available space with photographs of distraught Indians.

The one item which serenely and incongruously sat unperturbed in this maelstrom of international tragedy, was my 800-word profile of Mae West. Herbert Gunn was determined to prove to Beaverbrook in Bermuda that he had taken seriously his master's advice that he had a writer on his staff. A few paragraphs from that piece give some indication of the quality of the prose that was keeping me my job.

'It's my personality. Just like Charlie Chaplin's – it's unique!'
Mae West by Vicky.

'When Diamond Lil, an opulent, spheroid, deep purple synthesis of feathers, ribbons and furs, slithers into focus from the wings, the vast majority of her audience settle comfortably into their seats in anticipation. A minority wince with annoyance.

'When Diamond Lil in a voice that exercises her adenoids far more than her larynx confides (sings is hardly the word) to her listeners the arch sentiments of "You made me love you", a Niagara of applause lasting several minutes overwhelms the theatre and stops the show. Music lovers in the audience cringe and groan in their loneliness.

'There is one person, however, who fully understands this paradox in taste. She is Mae West, actress, author, playwright and very rich woman. She discovered the secret some twenty years ago when her first play *Sex* was alternately witnessed by cheering crowds and raiding police.

'"It's my personality," she told me. "Just like Charlie Chaplin's – it's unique. No one can do what Charlie does and no one can do what I do."'

At last the call came which every journalist in the Beaverbrook Group coveted and feared. I was summoned to Beaverbrook's penthouse flat in Arlington House, just behind the Ritz Hotel, on 5 April 1948. April was a significant month for Beaverbrook for that was the date which entitled him to return to Britain and not have to bear the punitive tax rates which, for him, would have been ninety per cent at the top rate. He was standing at a podium in front of a large glass window which had a sparkling view of Green Park and in the distance the roundabout hurly-burly of Hyde Park Corner.

His face opened into a welcoming smile as he shook my hand and led me to one of the many armchairs scattered in the large living-room. His wide mouth and softly simian appearance were already familiar to me through the many photographs I had seen of him. I had already equipped myself with details of his personal history – son of an impoverished New Brunswick preacher who became a multi-millionaire by thirty, Minister of Aircraft Production in Churchill's war cabinet, owner of the *Daily* and *Sunday Express* and the *Evening Standard* – he was probably the most successful and most controversial tycoon in the history of Fleet Street. He looked large even though he was only about five foot nine inches tall. He was already a legend and if I had never seen him again I would have thought it a privilege that I had once been in such close proximity to him.

Beaverbrook in a jaunty mood.

He signalled me to take the chair opposite him and asked me about my Toronto background. Then he switched to *Defeat in the West* and asked me about my views of the senior German generals and whether or not I thought a Second Front could have been undertaken in 1943 instead of 1944. He had read some of the interviews I had done for the *Standard* and had enjoyed them, particularly the ones on Danny Kaye and Mae West.

'Now, Mr Shulman, what do you know about films?' he suddenly asked me, for no particular reason.

'Not very much,' I replied, not knowing what he expected me to say.

'Do you go to them?'

'Not very often. About once or twice a month, I would guess.'

'Good!' said Beaverbrook, seemingly having got the answers he had been waiting for. He stood up and walked to his podium and began to scribble on a sheet of paper. 'Just the man we want. A fresh mind on the subject of films. Starting in two weeks time you will be the film critic of the *Evening Standard* and your salary will be raised by £10 a week.'

He didn't ask me if I wanted the job. I listened to him, somewhat stunned, as he talked into his dictaphone. 'Mr Millar,' he said to his secretary, 'tell Mr Gunn that Mr Shulman will be taking Margaret Lane's place as film critic of the *Standard*. She is going in two weeks and she will show him what to do. He will be getting £10 more a week.'

Having settled my future without hearing a word from me, he started to walk me to the door.

'Margaret Lane is giving up the job,' he said, 'and she will take you to next week's film press shows. Mr Gunn will organize it.'

He shook my hand and with a twist of his wrist indicated by his strong handshake that he expected me to leave.

'I will be in touch with you soon,' he said. 'Being film critic of the *Evening Standard* is a very important job. All the film companies will want you to say nice things about their pictures. They will try to bribe you with money, liquor and women. Goodbye.'

I wandered into Piccadilly, bemused at what had happened to me. What did I know about films? How long could I possibly keep that job? But his last words were still echoing in my ears. Money, liquor and women! Even if it lasts for only a short time, I consoled myself, this is easily the best job I've ever been offered. And ten pounds extra a week as well! My head was in the clouds and my feet barely touched the ground.

'Soon' turned out to be the very next day. I was told to go to Victoria Station and take a train to Leatherhead where I would be picked up by Lord Beaverbrook's chauffeur at 12.30. I would be having lunch with His Lordship at Cherkley, his country home. To those of us who became the object of Beaverbrook's whim, a peremptory summons to Cherkley or Arlington House always set up a tingling sensation of expectation and unease as we speculated about what fresh test we were likely to be asked to meet.

'No one who ever lodged for a while beside that Vesuvius will ever forget,' wrote Michael Foot, former leader of the Labour Party and once an acting editor of the *Evening Standard*. 'Some who came into contact with that bubbling lava were undoubtedly hurt and burned; others, like the relics of Pompeii, were encompassed and varied by the irrepressible flow and have remained ever since, durable evidence of the Old Man's touch.'

Cherkley was a nineteenth century country house with a large, rolling lawn, a splendid view and boring furniture. His butler, Nockles, met me at the door and Beaverbrook and I dined in solitary splendour in his ample dining-room. My only contribution to the conversation was a few answers about my work in MI14(b), which he knew little about. He then went on to tell me a few anecdotes about Bonar Law, a Canadian who had become British Prime Minister and for whom he had been a personal assistant before the First World War. But he was particularly keen on talking about Lord Louis Mountbatten, whom he blamed for Dieppe and other military disasters.

'Have you ever heard of Habakkuk?'

I hadn't.

'Mountbatten has a grand reputation he doesn't deserve. You'll live long enough to discover the truth about him. Take Habakkuk. That was one of his crazy ideas. There was this fellow Pyke on Mountbatten's staff. He had a plan for making a floating aircraft carrier made of a special mixture of ice and wood pulp. The material was called Pykerete. It was supposed to be unsinkable. To prove the toughness of this ice, Mountbatten had a chunk of it carried into a meeting of the Combined Chiefs-of-Staff. It was placed on the table and Mountbatten removed the burlap that was covering it. After explaining that no shell could penetrate it, Mountbatten drew a pistol from a holster and fired a bullet on to the ice. The bullet made no impression on the ice but it ricocheted around the room and missed by an inch killing Tedder, the Chief of the

Royal Air Force. What a fool that man was. What a story it would have made. Air Marshal Killed in Conference.' He burst into a loud guffaw at the very memory of the incident.

Throughout the lunch, not a word had been said about my new job as a film critic. Suddenly, as if remembering why he had asked to see me, he rose from the table and led me into a small private cinema which he had had installed at Cherkley. It was equipped with comfortable arm-chairs – about twelve of them – which were located on two levels of the room. When we were seated, Beaverbrook called out to his butler, 'Nockles, put on two reels of *The Big Clock*.'

The lights went down and hardly were the opening titles of this new film finished when I could hear gentle snoring sounds beside me. Beaverbrook was asleep. Since a reel was about ten minutes long, the screen suddenly went blank twenty minutes later and the lights in the cinema went up. This awakened Beaverbrook.

Up to this point, the preliminaries of the plot of *The Big Clock* had only just begun to unfold. The story was set in a newspaper office and I had been paying only casual interest to what was going on amongst the characters.

'Who killed her?' were Beaverbrook's first words, still shaking him-self out of his short nap.

'Who killed who, Lord Beaverbrook?' I asked. There had been no signs of any such impending violence in the two reels I had seen.

'The blonde. Who killed the blonde?'

'I'm sorry, sir,' I said, 'but I haven't seen any blonde. She hasn't turned up yet in the plot.'

There was a slight pause while he digested this information.

'Well, if there had been a blonde who do you think would have killed her?'

I decided not to guess because I had no idea what the characters were up to. I said I didn't know. I had the feeling I had let him down.

'Ah, Laughton did it. Laughton killed her.'

Since Charles Laughton had not yet made an appearance in those first two reels, it was not altogether surprising that I had not spotted him as a chief suspect.

Beaverbrook rose from his chair. 'Now if you were writing a review of *The Big Clock* what would you say about it?'

'It has lots of suspense,' I said, groping frantically for the appropriate adjectives I had associated with film criticism.

'Yaas. What else?'

'It's very tense.'

'Yaas. What else?'

'It's taut.' I wasn't sure what that meant but I thought it sounded knowledgeable.

'Taut. Ah, yaas.' We had now reached the exit door of the viewing room. 'All right now. You go home and write me two hundred words about *The Big Clock*. And let me see it tomorrow afternoon.'

I was ushered into a chauffeur-driven car and taken to Leatherhead Station. I was too pusillanimous to admit to my proprietor that he had given me an impossible job. All the way back to London I contemplated the fact that my career as a film critic was about to be the shortest in Fleet Street annals. I knew nothing about the story, the stars, the direction of *The Big Clock*. I would have to admit the next day that I could not write the review that was expected. Nor could I possibly bluff my way through it.

Suddenly it occurred to me that if Beaverbrook had a print of the film, there must be other prints in London. Perhaps if I phoned Paramount, who produced the picture, and told them of my plight, they might arrange a screening for me the next morning. Better still, I thought, the movie might be showing somewhere in London. Scanning the *Evening Standard* entertainment advertisements, I found it. It was at the Plaza Cinema in Lower Regent Street, and at 10 o'clock the next day I was at the first showing, practically alone, seeing *The Big Clock* for the first time. The two hundred words were duly written.

★ ★ ★

My credentials for being a serious film critic were not exactly zero, but almost. I did not actually know what a film critic was supposed to do. We called them theatres, not cinemas, in Toronto and my first theatre experiences were at the Red Mill where the screen was located behind you when you entered. I considered this a great advantage when I was very young because I was always reluctant to leave a film, which I had probably started to watch when it was half-way through, and at the Red Mill I could continue to watch the flickering shadows walking straight forward to the exit instead of being pulled out by an adult trying to linger on the illusion by walking out backwards.

Charlie Chaplin, Harold Lloyd and Douglas Fairbanks seemed to be in most of the films I was taken to before the age of ten. I fell in love with Janet Gaynor, Ida Lupino and Merle Oberon. The films that had lodged in my mind as unforgettable by the war's end were *City Lights*, *All Quiet on the Western Front, Nothing Sacred, Ninotchka* and *A Night at the Opera*.

The closest I had ever come to criticism was writing some flattering puffs for the *Varsity* for Hollywood films that reached Toronto. The understanding was that for two free seats, you were expected to outline the plot and not be too rude about what you had been watching. My six years in the army had curtailed my movie-going even further and it was only when I began to read British papers in order to familiarize myself with their style for my hoped-for future as a journalist that I paid some cursory attention to the film criticism of Caroline Lejeune in the *Observer* and Dilys Powell in the *Sunday Times*.

Margaret Lane, who was married to the 15th Earl of Huntington and was a respected biographer and novelist, had done a temporary spell of film criticism on the *Evening Standard*. She explained how invitations for press shows were received and took me to four or five of them in Wardour Street. About twenty representatives of British papers and certain magazines would be present in these small viewing theatres and they were usually scheduled for a morning and afternoon showing on Monday and Tuesday, and in an over-crowded week there would be a fifth film to be seen on Wednesday morning. Most of the films came from Hollywood and the rest from Britain, France and Italy. Those countries had the monopoly of film production and catching up with them all was not difficult. How different from the 1990s when a national film critic can be expected to cram in three, sometimes even four, film shows a day with product coming from Japan, Vietnam, Brazil, Australia, Canada, Israel and almost every country in the world.

Beaverbrook was determined to promote his new film critic with almost indecent vigour. He printed in the Diary my dashed-off piece about *The Big Clock*, which I synopsized as 'improbable people doing improbable things which will probably do very well at the box office.' I was asked to write an attack on the isolation of critics in press shows, which I duly did, and when it, too, appeared in the Londoner's Diary, Beaverbrook's own words were used to advertise my presence. 'His mind is lively,' ran the blurb. 'His views are fresh. He is unconventional. His pen is vigorous. He attacks.'

Early evidence of this ferocious beast that had been let loose on

Standard readers was a front page story containing my review of *No Orchids for Miss Blandish*. 'A disgrace to British Films' ran the headline in large black type. 'For 102 minutes today I was subjected to a most vicious display of sadism, brutality and suggestiveness,' ran my first line. My reward for this outburst of candour was a note from the editor telling me that 'Lord Beaverbrook has asked me to congratulate you on your attack on *No Orchids for Miss Blandish*. He says you are a man after his own heart.'

It was the beginning of dozens of such comments throughout the years – almost all were congratulatory. When he was displeased, such notes were never sent direct. They were communicated through his editors, who had to word them in the most diplomatic phrases they could invent. Tudor Jenkins, whose book *The Londoner* was a collection of reminiscences about his years as editor of the *Standard*'s Londoner's Diary, illustrates this shadowy technique of his proprietor. I had written in a review of the film *The Bad Lord Byron* that 'if Lord Byron were as colourless and fatuous a character as that portrayed by Dennis Price his only poetic contribution to mankind would have been doggerel on a wall.' Jenkins received a typical dictographed memo. 'I see a vigorous attack on Dennis Price in Mr Shulman's column. I wish you would have a really good note on Dennis Price in the Diary, for we have pounded him too much, hit him too hard, he is too good a man altogether. I am not complaining about Shulman, I don't wish you to convey to Shulman any such suggestion on any account.'

I realized that if I were to gain any respect as a film critic, I would have to fill in the deep voids in my knowledge about past movies and the history of the cinema. I scoured second-hand bookshops for out-of-print classics and for anything expected to be read by film experts. I still have on my bookshelves Paul Rotha's *Film*, Bardeche and Brassilach's *History of the Film*, Lewis Jacobs's *The Rise of the American Film*, Eisenstein's *The Film Sense*, Gilbert Seldes's *Movies for the Millions*, Leo Rosten's *Hollywood*, James Agate's *Around the Cinemas*, M. F. Thorpe's *America at the Movies*, Bela Balazs's *Theory of the Film*, Alistair Cooke's *Garbo and the Night Watchman* and many more.

I also tried to catch up with acknowledged film classics that would turn up in specialized cinemas in Chelsea or Hampstead. I managed to see *Battleship Potemkin, The Cabinet of Dr Caligari, Intolerance, Ivan the Terrible, Modern Times, An Italian Straw Hat, Ten Days That Shook the World, The Way of All Flesh, The Thin Man, The Four Horsemen of the Apocalypse,*

The Gold Rush, Greed, Metropolis, Scarface, The Ten Commandments and many more that every knowledgeable film fan could talk about. Whenever I could I dropped names like D.W. Griffith, René Clair, Cecil B. DeMille, Jean Renoir, Mack Sennett, von Sternberg, Keystone, Ufa, Fritz Lang into my notices to give myself an aura of expertise, which I decidedly lacked but was quickly acquiring.

The *Standard*, of course, was not particularly interested in learned appraisals of the art of the cinema. Most of the stuff I was shown weekly was quickie junk and since television had not yet emerged as a rival for the public's attention, almost any film if it was not too abstract or demanding could make a profit at the box office. Setting standards based upon my reading and my selective viewing of some of the best pictures that had been produced, I was, of course, far too critical. I was not deliberately trying to be provocative. Not being accustomed to the standard of film fare that filled cinemas, I just voiced my disappointment with what I was regularly shown in as entertaining and mocking style as I could muster. After all, I didn't believe my future career was destined to be that of a film critic.

I had only been on the job a month when Herbert Gunn called me in to tell me that my latest review of *The Good Time Girl* had received a challenge from the film's producer, Sidney Box of Gainsborough Pictures.

The plot concerned the dangers of London life to sixteen-year-old girls who get jobs as hat-check girls in night-clubs and end up with shady musicians and American deserters who teach them how to drink and rob, as a result of which – and here's the Moral – they become involved in a murder and end up in prison with a fifteen-year sentence. Jean Kent starred as the wayward adolescent, and commenting on her performance I said, 'When are British studios going to stop building up and starring boys and girls with as much personality as a thick wad of blotting paper? Jean Kent is almost indistinguishable on the screen from Patricia Roc, Greta Gynt and Margaret Lockwood. They all have the same stereotyped, glossy, manufactured features which have somehow become the hallmark of British female stardom ... I could find half a dozen more attractive girls any day on the Central Line. Since most of their screen moments are spent looking like petulant cream-puffs, it is impossible to say whether they can act or not.'

'Sidney Box has challenged you to find six more attractive girls on the Central Line,' Gunn told me, 'and I have accepted on your behalf.'

What had been meant as a light-hearted jibe now became a test of my judgement about attractive girls.

I looked up the stations on the Central Line and thought Marble Arch a reasonable place for decamping pretty working girls in the morning. I recognized that I might be misunderstood if I began accosting girls as they came off the underground escalator so I asked the *Standard's* woman's editor to join me to prove my credentials to any suspicious female, and with a photographer we set off at 7.30 in the morning early in May 1948. It was one of those days when heavy, unrelenting rain took over the sullen skies all morning. Every woman coming out of the station had an umbrella or a large scarf covering her head. In their rationed clothes, they looked drab, raindrops dripping from their sodden hair down their pale cheeks.

There was not a single photogenic prospect and I decided to call the hunt off for the morning. We would try again at five o'clock at Bond Street station on the Central Line. The prediction was that the rain would cease and I calculated that Bond Street, where some of London's smartest and most expensive shops were located, might disgorge some reasonably pretty girls. And I was right. They were aged between seventeen and twenty-two. For a week there were prominent stories in the *Standard* about the film tests they were all given by a prominent film director, Ken Annakin, who photographed them acting out five-minute film scripts.

I reported their debuts and had to admit that their acting ability came nowhere near their looks. A young actor, Anthony Steel, read the men's lines opposite them. 'There is only one moral to this episode of the Central Line,' I wrote when it was clear that no Garbo or Vivien Leigh had turned up in the experiment. 'It is that beauty and acting ability have very little in common. Our British films are full of pretty girls who act like animated meringues … My little girls on the Central Line need not despair about the fact that they cannot act – they have plenty of company in Mr Box's studios.'

This rumpus together with the front-page prominence given to my review of *No Orchids for Miss Blandish* delighted Lord Beaverbrook and ensured that my position as a film critic was going to be more long-term than I had originally thought. The time involved, together with other news stories and book reviews about the war which I was expected to do, meant that I had to abandon my night classes at the School of Slavonic Studies and my vague plans for a biography of Peter the Great.

To supplement my income from the *Standard* and to maintain my interest in international affairs and politics, I was doing a weekly broadcast to Canada and America on the BBC's North American Service called *Progress Report*. I dealt with one British industry at a time – steel, energy, motor cars, tourism, railways – and in a half hour tried to summarize its history and possible future development. I was paid twelve guineas a programme and since I received no reaction whatsoever from any listener I assumed my words of wisdom were only enjoyed by seagulls over the Atlantic. It was finally terminated as a regular feature because BBC executives in Canada thought that I was losing my Canadian persona through using words like 'lift' instead of 'elevator' and pronouncing 'drama' as 'drahma'.

★ ★ ★

Having been launched accidentally as a controversial critic, the readers of the *Evening Standard* made sure I remained one. Television had not yet arrived to take over as the nation's most important and absorbing entertainment medium. Almost anything I wrote set up furious duels of opinion in the paper's correspondence columns. My film notices appeared weekly, usually on Fridays, and three to four movies were assessed. Introducing each picture was its name, the cinema where it was showing and a succinct Opinion which was a one-line summary that often, if the film met my disapproval, was flippant or blunt. Thus a film called *Blood on my Hands* was dismissed with the words 'Get me a towel.' *My Brother's Keeper* was summarized: 'A convict escapes – so should you.' *The Fallen Idol* was hailed as 'A great British picture.'

Impatience with film critics was growing in intensity on the part of film companies who were big advertisers in newspapers and expected the kind of benevolent, fawning adulation they had received for their product during the war.

When I dismissed *Bonnie Prince Charlie* in October 1948 as 'history for the nine-year-old done up in tartan tissue paper', I received three long letters from Sir Alexander Korda, Britain's best-known producer and Chairman of London Film Productions, lecturing me severely on the functions of a film critic. 'I defend this film because I am sincerely convinced that, judging it as harshly as you and some other critics do was wrong. The picture with all its faults and, in spite of the series of misfortunes we went through in the making of it, is not a worthless effort.'

The legendary Sam Goldwyn condemned my review of *I Want You* in an open letter to the *Standard* as 'insulting'. My Opinion catch line read, 'Are you sure you mean me?' and I insisted that this expensive movie was little more than a cliché-ridden recruiting poster for the Korean war. 'Confused, well-meaning and bumbling' was my summary of its qualities.

'I concede readily every critic's full right to his own opinion on the merits of any work he is evaluating,' began Goldwyn with the usual disclaimer every critic receives before his outraged opponent is going to deny him just that. 'But I reserve the right to dispute vigorously any critic who writes from an ivory tower or who apparently does not pay enough attention to a film to know what it says and to answer any critic who seems to delight in taking pot shots at Hollywood on general principles.'

In spite of the steady barrage of complaints about my work, there was concrete evidence that I was pleasing Beaverbrook. And that it was the reader who really counted. I received a £10 raise seven months after I became a critic, another rise of £5 per week and a £50 bonus in 1949 and another £10 rise in 1950. I was now in the category of a £50 a week journalist, including expenses, and even though I was having to give the government 60 per cent of my top slice of pay, I was told by the *Standard* General Manager I could count myself among Fleet Street's highest-paid writers.

With all these epistolary and financial compliments pouring in, it came as somewhat of a shock to discover that these streams of verbal honey might soon be dribbling to a close. 'I really think you have got to find one film to give some praise to occasionally,' said a surprising memo dated 3 February 1948 from the editor. 'Again today your column consists almost entirely of castigation and condemnation of the week's pictures. I have no doubt they were a bad lot. But your criticism will lose all its power if you indulge in constant condemnation. Let us try, for a short time, to look for the virtues in pictures rather than the bad spots and weaknesses.'

Since I did not know of any other way of writing film criticisms other than the way I had been doing it, I realized that if I was to become a puff merchant for the cinema I would soon have to find other work. The accusation that I had not been able to find any films to praise all through 1948 was, of course, untrue. I had been lavish in my enthusiasm for Olivier's *Hamlet*, David Lean's *Oliver Twist*, Carol Reed's *The*

Fallen Idol, *The Naked City*, *Kiss of Death*, *Le Diable au Corps*, *The Winslow Boy*, *Call Northside 777*, *Scott of the Antarctic* and others. Indeed, only a fortnight before I was accused of never finding a film to praise, I was doing handsprings of approval for Powell and Pressburger's *The Small Back Room*.

Knowing that as far as I was concerned Herbert Gunn had long ago decided to act only as a mouthpiece for Beaverbrook's idiosyncratic passions and prejudices, I could detect the echoes of His Master's Voice behind Gunn's admonition to be kinder to films. Were his cronies in the industry – Korda, Sam Goldwyn, Spyros Skouros – indicating their irritability with my critical stance and was Beaverbrook preparing to switch me into something else? A war correspondent, perhaps? Not immediately but in due time.

★ ★ ★

There is nothing more gratifying for an aspiring writer than to see his name and his words between hard covers. *Defeat in the West* was my first experience of waiting anxiously for reviews, of haunting bookshops to see if your precious achievement is displayed on their shelves, of enjoying the thrill of talking about it on radio or TV, being despondent when some damn fool critic has misunderstood the validity of your argument or some literary editor has only thought it worth an inch of space in their miscellany section.

I had been writing interviews in the shape of profiles ever since Beaverbrook had urged Herbert Gunn to get my name into the *Standard* more often. Whenever some well-known figure arrived in London (Joe Louis, Alfred Hitchcock, Danny Kaye) I met them in their hotel for an hour or two and produced 800 words for the *Standard*.

One of my oddest meetings at that time was with the legendary Russian ballet dancer, Nijinsky. I had thought he had died before the war and it came to me as a shock when I was asked to interview him at a country hotel near Egham, Surrey. Since the dancer had been declared incurably insane in 1919, it was only the resolution of his wife, Romola, to lead him around from country to country, pretending one could communicate with him, that brought about this strange meeting with him in March 1948. For ten years – from 1909 to 1919 – Vaslav Nijinsky captivated an incredulous world with the magic, beauty, originality and technical perfection of his dancing. Then suddenly, with impresarios flooding him with offers, this brilliant light was dimmed. He became mystical, morbid, strange. Late in 1919, just twenty-nine years of age, Nijinsky was declared incurably insane, a victim of schizophrenia.

When the Ballet Russe Company, formed by Sergei Diaghilev, left Russia in 1911, never to return, Nijinsky was its star. Obsessed by him was a Hungarian society girl, Romola de Pulszki, who followed the Ballet Russe everywhere it toured just to be near him. She eventually married him in Buenos Aires and bore him a daughter. Between 1919 and 1938, Romola searched the world for a cure for her husband. Psychiatrists like Freud, Jung and Adler could do nothing. She tried Christian Science, healers and fakirs. Even Lourdes.

In 1938, after 270 'shock' injections of insulin, which would put him into a deep coma, he achieved a semi-cure which enabled him to be discharged from his Swiss sanatorium and, under the strict supervision of his wife, lead a subdued, normal life again.

When I saw him, his round face with the high, balding forehead and cheeks puckered in a fixed querulous smile gave him the air of a benevolent, elderly, quizzical doll. His bright, brown eyes danced into and away from you, while his fingers rapidly opened and closed in a series of nervous spasmodic movements. His voice seldom rose above a mutter and the only words I could hear him say were '*oui*' and '*non*'. I suspect that his capacity to communicate – he only spoke in Russian – was manipulated by Romola to give the impression that he was far more sane than he actually was. I played along with this charade, talking only to her but grateful, even if the interview was non-productive, to be able to see this legend, even if only in his days of decline. He died two years later at the age of sixty in Paris.

Apparently my approach was just what was wanted by the editor of the *Sketch*, who had been a submarine commander during the war and still retained his military title of Captain J. E. Broome. His society magazine had been running a regular feature of short cameos written under the pseudonym of Urtica. It was 1949 and I needed the money so I agreed to do them from time to time. My Urtica subjects included the actor John Mills, the playwright Terence Rattigan and the cricketer Denis Compton.

There were murmurings from some publishers about collecting these transient pieces into a book and I was truly surprised when Max Reinhardt, who produced books under the imprint of Reinhardt and Evans and later Bodley Head, actually offered an advance to print them.

What made the proposition intriguing from my standpoint was that Vicky, the political cartoonist of the *Standard* and probably the best caricaturist in Britain, had been contracted to etch each of my subjects in his own inimitable way. Although almost forty-eight years have lapsed since Vicky's brush caught their personalities, I still think his gallery of witty images can be numbered amongst the most amusing and revealing caricatures of the century.

I was grateful that each of these prominent people had agreed to subject themselves to the questioning of a relatively unknown journalist with a growing reputation as an acerbic critic. I had no intention of putting them through an ordeal in aspic. It was small wonder, then, that Michael Redgrave should write, 'Thank you indeed! The only fault I can find is that some of my friends will think I've written it myself.' Less keen on allowing my view of him to go into print unmodified was Laurence Olivier. Although it was not my practice to let my subjects see beforehand what I had written, Olivier was such a big catch at the time that I thought it advisable to let him make small corrections if he was worried about them.

His letter of 26 June 1950 was generous and found few faults but those that he did point out, I corrected in my final draft.

'Thank you very much indeed; I don't know how you can have had the patience to do it so beautifully,' he wrote. 'I think it most charming and generous, and I would not have the temerity to say a word about it if you had not been kind enough to ask me to.

'A tiny point, hardly worth mentioning, is that my Old Vic salary was £20, not £25. I wonder if the "palatial country house" could be soft-pedalled a trifle, at any rate the address be suppressed? This purely for reasons of convenience and privacy. Perhaps the "late hours in the tiny Chelsea house" had better not be too frequent occurrences, don't you think? As a matter of fact, when you are working, it isn't possible that they can be . . .

'I rather think that any crack from me about the critics is something I should probably live to regret, don't you think? . . . That isn't really the whole truth about *Othello*; actually I feel his voice should be a great deal deeper than is mine, and in my heart I know perfectly well I shall have a crack at it some time. Again, many thanks indeed for your splendid effort; it must have very nearly killed you.'

Laurence Olivier by Vicky

Bertrand Russell and Alfred Hitchcock by Vicky.

I called the collection *How to be a Celebrity*. It was published in November 1950, and being somewhat inflated journalistic pieces, adorned by Vicky's genius, it received what are euphemistically called 'mixed notices'. No critic was either very rude or very kind. Just what I expected. I was therefore very surprised and encouraged when it was chosen by Miss Christina Foyle to be honoured at one of her very respected Literary Luncheons. These occasions, started in 1930, organized by the proprietors of Foyle's bookshop in Charing Cross Road, managed to keep going even through the Second World War and took the form of a grand meal at a grand hotel like the Dorchester or the Grosvenor House. My luncheon was the 223rd that had been given and to see one's name added to the list of previous speakers – Bernard Shaw, Anthony Eden, Evelyn Waugh, Harold Macmillan, A. A. Milne, Peggy Ashcroft, Chico Marx, Dorothy Sayers, Mistinguett, De Gaulle, John Gielgud, Aneurin Bevan, Arthur Koestler to name but a few – was not only good for the ego but good for book sales as well.

Over 300 guests had paid for the opportunity of hearing those at the top table give amusing speeches on the subject of being a celebrity. It was obviously the reputation of the Foyle's Literary Luncheon that had brought out such a large following but the eminence of those at my top table truly astonished me. Sir Michael Balcon, whose Ealing Films – *Passport to Pimlico*, *Whisky Galore*, *Kind Hearts and Coronets* – had lifted British films to an international stature, had agreed to be the Chairman. Emlyn Williams, Michael Redgrave, the novelist Peter Cheyney were seated near me but, most gratifying of all, the eminent philosopher Bertrand Russell was going to make the main speech. He was then seventy-eight years old and my single meeting with him had been late in the evening in a dusk-filled small room in Chelsea. It was clear from his amusing but rambling talk on the nature of celebrities that he had not read the book. I concluded that it was loneliness rather than admiration for my profiles that had encouraged him to accept the invitation. His popularity at the time had taken a knock in the tabloid press because of his anti-nuclear campaign. Having a free meal in congenial company probably seemed to him a better way of spending an afternoon than being incarcerated with one of his ideological secretaries in his glum London home.

Having become identified with the film industry, even if only as a baleful nuisance, the editor of the *Standard*, no doubt pushed by Beaverbrook, decided that I should discover what Hollywood looked like. First class passage was booked for me on the *Queen Mary* and a return booking on the *Queen Elizabeth*. I was to leave on 29 October, spend a few days in New York, fly to Toronto for five days, then to Los Angeles, back again to New York and return to England on 17 December. The *Standard* would be paying for most of this expedition even though it was understood that spending time with my parents in Toronto and my brother's family in Los Angeles was something of a reward for my satisfactory work on the paper.

Naturally I was treated as a home-town boy who had made good by my relatives and no one this time asked me if I was coming back to Canada. They knew I wasn't. In Hollywood the press officers at such major studios as Paramount, United Artists, Columbia and MGM had arranged to have me watch the films they were making in their studios, and to have me photographed with some of the stars so I could snatch a bit of banal conversation with them while they were being made up for their next action. I soon realized that the British or foreign market was of little moment to those who produced, directed or acted in American pictures. They were polite to visiting critics from London, but the publicity men were far more anxious to cater to the needs of a gossip columnist from the tiny circulation *Podunk Gazette* than to requests for interviews with stars from the four million circulation *Daily Express*. I managed to get a quick word with Montgomery Clift on the set of *A Place in the Sun* and thought him a level-headed fellow who still retained a tiny flat in New York and had no illusions about the transitory nature of his success in films. Bing Crosby seemed casually unconcerned about his next shot on the set of *Mr Music* and was too involved with his lines to talk to me. Joseph Cotten, being an Anglophile, was willing to talk to me enthusiastically about *The Third Man* in his dressing-room. He was the only actor who appeared genuinely interested in trying to make a good impression on a foreign journalist.

Although I also watched Gene Kelly, Betty Hutton, Broderick Crawford, the director John Huston going through their bits of action for the films they were on, it was the memento I have of a few moments with Humphrey Bogart, directed by Nicholas Ray on the set of *Knock On Any Door*, that was my most pleasing experience of this publicity-oriented tour. Although he was dragged away almost every ten minutes for some camera shot, he managed to convey to me his enthusiasm about the English MG car he was driving, his hopes that the Labour Party would win the forthcoming British election and his dismay at the quality of the Los Angeles newspapers. The usual photographs were taken of us together and when Mimmo of the small Italian restaurant, Mimmo d'Ischia, in Belgravia, asked me for a photograph of myself to join the dozens of showbiz personalities – Roger Moore, Elizabeth Taylor, Joan Collins – festooning his wall, I gave him this shot of myself with Bogart. I told Mimmo about Cohen in the Champs Elysee seeing his friend, Goldberg, riding in a state carriage beside General de Gaulle. 'Who is that man sitting beside Goldberg?' asked Cohen of his wife. Similarly, I explained to Mimmo justifying this photo for him, his customers would not recognize me but like Cohen, they might ask, 'Who is that man talking to Humphrey Bogart?'

Before I had taken my six weeks' trip to America, after which I wrote a number of long articles for the *Standard* on the American movie scene, there had already been indications that Gunn's urging me to be kinder to pictures was symptomatic of unease about my critical stance in much higher reaches in the *Express* Group. When in April, 1949, Beaverbrook returned to England from Bermuda in accordance with the rules of his tax regime, he not only asked me to review the second volume of Churchill's war memoirs, *Their Finest Hour*, to which the *Standard* gave a full page, but to come and see him at Arlington House for a talk about my future.

The suspicions aroused by Gunn's memo hardened when Beaverbrook, in a complimentary tone of voice, told me that he thought I could be of much more use to the *Express* newspapers if I gave up film criticism and took on an executive or administrative job within the Group. What would that entail, I asked, wondering what he was up to. 'I want you to become a qualified newspaper man,' he said. 'Learn all the technical problems of putting out a paper. Eventually if you prove satisfactory, you could become an editor of an *Express* paper.' I should have been elated by such an opportunity to be offered the chance of attaining one of the most important posts in Fleet Street, but I wasn't all that sure I wanted it. An editorship with a salary of over £10,000 a year? Of course. But how long would I last at the end of Beaverbrook's demanding dictograph machine? What specifically would I have to do if I gave up film criticism?

'You would go to Manchester and work as an executive on the northern edition of the *Daily Express*. Learn the business.'

There was a long silence on my part. 'It is a very exciting prospect,' I said, 'but I would need some time to think it over.'

Bogart gives me his views on the Labour party.

Beaverbrook had not expected such a hesitant reply to his offer.

'How much time?'

'I'd need at least a month.'

'A month!' To Beaverbrook, who expected positive action to his demands in a few hours or at most a day, it was clear I had not reacted with the gratitude he expected. I also sensed that his enthusiasm for me as a dedicated Beaverbrook acolyte was ebbing away. He was standing at his lectern and wrote something down on the pad in front of him. 'Alright, I'll give you a month. I'll be in touch with you then,' he said. 'Goodbye' and grasping my hand ushered me towards the front door.

A month to the day, I was summoned to Arlington House. I knew why. I had agonized about the issue in the intervening days. I was then a dedicated socialist, representative of the Canadian CCF and opposed to the political views, expressed in their leader and news columns, in his papers. Although Beaverbrook employed journalists of the Left – the two editors of the *Standard* before Gunn had been anti-Tories – I did not believe such freedom would be available in the course of the election campaign about to begin. In addition to the moral crisis of reconciling my convictions with Beaverbrook's eventual demands, I was then too much in love with Jackie to want to spend one or two years away from her in Manchester. She had just begun to train as an actress and the thought of long journeys, perhaps once a fortnight to see her, was too painful to contemplate. Although not living together, we saw each other almost every day. If I am honest with myself, I suspect it was my heart rather than my political conscience that dominated my decision.

'I am very troubled by your offer,' I said, when Beaverbrook asked me as soon as I arrived, what I was going to do about the job. 'Although I want to expand my career as a journalist, I feel that I cannot accept your offer at this time. My political views do not agree with those of your papers and I feel that if I became a senior executive or an editor of one of them, I would have to compromise my principles or compromise my responsibilities as an editor. I do not want to do either. With a general election soon coming up, I feel that readers would be losing their sense of humour about politics and would not be tolerant about a non-enthusiastic point of view about the government. Perhaps if a decision could be postponed until after the election, I might see matters in a different light. I'm truly grate-ful for your confidence in me and I'm sorry that I am turning it down.'

There was a long silence.

'Are you a communist?' he asked.

'No, sir, I'm not.'

'Then you must be a socialist?' He pounded the lectern as if he had made some startling discovery. 'But there are no socialists in Canada. Unless you mean that new-fangled party in Alberta.'

'I am the CCF representative in this country,' I said, rather abashed and uncertain of his reaction.

'Oh, they'll never get anywhere,' he said. He then dropped the subject and amicably talked to me about films and Churchill's war memoirs about which he had certain views about the Second Front which, fortunately, I agreed with. Half an hour later he indicated that the meeting was over and ushered me to the front door of the flat. 'About that other matter,' he said, not having mentioned it since he had assured me the CCF had a hopeless future in Canada, 'I'll get in touch with you after the general election.' He never did.

(ii) Bernard Shaw has fallen off an apple tree

Whenever a summons came from the Old Man – all who worked for him called him that but never within his ear-shot – everything had to be dropped to get to him as soon as possible. What impossible or difficult task would you be faced with? An article to write by tomorrow, a book to review that had not yet been published in Britain, a film to see which you had to guess whether he loathed or loved?

It was in late September, 1950, that I once again joined him in his living-room at Cherkley. We sat opposite each other on the long sofas that paralleled the fireplace.

'George Bernard Shaw has fallen off an apple tree and he has six weeks to live,' were his opening words as soon as I had sat down. 'I want you to write his obituary for the *Sunday Express*.'

This came as a surprise to me since I worked for the *Evening Standard*, not the *Sunday Express*, a paper with almost ten times the circulation of the *Standard*.

'I have spoken to Mr Gordon about it,' he said, seeing my puzzled expression. 'I told him I will be speaking to you about it and he has agreed with me that you would be the best man to do it for him.'

Having disposed of that matter of editorial protocol, he launched into a monologue so that I would be aware of the background of the job I had just been given.

'Before you write that obituary, I want to give you my views of Bernard Shaw. Shaw is a vastly overrated writer. I have lived much longer than you and I have seen reputations of writers as popular as Shaw sink with time. His name will fade away just like other overrated writers. Take John Galsworthy. Who puts on his plays and who reads his novels now? Arnold Bennett? Who reads Bennett now?' He did not pause long enough for an answer as he was not expecting one. 'Warwick Deeping? Who reads Deeping now? Thomas Hardy? Who reads Thomas Hardy now? The same thing will happen to Shaw. There will come a time when no one will read his works or put on his plays.'

At that moment his son, Max Aitken, entered the room. 'George Bernard Shaw has fallen off an apple tree,' he said, turning to his son, 'and he will be dead in six weeks. He has broken his hip. Shulman is going to write his obituary for the *Sunday Express*. I've been giving him my views of Bernard Shaw.'

'And what does he think of Shaw?' asked Max Aitken.

'I don't know,' replied Beaverbrook. 'He hasn't opened his mouth yet.'

I really didn't know what to say having disagreed with almost everything I'd heard. I had learnt long ago to never dissent from the Old Man in public. If you weren't prepared to follow Beaverbrook's line either procrastinate long enough in the hope that he would have forgotten about it or write what you thought and be prepared to take the consequences. I made a few innocuous comments and left. Shaw duly died on 2 November 1950, within the predicted time scale, and I wrote his obituary for the *Sunday Express*.

It occupied the entire leader page of that paper on 5 November 1950. The headline read 'How Shaw Would Have Loved It All!' Because John Gordon had been told I was being briefed by Beaverbrook, he naturally assumed the obituary I had written would have been along the guidance lines I had been given. Beaverbrook had gone to Bermuda and would only have seen the paper when it was too late to pull the obituary, had he desired to do so. It hardly accorded with his views that Shaw was a vastly overrated writer bound to dwindle in significance with the passage of time.

'George Bernard Shaw believed that the bereaved needed a little comic relief,' I began, and the following extracts indicate the overall tone of the piece.

> The reception of his own death would have tickled him hugely. He must have regretted his inability to be present.
>
> For would he not have found the tributes and obsequies fun?

Broadway dimmed her lights at midnight; Australian theatre audiences stood silent for two minutes; a Cabinet meeting in India was interrupted; H. G. Wells was summoned from the dead for a few words on the newsreels; and a first leader in *The Times* was accorded him when he might have considered a fourth leader more appropriate.

If there is any doubt about Shaw's relative position in the hierarchy of English language dramatists, one needs only to consider his opposition. Who stands next to Shakespeare? Congreve, Sheridan, Marlowe, Jonson, Ford, Wilde, Synge, Pinero, Barrie, O'Casey, Galsworthy, O'Neill? ...

One need never to have known him nor have seen him to feel the exhilarating impact of his personality upon his day. It exudes from every page of the memoirs, biographies and letters of those who came in contact with him or his work.

He made thinking a religion and pretence a heresy. He routed smugness by laughter, dissolved humbug in buffoonery, and destroyed false sentiment with irresistible logic. And he bequeathed us the technique and the inspiration in the word Shavian. It means the penetrating scepticism of Voltaire, the caustic satire of Swift and the irreverent, high-spirited wit of Bernard Shaw.

I normally received some acknowledgement through his editors when I wrote something in which Beaverbrook was interested, but over this obituary, there was only silence. I knew that I was the object of his displeasure because I was off his guest list – I was a frequent recipient of his hospitality at lunch or dinner – for at least six months. That, I believe, was my punishment for deviating from his instructions.

★ ★ ★

In the early 1950s I unwittingly consolidated my reputation as a controversial film critic who rarely enjoyed himself in the cinema. The *Standard* took some masochistic delight in running pro and con Shulman letters almost once a week. They tended to balance each other like a see-saw but most had some complaint to voice against me.

Fans of Jean Kent resented my view of her performance in *The Woman in Question*. 'Miss Kent makes a brave try at running the alphabetical gamut of emotions, but her range hovers relentlessly in the neighbourhood of high V – virgin to vixen. Properly lit, she displays the ethereal nobility of an advertisement for talcum powder.'

I didn't think I was particularly witty when, writing of Noel Coward in *The Astonished Heart* I wrote, 'Mr Coward tries so desperately to conceal his emotions that he has about him the harassed air of a woman who is afraid her slip is showing.' I realized, however, how deep even the slightest jibe can cut into an actor when, some ten years later, Coward reminded me at a cocktail party that I had used those exact words about him. Considering how much abuse and praise has been heaped upon this off-and-on genius over the decades, one would have thought a mild quip like mine would have been instantly dismissed and forgotten.

The urge to unburden oneself to a critic sometimes affects even the most seemingly confident and secure performers. I was certainly very surprised when I received a letter from Bing Crosby in 1950 about a notice about a not-very-significant film called *Mr Music* which had obviously been made to cater for his particular talent.

'The ideal American is a man who can make the most money doing nothing,' I began. 'This probably has much to do with the prolonged success of Harry Lillis Crosby, Jr., who, as Bing, has hardened into an institution. By appearing to be the most leisurely man in creation, he has acquired a cattle ranch, a race track, a gold mine, an orange juice factory, a baseball team and an income in the vicinity of one million dollars a year ... In a world tense with the after-effects of a depression, the threats of Hitler and Mussolini, and the prospect of an Armageddon, Bing Crosby was as relaxed as a slumbering oyster. To sing he barely parted his lips. To walk he hardly moved his feet. To joke he just twinkled an eye. To act he scarcely lifted an eyebrow ...' The film itself, I said, was as restful as a sleeping pill and 'if you keep awake you should enjoy it.'

This glib analysis of his on-screen presence provoked him into a reflective letter.

'Our publicity man at Paramount brought me a clipping from the *Evening Standard* containing your impressions of *Mr Music* and also containing some highly complimentary remarks about my poor efforts,' he wrote. 'I particularly appreciated your reference to the film being as restful as "a sleeping pill". In these parlous times, if one can provide entertainment suitable for rest and relaxation, even if it's sleeping, we certainly should be grateful.

'I hope the film has a good reception in England when it's released. My last three or four efforts haven't been too successful over there, or over here either, for that matter. I'm beginning to wonder if the public is getting wise to me, or weary of me, or if the stories have been susceptible to criticism or what. Possibly a combination of all these factors. After all, I have made forty-some pictures, I believe, and my talents are limited and it's pretty difficult to come up with anything original or new, when faced with me for a leading man. But we keep trying, and maybe we'll be able to develop another story such as *Going My Way* before they cast me aside entirely. There are some thoughts in your article that I am going to retain ...'

(iii) Why did you want to drop an atom bomb on Hollywood?
It was obvious from the personal letters I was receiving from important film moguls like Alexander Korda and Sam Goldwyn, from anti-critic articles in the film trade press such as the *Hollywood Reporter* and *Today's Cinema*, that leading figures in the industry were contemplating retaliatory action against what they considered a hostile atmosphere against the cinema in the British media. After all, they could justifiably reason, they were contributing millions of pounds through their advertisements and they were receiving in return a hail of brickbats against most of their product from an ungrateful press.

The first report of a major concerted effort to cow British papers into a more complimentary attitude to films appeared in the left-wing journal, *Tribune*, which was no doubt tipped off by Lord Beaverbrook who was a great admirer of its editor, Michael Foot, in later years to become leader of the Labour Party. 'Film Bosses Declare War On Fleet Street' ran the front-page headline reporting a war that had been raging in secret for four weeks, in which most of the American-controlled film companies and some British companies had withdrawn their display advertising from the *Sunday Express* and the London *Evening Standard*.

'Not until Logan Gourlay of the *Sunday Express* and Milton Shulman of the *Standard*, particularly Shulman, were tamed or fired would they put back their advertising estimated at being worth £250,000 a year. The American companies involved were MGM, Paramount, Columbia, 20th Century Fox and all members of the Motion Picture Producers' Association of America. By a strange coincidence, at the same time the J. Arthur Rank organization withdrew their advertising from the Beaverbrook papers claiming that it was not an anti-critic move but as an experiment they were severely cutting their advertising budget for British national papers and concentrating on the provincial press. Alexander Korda refused to join the conspiracy.'

Beaverbrook's opening act of retaliation was typical of him. The first targets were confined to the *Sunday Express* and the *Standard*. On 2 January 1953 the *Express* management blandly announced that in view of the boycott against his fellow critics, Leonard Mosley, the film critic of the *Daily Express*, which was still receiving advertisements, would find it embarrassing to continue to visit the boycotting companies' press shows and that the *Daily Express* would no longer carry their display advertising. Since the *Daily Express*, with a circulation of 4,000,000, was estimated to have about 12,000,000 readers, this blacking out of their access to the film-going public caused a certain amount of uneasiness amongst the American moguls.

Early in the war, I received a personal cable from Beaverbrook in Montego Bay in reply to a letter of mine explaining my position about this affair.

'Letter Received Stop The Boycott Is Not A Bad Thing Stop It Teaches The Newspapers To Meet And Deal With Difficulties Stop There Is Altogether Too Much Ease And Comfort Stop Trouble Makes For Efficiency Stop In No Circumstances Will The Newspapers Yield To Any Form Of Coercion ...' was how it read.

From then on, the issue was no longer a matter of revenue but one of freedom of the press. Under that banner Beaverbrook received the most supportive press – national and international – he had ever received in his career.

In the following days the clamour against the film companies became more angry and self-righteous. The important *Sunday Times* in a leader wrote, 'Conspiracy is an ugly word, but unless the account of this action published by our contemporaries, and not denied by the film companies, is quite false, it is a conspiracy to coerce the papers into giving favourable notices of American films ... Once advertisers begin to impose their interests on editorial policy and appointments, the freedom of the Press is prostituted, and the newspaper's comment becomes worthless to its readers. Critics, like the films and plays or books they criticise, may be good, bad or indifferent, but so long as they hold their posts, it is their duty to write what they think, and the newspapers' duty to protect them.'

Diogenes, a columnist in the political magazine, *Time and Tide*, brought my name into the debate.

'The *Evening Standard* runs as a regular feature, film criticism by Mr Milton Shulman,' he said. 'They are very good criticisms, as I think, the best that appear anywhere in the daily Press. They are, however, often very pungent and outspoken – he does not suffer bad films gladly. Judging by my own observation the pungency and the outspokenness are fully justified. The film industry turns out an immense number of thoroughly bad films which deserve all the criticism Mr Shulman gives them. In this criticism he is not the enemy of the industry; indeed the honest critic is the industry's best friend. It is the function of criticism to applaud the good and condemn the bad and, if condemnation is more frequent in Mr Shulman's column than is applause, that is because a good film is the exception and bad films unhappily abound.'

The row was taken up by the international press. The American news magazine, *Time*, led its Cinema section with the explosive words of an American film executive who told an *Express* official 'We're not going to spend another goddam penny until you change your critics.' It said that the chief target was the *Evening Standard*'s Milton Shulman who recently joshed the plot of *Affair in Trinidad* which contains some schemers fiddling with the V-2 rocket.

Time claimed that the boycott had already backfired since the companies were getting no more recruits for their action. They quoted Alexander Korda as dismissing it as 'Disgustingly silly'.

'Unruffled and unrepentant was the *Standard*'s critic Shulman. Said he last week: "I tell them, 'You confuse the whole conception of criticism. What you want is free publicity but three-quarters of the films are designed for adolescents. When you put in an ad for Esther Williams in a one-piece bathing suit, you do it just to tell people it's there and available. Nothing I say will deter those people who just want to see Esther Williams floating on her back. But if I say it's a good film too, a lot of people who wouldn't go otherwise, will go.'"'

The row bubbled over into the non-English language media with the large-circulation magazine, *Paris Match*, giving it two full pages under the headline, '*Le Grand Lord de la presse dit non dans son dictaphone aux millions de Hollywood*.' A long article in the Dutch newspaper *Vrij Nederland* was graced with a large smiling picture of myself under the heading '*Film Magnaten Contra Critici*'.

*Conversations with the stars. (Clockwise; Milton Shulman with
Kirk Douglas, Burt Lancaster and Gary Cooper.)*

There was by now no doubt who was coming off worse in this propaganda battle. Except for the toadying film trade publications, no one had a comforting word for the companies. Not only was it an opportunity for the European media to proclaim their dedication to the freedom of the press, but even more galling for the conspirators was the fact that financially it was in no way hurting *Express* profits. The papers at that time were so small that advertisers would come cap-in-hand to the papers' advertising departments, practically begging for space for their ads. The column inches hitherto taken up by film advertising were quickly filled up by a queue of retailers and manufacturers, eager to display their products to the vast readership of the *Express* Group.

Clandestine meetings were taking place between executives of both sides, eager to bring the unseemly war to an end. It was decided that this might be served if a meeting were held between the London representatives of the American companies and myself. They all sat around a large oval-shaped executive table as I was taken in to a conference room by Leslie Needham, the advertising chief of *Express* Newspapers. Needham was a florid, tall man who always wore a red carnation in his buttonhole and had the manners and sartorial elegance of an affluent country gentleman.

Almost a dozen heads turned in my direction as Needham introduced me and I took my place amongst them. 'Why did you want an atom bomb dropped on Hollywood?' was the first remark directed at me by the London representative of Columbia Pictures.

I was taken aback by the question.

'Me? Me want to drop an atomic bomb on Hollywood? Where did I say that?'

'In a review of one of our films,' I was told.

I didn't ask him what film because the proposition was so ridiculous.

'But why would I want to bomb Hollywood?' I asked. 'My mother lives in Hollywood.'

There was no reply.

Pressing home my advantage, I went on, 'My brother and his family live in Hollywood. Why would I seriously want to atomize my entire family because I didn't like one of your pictures? Surely if I said anything like that in one of my reviews, it could only have meant to be a joke.'

Nothing more was said about this accusation and I felt a suspicion of embarrassment amongst the others that the discourse had taken such an awkward turn.

It was only when I returned to my office and looked up some former reviews that I realized why I was being accused of wanting a nuclear holocaust to descend on the film capital. It was a film called *Affair in Trinidad* in which Rita Hayworth, in between dancing the rhumba, gets involved with international villains called Dr Hoebling, Wittol, Blonec and Ulaf who have developed a monster V-3 rocket with which, as was reported in *Time* magazine, I said they hoped to 'destroy most of the major centres in the United States and presumably, with any luck, Hollywood.' It was no doubt indicative of how fragile their case had become that this patently absurd jest was being flung at me to justify their increasingly hopeless boycott.

Meetings were taking place between Lord Beaverbrook and Spyros Skouros of 20th Century Fox to bring this unseemly dispute to an end so that the film companies would not have to lose too much face. During these rancorous weeks, I continued to review films to which I was invited, chiefly British, but eventually American as well. If any pressure was exerted upon me to modify my values, it certainly was not evident in the judgements I was still making. Of *Cosh Boy*, reviewed on 5 February 1953, I said, 'The fact that this picture is unrelieved by any distinction in direction, dialogue or story should not seriously affect its box-office potentialities.'

In those early years as a film critic, I was also expected to earn my keep by writing book reviews, doing interviews and contributing general features whenever Beaverbrook or the editor had something in mind. Herbert Gunn was replaced as the editor in 1950 (he was the first of the eight editors I served under for the *Evening Standard*) by an earnest, constantly anxious Yorkshireman called Percy Elland. While Elland was efficient at understanding the twists and turns of the Beaverbrook political line, he was out of his depth trying to cope with the sophisticated artistic topics like theatre, films and books that were fundamental to the appeal of the *Standard* as the most cultivated paper in the nation's capital. I often found him on the floor trying to decipher some garbled message that had been badly transcribed on the dictaphone machine. He would call me in for help, apparently presuming that my Canadian ear might be helpful at understanding the broad, Canadian vowel sounds of the barking Old Man.

Any book to do with the war was inevitably given to me to review and I was allowed plenty of space to express my views about all the five volumes of Churchill's *Memoirs,* Chester Wilmot's *Crusade in Europe,* the memoirs of American Mark Clark, head of the 5th Army in Italy, and many more...

★ ★ ★

Although I have contemplated adopting many careers in my life – soldier, lawyer, historian, biographer, crooner, critic, foreign correspondent, TV executive, editor, playwright, novelist, broadcaster – I never thought anyone would ask me to become a film actor.

But it was a telephone call in 1964 from David Deutsch, head of Anglo-Amalgamated Films, that set expectations jangling about a chance of seeing myself emoting on a cinema screen. He said he had a part in a film that he would like me to play and was I interested.

Taken aback, I spluttered about needing more details because as a threatre critic such a performance on my part could be extremely embarrassing. Could I have more information? We met in his office.

'I'll be quite frank with you,' said Deutsch, 'I have to start shooting this picture in Cornwall in a fortnight's time and I haven't been able to find anyone to fit this part. The picture is called *Catch Us If You Can* and will star the Dave Clark Five. This script has been written by Peter Nicholls, the playwright whose work you know, and will be directed by a new man, John Boorman.

'I would like you to play a big-time advertising executive. I've been telling people to look for someone like Milton Shulman. The big names like Robert Morley are either too busy or too expensive. Other actors we have tested haven't the authority. It suddenly occurred to me that I ought to ask you instead of trying to find someone like you. I'm sure I could straighten things out with Equity.'

I wasn't sure. It was a risky gamble. Trying to make up my mind, I asked facetiously, 'Do I get the girl, Barbara Ferris, in this role?'

'Yes,' he said, much to my surprise.

That settled it. I took the script home, was impressed with it, and I told Deutsch I would take the part. I had worked out that the four weeks on location demanded for the film could be done during my four weeks' annual holiday.

Next I met John Boorman, who was then basking in the light of good reviews of his film, *Where The Heart Is*. He surveyed me through oblonged fingers in an empty penthouse in Victoria which was going to be one of the London locations for *Catch Us If You Can*. He seemed resigned rather than over-enthusiastic about my involvement.

A few days later, just when I was beginning to have sinking feelings in my stomach and second thoughts about what I had let myself in for, Deutsch telephoned me.

'You know I told you when we first met that we had been talking to other actors about the role and that the ones we wanted were unavailable,' said Deutsch. 'Well, an actor we are very keen on, David de Keyser, had just told us that he *is* available. I'm sorry to have put you to so much trouble but would you mind stepping aside?'

'If you can get David de Keyser, you'd be a crass idiot to keep me,' I said. 'He would be perfect in the part. It's been a lovely experience. Goodbye.'

I hung up the receiver with one of the greatest waves of relief I had ever known. My ego had been driving me relentlessly on to what would probably have been a histrionic disaster. My daydreams of being a Marlon Brando or Spencer Tracy had come to an abrupt stop. But I had begun to realize when my ego stopped dominating me, that I was stupidly risking in this venture my authority and reputation as a critic. And there would have been few tears shed if the notices had been disparaging, by those who have been pained by my critical attentions over the years.

6

I'M NOT GOING TO TELL MARLENE
YOU'RE TOO TIRED!

*Kenneth Tynan and a case of mistaken identity... Becoming a theatre crit-
ic... The worst Hamlet ever... The Frog princess... PG Wodehouse keeps to
his period... Beaverbrook puts a policeman in his place... Meeting
Drusilla... Losing a Lowry... Some observations on women*

(i) Nights on the aisle seats

It was my relationship with Jackie that put me in touch with Kenneth
Tynan. She had given up nursing to study acting and when she was
moderately qualified wrote to a number of provincial repertory companies for work. To her surprise the new young director of a company at
Litchfield wrote her a long letter setting out his requirements for anyone joining his company, took her out to lunch where (as he did with
most women then) he hinted he would like to marry her, and then
hired her. He had only just come down from Oxford where his tall,
ethereal-like figure with its pallid, almost skeletal face and long, jumpy
fingers had etched itself on the undergraduates of his generation as one
of the university's legendary personalities. His witty writings in college
magazines, his participation in Oxford theatricals, his talked-about parties had become known to me through gossip from Jackie.

Because I had already been established as a talked-about film critic
(Ken was a passionate celebrity catcher) and because of my closeness to
Jackie, he had invited me to some of his Bohemian parties in a top-floor
flat in Hyde Park Gardens in Bayswater. In his long string ties and fake
leopard-skin trousers, his conversation, in spite of an obvious stutter,
dominated the chatter as it leapt from theatrical heroism to Marxism to
Wilhelm Reich.

He had published his book in defence of grand characters on the stage, *He Who Plays The King*, which was a remarkable *tour de force* for one so young. As someone labouring in a similar field, I was vastly impressed by his descriptive ability which could preserve a performance with the accuracy of a camera and the wit of a cartoon. It was precisely this mercurial genius, his ability to pass on to posterity the detail and excitement of great or disastrous acting, that guarantees that his name will rank with those of Hazlitt, Shaw, George Jean Nathan and Agate as amongst the most enduring of this minor art form. His judgement as displayed in his passionate advocacy of Bertolt Brecht, Hochhuth's *Soldiers* and the semi-pornographic musical, *Oh! Calcutta!*, is likely to be treated with increasing disdain with the passage of time.

It was Jackie, I think, who gave me a copy of an undergraduate magazine called *Panorama* which contained a coruscating assessment of Fleet Street critics under the obvious pseudonym of John Knox. I recognized it immediately as having the stylish, wicked wit of the young Kenneth Peacock Tynan. The article was a sardonic knifing of all of Fleet Street's working theatre critics but was particularly derisive about the 'merciless volubility' of Beverley Baxter of the *Evening Standard*. I thought our feature editor, Charles Curran, would be amused by the piece and gave it to him with the words, 'If you are looking for a really bright young man to write for us, read this attack on the critics, especially what he says about Baxter. John Knox is a pseudonym for Kenneth Tynan.'

Inevitably, and I should have expected it, Curran showed the article to Baxter, told him that it was by Tynan, and Baxter was not amused. About a year later, Baxter was presented with a golden opportunity to get his own back on the young man who had so ridiculed his critical reputation. In casting his production of *Hamlet* in 1951, Alec Guinness made the eccentric decision to offer the part of the Player King to Tynan. Because Ken had to suppress and discipline a severe stutter to deliver his lines, he sounded weirdly like a mechanical robot speaking through a hole in a barrel.

Baxter's review with the headline 'The worst Hamlet I have ever seen' paid particular attention to the small part of the Player King. 'I am a man of a kindly nature,' he wrote, 'who takes no joy in hurting those who are without defence, but Mr Ken Tynan would not get a chance in a village hall unless he was related to the vicar. His performance was quite dreadful.'

Tynan with characteristic bravado, defended himself in a letter claiming his performance was not 'quite dreadful' but 'only slightly less than mediocre'. The feature editor, being an admirer of some theatre pieces Tynan had written, asked him to produce profiles of Danny Kaye and Vivien Leigh which delighted Beaverbrook, and it was clear that an obvious successor to Baxter was now waiting in the wings.

There were rumours that Beaverbrook was displeased with Baxter's record as a critic since he often had to miss first nights because, as a Conservative MP, he had to obey any three-line whip that his Party might call. There was a deeper, more personal reason why Baxter's days as a critic were numbered. Although Baxter, when he was editor of the *Daily Express*, had once been a close friend of Beaverbrook's, the relationship had cooled and reached a decidedly frigid point when Baxter unwisely hosted a joint party for his daughter with Vivien Leigh's daughter, on the very same night as Beaverbrook gave a birthday party at Claridge's for his granddaughter, Jean Campbell.

The guest list for both affairs overlapped, with many special guests declining Beaverbrook's invitation so that they could attend a more glamorous occasion where they could be in the company of Vivien Leigh and Laurence Olivier. Baxter was not forgiven for such a brazen lapse of judgement and, when the opportunity came to replace him with Tynan, Beaverbrook was ruthlessly quick to seize it.

Tynan's criticisms were flamboyant, controversial and compulsively readable. The theatre world viewed this fiery verbal geyser with admiration and apprehension, but his growing reputation did not deter readers of the *Standard* from reminding him of his disastrous performance as a Shakespearean actor.

Whenever he was dismissive of some performance, letters would be printed in the paper asking how 'the worst Player King in history' had the audacity to criticize other actors doing Shakespeare. Tynan, who imagined conspiracies everywhere, suspected that some of these letters were written in the office. Tynan had now been the *Standard*'s critic for thirty months and was earning £35 a week plus £10 expenses.

'In mid-July Ken could take no more,' wrote Kathleen Tynan in her magnificent biography of her husband, 'and wrote to the paper threatening to sue them for libel if they published a proposed page of letters headlined "Should Actors Be Critics?" Explaining this curious outburst of sensitivity, Ken said, "Since I'd made only one appearance as a professional actor in my life, I resented being cast as the punching-bag in this debate."'

Critical shooting star Kenneth Tynan.

It was at this stage in the crisis that I was called to Arlington House. Beaverbrook opened up our conversation by telling me that Tynan had threatened to sue the paper for libel if they printed any more letters questioning his fitness to be a critic.

'What are you going to do about it?' I asked.

'I've fired him. Can't have a fellow threatening to sue his own paper for libel.'

'What has he done about that?' I said.

'Oh, he's apologized.' He waved Ken's letter in front of him. 'He wants his job back.'

'Are you going to give it to him?'

'Naw. His wife has also written a letter saying he'd done a foolish thing and asking for his job back.' He waved a second letter in front of him.

'Has *she* changed your mind?' I asked.

'Naw.' He stood up and walked to his podium. 'I want you to take over as the *Standard*'s theatre critic.'

I knew there was no question of being allowed to refuse the job. Again the wayward fingers of Fate had clutched my destiny. I suspected that my travails with the film industry may have had something to do with his decision to switch me over to theatre criticism. From my standpoint, the theatre was a more prestigious and respected area of criticism than films, and although I was uncomfortable about the circumstances that had created it, I was happy about the prospects of this fresh vista of journalism.

Several years later, when Tynan's work on the *Observer* had established him as the foremost critic in the land, I reminded him that he owed his first job as a professional critic to me because I had told the *Standard*'s feature editor that he was the pseudonymous author of that *Panorama* attack on the critics.

Tynan gave me a severe, puzzled look. 'But I never wrote that article,' he said. 'It was written by Gavin Lambert. I had nothing to do with it.'

Lambert had been a contemporary of Ken's at Oxford, a well-known film critic and eventually a scriptwriter in Hollywood. According to Kathleen Tynan, Lambert knew all along about this false attribution but, for his own reasons, decided to keep mum about his authorship.

Thus another Big Accident had rolled a huge boulder in the path of my career and forced it to take a detour not of my making.

Tynan went on to great fame as a theatre critic. I went on to be the

Standard's critic for many decades. How would Fate have treated both of us if I had only kept my mouth shut?

★ ★ ★

Switching to theatre criticism from film was not nearly as traumatic or forbidding as my first days as a cinema critic had been. By now I had acquired the technique of writing 500 to 800 words about an imaginative artistic endeavour for a popular British newspaper. What was definitely not wanted in such a small space, and for such a non-involved readership, was a philosophical or historical or profound attempt to assess the cultural merits of the work.

The plot had to be set out in as concise a manner as possible. Even *Hamlet* had to be summarized in about six lines. Then followed the overall impact of the quality of the dialogue, the imaginative nature of the action, a comparative assessment of other similar plays written in the past or the present, the originality of the production and the director's contribution to that effect and, finally, the ability of the cast, particularly its main actors or actresses, to grip the mind or heart of an audience and hold it. A big menu which could rarely be met because space and time prevented it. Above all, more important than being right or wrong, it had to be readable.

Because of my notoriety as a film critic, the feature editor would ask me to fill in for Beverley Baxter whenever he was on holiday or his duties as an MP made him miss a first night. Even as a substitute critic I was embroiled in rows, particularly over my lack of enthusiasm for the British musical. Why could they not match the vitality, tunefulness and high spirits of such American musicals as *Oklahoma!*, *Annie Get Your Gun* and *Brigadoon*? The problem seemed to me to be 'authors who wrote an inane book aggravated by painful lyrics, composers who concoct tuneless rhythms and producers who stage spiritless and hackneyed routines.'

I took on an even more sacrosanct idol a few weeks later with my review of Ivor Novello's *King's Rhapsody*. 'Critics are realists,' I wrote, 'and most of them have given up the unrewarding experience of stubbing their pens tilting at sugar-cake windmills and firing at the loopholes in the Ivor tower. To complain that *King's Rhapsody* drips with cloying sentiment, that its situations are contrived and ludicrous, and that it is practically empty of wit, would only unnecessarily raise one's blood pressure and make one vulnerable to early stomach ulcers.' The abuse that was showered upon me over Ivor Novello converted the *Standard* letters pages into ribbons of hate.

For the next four years, because Baxter's ability to attend first nights was somewhat erratic, I had numerous opportunities, while still functioning as a film critic, to acquire some knowledge and to test my judgement about the theatre. Before coming to England I can recall having seen only one professional performance of a play in my life. It was *Winterset* by Maxwell Anderson, which was set in the basement of a New York tenement and had a large steam-pipe crossing low on the stage. Where I was sitting in the loftiest and cheapest seats of the top gallery of the Royal Alexander Theatre in Toronto, most of the cast were decapitated unless they were almost on the footlights. It was an experience that put me off the theatre for years.

As I had done about films, I undertook a self-education course about the theatre. Whatever collected works there were on theatre criticism I bought in second-hand bookshops or borrowed from a library. Shaw, Hazlitt, Beerbohm, George Jean Nathan, Agate, Stanislavski and others were pored over for style. The great playwrights, of course, I read from Sophocles to Oscar Wilde. I read most of Shakespeare although I never got around to looking at *Pericles* or *Henry VIII*, until in later years I had to review them. During this period as a second-string critic I said my bit about plays by Ben Jonson, Pinero, Chekhov, Ibsen, Bridie, Anouilh, Molière and two productions of *Hamlet*. I conscientiously did my home-work about the classics I was sent to see, not only by reading them before the curtain went up but also by finding out what other authorities had said about them.

Inevitably I managed to get myself involved in controversy, especially over my reaction to Christmas pantomimes, a theatrical treat as unknown to me as Japanese Noh plays.

'Until this Christmas I had never been to a pantomime,' I confessed on 29 December 1950. 'I have now seen three – *Babes in the Wood*, *Mother Goose* and *Goody Two Shoes*. I am baffled.

'Measuring my words carefully and taking into account the appropriate restraint demanded by the Christmas season, I would say that on this year's evidence, this form of entertainment is unsuitable for children, boring for adults and an excellent argument for the anti-traditionalist.

'The children, I imagine, suffer most. Not only are their little minds baffled by a confusion of the sexes and incidents that shift inexplicably from the Highlands to Gooseland, but they are wearied by three hours of questions from accompanying adults anxious to find out if they are enjoying it. They are, of course, too polite to say no.'

More virulent fodder for the *Standard* letter pages was provided by me in my notice of Judy Garland's appearance at the Palladium in May 1951. Not being an assiduous reader of showbiz gossip columns, I did not realize that she was tackling a drink problem at the time, which accounted for her swelling figure and the diminished quality of her voice. I hope that if I had known, I would have been more sympathetically understanding.

For the past two weeks the Palladium has witnessed everything but a ticker-tape reception for the nightly appearance of a buxom young lass named Judy Garland. I doubt if Sarah Bernhardt, Jenny Lind or Vesta Tilley would ever have asked for more from their admirers. Yet it is difficult to analyze the objective basis upon which all this adulation is founded. If any other young lady were doing exactly what Miss Garland does she would be sited somewhere between the seals and the acrobats on the Palladium agenda ...

But perhaps it is unfair to look for exceptional talent in this kind of entertainment. Gratitude for past pleasures is probably the real explanation. We were therefore determined to love her – fat or thin. Next to animals, sailors and roses the British probably love troupers best. At least they command our steadfast loyalty. But we must not mistake affection for art. To expend our enthusiasm on mediocrity leaves us nothing left for real genius. Surely we can be polite without being sycophantic or hysterical ...

* * *

Although I was kept busy doing book reviews and interviews in addition to my film criticism, which was really only a three-day full-time occupation, I decided to try my hand at writing a play. Every critic is aware of the cliché jibe that those who can do and those who can't criticise. I thought the idea of placing a man like Beaverbrook in a situation where his resources would not depend only on his minions but solely on himself, might provide an interesting psychological drama.

Together with a close friend, Stephen Watts, who had been reviewing plays for the *Sunday Express*, we invented Lord Drumdhu, a newspaper tycoon, who owned a large remote stately home in Scotland where, one week-end, he had invited six guests to stay. They were a senior civil servant, a top investigative journalist from a rival paper, a woman novelist, a film producer, a junior girl reporter and his leader writer. On this particular week-end a violent storm and a fog cut off this section of the Scottish Highlands from the outside world for forty-eight hours.

A renegade journalist, once employed by Drumdhu, turns up out of the fog with a story he believes Drumdhu will buy for a large sum of money. He claims to have Hitler with him and the Führer is prepared to explain what happened to him in the two years since the war ended. Drumdhu meets Hitler (off stage), is impressed by his *bona fides* but has to check with the people he has with him (without letting them know it's Hitler he's talking about) whether he is the subject of a clever hoax or whether he has the newspaper story of the century.

The plot, of course, could be dismissed as preposterous nonsense, but Stephen and I had supplemented it with so much supportive evidence that the great man had to at least have it tested and it was the methods he used that constituted the essence of the play. The dialogue was amusing and cynical and everyone who subsequently read it testified to the verisimilitude of Drumdhu's personality.

I liked the opening, which had Drumdhu's favourite journalist addressing the audience. 'My name is Madden, William Madden. You don't know me. My profession is anonymity. Technically, I suppose, I rank somewhere between a backroom boy and an *eminence grise*. I provide opinions. That's not strictly true. I provide reasons for opinions. Tell me what you're thinking and I'll tell you why. In my job I am by turns a counsellor, a patriot, an elder statesman, a defender of the faith, a judge, a jury, a protector of human rights, a psychiatrist, a bulwark of liberalism (with a small L), a soothsayer, a hairshirt, a philosopher, a friend, a father and, naturally, a common man. In other words, I am a leader writer. I apologize for the anti-climax ...'

We called it *Man of Decision* and because we were both critics we decided to submit it, through an agent, to managements under the pseudonym of Anthony Frost. We were only too aware of the humiliating consequences that would descend on us if it were produced and our colleagues found it a pathetic or laughable exercise. I personally had serious doubts about our third act, and would only have allowed it to go any further if a major amount of re-writing were exercised on the play's climax.

One of the most knowledgeable agents in theatre production was enthusiastic about its prospects. Of course, it was far too long and some revision was necessary, but he didn't think the defects were insurmountable. To his surprise, the managements he sent it to didn't agree with him.

As far as I was concerned that was the end of it. Since I agreed with the reservations that had been expressed, I thought there was no point trying to put fresh make-up on a hollow portrait. It has languished in my files ever since, and from time to time I glance through it and wonder what can be done with all that sparkling dialogue. But I suspect that it is only my ego that keeps me looking at it so fondly after forty-five years. I did eventually get a play of mine produced, but it was in the early days of BBC2, some ten years later, and was seen by only a few dedicated TV critics. But more of that later.

* * *

When I took over on 11 September 1953, from Kenneth Tynan, *Standard* readers were told I was shifting 'my critical perspective from Wardour Street to Shaftesbury Avenue. The lively and unconventional approach which has won him fame as a film critic will now be directed towards the London stage.' The transition, as far as working practices were concerned, was not too difficult, because both Baxter and Tynan had never had to write overnight notices, which became my lot almost a year later in June 1954. My weekly column would usually consist of an assessment of the two or three first nights I had attended that week, and there was plenty of time for reflection and considered words.

Because Lord Beaverbrook was inordinately lavish in his praise if he liked something, his editors, too, were bountiful in the memos in which you were congratulated. It was a practice that all *Express* and *Standard* editors employed and one which has now apparently gone out of fashion. Although the first five editors I worked with continued rewarding their writers with compliments, the last three I dealt with on the *Standard* – stretching over some seven years – never thought anything I wrote worthy of an extraordinary pat on the back.

From a management standpoint, I always felt the old technique could be more rewarding for them. In the first place, it massaged the ego and enhanced loyalty in a profession where doubt about one's standing was an occupational disease. As far as I was concerned, an extravagant compliment always deterred me from asking for a rise, because it might appear I was taking advantage of my boss's good will. Praise, therefore, deterred much sought-after journalists from accepting tempting offers from rival papers – and cost nothing. It is a custom contemporary editors might think of restoring.

My job as a critic was made much more difficult late in May 1954 when my weekly theatre column was replaced by overnight notices. This meant that instead of at least a day or two of reflection for one's column at the end of the week, a deadline of 7 a.m. had to be met after every play. The morning dailies that had to telephone their notices to the paper's copy takers before 11 p.m. would rarely have more than an hour to collect their thoughts, find a telephone kiosk and breathlessly communicate what they had to say. It was usually a triumph of energy over content.

The task of making sense of difficult, unfamiliar plays like *Waiting for Godot* or *The Birthday Party* often resulted in judgements that were either non-committal or bizarre. No critic whose work is respected by posterity ever seriously, or for many years, wrote overnight notices. When Kenneth Tynan tried it after leaving the *Standard*, he failed miserably at the *Daily Sketch*. The fame he subsequently acquired was because of his column on the weekly *Observer*. Hobson, Shaw, Agate, Beerbohm, Hazlitt never had to organize their thoughts in a heart-straining race against the clock. There are no collected works – except a few selected pieces by Philip Hope-Wallace of the *Guardian* in a book edited by his sister – by any critic who devoted his career to overnight notices. Jack Tinker of the *Daily Mail* was the last national critic to regularly maintain the tradition. Few editors still demanded them when he died in 1996 and, I suspect, like productions in New York or Paris, previews before the first night will become the basis of most dramatic criticisms in national dailies.

On the *Standard*, because it was theoretically an afternoon paper, I could have a civilized meal before starting to write my review at about midnight, be in bed about 1.30 a.m. and on the telephone dictating my copy five hours later. It was primarily the sleep factor that I had to tussle with in almost forty years of theatre criticism. The minor miracle was that I managed it while, during the same years, I wrote a political and social column for the *Standard* and *Daily Express*, film reviews for the

Sunday Express and *Vogue* magazine, produced television programmes for Granada and Associated Rediffusion, was a member of a BBC radio chat show for fifteen years, was book critic of the *Sunday Express*, wrote two novels, three children's books and two serious books on TV, and when I had nothing much to do managed a ninety-minute play for BBC2 and provided book reviews, interviews, profiles and short stories for other publications. I suppose the secret of so much industry was that I never needed a lot of sleep.

Although I had made it a rule never to review amateur stage productions, since whatever criteria you used – too lenient or too harsh – would depend upon unfair or arbitrary values, it was an amateur show that inspired one of my earliest overnight notices. This was an adaptation of Edgar Wallace's thriller novel, *The Frog*, put on for charity at the Scala Theatre by a group of Princess Margaret's friends. Billy Wallace, Mrs Gerald Legge (later to become the stepmother of Diana, Princess of Wales) and the American socialite, Miss Elsa Maxwell, had the leading roles. Gossip columns had spoken of Princess Margaret herself being present at rehearsals and being part of the production team. The Queen, Prince Philip and the Queen Mother were in the audience. No editor could resist such a tempting morsel of royal news, and I was sent to cover it as if it were a routine first night in the West End.

'Amateur dramatics have added a fresh burden to charity,' I wrote. 'Contributions to funds for orphans, invalids or sailors are no longer enough. Your friends expect you to watch them act as well ... *The Frog* is hardly a happy choice for amateurs. While Shakespeare and Shaw can usually be relied upon to cover up weak acting, this kind of thick-eared thriller is more likely to show it up ...

'On the whole, this largely unknown cast is best in the noisy bits. When emerging from explosions, firing pistols, shouting denunciations or ordering double whiskies, they achieved a remarkably high standard of verisimilitude. But the subtler passions like romance, completely eluded them. When Mr Wallace says, "What are you doing in my bed at six in the evening?" and Mrs Legge replies "Well, I don't quite know," we had no difficulty at all in believing her ...'

Inevitably, even if only by proxy, the Royal Family felt the backlash of the ridicule heaped on this silly production. This time I was singled out as being kinder than most of my colleagues. 'This is the first unsporting thing I have met in Britain,' said Elsa Maxwell, rounding on us in an interview the next day. 'The critics have hit below the belt. These babes-in-the-wood are doing the job for charity and shouldn't be criticised at all.' Asked how she felt about my description of her looking like 'a small stranded whale', she replied, 'That's pure heaven. I love other people poking fun at me almost as much as I love laughing at myself.'

★ ★ ★

When Marlene Dietrich came to the Café de Paris in June 1954, she was already in her mid-fifties. She had been in dozens of films with her chiselled beautiful face, her unforgettable legs and her sultry German accent having made her almost as memorable as Garbo in films like *The Blue Angel* and *Destry Rides Again*. With her latest films casting her more and more in bit parts, she had converted herself into one of the most popular one-woman shows on the cabaret and variety house circuit. She was one of a small number of star personalities – Frank Sinatra, Eartha Kitt, Noel Coward, Judy Garland, Ella Fitzgerald, Tony Bennett were others – whose names could guarantee full houses at any nightclub or hotel restaurant from Las Vegas to Melbourne lucky enough to book them. We critics were given a meal while we waited for Marlene's late night entrance. The food was satisfactory but the wine that night at the Café de Paris should have been more apologetic. When I called the waiter over and complained that my bottle seemed to be corked, he just shrugged his shoulders and said, 'No, sir. It's not corked. It's just the wine.'

'Marlene Dietrich is as susceptible to criticism as Niagara Falls or the Leaning Tower of Pisa,' I wrote in my next day's notice which, because of the lateness of her act took me to almost four in the morning to finish. 'The wonder is that she exists at all. For she has conquered where so many of her sex have failed. She has managed to convert the ravages of Time into handsome compliments.

'At the Café de Paris last night she was still every man's version of what every woman but his own should be. She was beautiful, overpowering and unapproachable. This lady was definitely not for yearning.

'Leaders of café society – most of whose pedigrees go back no farther than their cheque stubs – had gathered to do her homage. And the full glory of the occasion did not strike us until it was realized that Mr Noel Coward himself had written, and was actually there to speak, a poem to usher her in. As a one-night Poet Laureate, Mr Coward was a sibilant success.

'Then slithering down the famous stairs like a glazier glinting in the sunlight came a fantasy in white furs and rhinestones that politely kissed Mr Coward, wrapped itself round the microphone and turned out to be Miss Dietrich. She was wearing a dress that can only be described as a masterpiece of illusion. It was transparent enough to make you think you were seeing everything and opaque enough to make you realize you were seeing nothing. Houdini must have designed it.

'She surveyed us, hands on hips, with something between cosy disdain and amiable tolerance, and plunged into her act with the resolution of a housewife tackling a formidable pile of dishes. She sang about a dozen songs and no Dietrich fan could have complained about the selection. She asked what the boys in the back room would have; she fell in love again and never wanted to; and she protested that she was not the marrying kind. They were the words she had sung in films like *The Blue Angel* and *Destry Rides Again*.

'The voice had its familiar, loveable, limited range, never straying from its narrow vocal path between melody and laryngitis. The perfect features, as smooth as something carved out of velvet and butter, conveyed the emotion of her songs as impersonally as smoke signals. Each number was followed by the swirl of the white fox cape, a drink of white liquid which should have at least been vodka but which I am sure was only water, and then a delighted survey of us all which seemed to say "Oh, you lucky, lucky people!"

'Two songs she sang in German and a third, which she told us she had sung everywhere from Alaska to Czecho-Slovakia, turned out to be that favourite of the Afrika Corps, "Lili Marlene". Rommel could have had no complaint about the enthusiasm with which she sang it. Some of the rest of us were less keen.

'Yet, though here was the Dietrich we had expected, something warm and intimate was missing. It was as if Sex had been replaced by Authority. So completely did she dominate us that I felt if she had shouted "Achtung!" we would all have leaped to attention.

'When she told us she was going to sing her last number, we knew that no matter how hard we applauded, there would be no more. And there was none. Discipline is discipline.

*Marlene on stage; with a voice ranging between melody and laryngytis it
was as if sex had been replaced by authority*

'Perhaps beautiful dreams are best left unrealized. It is sad enough when they harden into reality. But it is even sadder when they become an institution or, worse still, a spectacle. Before it is too late I must hurry off to see once more *Destry Rides Again* or *The Blue Angel*. And renew my faith in that beautiful *woman,* Marlene Dietrich.'

Reading it the next day through very tired eyes, I thought it was perhaps too rough. Maybe I ought to have left out all those oblique hints at her Teutonic origins and that her personality reiterated the defence of every German war criminal when he insisted that he was only obeying orders.

I was coming out of the Watergate theatre the next night, having just seen a moderately entertaining revue called *Reprise*, when I was approached by a dapper little man who introduced himself as Major Willing. I think he was wearing a monocle but if he wasn't he was dressed like the kind of man who ought to have worn one. Because the Watergate was a tiny fringe theatre behind Charing Cross station, I was planning to take a taxi to the *Standard*, not far away in Fleet Street, where I would dash off about 400 words and then go to Elizabeth's Bistro in Chelsea for some scrambled eggs, coffee and noisy conversation.

'Marlene would like to see you in her dressing room at the Café de Paris after her performance tonight,' he said, informing me that he was the Café's press and publicity man.

'What does she want to see me about?' I replied rather suspiciously. 'I suppose she wants to complain to me personally about my notice.'

'No, not at all,' said Willing. 'She loved it. She wants to have dinner with you at the Café when her act is over. She just wants to meet you, that's all. She was intrigued about it.'

Ever since the day Lord Beaverbrook had warned me that as a critic I would be bribed by liquor, money and women for complimentary reviews, I had been waiting to have my integrity tested. So far all I had ever received from the entertainment industry was a dry martini with a sad olive in it. Normally I would have considered an invitation to have a tête à tête dinner after midnight with one of the world's most glamorous women the fulfilment of the welcome warning Beaverbrook had made to me. But because of the overnight notice I had written on Marlene, which had left me with only three hours' sleep, and because of the need for another notice immediately after the Watergate revue, I knew that I would only be presenting a limp, exhausted critic to the glamorous Marlene.

'I'm very honoured by Miss Dietrich's invitation,' I said to Willing, 'but I have had little sleep after her show last night and I'm sorry. Will you thank her and tell her I am too tired to accept it.'

Willing reeled back as if I had struck him between the eyes.

'Too tired to have dinner with Marlene?' he said. 'I can't tell her that. You'll have to tell her yourself. You can't expect me to tell Marlene you're too tired.' He kept shaking his head at the very thought of such a bizarre proposition. 'It's as much as my job is worth.'

I explained to him again that I still had another notice to write before I could meet her, but if he wanted me to tell her that myself, I was ready to do so and offer my apologies.

He took me by the elbow and hustled me into a nearby telephone kiosk. Having dialled her number, he told her I was on the other end of the line and waved me in to talk to her. I grovelled with regrets about my inability to see her because my first night commitments had exhausted me. She was very understanding, discreetly complimenting me on my writing style but saying nothing about my opinions. She was staying at the Dorchester Hotel and was there some other time we could meet, like lunch the next day? I leapt at this second invitation.

At noon the following day, clutching three dozen long-stemmed roses, I went to the Oliver Messel penthouse suite in which she was staying and where a delicious meal had been organized. In the unkind glare of day, and without the help of stage make-up and lighting, tell-tale signs of her age were already emerging in that seemingly timeless face. Our conversation can not be reported as anything but polite, routine and domestic.

Knowing I was Canadian she told me how much she had been impressed by Dr Banting's discovery of insulin for the treatment of diabetes. The main course of our lunch was occupied with her experiences with the impact of penicillin in poverty-stricken hospitals she had visited and her admiration for Sir Alexander Fleming who had developed it. During dessert, her talk become more domestic, with loving tales about her granddaughter and accounts of her experiments with cooking.

What I wanted to ask her about – her early films, her many love affairs, her difficult position as a German film star in America – we never got round to, because I was so impressed with just watching her that I did not want to risk anything uncomfortable arising. It was all smiles and pleasant remarks as I left two hours later. Not a word that I can recall was said about my review, newspapers or her performance. I never met her in person again.

★ ★ ★

It was Harold Keeble's suggestion that I become the book critic of the *Sunday Express*. The furore over the film boycott had died down with the companies sheepishly returning to the *Standard*, but not enthusiastically to the *Daily* and *Sunday Express*. I suspect that during the boycott they discovered that audiences, without being urged by these mass circulation papers to see their product, had not substantially dwindled. With circulations in the millions, their rates were very high and it was probably decided that regular film ads in these papers were economically unnecessary. I was still being allowed to write what I liked for the *Standard*, and with book reviews, interviews and radio programmes I still had enough time on my hands to plan the future production of books and plays.

Harold Keeble was the feature editor of the *Daily Express* when he read my article about Canadians and British publications and bought it in 1946 without ever printing it. In 1953 he was editor of the *Sunday Express*, with a reputation for having so many ideas and such a quicksilver mind that articles he printed in the first edition were often thrown out in the following editions because something fresher had just come in. Fresher, not necessarily better.

The *Sunday Express* had never had a regular book column and when Keeble put the idea up to me at a lunch I told him that, with my film review requiring three and a half days a week, I could not do a conventional coverage of three or four books a week. At the most, I could handle one book a week and I suggested we call the piece A Book To Talk About. Under that title topicality would not be imperative, and I could use a chosen book to write a personality piece about the author and the relevance of his other work. It didn't occur to me at the time that, in the event, I would have to absorb three or four other books during that week.

I suspected that the whole idea was Beaverbrook's. Although I never had that suspicion confirmed, the manner in which he displayed an interest in the column and his suggestions for books I was to review, indicated to me that this was part of a long-term strategy designed to get me out of film reviewing and into something which might serve his interests better. He was, after all, an author of two very successful books, *Politics and the War* and *Men and Power*, as well as some less auspicious ones, and his involvement with films was always an amusing, but mischievous, concern.

Having decided that his views about the conduct of the war were roughly in line with my own, there was no book written by a major military or political figure about those years that wasn't sent to me, either to review or comment upon.

Occasionally I would be invited to lunch at Arlington House which, as ever, I faced with a degree of apprehension because I suspected some extra work would be involved. After one of these lunches, he asked his butler to bring in the Harry Hopkins papers. These turned out to be a biography written by the American playwright, Robert Sherwood, about the life and war-time career of Harry Hopkins who had been one of Roosevelt's Cabinet members and a special envoy to Russia and Britain about such matters as Lend-Lease and the Second Front. Beaverbrook, as Minister for Aircraft Production, had been deeply involved in these meetings and negotiations.

In front of me on the dining-room table were placed four bound volumes of foolscap. The manuscript in that form was over 1,200 pages and stood about two feet high.

'The Harry Hopkins papers have been sent to the *Sunday Express* by the publisher for serialization,' Beaverbrook said to me. 'I'm sure they are very interesting. Sherwood is a great writer. He writes Roosevelt's speeches, you know. I would like you to read the book and tell me whether you think we should buy them. I've not yet had time to read them myself. Could you give me your opinion by tomorrow afternoon.'

Beaverbrook could see the look of consternation on my face.

'I don't want a long, detailed summary of what's in it. Just a brief note from you – yes or no – about whether you think it would interest the *Express* readers.'

He pushed the pile of papers towards me and I stood up, finding it difficult to lift them under my arm.

'Now there is no index in this manuscript,' he said, as if by way of an afterthought, 'so when you are reading it will you put a slip of paper at every page where you see my name. That would be of great help to me. Goodbye.'

I staggered out into Piccadilly, realizing that my opinion about the Hopkins Papers was of minimal interest to the Old Man. He was a personal friend of Sherwood and had already agreed to buy them. What he wanted to see was how the author had treated him in the book and he couldn't wait until the printed volume which would, of course, have an index.

I was up until four in the morning skimming through the pages, inserting a slip wherever I saw Beaverbrook's name, and made no serious effort to read what was in it. I returned it the next day with a short ten-line note waxing enthusiastic about the book and agreeing that it would be a major coup for the *Sunday Express* if they could buy it. I heard nothing more about my recommendation, but several months later it was duly serialized as Beaverbrook had always intended.

The projection of the Book column on 29 March 1953 was a typical Keeble topographical extravaganza. An entire page was devoted to *Picture* by Lillian Ross, in which the bizarre and comic antics of making a film like *The Red Badge of Courage* are recorded by the ubiquitous Miss Ross in what I claimed was 'the most devastating account of the inanities and frustrations of that place called Hollywood'. There was a huge photograph of me, chin cupped into my right hand trying to look profound, with a short biography announcing me as 'the most discussed newspaper man of the day'. From then on the column was displayed erratically, usually generously, moving with time further back in the paper and lower down on the page.

But controversy seemed to be my lot in almost any area of criticism that embraced me. My third column dealt with five books about Jeeves and Bertie Wooster which Penguin were re-issuing in a commemorative edition to mark the thirty years since P. G. Wodehouse revealed this remarkable pair, oozing and shimmering in and out of the stateliest homes in the land.

I was truly astonished and I admit, rather elated, that these casual comments should have provoked a letter from the comic genius himself, P. G. Wodehouse. It was dated 30 April 1953 and came from New York.

'I was very pleased and flattered that a critic of your eminence should have given me so much space all to myself,' he said. 'Your article has decided me to go back to the old "period piece" stuff and not try to keep up with the times. I don't know if you saw my last one – *Pigs Have Wings* – but it was overflowing with butlers and footmen and completely

Edwardian, and it has sold about 25,000 so far, so apparently my Public doesn't mind me being out of date. I propose from now on to fight it out along those lines. No good leopards trying to change their spots.

'*Ring For Jeeves*, as a matter of fact, is really a collaboration. It is a novelized version of a play which Guy Bolton and I wrote last summer, and all the best things in it are his.

'A pal of mine who was in the prison camp with me sends me the *Sunday Express* each week, so I shall be able to enjoy your reviews regularly.'

A month later I had to walk relatively blindfolded into the minefield of criticizing a new Evelyn Waugh novel. Although I was not familiar with everything he had written, I counted *Scoop* and *Put Out More Flags* amongst the most brilliantly funny novels of the century and *Brideshead Revisited* was my idea of a masterpiece. How disappointed I was with *Love Among The Ruins* can therefore best be judged by the intemperance of my language. I would imagine, too, that my pro-Labour Party sentiments at the time could not see much that was hilarious about all the ideals socialists held dear in 1953. With hindsight it may be that what was chiefly amiss about *Love Among The Ruins* was that it was written twenty years too soon.

'After reading *Love Among The Ruins*, it may well be predicted that Evelyn Waugh's future novels are unlikely to be enjoyed by anyone not a snob,' I wrote. 'For this short work of fifty-one pages brings to an angry boil the indignant simmerings in his post-war novels, *Brideshead Revisited* and *Men At Arms*. He has signed up against the Common Man and the Welfare State for the duration...

'What he is against he makes clumsily obvious – penal reform, psychiatry, politicians, television, Picasso, modern architecture, trade unions, central heating, sex, doctors and divorce.

'By implication he prefers a return to the good old days of the lash, slums, Victorian painting, the landed gentry and unlanded peasantry, the dole, the inquisition and the rack. But Mr Waugh is not likely to make many converts to the past if he abandons his natural gifts of good writing and sharp wit ...'

Unusually, Evelyn Waugh was so stung by the negative tone in most reviews, including mine, that he decided to take them on. The *Spectator* magazine had instituted a feature in which authors would be given a chance to reply to the reviews of their books. Waugh accepted their invitation to hit back on 3 July 1953.

In his two-page offensive he first of all condemned the general quality of all British literary criticism, claiming that even such subtle critics as Raymond Mortimer, Cyril Connelly and Peter Quennel are never given enough space to treat an important work adequately and that therefore they have had little influence on the book-buying public ...

Inevitably my turn came round. 'Mr Shulman of the *Sunday Express* accuses me of snobbery,' he complained. 'He goes further and predicts that "in future" only snobs will enjoy my books. This seems very odd since the book under review is the only novel I have ever written in which there appears no member of the upper class, either as buffoon or heroine.'

It would have been pointless for me to have written to Mr Waugh protesting that I had no idea what any other critic anywhere was going to think about the book, or whether Beaverbrook did or did not admire Waugh's novels, since we had never discussed the matter. He wouldn't have believed me. But considering how my colleagues had been treated by this master of the literary stiletto, I think, on the whole, I got off rather lightly.

★ ★ ★

In the next few months my books to talk about dealt with Senator McCarthy, Edward Carson who prosecuted Oscar Wilde, Consuela Vanderbilt who became the Duchess of Marlborough, Emperor Hirohito, Noel Coward, Julius Caesar and novels by Nigel Balchin, Vicki Baum, C. S. Forester, Anita Loos, George Orwell as well as others. My perpetual complaint to Harold Keeble was that the column was a restless feast with no fixed location in the paper, and veered from typographical prominence to visual obscurity. We never resolved this clash and it was eventually the reason why I gave the job up.

Most of my reviews were accepted with reasonable equanimity by my readers, but when I pricked some conventional social balloon or was less than idolatrous about some popular novelist, their letters sometimes displayed a mastery of venom which I reluctantly had to envy. One should not exaggerate the representative value of this form of public opinion. It would be remarkable if any serious topic ever provoked more than a dozen letters all told. As Alan Brien remarked about the response to one of his controversial film criticisms – 'Two postcards poured in.' To really flood the letters-to-the-editor with hundreds of epistles, the paper would have had to stop printing a children's comic strip like Billy The Bee or accidentally put the wrong list of clues under the day's crossword puzzle. TV has replaced the press as the receptacle for the public's complaints and anxieties.

My book column provided me with many opportunities to glimpse Beaverbrook's lifestyle since something in one book or another could provide him with an excuse for having me to lunch or dinner at Cherkley or Arlington House. Beaverbrook was rarely on his own, since he relished company and conversation attended by good champagne, wine and brandy. He had a coterie of personal acquaintances who could be counted upon to exchange political and social gossip with him at the height of their voices and with much ribaldry. They included Brendan Bracken, Randolph Churchill, Lord Grantley, Lord Queensborough, Stanley Morison (the *Times* leader writer and typographer), Gertrude Lawrence, Michael Foot, Frank Owen, Lord Castlerosse, Sir Alexander Korda, who would be joined at a table for ten or twelve by senior politicians, editors, visiting Americans and literary figures who happened to be in the news.

The banter between the food and drink often ended up in puzzling memos landing on an editor's desk the next morning, with journalists having to scamper through their newspaper libraries to find the facts that would resolve some bet or argument amongst the guests. Typical of this was the note I received from the *Standard*'s deputy editor, Charles Wintour, which read: 'We still have to reply to the inquiry about the origin of the story re Churchill and Roosevelt arguing about the second line of 'Mad Dogs'. Perhaps you could give me the exact quotation from Coward's book.'

Some similar sort of light-hearted disagreement must have sparked off the *Express* editor's request to me that I review Charlotte Bronte's *Jane Eyre* in my column. *Jane Eyre*! Why? Was there a film being made of the book? A comprehensive edition of the Brontes being planned? An undiscovered aspect of the Bronte family found in the Lake District? No, none of these. The Old Man just thought it would be a good idea and he didn't say why, Keeble reported back to me. Being the inventive editor he was, Keeble put a good spin on my review when it appeared in July 1953, with the heading 'For Your Holiday Reading ... One of the World's Most Exciting Stories To Be Discovered By New Generation.'

It turned out that Beaverbrook had read somewhere, or been told, that Penguin had just brought out a commemorative edition of *Jane Eyre* and had sold 50,000 paperbacks of it in only three weeks. Trying to decipher the phenomenon, I said it was not simply the mystery of the stranger in the attic, who set the house alight at midnight and plunged a knife into the breast of the visitor from Madeira. These were routine incidents of a Victorian novel. What gripped generations of *Jane Eyre* readers was the story that had single-handedly sustained all those fortunes made out of scullery fiction and soap operas – the poor governess who marries the rich, Byronic master. Today it has become the secretary and the influential advertising executive.

'Charlotte Bronte can also thank for her popularity in 1953,' I wrote, 'the fact that she had to describe passion without the aid of the jargon of the psychiatrist. Forced to break through the veil of Victorian propriety, her words glow with a violent urgency that is so compelling because it is so innocent. If she had been writing today she probably would have taken the easy way of describing sex in terms of suppressed urges, substitute wish-fulfilments and very small explicit words. *Jane Eyre* kindles our imagination because we are allowed to use it.'

(ii) Time with Beaverbrook

In the years between 1948 and 1958 I was a particularly frequent recipient of Beaverbrook's hospitality and attention. I remember the first time I was asked to stay the weekend at Cherkley, I found my tattered underpants, undarned socks and crumpled shirts laid out on a massive double-bed where the butler had neatly put them. I hadn't realized that in stately homes, emptying the contents of your luggage was one of a butler's first jobs. I learnt the routine of drinks a half-hour before dinner; the men remaining behind after dessert to exchange gossip or political secrets while the women left to join them later in the drawing room; the obligation to say 'yes' when you were offered one of Beaverbrook's special rum cocktails; the signal that said the evening was over when the Old Man walked towards the tiny lift that cranked its way noisily to the next floor.

Although Beaverbrook had presumably abandoned his plans for trying me out as an editor, he would often have me accompany him on long walks through the countryside. I would be told of his child-hood in New Brunswick, where he described himself until about the age of eleven as being a normal boy with no distinctive qualities until he was hit by a mowing machine and was unconscious for several days. After an operation on his head he recovered with fresh energy, more brain power and a questing, restless personality that marked his life from then on. How much credence one can place in this tale, I don't know, but I was always impressed by his feats of memory when he could name, at the age of seventy, the shops and personalities on the main street in Newcastle, New Brunswick, that were there when he was five.

He liked to reminisce about his days with Bonar Law and Lloyd George, attack Mountbatten about the disaster at Dieppe, reiterate his views about the timing of the Second Front and wait for me to tell him any gossip about people in Fleet Street of which I had very little. He told me about his chauffeur-driven car being stopped for speeding on the way to Cherkley late at night.

Poking his head out of the back-door window, he said to the motor-cycle cop, 'Do you know who I am?' The policeman said he didn't. 'Well, I'm Lord Beaverbrook. And do you know where I have been?'

The cop shook his head.

'I've just come from Downing Street where I've been talking to Winston Churchill, the Prime Minister. And do you know what we've been talking about?'

'No, Lord Beaverbrook.'

'We've been talking about how to get more money for the police.'

'Yes, Lord Beaverbrook,' said the overwhelmed policeman, waving the car on.

It was with great glee that he told me about Tom Driberg, a Labour MP, former *Express* gossip writer and homosexual, who had been fol-lowed by detectives after he had been seen picking up a young man in Leicester Square. 'The two detectives knew which room they were in in Driberg's house,' said Beaverbrook, 'and one of them reported to his superiors that they would have caught Driberg in the act if the window-sill had only been six inches lower.'

As far as I was concerned a summons from Beaverbrook was a com-mandment I could never reject. I was rarely given more than a day's notice and I was usually expected to come the same evening, occasion-ally in black tie. But when Beaverbrook himself was on the phone asking me to be at dinner that day, I, for the first time, had to turn down his invitation.

'As you know, Lord Beaverbrook,' I said in as apologetic a tone as I could muster, 'I have been only too happy to join you at Cherkley but tonight, I'm afraid, for the first time, I trust you will forgive me if I tell you I am obliged to be somewhere else this evening. My wife has prepared a dinner for ten people and she has been involved with it for many days. I suspect it might be grounds for divorce, if I were to tell her now I couldn't be there. I hope you will understand.'

'Aw, so you are busy elsewhere, are you?' he said.

'Yes, Lord Beaverbrook. I'm afraid so.'

'Well, that's too bad. I'm sure you would have liked to meet Sir Winston Churchill. Goodbye.'

I had never seen Churchill in person and being at close quarters at dinner with him would have been one of the fulfilling moments of my life. For a moment I flirted with the idea of phoning him back and saying I could, after all, come. But I realized that would be a humiliating retreat for which my wife would not easily forgive me. And the suspicion also dawned on me that perhaps Churchill was not really going to be present after all and Beaverbrook was up to one of his mischievous tricks, designed to make me regret my temerity at turning down his invitations. I never did discover whether Churchill was there that night, but I have always been sorry that I did not take the chance to find out.

Trying to make conversation with him one day, I asked Beaverbrook if he had ever met Gilbert Harding. Harding made himself a love-hate figure with TV audiences because of his curmudgeonly outbursts on a family quiz game. He could be eccentric and rude and resented the fact that he had become temporarily famous by taking a part in an activity for which he publicly displayed his contempt. Privately he was an erudite and cultured man. Beaverbrook had heard of him. 'Why should I meet him?'

'He is a good conversationalist. He has a fund of good anecdotes and tells them very well. I'd think you'd find him amusing.'

'Does he tell his stories twice? Does he repeat them?'

'Not as far as I know,' I answered, taken aback by the question. 'He's never repeated any anecdote he's told me. I don't know him that well but I can't guarantee it. I'm sure your other guests would find him interesting.'

'Can't stand a fellow who tells his stories twice,' repeated

Beaverbrook, as if he hadn't heard me. 'I remember once travelling from Cannes to Nice with Lord Castlerosse.' Castlerosse was an Irish peer who wrote a gossip column for the *Sunday Express*. 'We were going to a grand ball. On the way we could see an overturned car and some women lying on the grass. I asked my chauffeur to stop and find out if we could be of any help. He was told an ambulance was on the way and there was nothing we could do. That night at the ball in Nice, I was telling a story to some women friends when Castlerosse stopped me and asked, "I've been thinking about those women in that accident. Do you know what happened to them?" I was annoyed at his interruption. "Here I am telling a story and just reaching its climax when you spoil my story by asking me a silly question about that accident. Why have you done that, Castlerosse? Tell me why." "Because you were telling the same story when we passed those women on the road."'

I never knew why Beaverbrook so often placed himself in a position where some sort of embarrassment was likely to be the ultimate outcome. One of the most nerve-wracking experiences I had with him was when he summoned me to lunch at Arlington House and I found him in his drawing room where he was serving his inevitable rum cocktails to a number of men strange to me, except for Michael Foot. He introduced me to the strangers. 'The Deputy Prime Minister of New Zealand, the High Commissioner of New Zealand, the Agriculture Minister of New Zealand, the Information Officer at New Zealand House.' I don't think he told me their names, only their titles. I shook hands with each of them and nodded to Michael Foot.

He then led us into his dining room where I was seated at one end of the table and he at the head of the table at the opposite end. On his left was Michael Foot and arrayed at each side of the table were the New Zealand luminaries he was entertaining. Since I was a film and theatre critic, I hadn't the faintest idea why I had been selected as a guest, except perhaps that being a Canadian, the Old Man thought my presence would be some sort of gesture of solidarity towards the Commonwealth.

Never having been to New Zealand, I found conversation with both my neighbours rather sticky and was relieved when, during the coffee, Beaverbrook beat a spoon on his glass, calling for silence.

'We are gathered here,' began Beaverbrook in his most magisterial voice, 'to see what we can do about New Zealand's butter problem.' What in the world can I say about that, I thought to myself. 'Sales of

New Zealand butter have been sinking in the British market. They are finding it increasingly difficult to cope with the competition from Dutch and Danish butter. The *Express* Newspapers want to do all we can to help our New Zealand cousins over this matter. Shulman, what's to be done about their butter problem?'

Never having given butter or New Zealand a single thought, I rose to my feet feeling nothing but panic in my stomach. All the visitors' heads swivelled in my direction and waited expectantly for me to open my mouth. Beaverbrook sat back in his chair, obviously unperturbed by the fact that he had given me no warning at all about my having to speak, nor did he look at all concerned about my ability to say something on this arcane subject. The New Zealanders assumed I was the *Express* papers' agriculture or Empire expert.

Deep down in my subconscious I could feel memory banks being stirred. New Zealand butter? What the hell did it look like? Was it Anchor butter? I thought I'd ask.

'If I am right,' I began, 'I think New Zealand butter is sold in this country as Anchor butter.' They all nodded. I pushed my luck a bit farther. 'And wasn't that butter, and still is, wrapped in wax paper?' They all agreed again. I could sense panic receding and confidence taking its place as a glimmer of an idea began to take shape in my mind.

'And don't the Dutch and the Danes wrap most of their butter in silver foil? Oblong blocks of butter in silver foil?' Again I was right. I had my theme!

'I may be wrong, but I suspect the English housewife now identifies Anchor butter and its wax paper with the austerities and rationing of the war. Dutch and Danish butter in their neatly-packed silver foil have a richer, more modern image. And it may be that English women are fed up with all the restrictions of the war and see in your competitors' product something on their table that doesn't remind them of the past and promises a freer and more fulfilling future. What I think New Zealand butter needs is a new, more attractive image.'

No one said a word when I sat down until Beaverbrook turned to the man on his right.

'Well, what do you think of that, Mr Deputy Prime Minster? Has Shulman got a point?' he asked.

'Yes, Lord Beaverbrook, he certainly has,' came the answer. 'We've been giving a great deal of thought to our packaging methods. We'll probably have to do something about it.'

Beaverbrook then turned to Michael Foot. 'And what have you to say about New Zealand butter, Mr Foot?' Foot was an experienced politician and had had at least five minutes to think of something to say while I was talking. I was still so relieved and mentally exhausted by my experience that I didn't hear a word he said. I got no special thanks for my quick thinking but I kept wondering what would he have done if, when asked to speak, I had said, 'I am sorry, Lord Beaverbrook, I know nothing about butter or New Zealand and I have absolutely nothing to say on the subject.'

(iii) Women and marriage
In 1951, two days before Christmas, I found a brief letter on my bed in my one-room flat in Kensington Close. It was from Jackie, telling me that she knew I was seeing someone else and that she was ending our relationship. The man she was going off with was John Boulting who, with his twin brother Roy, was to achieve a formidable reputation as producer and director of some of Britain's best post-war pictures – *Brighton Rock*, *Seven Days to Noon*, *Lucky Jim*, *I'm All Right Jack*.

I couldn't believe that what I had seen happen in many Victorian melodramas was happening to me. Betrayed! By the one he loved! And at Christmas! I could envisage the sub-titles in some early silent film. I had known she dined with him from time to time. I had even encouraged her to accept one of his invitations. But I hadn't had the slightest suspicion that anything more than a platonic friendship existed between them.

When, after a couple of days, I stopped feeling sorry for myself, I began to realize that wounded pride was fuelling my pain. It was pure hypocrisy to feel betrayed by a situation that I had brought upon myself.

I had for months been meeting Drusilla Beyfus in cocktail bars and restaurants. She was the most decorative aspect of the *Daily Express*, where her elegant figure, piquant face and ever-smiling personality were in constant demand by feature writers and columnists who competed for her services as a junior reporter and researcher.

Her father, the son of a wealthy wool merchant, had rejected the family business to become a not very distinguished poet. He went blind as a young man and subsequently financial circumstances were always rather tight, since his main source of income – Drusilla had a sister, Angela – was a modest family trust. Having acquired her matriculation papers at a school for the children of naval officers – she was given a place as an exception – she decided not to try for a place at university and wrote to over a hundred provincial newspapers and periodicals for a job as a trainee journalist. The *Reading Mercury* took her on and, a year later, she was in London, first with a news agency and then the *Daily Express*. It was at a Fleet Street pub, the Cock, that I managed to get myself introduced to her. She had just broken off a relationship with Derek Monsey, a critic and novelist, who was later to marry the actress Yvonne Mitchell and move to the south of France to write some reasonably well-received books.

Drusilla was acquiring a rather eccentric reputation as a journalist. Her most unusual exploit when I had met her was managing to get into Berlin during the blockade which denied Allied planes, except for a narrow corridor, the right of access from East Germany into the British, American and French zones of Berlin. Having missed the travel connections that the *Express* had made for her, she had succeeded in charming the pilot of an American transport plane carrying coal into the city to hide her amongst the sacks and then crawled into one for delivery when the plane landed. It was an enterprise that might have broken one of her bones, but she got her story.

Because Jackie was out of London much of the time, acting in plays in provincial towns, I found myself more and more involved with Dru. At first she positively disliked me, since among her friends I was being dismissed as a brash Beaverbrook man with few qualifications for my job as a film critic. But, she has told me, it was my ability to guess who-had-done-it in the first twenty minutes of any thriller we saw together, that made her contemplate me in a more sympathetic light. Jackie and I had already come to an understanding that marriage was not likely between us. I was still recovering from my divorce and, although we were still intimate, I was very wary of entering into a permanent liaison with an actress. If successful, her husband never sees her; if she is not successful, he has to share the burden of her failure.

Drusilla was rapidly moving up the rungs of women's journalism. At twenty-six she had become the youngest women's editor in Fleet Street and was writing a joint weekly column with Anne Edwards for the *Daily Express*. Together they had also written a light-hearted but authoritative book on modern etiquette, *Lady Behave*.

She was slowly taking over my social and domestic life. After Jackie left, we were being seen more and more together as a recognizable couple amongst our friends. At that time Michael Foot and his wife, Jill

Craigie, the film director, would invite us regularly to dinner parties at their home in Hampstead where other guests were likely to be Aneurin Bevan and Jennie Lee, Barbara and Ted Castle, Harold Wilson, Richard Crossman, the film director Frank Launder, Ian Mikardo, the TV journalist John Morgan, the actor Roger Livesey, and a couple of young journalists who, Michael assured me, would one day have an explosive effect on Fleet Street. He was quite right. They were Paul Foot and Paul Johnson. And to demonstrate his eclectic taste in friends, Dru and I once spent a very argumentative evening in Hampstead with Randolph Churchill and his second wife, June.

Although my loyalty to socialism had been steadfast in the immediate years after the war, reports of the gulags in Russia recalled the purges conducted by Stalin and Lenin in the 1920s and 1930s. We thought that the struggle against Hitler might have wiped clean the memory of those excesses, but I was becoming more and more alarmed at the brutality needed to sustain a dictatorship of the proletariat. Nor was there any evidence in any Marxist state that such a dictatorship would eventually wither away. I realized there was a distinct line between socialism and communism about the acceptable methods required to maintain enough economic and social control to make governmental centralization workable. I was beginning to realize that freedom in any real sense was incompatible with any form of Marxism. I found myself at increasing odds with my Labour Party friends, who were still thrashing about intellectually trying to find a political system that could blend Marxism and democracy. The crushing of the uprisings in Hungary and Czechoslovakia revealed the impossibility of that task. Nonetheless I was not yet ready to abandon my early ideology. That would come later.

Drusilla was also determined to raise me out of the cramped, parsimonious bachelorhood in which I had been living since leaving the army, and find some dwelling more in keeping with what she thought I would like and could afford. With my regular book and film criticisms and freelance articles for other publications, I was earning about £85 a week, which would have made me reasonably affluent had it not been for a top tax rate of 80p in the pound which guaranteed that no journalist would ever become rich.

Eaton Square, which was owned by the Duke of Westminster, was slowly being given back to its owner, having been requisitioned during the war for bombed-out families from the East End of London. At No. 65, facing east down the square and with a splendid view of these

Drusilla in St Tropez on our honeymoon

luxurious, green gardens, was a freshly decorated flat on the second floor. It had a large drawing room, a large and a small bedroom, a newly converted kitchen and bathroom and a separate lavatory. For this sumptuous residence I paid £9 a week, which included central heating, porterage and rates.

I didn't know at the time that before the war Eaton Square had been one of the most desirable locations in London, and therefore one of the most expensive. I have lived in the square ever since with neighbours like the millionaire Labour MP Harold Lever, Lord Rothermere, the Aga Khan, Andrew Lloyd Webber, Vivien Leigh, Terence Rattigan, the Crown Prince Frederick of Prussia. I assure you, they pay much more than the modern equivalent of £9 a week. I manage it with difficulty – and understanding landlords.

Having to furnish such a flat with carpets, curtains, beds, kitchen equipment – I did not own a single piece of furniture – meant not only spending all my accumulated capital but also acquiring a bank overdraft which has been my financial companion ever since. It was during this trawl for possessions that I discovered an interest in and taste for modern art.

My interest in paintings had been first aroused by Felix Lichtblau, a charming Austrian Jew, who was stuck in Toronto for almost a year just before the war, waiting to get the much prized visa that would enable him to take up residence in America. Louis Herman, whose firm I had joined as soon as I was called to the Bar, was a specialist in the administrative quagmire which refugees from the Nazis had to go through to get the necessary papers to freedom. The procedures often required a temporary residence in Canada before being accepted by the Americans, and Herman had cultivated contacts that gave him both a merciful and lucrative role in these complex manoeuvres.

Felix was in his early thirties and had abandoned a prosperous jewellery and art business in Vienna. We became close friends and he felt it was his duty to introduce me to the finer aspects of European culture. We would haunt the Toronto art galleries together, and it was here that I made my first contacts with the Impressionists, the Fauvists, the Surrealists as well as such masterpieces as works by Goya, Raphael, Bruegel, Vermeer, Rembrandt and others.

In the first years of the war, I visited him in New York where he had set himself up in an elegant Fifth Avenue shop, trading under the name of Felix Lawrence. He was particularly excited to see me, not only because I was in uniform but because that afternoon he was trying to sell three paintings to a representative of the Duveen gallery. In a large attic room Felix just had time to name the painters and give a short account of their provenance when the man from Duveen arrived looking like a trim, non-smiling banker. The two large paintings were attributed to van Dyck and Palma Vecchio. The third appeared to be a wooden panel about three feet wide and two feet deep. Felix was hoping it could be ascribed to Giorgione, a 15th century Italian artist whose works were very rare and had often been completed by other painters. A fragment of a Giorgione would have been a very rich find indeed.

The Duveen man studied the van Dyck and Palma Vecchio very carefully, squinting intensely at various corners of the canvas. He gave the Giorgione a quick, cursory glance. After a few social words and handshake, he was gone. My friend lay down on the floor and began to kick his legs in the air while his face was suffused with delight. What was the dealer's opinion?, I asked Felix.

'He doesn't think much of the van Dyck and the Palma Vecchio. He suspects they're fakes,' said Felix, 'but he was impressed with the Giorgione. He wants to see it again.'

'But he hardly looked at it,' I protested.

'That's a dealer's trick,' said Felix. 'They give you the impression they're not interested. They think it'll help them with the price.'

A few years later I heard in a letter from Felix that the Giorgione had ended up in a Washington museum. But it had to go through four sales by experts before the museum would accept it. 'I didn't have the authority to push the claim that it was a Giorgione myself. I made a small profit but it had to go through other experts' hands before a really good price was paid for it.'

This was a valuable lesson for me when I started buying paintings for myself. I realized that no painting was ever worth what a dealer said it was; only what he could get. I went to the Leicester Gallery for my first purchase, explaining that I had a large flat which with its empty white walls looked like a warehouse waiting for some crates to arrive.

They thought I might be interested in a small seated Madonna, about a foot high, that had been sculpted by Henry Moore. I believe there was an issue of nine. The price was £80. I explained that it was more than I had intended to pay and that it didn't really solve my furnishing problem. A Henry Moore would enhance my mantelpiece, but the walls would still be bare and unwelcoming. When I had some pictures, I might come back for it. My eyes lighted upon a small oil by Venard of a table holding some fruit, papers and playing cards with a guitar on a chair beside it. It had echoes of an early Braque. It cost £40 and I still have it. I could probably get £1,000 for it now. When I last saw an auction estimate, the Henry Moore which I had turned down was worth £12,000.

I was buying, and occasionally selling, pictures for about twenty years in the sixties and seventies. I am content with those that I fancied then. If, when my finances got tight, I had to dispose of one or two, my taste was well rewarded by prices well over inflation. Inevitably I made some costly blunders. In the early sixties I had purchased a splendid L. S. Lowry showing sixty-three of his spindly, sad characters waiting for a train at a small provincial railway station. Counting those passengers was a most relaxing exercise, rather like counting sheep to help you fall asleep.

I had lost more money than I could afford on the horses. This was an expensive hobby that I had indulged in since the 1950s when Woodrow Wyatt, later Lord Wyatt, came to my flat for a drink on Boxing Day and introduced me, on the phone, to his bookmaker. Lord Wyatt, then a Labour MP, later became head of the Tote, which he had revolutionized by the time he died in December 1997.

My overdraft was becoming uncomfortable as I helped enrich the coffers of bookmakers. I had read that a Lowry had been sold to the Queen for something like £2,300. I had paid £100 for mine. Taking the Lowry to the gallery from which I had bought it – tactically a mistake because it reveals too much eagerness to sell – they offered me £600. I thought this was very low in view of what the Queen was paying for hers. There was no comparison, they assured me. That other picture was much larger, a better period, a much rarer painting all round. They'd raise their offer to £700. I hesitated, decided I was not that desperate for the money and walked out.

I hailed a taxi and, just as I was about to get in, the dealer came running out. 'How much do you want for it?' he asked. I hadn't any specific figure in mind but my expectations had been considerably punctured by the amounts I had been offered. 'A thousand,' I said, thinking they would refuse it. 'Come inside,' said the dealer. 'I'll pay off the taxi.'

After a few minutes he came out of his office with a written cheque. I handed over my precious Lowry with a heavy heart. I'd really relished that painting. 'I hope some day,' I said to him, 'I'll come back to you and, if you haven't sold it, buy it back.' He gave me a wicked smile. 'You won't be able to afford it.' And he was right. A year later the picture was the centrepiece of their window display. It had a price tag of £22,000! By 1997 a Lowry of the same date and about the same size fetched £310,000 at auction!

* * *

My relationship with Drusilla had become much closer since Jackie left me but neither of us felt we wanted it socially recognized by living under the same roof. My Eaton Square flat was acquiring paintings for every room with Abstract Expressionists like Sam Francis and Hans Hartung dominating the growing collection. Drusilla had her flat in Shepherd Market where she shared two floors above a corner tobacconist with Toni Frost, a South African actress with a part in *The Seven Year Itch* and, whenever she came to London, with Inge Morath, then a photographer learning her craft with Henri Cartier-Bresson and who later married Arthur Miller after he divorced Marilyn Monroe.

Marriage was certainly something we never had in mind and we asked no questions about any connections we might have had with any other people. I was, therefore, not surprised when, in 1955, Drusilla said she was going to America for an unspecified period of time, to try and get her book, *Lady Behave*, published, and that she would write some articles about America as a freelance for the *Express* and other publications. Although I never told her so, I sincerely believed that with her beauty, vivacity and talent there would be scores of American men trying to lure her into a permanent liaison with them in the United States. We wrote long letters to each other but I had more or less reconciled myself to losing her.

Being free of any social or romantic entanglements for the first time in my adult life, I discovered that England was full of young women eager for close companionship. I realized I possessed the magic ingredient guaranteeing my popularity – availability.

Kenneth Tynan once said that he always asked a woman for another date after he had been to bed with her. He considered it a matter of good manners, no matter how unsatisfactory their mattress liaison had been. I, too, always felt an obligation to check that no one had been hurt when there had been little time to get to know one another. Sometimes, however, one was reluctant to organize such a congenial reprise when one suspected the next time would be as dampening a test of one's virility as the last.

My experiences with women have taught me, as far as sex is concerned, that they are divided into two categories – those who eagerly welcome the hurly-burly and intimacy of a sexual contact and those who are indifferent to it. There is no in-between. A modest interest in sex is equivalent to none at all. If that is the goal desired, then it is important to try to sort out in advance what the odds are of achieving it. A great deal of time and money can be saved if you discern early on what type of prey you are stalking. Very long, stiletto-like fingernails and complex, expensive, bouffant hair styles are warning signs that the lady is not for ruffling.

The techniques of courtship have changed considerably since my most predatory days. For me, getting a woman into bed was a long, patient, conspiratorial activity. There were walks in the park, visits to the cinema and restaurants before a truly passionate kiss evolved. That made no definitive statement about what was promised, but it was a hopeful beginning. Judging from the cinema and TV, the process these days is much quicker and less subtle. In films, a few hours – often only moments – of eye contact, suggestive or witty verbal exchanges, proximity on a beach or hotel balcony or in a taxi, will result in a romantic kiss. The next scene, almost inevitably, is their bodies in bed together with him or her asking, after consummation, 'What's your name?' I rarely had such luck.

I had been intrigued by a small woman – just over five feet tall – who had a penchant for two huge dogs. They were a tall Afghan wolfhound and a dark-brown Alsatian. When she took them for a walk, they almost pulled her arms out of their sockets as she tried to control them. When she opened the door for me, they leapt at me with something she assured me was pleasure, although I wasn't so sure. When we eventually moved into her double-bed the Afghan curled up near my feet at the bottom of the blanket and the Alsatian took his place on the floor at her side of the bed. They both watched me with what looked to me like hate-filled, baleful eyes. Any undue movement on the bed caused the Alsatian to emit a menacing growl. I made a hasty, apologetic exit that night. I took her to a cinema a week later but never ventured into her bedroom again.

Celia had a houseboat on the Thames near Cheyne Walk. I had already taken her to a cinema and a Chelsea restaurant when she asked me to have dinner with her. It was one of those windy nights when the weatherman assures you that London is not in the midst of a hurricane although it certainly feels like one to you. By the time we had finished the spaghetti bolognese and the cheddar cheese, the howling wind had settled down into a soft purr and the river's waves were lapping only gently against the houseboat.

By the way we kissed and held hands, it was obvious we were going to share that narrow couch-bed with each other. It was not very amenable to someone of my bulk and took some settling into. Suddenly I noticed that small rivulets of water were flowing in under the front door. I said nothing at first, not wishing to spoil the moment, but in no time two inches of water had covered the carpet and it was rising rapidly. Under the circumstances, I was not performing particularly amorously.

'Celia,' I said, into her shoulder, 'is it usual for your houseboat to flood from time to time?'

She sat up with a jolt.

'Oh, my God,' she said, leaping out of the couch. 'It's done it again. There are towels in that bottom cupboard. Help me stuff them under the door!'

Naked as we were, we began to bail out the accumulated water, mop up the carpet and erect a barrier of planks on the deck to prevent the river sneaking on board. By the time all this was done, sex had lost its imperative. We met again but never on her houseboat.

There are some women who seem impervious to the effect their particular taste in cosmetics, perfume and grooming will have on a man's libido. I cannot abide women who announce their presence with clouds of perfume, not so much because the odour might offend me, but because they have imposed a particular environment around us without bothering to discover whether or not it would irritate or offend me. Lipstick or make-up that requires dry-cleaning one's favourite suit the next day are also minor penalties of an unsettled single life.

Some women seem oblivious to what the revelation of their beautification techniques can have on a man in the early days of a courtship. I had been enchanted by the stunning looks of a girl I had met at a cocktail party. Her father was a North American Indian and her mother an Ethiopian. Her patrician features and graceful body had given her a certain amount of work as a catwalk model. After taking her to the theatre she invited me to see her again in two days' time at her Kensington flat, where she would treat me to a meal of African cooking.

When I arrived at 8.30 pm I was greeted by an apparition that might have been a character out of a zombie film. Her face was completely coated with thick white cosmetic cream so that only her eyes were visible, like black grapes in a bowl of semolina. Her lustrous black hair, which had been a wig, was replaced by erratic tufts of tiny curls that made her look as if she was recovering from some sort of incipient baldness. She apologized for not having a meal ready, saying some unexpected work had come up, and asked could we go to a restaurant instead? We did. I paid the bill. I never saw her again.

Drusilla's stay in America concentrated both our minds on the likelihood of marriage. When I did my story of Marilyn Monroe, I stayed with her for a few days in New York. We had been writing letters and they were becoming more romantic and more possessive. She came back to England to take up a job on *Queen* magazine in March, 1956. We were married at Caxton Hall on 6 June 1956. Michael Foot and his wife, Jill Craigie, were our witnesses.

7

THE DAY KENNEDY WAS SHOT

Juggling Bernstein and Beaverbrook...Joy Adamson, Desmond Morris and the one-eyed electric eel...Head On with Randolph Churchill...The good ship Associated Rediffusion...Harold Wilson objects to Bernard Levin...JFK gets shot, Eli Wallach hit and George Brown wounded

(i) There's a sucker born every minute
My career as a book critic for the *Sunday Express* lasted just over a year and A Book To Talk About often became A Book To Argue About between myself and the editor, Harold Keeble. He was being harassed by Beaverbrook to make sure the column was not too 'highbrow' and I was picking books to review that were not of much interest to the majority of the 5,000,000 readers of the *Sunday Express*. Whenever I reviewed anything that was slightly demanding in a social or philosophical sense, Keeble tucked it away in some remote corner of the paper probably hoping that Beaverbrook in Bermuda would not see it there.

My complaints about the treatment I was receiving came to a climax when I wrote an angry article denouncing the appointment of a Herr Zimmermann as the official publisher to the future German forces. NATO had agreed that Germany could raise twelve divisions and 1,746 planes to make a contribution to the defence of Europe. The re-armament of Germany was a subject not much discussed in 1954, but the fact that their troops were to be issued with training pamphlets advocating a nuclear preventative war against the Russians was something certain Labour politicians were alarmed about.

The review took up the entire leader page of the *Sunday Express* and then, for some inexplicable reason, Keeble dropped it for later larger circulation editions. It was replaced by an article about South America which could have been of absolutely no interest to Keeble's readers. Having spent a great deal of time researching this article, I was furious about its short life and said so in a memo to the editor. To compound the problem, a week later Michael Foot raised the issue in the Commons but had to concede that his denunciation of what General Zimmermann was up to was somewhat blunted by the way the article had been treated. 'For some unknown reason, the editor removed the article after it had appeared in the first edition,' Foot told the Commons.

The Government spokesman, Mr Paget, said he did not believe one word that he read in the *Sunday Express*, whether it was a quotation or not. Foot replied, 'When I read an article by one of the most responsible and brilliant journalists of this country, Mr Milton Shulman, in which all these facts are revealed, then I think it is very foolish of my honourable and learned friend to contravene them.'

The next day no other paper got excited about the matter and it died in the morgue of newspaper cuttings. Nevertheless I felt that in some way I had embarrassed Michael in the Commons because not even the Beaverbrook papers were backing his concern. I told Keeble I would no longer write a weekly book review for the paper. He was fired a few months later, but I do not know if the Zimmermann affair had anything to do with his dismissal.

Keeble was succeeded by John (later Sir John) Junor, a canny, ebullient Scotsman who played the games of journalism and politics with such shrewd skill that he held the editorship of this high-circulation weekly for no less than thirty-two years, from 1954 to 1986. He was still writing a pugnacious, wayward column in the *Mail on Sunday* right up until his death in May 1997 and seemed indestructible. The secret of his success was remaining loyal to his staff and to a consistent unwavering editorial formula that was precisely what his middle-income, middle-class readership wanted.

And he could lay on the compliments in just the manner he'd been taught by his master, Lord Beaverbrook. Alan Watkins, who wrote political articles for the paper, reminisces about how he once offered a commissioned piece to Junor for his perusal. 'There's only one word to say about this article, Alan – brilliant. If I were going to print it, I wouldn't change a single comma in it.'

My differences with Keeble did not seem to have any negative effect as far as Junor was concerned. In June 1955, I became his film critic. The animosity about film criticism had died down amongst the film companies and although I was just as acerbic as before they never protested. Maybe they realized that film critics had very little impact on the box-office and they could shrug off bad reviews as they whined all the way to the bank. I now had two regular jobs again with the Beaverbrook papers – films for the *Express* and theatre for the *Standard* – and with a family on the way, the double money was very handy.

However, I was restless for something different. Having turned down the editorship of a Beaverbrook paper, I began to have doubts about my ideological rectitude now that disillusion about socialism was beginning to set in. I decided that what Britain needed was a weekly Arts magazine that would treat culture not as if it were something arcane and dainty, but as robust and controversial as aspects of politics and finance.

I had a dummy made up with the help of the best page designer on the *Standard*. Not only were there sections for the predictable criticism of plays, films, books, dance, painting and pop music but there were also interviews and profiles of artistic figures in the news, articles that aired current rows and debates such as entrance charges for public museums, the case for Public Lending Rights for books, an amusing piece about what visitors to galleries looked like if seen from the painting's point of view, the dire state of British film financing and a few more ideas of that kind. The emphasis was on a lively, graphic design to ensure the magazine was not tagged with a non-popular highbrow image. Its aim was to show that culture was something anyone could enjoy and argue about. I had a business plan requiring an initial capital sum of £100,000 and a list of potential advertisers. A circulation of 50,000 at £1 a copy would just make it viable. I called it *Today*.

The big publishing houses that I went to said they were impressed but it was much too small a printing order for their involvement. Smaller houses doubted if there was a market for an Arts magazine. Because he was a friend of mine I contacted Sidney Bernstein, head of Granada, which had just announced huge profits for his TV company. Considering himself a recognized, left-wing supporter of the Arts, he said he did not think his TV company had the mandate to diversify into such a non-TV enterprise, but added that if I wanted individual investors, he was prepared to give me £5,000. He felt that such a sum would enable me to set up an office, print stationery and hire a secretary. This was the only positive gesture made by anyone I had been to, and since I have little staying powers in such matters, I abandoned the project and, as they say, chalked it up to experience.

Early in 1958 Sidney Bernstein asked me to see him in Granada's offices in Golden Square. We had met socially at a number of parties given by Michael Foot and other members of the Labour Party. He was a secret financial supporter of the Party although his contributions were not large. Of the many consortiums that had applied for a franchise to present commercial TV, Bernstein's was the only one that could be said to have left-wing leanings. His group was financed primarily by the Bernstein family whose money came from the ownership of a chain of cinemas and from a substantial loan from one of the major banks. Granada provided the necessary political balance in the distribution of these contracts.

Bernstein was a tall, always elegantly dressed man with a slightly crushed nose due to a boyhood accident when it had not been set properly. He was an ardent collector of modern paintings and owned a Modigliani I always envied whenever I visited him. He loved arguing and debating politics, but his intellectual side never dulled his enthusiasm for show business and his recognition of the sources of his wealth. In every Granada office there hung a framed lithograph of the famous American showman, Phineas T. Barnum, to remind his young, sometimes anti-authoritarian employees that even the most serious and controversial programmes could best be sold to the public in bright, even razzle-dazzle presentation packages. Barnum's favourite dictum 'There's a sucker born every minute' guided the behaviour of the Granada workers, even in their most idealistic ventures.

In the first few months of their appearance on the air early in 1956, Granada had lost so much money that their staff had to wait a few weeks for delayed wages. But in 1958 the commercial companies were overwhelmed by an avalanche of money and Granada, with its northern franchise, matched its brother companies with profits of about £5,000,000. It stimulated Lord Thomson, who headed Scottish TV, to foolishly boast that 'Television was a licence to print money.' Commercial TV has tried to dampen down that encomium ever since.

At our meeting Bernstein asked me if I had ever considered going into television. It hadn't occurred to me, I said, but I would be interested in any proposition as long as he realized, of course, that I knew very little about the production of TV programmes. Bernstein replied that my technical ignorance didn't matter very much. After all, his own staff had very few professionals on it and had had to learn how it was done in less than three years. He had been impressed by the magazine I had offered him and the business acumen I had displayed in my presentation. He was also a great admirer of my criticisms and thought my judgement about programmes would be helpful to his company. Would I consider taking on the job of an executive producer? He realized it might mean a diminution in my income, since I would have to give up being the film critic of the *Sunday Express* because I would be expected to be in Granada's offices in Golden Square from 9 a.m. to about 5.30 p.m. Since films were screened during the day I could not possibly do both jobs. If I thought I could manage it, and the Beaverbrook papers had no objection, he was quite amenable for me to continue as the *Standard*'s theatre critic. If I was prepared to join him, we would talk about money later.

Again the unpredictability of Fate had presented me with a decisive and difficult dilemma. I knew that Lord Beaverbrook's policy towards television was that of implacable opposition and resistance. He considered the BBC and ITV as media rivals capable of eventually putting many papers out of business as they competed for audiences and advertising. No one who worked for any of his papers would be allowed to take a regular job on TV or even appear on it.

However, I was in my late forties and I hesitated about rejecting this chance of trying my luck with a medium that would eventually transform this country. Lord Beaverbrook had been extremely generous to me. I had gained a healthy reputation as a critic and journalist. Only that year I had been named by the *World's Press News*, an influential trade journal, as the Best Theatre Critic of 1957. Should I abandon it all for the uncertainties of a new career? I had two more meetings with Bernstein and some of his chief executives. The money on offer was more than I was being paid by the *Sunday Express*, but it was not enough to compensate for my salary on the *Standard* if Beaverbrook fired me.

Since I had already turned down the chances of an editorship, I had to decide if I wanted to spend the rest of my working career solely as a newspaper critic. Should I not take the gamble and if it didn't work out, couldn't I always get some newspaper to take me on as a critic in a few years' time? I talked it over with Drusilla and made up my mind to join Granada.

Bernstein had assured me I could carry on as a theatre critic because he could see very few occasions when I would be expected to be involved in any evening work. I told Bernstein I would take the job and we did not fix a start date. I said I was going to try to make the Old

Man change his adamant stance against TV in my case. I had a Machiavellian plan in mind.

I knew that the only way to win in such a game with Beaverbrook was to play from strength. He had to know that if I left the *Standard* I would probably work for a rival newspaper as a theatre critic. Marius Pope, a friend of mine who had been features editor of the *Standard*, was now doing the same job on the *Daily Mail*. I took him out to lunch and disclosed my problem. I couldn't be sure, but it was highly probable that I would soon be looking for a post as theatre critic. If that happened would his paper take me on, as I knew their present critic's work was not particularly distinguished and that they might be in the market for a replacement in a few months' time? Marius was very enthusiastic. He couldn't definitely promise me the position but as soon as I heard about my future would I get in touch with him? In the meanwhile he would have a word with his editor.

The very next day I went into Percy Elland's office and told him that, with very many regrets, I had decided to try my luck as a producer with Granada TV. Percy was not a man who took shocks easily, nor did he fancy the prospect of having to tell Beaverbrook the news. He tested me out on my resolution and, finding that it was not just a ploy to get a rise, he told me not to do anything until he'd spoken to the Old Man. I could see by the colour that had drained from his face that he didn't relish the prospect.

Just before leaving, I told him in a conspiratorial tone of voice that I thought he should know something which I did not on any account want him to convey to Beaverbrook. I did not want Elland to think I was doing anything behind his back. I had already made contingency arrangements, so if I was forced to quit as the *Standard*'s critic I would very probably be offered that job on the *Daily Mail*. But I didn't want the Old Man to think I was attempting to blackmail him. After all, I needed that extra income and it would be unreasonable for me not to try and work for another paper because of Beaverbrook's personal vendetta against television.

I was not surprised that when I got to my office there was a message from Lord Beaverbrook asking me to see him immediately at Arlington House. Elland had done precisely what I had expected him to do and, knowing the ways of Beaverbrook editors, had no doubt also reported my offer from the *Daily Mail*.

'Mr Elland tells me that you want to join Bernstein's TV company,' he said in an affable manner, 'but you know it is the policy of our company that our employees will not take jobs on television. I understand you want to continue as the *Standard*'s theatre critic. How can I do that, Shulman? Tell me why I should break our policy in your case?'

'First of all, Lord Beaverbrook, I want to thank you for your generous support over all these years and your personal friendship to me and Drusilla, which has been greatly appreciated. I would hate having to give up my job as critic on the *Standard*, which has done so much for my career, but I am not asking to be made an exception. I just want to have applied to me conditions of employment enjoyed by other writers on your papers.'

'And what do you mean by that?'

'Well, there's Clive Graham and Peter O'Sullevan. They are the BBC's regular racing commentators on TV. They are also the staff racing correspondents of the *Daily Express*. Every betting man associates them with BBC TV.'

'Aw, yaaz. And who else?'

'There's Godfrey Winn. He produces a weekly column for the *Daily Express* and has regular broadcasting slots on the BBC.'

'Aw, yaaz. And who else?'

'There's Nancy Spain. She does a weekly book column for the *Sunday Express* and chairs a regular quiz show about books on TV.'

'Ah, that's just a tax dodge,' said Beaverbrook, perhaps feeling he was losing the argument. 'Who else?'

'It may be a tax dodge about Nancy Spain,' I said, 'but as far as the TV viewer is concerned she is linked with the *Express*. Then there's Wolf Mankowitz.'

'That's a bad one,' interrupted Beaverbrook, not wanting to hear any more. 'He's got nothing to do with us.'

I repeated my plea for equal treatment, my intense gratitude for all he had done for me and my hopes that my association with his papers could continue, by my being permitted to carry on as a theatre critic.

'Write me a letter setting out your case,' he said, leading me to the door. 'I'll let you know. Goodbye.'

Not a word was said about the *Daily Mail* or my working for another paper, but on 3 April 1958 I received the following letter, which showed that Elland had told him about that offer.

'Thank you for your letter,' it read. 'I have the greatest appreciation of your work, with the added advantage that I have a great liking for the writer. The idea of your ever appearing anywhere except in our news-papers is quite intolerable, and I never allow such a notion to enter my mind ...' The day before, after a meeting with Beaverbrook's son, Max Aitken, I had signed a new contract confirming that I would continue as theatre critic of the *Evening Standard*, on a freelance basis, at £30 per article with a minimum of one hundred articles. The editors of the *Daily* and *Sunday Express* could continue to call upon me to write for them at negotiated fees for each article. It was agreed I would confine all my newspaper articles to the Beaverbrook Group.

During the six years I worked in television, I never saw Beaverbrook socially or professionally again. I had been the recipient of a Top Hat pension scheme which was to comfort me in my old age. This was can-celled, the accumulated fund to which I had contributed nothing was withdrawn, and although there was talk from time to time about an alternative pension, one was never arranged. That was Beaverbrook's final comment about my joining television.

★ ★ ★

I arrived at Granada on 19 May 1958 and was welcomed by the man-aging director, Victor Peers, a wiry, taciturn man who acted as both a conduit pipe and a blocking mechanism for Sidney Bernstein. To get to the chairman one usually had to go through Peers. Almost every con-versation that I had with Bernstein that needed some action ended with the words 'Tell Victor' or 'Ask Victor'.

I was given an office, an attractive secretary, a company car and expense accounts at two West End restaurants where I had only to sign the bill if I entertained anyone. I was not expected to do anything but sit in on discussions, listen in on production meetings for programmes, put on paper any ideas I had for the Monday morning conferences, become familiar with the technical jargon used in transmitting shows, make myself known to the staff and visit Manchester to see how the company worked there. Plans were afoot for a huge TV complex, to be built in the next two years.

My one constructive job was to occupy the viewing theatre, assess-ing material from American serials or independent producers which Granada might buy. I also watched old films made in the thirties and during the war which were being offered to TV companies very cheap-ly. Films like Arthur Askey or Jack Hulbert/Cicely Courtneige comedies and musicals could be bought for tiny sums with a small repeat fee for three showings, after which transmission rights would pass to Granada in perpetuity. Some of these films, costing the companies nothing, can still be seen in the mornings or late at night. With the proliferation of channels due to digital TV, they will probably soon be turning up again to keep the screens full economically.

I discovered that, like most tycoons, Sidney Bernstein had his idiosyncrasies. He had a passion for neatness and an obsession with detail. When he used to make a surprise visit to one of the Granada cinemas, it was the lavatories that were likely to receive the most diligent scrutiny and the state of the hand towels and toilet rolls his most pointed criticisms.

Once he stopped at my secretary's desk to tell her that the telephone directories were stacked in the wrong alphabetical order, and that the books on my shelves should all be standing vertically and none should be lying on their sides.

He had odd foibles about clothes and people. He would not hire anybody with a beard and he took against anyone applying for a job who wore suede shoes or had a metal wristwatch band on display.

Although he was a shrewd judge of news and current affairs programmes, he was never too sure of himself when he had to decide to commit Granada to a series like *Coronation Street*. Its tatty, working-class ambience offended his sense of style. The only comment he made after the producer revealed the first episode to him was a query about why one of the characters was wearing a shirt with the same pattern as the wallpaper in the pub. When Bernstein died in February 1993, at the age of ninety-four, Anthony Howard's obituary in the *Independent* read that 'there would be trouble to even the humblest presenter in a local programme who disregarded the chairman's prohibition against the display of a handkerchief in a breast pocket.' It would have tickled Bernstein's sense of humour had he seen that the photograph accompanying the obituary showed him with a handkerchief prominently revealed in his breast pocket.

One of the more bizarre episodes of my career as a buyer of original film material came after I had been with Granada for a few years and was fairly confident in my post. One day a young man named Peter Watkins turned up in my office with a remarkable piece of film. I hadn't listened too carefully to the details of how he had come to shoot the film, and it wasn't with very much optimism that I joined him in the company's viewing theatre to see it being screened. Watkins was an amateur film-maker and my experience of the kind of movie usually shot by amateurs had not been very encouraging.

But hardly had the first images begun to flicker in front of me when I found myself riveted by this extraordinary example of documentary filming. It dealt with the last ten days of the Hungarian uprising against the Russians in 1956. In a corner of Budapest a small group of students and workers were seen defying the Russian tanks and artillery – until most of them were either killed or captured.

The startling, dramatic quality of the film was achieved by the utter realism with which it depicted the violence, the agony, the despair and the courage of those involved in this microcosm of a revolution. The shuddering film frames during moments of violent action indicated the use of a hand-held camera. The rough photographic work, the crude lighting, the texture of the celluloid, the chaotic shot of fighting, tussling men had that quality of immediacy and involvement reminiscent of the work of cameramen covering the front-line fighting during the Second World War in places like Stalingrad and Arnhem. It could only have been shot on the spot.

When the picture was over – it was just under an hour in length and called *Forgotten Faces* – I asked Watkins how he had managed to be in Budapest in 1956, and how he had contrived to get such a record of the fighting out of the country.

'But I have already explained all that to you in your office,' said Watkins, patiently. 'It wasn't made in Budapest. It was shot in Canterbury and all the actors are English amateurs. That location is not very far from Canterbury Cathedral.'

My first reaction was incredulity. The faces, which I had seen in such lingering close-ups, seemed so utterly un-English and the locale so thoroughly Balkan that I found it very difficult to accept my own self-deception. Would other people find this re-creation of those real events as convincing as I had?

Before showing it to anyone else in Granada – and to test whether or not my own reaction had been merely one of gullibility – I decided to work with Watkins on getting the film into better shape. The commentary was, in my opinion, too strident and too anti-Russian and gave the film a heavy propaganda flavour which needed toning down. It also needed technical work on the soundtrack and some re-editing that Watkins himself wanted to do.

An intense, handsome, non-smiling young man of about twenty-five, Peter Watkins was not someone whose views about his own work could be easily shifted. After a number of letters and meeting, I finally thought the film was in a reasonable enough shape to be shown to two senior Granada executives who would make the final decision about whether or not we should try to find a slot for it in the company's schedule. The commentary was still not to my liking, but Watkins and I had agreed to differ about it.

I had decided not to tell my two colleagues – both very experienced film men – anything about how the film was made to see if their views would be the same as mine. One of them was Cecil Bernstein, Sidney's brother, and the Vice-Chairman of Granada. They sat through the film in absorbed silence. When the lights went up, one of them, not Cecil, turned to me with exactly the reaction I'd expected.

'How did that boy shoot such a film in Budapest during the fighting?' he asked.

'But it wasn't made in Budapest,' I replied triumphantly. 'That's the remarkable thing about it. It had me fooled, too. It was made in Canterbury and all those people in it are amateur actors – English amateurs. During the rolling of the end titles you can catch a brief glimpse of Canterbury Cathedral.'

There was a long silence.

'Oh, we couldn't possibly show it then,' said Cecil, very quietly but firmly.

'Why not?' I asked.

'If we show a film like that,' he replied with impeccable logic, 'no one will ever believe our newsreels.'

'In the event *Forgotten Faces*, although some extracts from it were shown on a BBC programme about amateur film makers, was never transmitted in its entirety on television. Peter Watkins, however, went on to use the same realistic techniques in his prize-winning film for the BBC reconstructing the battle of Culloden and in *The War Game* – his fierce, imaginative account of what England would be like after an H-bomb attack.

Indeed *The War Game* so vividly and convincingly depicted the horrific consequences of nuclear destruction that the BBC, who had financed its production, did not have the courage to transmit it when it was finished. Its stark and brutal scenes were considered too upsetting and gruesome for TV viewers. It was seen, however, in cinemas throughout the world. When the BBC did eventually show it, many years later, all the heat and controversy had gone out of the subject and it provoked hardly any ripples of interest.

★ ★ ★

Although I can claim some modest success as a talent-spotter in the case of Peter Watkins, I must admit that when I was offered another opportunity for vicarious fame, my crystal ball turned out to be very clouded indeed. Her name was Joy Adamson and she had written in for an appointment to show me film she had shot in Africa. When she turned up in my office in 1959, I was startled and rather apprehensive about her unusual appearance. She was a middle-aged, tawny-haired blonde who spoke with a pronounced German accent.

It was her clothes that troubled me. She was wearing a leopardskin coat and hat, and carrying gloves made of the same material. She seemed to be proclaiming some sort of affinity with big cats. It was a costume that often got her into trouble in her later career as a dedicated lover of animals. It was incongruous to see a person lecturing about animal conservation decked out in spotted cat fur.

She talked to me enthusiastically about a young lioness she had been rearing in Kenya which she thought might be the basis of a TV programme. She had with her some film which she and her husband had taken.

Seated in Granada's viewing theatre watching her scrappy, amateur film, my unease about this curious woman grew. She was on very intimate terms with a large lioness, romping through the jungle, playfully stroking its head and body and at times appeared almost sexually entwined with this mature beast. Coupled with the outfit she was wearing, I thought there was something unhealthy in that relationship which would not be appropriate for family viewing on Granada. I politely said that I doubted if there was enough film material for a TV documentary and that I would let her know.

It turned out that I was one of a large group of media people who saw no commercial future in her adventure story. In addition to the film, she had offered publishers a large pile of typed papers as a book. Thirteen of them turned her down in quick succession. Eventually an executive at Collins reluctantly saw her, was entranced by her story and offered her a £1,000 advance. After being entirely re-written, *Born Free* was published in 1960. It has been one of the most phenomenal successes in British publishing history and within months it had been translated into twenty-five languages. It made Joy Adamson a very rich woman.

If I'd only seen its potential, who knows what financial rewards Granada might have reaped?

As it is, I joined the list of blind talent-spotters and agents who could not recognize a gold mine when it lay glittering at their feet. There was the executive at Decca Records in 1962 who preferred to give a recording contract to Brian Poole and the Tremeloes rather than the Beatles. There were the dozen publishers who rejected Frederick Forsyth's *Day of the Jackal*. And then there was the familiar story of the Hollywood talent scout whose written report about Fred Astaire's movie potential read: 'Can't act. Can't sing. Slightly bald. Can dance a little.'

★ ★ ★

My first job at Granada involving the production of actual TV programmes was as the executive producer of the animal programmes being made at the London Zoo. As had so frequently happened in my career, I was handed this responsibility although I knew nothing at all about animals. It is true we had a King Charles spaniel and two goldfish in our flat, but that hardly equipped me for the task I was now given.

Because of Sidney Bernstein's close friendship with Professor Solly Zuckerman, the eminent zoologist, Granada had received exclusive rights to transmit programmes using the resources and facilities of the London Zoo. A small office and studio had been built and a staff of twenty-eight were employed. My mentor and guide in those early months was Dr Desmond Morris, the Curator of Mammals, who later became rich and famous as the author of *The Naked Ape*.

Desmond did a weekly live children's programme called *Zoo Time* in which he took youngsters on a tour, showing them the treasures of animal life behind the bars and in the cages and in the tanks at the Regent's Park Zoo. Although I was theoretically responsible for its scheduling and financing, I really left it all to Desmond. My involvement was chiefly with a series called *The Animal Story*, which was a more serious effort to capture animal behaviour on film. We would build up a series and then transmit them weekly for some months. The chief photographer was Douglas Fisher who was a monument of patience as sometimes the cameramen would have to wait hours – even days – for the stickleback to build a nest of waterweeds, perform a zig-zag courtship dance and lead the female of his choice into his nest so she could lay eggs for him to fertilize.

As its producer I would have many anxious moments waiting for film material to arrive so that it could be cut and edited into shape for a programme that was scheduled to be transmitted before we actually had anything to show. The journalist, Philip Oakes, a friend of mine, wrote the scripts which Desmond Morris read. You can hardly go wrong with animals like seals, penguins and chimpanzees, particularly when Desmond had cultivated a star artist called Congo who, at three years old, could paint abstract canvases that could match, and even better, the images sploshed about by any three year old human child.

The reviews we received were so enthusiastic that I began planning an even more ambitious series called *Breakthrough* in which attempts would be made to get original film material on such topics as whether or not animals really laughed, and what level of intelligent communication was there in the sounds they made. *Table Manners*, which showed the complex methods used by animals to feed themselves, won first prize in the Children's Division at the Venice Film Festival. *Breakthrough* never got very far because there was no one at Granada to push for it after I left in 1962.

The question of setting up situations so that animals could be seen at their most ravenous eating other creatures was obviously a ticklish moral problem, particularly in England where its inhabitants often give the impression they adore animals more than they do children. A few years ago I was reminded that we had such problems at the London Zoo when an Irish woman posted a tarantula in a brown envelope to her home in County Londonderry. It was spotted by airport security staff and she was charged with abandoning it. She pleaded guilty before West Midlands magistrates and although it was not imposed, she was liable to six months in jail or a £2,000 fine. 'We have prosecuted several people in the past for abandoning spiders,' said an RSPCA inspector, justifying this draconian measure.

We discovered at the Zoo Unit that there was a host of legislation which enables the authorities to have you up before the magistrates for swatting a fly. Today it is the Animals (Scientific Procedures) Act 1986 that lays down that experiments should not cause animals any unnecessary 'pain, suffering, distress or lasting harm'. But how far down the evolutionary ladder must we go before we are sure a creature feels pain or distress? Can an amoeba suffer, or a caterpillar or a spider? Or indeed, are insects animals within the meaning of the act?

Making our films, we were advised that only vertebrates could feel pain and other creatures probably not. If any creature had a sophisticated nervous system then any experiment that might inflict pain on it had to be approved by the Home Office before we could do it. This dilemma confronted me when we were doing a documentary about how animals defend themselves and Desmond Morris wanted to show how a cuttlefish releases a fog of black ink to escape a predator.

To frighten the cuttlefish enough to perform its survival act we wanted to borrow a conger eel from the zoo's aquarium. To our surprise the curator of fish was not keen on putting one of his eels in the same tank as a cuttlefish. This was not because of any special concern for the cuttlefish, but because he was afraid that if the cuttlefish failed to escape behind its black cloud and it was swallowed by the eel, the fish's bone might get stuck in the eel's narrow throat and choke it. However, trying to be helpful, the curator offered a one-eyed conger eel that they wouldn't mind risking for such a film. We accepted the offer and our cameraman had a busy time racing around the tank making sure that only the non-blind profile of the eel was kept in shot. The cuttlefish easily escaped its attentions.

Intrigued by the dilemma which we had managed to solve, I pressed the head keeper of insects at the London Zoo for guidance should we plan other experiments on insects for future programmes. He admitted that while he himself was rather affectionate towards spiders, it would be a difficult humanitarian enterprise to lay down special rules for avoiding pain for every kind of insect. 'After all,' he explained, 'there are no less than thirty million species of insects. Which of them should be protected has to be just a matter of common sense.'

★ ★ ★

Most of the other programmes I produced at Granada had a political or social orientation. Since the format for such shows was fairly predictable because of the imperatives of balance, there was not much room for originality. A witty comment on this opinion strait-jacket was conveyed in a cartoon showing two men in a studio facing a TV camera. The commentator is saying 'Yesterday the manager of this station wished all

its viewers a Happy New Year. Here is Mr Witherspoon with an opposing point of view.'

Who Goes Next? was my idea. Politicians on television, I had learnt,
were rarely permitted to give a scripted, considered reply to the questions they were asked. In live programmes there was little time for
reflection or for the shaping of opinions in a reasoned, articulate manner. The novelty of this programme was that its participants would not
be questioned or hectored by commentators, and that what they had to
say had been written beforehand and would be read as they wrote it
from an autocue. Its other innovation was its brevity. It was transmitted
on Mondays on the commercial network at 6.10 p.m. and was only
twenty minutes long.

Each week I personally formulated the questions, relying upon topical news events for my inspiration. There would usually be three serious topics and a light-hearted one. Have the trade unions too much
power? Do you believe in miracles? There was a strict time limit
imposed on every answer – thirty seconds to ninety seconds – and the
same question would be answered in turn in large TV close-ups by the
three participants. The hope was that the viewer would see in the round
the positions taken up on the same issue by a Conservative, Labour and
Liberal or Independent speaker. Balance demanded the major parties
being represented on every programme, while Independents and
Liberals shared the third slot. The programme had no chairman and the
faces came on in a fair sequence.

The trick was to find three prominent figures willing to spend their
Sundays writing their required answers, take the sleeper from King's
Cross to Manchester the same night, do the programme on tape at noon
on Monday and then return to London. Occasionally the programme
was made in London. None of them knew what the others had written.

There was no difficulty at all in finding volunteers, for politicians had
begun to realize that exposure on TV was by far the most rewarding
media asset. My regular team consisted of Peter Thorneycroft, a former
Tory Chancellor of the Exchequer, Richard Crossman, a journalist and
member of Labour's Shadow Cabinet, and Malcolm Muggeridge,
author and gadfly commentator. When they were on holiday or had
other commitments, Harold Wilson stood in for Labour, William
Deedes, later Editor of the *Daily Telegraph*, for the Tories and Jo
Grimond, the Liberal leader, for the middle political view.

At first they all protested that they couldn't possibly be expected to express an intelligent view about such complicated subjects as Clause Four or NATO in ninety seconds. But when I explained that they could speak about three hundred words in the time, which was about the length of a leader column in a tabloid like the *Daily Mirror*, they all gave it a try and most of them enjoyed it. Indeed Dick Crossman complained to me that having to compress his opinions so drastically on the programme had played havoc with his speaking style in the Commons. 'While I used to be able to stretch out any topic for at least half an hour in a Commons debate, I now find that after I've talked for five minutes I have practically nothing left to say.'

Who Goes Next? survived for over a year and it was a rich source of gossip and anecdotes as the team shared the same carriage for many hours, going up and down to Manchester every week. I was allowed to handle these egotistical, temperamental political prima donnas with no interference from Sidney Bernstein.

★ ★ ★

Head On was another idea of mine. Because of our stringent libel laws, TV has been particularly sensitive about belittling or ridiculing or insulting well-known personalities in its programmes. The more normal format was something like *This Is Your Life*, where the central figure's life was held up as a model of courage, talent, skill or determination as his or her friends were paraded in front of them recalling anecdotes of various forms of achievement. Not a critical word was allowed to crack this mirror of admiration and goodwill.

Wasn't there a more objective way to create a TV portrait if the subject was prepared to take the brick-bats as well as the bouquets? By filming friends and enemies giving their candid opinion of someone they knew, wouldn't the resultant mixture of insults and compliments be fascinating to see – particularly where the subject himself was given the right to answer back?

But who was confident enough of their ability at repartee to expose himself to such a challenge on TV? I tried out the programme on several prominent, controversial figures but none would bite. Finally Randolph Churchill, Winston's son, a man with a reputation for quick wit and ready rudeness agreed to be the first subject. We filmed such acquaintances and friends as Lord Birkenhead, Michael Foot, Lord

Stanley of Alderney and Sir Fitzroy Maclean, along with less enthusiastic contacts such as the landlady of his local pub, Nigel Nicholson and
others.

Their interviews were cut to the few pertinent minutes needed, and
then shown on a large screen in a studio with only Randolph watching.
Cameras were on him all the time to catch his reactions to the insults
being heaped upon him. After each edited statement was over, the cameras turned on Randolph to get his reply to these reminiscences and anecdotes. It was all edited together into a unique fifty-minute TV profile
which, with a couple of exceptions, the TV critics enjoyed and praised.

They heard about how, when he was behind the lines in Croatia with
Lord Birkenhead and Evelyn Waugh, he talked so much that his com-
panions each bet him £10 he couldn't stop talking long enough to read
the Old Testament in the Bible. 'Unfortunately it made him talk even
more because everything in the Bible seemed to surprise him as if he
had never read it before,' said Lord Birkenhead. 'He kept muttering
"What a swine!" or "God is a shit!" as he lost his bet.'

They also heard about how he accused a Cabinet Minster at a party
of cheating at bridge. 'They're quite wrong,' replied Randolph. 'I didn't
accuse him of cheating. Only of adding the score up wrong.' The local
pub landlady told of how he was so rude to the villagers where he lived
that the taxi drivers stuck matches into the keyholes of his car doors,
forcing him to clamber in the car's rear window.

Peter Black, the *Daily Mail's* TV critic, summed up that the total
opinion of all these voices was that Randolph was charming, testy, frank,
courageous, loathsome, interesting, litigious, nonconformist, pompous,
haughty, a fascinating raconteur and impartially rude. 'It seems a long
while since ITV offered in the evening a programme so alive and rich
in interest.' The critic of the *Sunday Telegraph* hit upon the programme's
main weakness as a series: 'A jolly good programme idea,' was his verdict, 'as long as the supply of Randolph Churchills keeps up.'

That was precisely the trouble. They did not keep up if, indeed, many
of them ever existed at all. Invitations were sent to almost any important person who had ever taken part in a public debate and was willing
to test his skill at repelling with wit any ruderies flung at him by his
friends and enemies. Amongst those who were invited and declined
were Anthony Eden, Graham Greene, Evelyn Waugh, Henry Moore,
Lord Mountbatten, Lord Reith and others.

It was eight months before another version of *Head On* was seen –

which caused the *Daily Mail* critic to comment that programmes in this series were about as frequent as quadruple births. Since we could get no one else who fitted the criteria of being well-known, controversial and available, it was Dr Hewlett Johnson, the 'Red Dean' of Canterbury, who was shown facing the critics of his long, outspoken, left-wing career. I felt rather guilty encouraging a man of almost ninety to take on such a task but, in the event, he emerged cool, confident, unperturbed and thoroughly batty.

One discovered that he had never been a card-carrying member of the communist party, that he still believed in the invigorating effects of the youth-enhancing drug H.3, that he thought the Soviet regime 'profoundly Christian', that he had invented zip fasteners for his gaiters and that much of what Stalin had done would have the 'benediction of Jesus'. That was the last we saw of *Head On*. British TV was not yet ready for so frank, brutal and revealing a dissection of a personality on a small screen. A similar idea was tried again in 1996 and had a similar wary and tepid reception.

That was the last programme I produced for Granada. I was coming under increasing pressure to move to Manchester, since Granada's entire operation, except for the zoo unit, was now up there and I was an anachronism, trying to retain some sort of authority over my productions from an office in Golden Square. It was obvious that to do the job properly I would have to stop being a theatre critic, and there were no indications that Bernstein was prepared to double my salary so I could do just that. Sadly, I told him I had accepted an offer to become an Assistant Controller of Programmes at Associated-Rediffusion. Reported in the Londoner's Diary in the *Standard* as to why I was making this change I said, 'I am going because it's a better job.'

* * *

It was once again an accident that brought about my next important career move. I happened to meet John McMillan, Controller of Programmes at Associated-Rediffusion (A-R), at a dinner party. As was the custom in those days, the women left to tidy up leaving the men with their port and an opportunity to gossip about business and politics. I must have given the impression to McMillan that I was finding it irksome justifying trying to do a job in London for a Manchester-based company.

A few days later he asked me to a meeting at their Kingsway offices when I met their general manager, Captain Tom Brownrigg. I must have made a favourable impression because I was soon invited to take on the post of Assistant Controller of Programmes with a much higher salary, a chauffeur-driven company car and permission to carry on with my work as theatre critic of the *Evening Standard*.

I was ensconced in my new offices in May 1962, and since Kingsway was very close to the West End theatres in the Strand and Shaftesbury Avenue, I could carry on working for A-R until six in the evening and still make the first-night openings at 7 p.m. My brief was much the same as the one I had at Granada. I was to buy films for the company and advise on the quality of films which A-R was contemplating producing. In addition I would stand in for the heads of the Drama and Current Affairs whenever they were absent or on holiday. I would also take on the production of programmes, probably about current affairs, as I had done at Granada.

A-R's franchise was for the five weekdays in the London Area, whereupon it gave way for the week-end to ABC Television. The fourth of the large franchised companies was Associated TV (ATV) whose major shareholders were showmen like Lew Grade, Val Parnell and Prince Littler and others such as the *Daily Mirror*. There were ten other franchises for smaller regions, e.g. Scotland, Wales and Northern Ireland. These fourteen companies provided a daisy-chain of networking with the Big Four usually monopolizing the programmes transmitted throughout the nation, while the other ten confined themselves to the making of regional programmes and local news.

When I joined A-R it was also making annual profits of between four to six million pounds. I always thought this was a remarkable achievement since their programme philosophy, their budgeting methods, their production techniques seemed to be almost contradictory in every important aspect to those of Granada. It was, indeed, an opportunity to 'print money', and the audiences and the advertisers didn't seem to care what appeared on that small screen as long as it was a moving picture.

Associated-Rediffusion was owned by a group of City businessmen with very little experience in any branch of the entertainment or newspaper business. Its major shareholder was British Electric Traction, a conglomerate with large financial interests in laundries and buses. It was a Board – contrary to the Granada Board – that made almost a fetish of not becoming involved with the content of its programmes. Its strange choice as general manager was an ex-naval officer, Captain Tom Brownrigg, who treated his fellow executives as if they were on board a British battleship. Manners and conversation in the executive dining suite resembled a naval mess, with formal standings and sittings and gin as the preferred lunch tipple.

Captain Brownrigg's awareness of what should be shown on his company's screens was practically nil. A professional sailor, he had rarely gone to films and until he was given this role his observation of TV content was minimal. He used to boast about the fact that when he had gone to Hollywood for the first time to familiarize himself with the cinema world, he had had an amusing conversation with one of the guests at a reception. When he asked a colleague who he had been talking to, he was told 'Bing Crosby.'

It was John McMillan, the Controller of Programmes, a shrewd, gregarious Australian who recognized that if commercial TV was to compete successfully with the BBC for mass audiences then frivolity and triviality had to be the order of the day. There were a few serious programmes scattered through the ITV schedules – *This Week*, *Armchair Theatre*, *What The Papers Say* – but basically it concentrated on silly quiz games like *Double Your Money* and *Take Your Pick*, both supplied by Rediffusion.

But McMillan was aware that when the franchises came up for renewal in 1967, their record would be judged not only by the viewing figures but by the programmes which might be labelled as having a public-service, educational, social-uplifting content. I suspect that I was hired to give some minor respectability to their choice of political and drama programmes because of my reputation as a theatre critic and because of the political programmes I had done at Granada. There were five assistant controllers of programmes at Rediffusion, each with an area like light entertainment, drama, engineering, scheduling to look after. I had no special arena of responsibility but the purchasing of new material occupied most of my time.

Before I took on my first programme, it was already surrounded by controversy. It was going to be called *Division* and to be edited and compered by Ian Trethowan, who in 1972 became Director-General of the BBC. But he objected to the amount of control demanded by the General Manager, Brownrigg, who insisted his approval should be obtained about any issue or MP that was planned for the programme. It was a task that Brownrigg had taken on for himself for the previous late-night political programme transmitted by A-R. Trethowan wanted a much more hard-hitting, less reverential approach to politics but Brownrigg, always eager to please authority, refused to grant him this independence.

Trethowan left and the programme which was to begin on 30 October 1962, coinciding with the State Opening of Parliament, was postponed until 27 November for a re-think. When the political slot was eventually filled for 10.30 to 11.00 viewing every fortnight, its name had been changed, so had its brief and I was its producer.

Now called *Decision* its aim was to investigate how political decisions are made, how real power is wielded, the crucial issues facing Britain and how they are being tackled. Our first programme examined public opinion polls and just how much parties are influenced by them. It dealt with the role of shop stewards, the organization of the defence services, the part universities play in the production of practical brain power for the nation, the qualifications Dr Beeching possessed for sorting out the railways, the shortage of resources for medical research. One of my roving reporters was Michael Heseltine, later to become Deputy Leader of the Tory Party, whom I described in an interview as 'A good-looking young man, argumentative and fluent.'

By ITV standards it was fairly onerous stuff, yet it managed a regular viewing figure of 2,000,000 for a late hour slot. Talking to the *TV Times* about *Decision*, my final comment was, 'When you remember that this matches the circulation of many national newspapers, it makes you think, doesn't it?'

The item that gave me most trouble concerned Harold Wilson and what impression he was making on the political commentators and experts in his first few months as Leader of the Labour Opposition. Wilson was easily the politician most conscious of the power of the media – newspaper and TV – and the most determined to use it as a tool to gain victory for Labour. The Kennedy–Nixon television debates had convinced him of the importance of the TV image. He recognized the importance of spin doctors long before Clinton or Blair had ever heard of them. In 1963 they were called press officers, and their duty was to keep an eagle eye out for any report or comment that reflected adversely on Wilson or the Labour Party. I was often the recipient of polite, sometimes hectoring, even threatening protests about something they had heard was going to be on a programme of mine which, they warned me, would be seen with much displeasure at Party Headquarters.

Complaints of this nature came from all parties, if they thought they could get anything changed in their favour. Wilson, behind a smoke-screen of spin doctors, manipulated TV like a virtuoso organist aware of the nuances of every pedal, lever and stop. The press officers were particularly sensitive about balance – seconds were counted up as if they were gold nuggets – and my researchers were frequently harassed by them. Of course, the spin doctors themselves were egged on by their political masters to complain about the most trivial sign of unbalance. Labour was most guilty of this kind of pressure because it claimed, probably rightly, that it was beleaguered by an overwhelmingly Tory press, and that therefore it deserved special attention in this area from a state media like TV.

On the day that Wilson was elected as Labour's leader, I invited three journalists and four politicians to come to Rediffusion's studio in Kingsway to answer three short questions about him for the television cameras. Do you think Wilson's leadership will be good for the party? Do you think he will be good for the nation? What are Wilson's strengths and weaknesses as a political leader?

The answers were not transmitted at that time. My aim was to discover a long-term assessment, and five months later the same people were brought before the TV cameras again, and asked, in the light of Wilson's performance in his job, whether their opinions of him had changed. The programme containing both the earlier and the later interviews was scheduled for transmission on 16 July 1963.

With so many individuals involved, I was conscious of the delicate problem of balance that had to be maintained, since I had assembled a wide political spectrum of opinions. It could be said that the journalists tended to be suspicious of Wilson, but I thought their negative bias was adequately countered by a surprising eulogy from the late right-wing journalist, Henry Fairlie, who had said, 'I think it's one of the most skilful performances by any politician, certainly in my time and possibly in this century.' Bernard Levin disagreed. 'I believe that his short-term effect on Labour's fortunes will be very good for it. But his long-term effect, both on the party and the country, will be bad and possibly disastrous.' To fill out the rest of the fifty-minute programme there was to be a discussion between the Labour MP Barbara Castle and the Tory MP Charles Curran, to be followed by a personal interview with Wilson himself, conducted by Kenneth Harris, which would last nine minutes.

To make sure there would be no trouble about all this I sent a transcript of the statements to Wilson's press officer, who told me in no uncertain terms that Wilson had no intention of appearing on any programme with Bernard Levin. I was told that the taboo against Levin was due to his consistent portraying of Wilson in a mocking and deprecating light in his column.

I indicated that I was not prepared to drop Levin, and for the moment I heard no more about that particular demand. With his spin doctors, I discussed other suggestions they put forward to please their master. They wanted another pro-Wilson commentator and I inserted a respected journalist who was willing to make a brief favourable statement about Wilson's record. Everything seemed to be settled. On the agreed morning, I waited with a large camera crew for Wilson's arrival.

At 9.30 a.m. I received a message that Wilson wasn't coming. Frantically, because a great deal of effort and money was now involved, I asked to speak to him personally. His voice was cold and dismissive. I had known him on more friendly terms when he occasionally sat in for Richard Crossman on Granada's *Who Goes Next?* He said that the matter had already been fully discussed with his people and that he had no intention of talking to me any more about it. If the television company wanted to know anything more about the reasons for his refusing to appear, he would only explain those reasons to Rediffusion's General Manager, Captain Brownrigg, and not to me. If a meeting could be arranged he would turn up at 10 a.m.

Brownrigg, of course, knew nothing about the details of the programme and I had to brief him in a few short minutes about all the negotiations that had taken place. I confessed I wasn't precisely sure why Wilson had suddenly taken this recalcitrant stand. Shortly afterwards in Brownrigg's office, Wilson, accompanied by two press offices, voiced his objections to the proposed programme. He pointed out that Bernard Levin had run a sneering vendetta against him, and had even written that if Wilson ever became prime minister he would emigrate.

I defended the balance of the programme as being, if anything, too pro-Wilson. I also warned Brownrigg that if Rediffusion were to remove Levin at that late stage, there would be too many people who would know, including Levin himself, that the company had caved in under party political pressure. It would be impossible for such a juicy morsel to be kept out of the papers. The resultant publicity could only be unfavourable to the Wilson image.

Brownrigg saw the merit of this argument. He thought Wilson might be letting himself in for some awkward press comment. Was he adamant that Levin be removed from the programme? There was a long pause. 'Oh,' said Wilson airily, puffing at his pipe. 'I don't want Levin taken out. I was just explaining why I didn't like being on the same programme with him.'

That left us all baffled. What changes, asked Brownrigg, did he want then? It turned out that Barbara Castle was the one he wanted taken off the programme. I had no objections to this surprising development but how should I explain her ejection to her at this late hour? I needn't worry about that, Wilson reassured me. He'd explain it all to Barbara himself.

The programme was duly transmitted with Levin in and Castle out. I received a letter from Wilson thanking me for my efforts, in spite of some early difficulties, and telling me that he had received extremely favourable reports. No explanation was ever offered for this sudden shift in demands, but it would appear likely that the possibility of facing ridicule for censoring a programme caused him to draw back.

Castle was probably removed because she was a prominent, vociferous member of the left-wing of the party and Wilson, facing an early election, was – like Tony Blair in 1997 – trying to woo the voters by cultivating a moderate image. Barbara Castle was, at that time, just too radical for his liking. I suspect that Tony Blair's spin doctors would have perpetrated similar manoeuvres had they been confronted with a programme inviting Ken Livingstone or Tony Benn to speak up for Blair on TV just before the 1997 election.

As Wilson started so he went on in his efforts to cajole and intimidate television executives and commentators. Of course politicians of every persuasion have used press officers or spin doctors or arm-twisting techniques against the electronic media to get favourable publicity for their parties. Harold Wilson was the most efficient and ruthless of them all.

* * *

It was gratifying to me that even before I joined A-R, it had bought my book, *Defeat in the West*, as the basis for one of their major documentaries. The script was written and narrated by Paul Johnson, and directed by Peter Morley. It supported my thesis for the three causes of Germany's defeat – Ignorance, Discipline and Hitler – and contained some stunning newsreel material of the Normandy invasion and the battle of Stalingrad, which had cost the lives of 600 German cameramen to obtain. There were also extensive interviews with General Gunther Blumentritt, von Rundstedt's Chief of Staff and General Walter Warlimont, Deputy Chief-of-Staff at Hitler's headquarters.

My final task for Rediffusion, which I left in 1964 to become the TV columnist on the *Evening Standard*, was being the British representative of the judges for the seventh international TV film festival, which had become an adjunct of the world-renowned Cannes film festival. The product we saw was film material that had been made specifically for television and no less than twenty-six countries had submitted entries.

In small viewing theatres we stared at five or six films a day giving us no chance to enjoy the sunny, swimming delights of Cannes. Our task had to be concluded by 2 May when the opening ceremonies of the grand Cannes Film Festival would take place. There were eight judges representing countries like France, Hungary, America and myself for Britain. René Clair, the renowned and respected director, was president of our jury. When we had made our choice of categories like the Best Film, Best Director, Best Photography, I agreed with the American representative that some countries had been the best in two or three of the categories and deserved two or three of the prizes.

We were taken aside by the organizers of the Festival and politely told that we had misunderstood one of the fundamental conventions of these occasions. The products were submitted over the past six years by nations hoping they might get a prize even though their facilities could not compete with such leading TV countries as America, Britain and France.

To encourage smaller countries to participate, the honours had to be evenly distributed – so that national representatives could go home clutching their little statuettes. This was like a children's party where everyone got a prize or a conciliatory balloon or bag of sweets to prevent tears spoiling the occasion. The American and I decided to play along and re-allocate our votes to please the organizers. I remember a prize was given to a Japanese director who filmed his father dying over his last few weeks. It was very slow, long and depressing. Just the kind of film that often won prizes at these festivals.

(ii) Kennedy's assassination wounds George Brown

Knowing how to handle television was a technique not yet mastered by many politicians back in 1963. But some arrogantly assumed they were capable of handling any demand of the electronic box on any occasion. George Brown, later to be Lord George-Brown, was a Labour politician whose career was seriously blighted by his miscalculation of the appropriate treatment of television.

He was easily the most volatile, unpredictable and controversial of Harold Wilson's Shadow Cabinet. 'His strengths far exceeded his weaknesses,' wrote Wilson, assessing his colleague, 'but it was his weaknesses that ended his ministerial career.'

He had contested the Labour leadership against Wilson and was well-backed. He was Deputy Leader of the Party and at the end of 1963 was the likely heir-apparent should there be a revolt against Wilson. I believe it was his TV appearance on the day of President Kennedy's assassination that effectively put paid to any chances of his succeeding to party leadership.

On 22 November 1963 I was having an early drink in Rediffusion's executive dining-room with Geoffrey Whitaker, the Assistant Controller of Programmes in charge of engineering. Usually seven or eight executives would be expected to relax for gossip and a drink before slipping off home, but that evening most of them – all the top men – were attending the annual dinner of the Guild of Television Producers and Directors, where awards for the best performances of the year were to be announced and handed out. The waitress who had been serving us drinks rather diffidently told us that President Kennedy had been shot in Dallas, Texas. She had heard it on the radio and wasn't sure that she had got it right. It was several minutes of busy telephoning before we could get confirmation that a shooting had taken place, and not long afterwards we heard that the President was dead.

Switching on the TV set in the dining-room to pick up further details of this numbing news, we saw to our horror that while the BBC had discontinued their regular programmes and were transmitting solemn music out of respect for Kennedy's death, Rediffusion was still churning out the bi-weekly medical soap opera, *Emergency Ward 10*.

We raced around to the office of Cyril Francis, the executive responsible for scheduling and coordinating the programmes of the fourteen companies that made up the commercial network, and protested that Rediffusion could not go on pumping out *Emergency Ward 10* and that something more appropriate for such a serious occasion should be substituted. If the BBC's screen had gone blank, we argued, we would have had to follow suit or be subjected to severe criticism for bad taste in the morning press. Francis pointed out, however, that his hands were tied by the formal Obituary Procedure that had been laid down, to be activated whenever the death of a prominent figure occurred.

According to these rules, different transmission arrangements were to apply depending upon the rank and importance of the deceased. In Category A, covering the immediate members of the Royal Family from the Queen to the Prince of Wales, all normal programming would cease immediately after the formal 'Announcement To The Nation' was made, and all commercials would be cancelled for the remainder of the day. The death of lesser categories of individuals would not have such drastic repercussions on the scheduled programmes or the commercials. For instance, the death of the Duke of Gloucester, who was in Category C, would mean only the cancellation of commercials in the programme break in which the formal announcement took place.

President Kennedy was in Category D, along with the Pope, the Archbishop of Canterbury, Harold Wilson, the Duke of Kent, Kruschev, Nehru and a few others. For their deaths no commercials were to be cancelled and no programmes would be altered or amended, unless it was felt that their theme was unsuitable in some specific way related to the death of that particular individual. It was this procedure that was being conscientiously carried out by the entire ITV network, immediately after the announcement of Kennedy's assassination.

Whitaker and I insisted that if we persisted in carrying out this obituary procedure, we would be affronting the mood of the nation, which would be extremely shocked and disturbed by the tragic circumstances surrounding the death of this much-admired and much-loved youthful President of the United States. Francis agreed.

Emergency Ward 10 was taken off, the commercials cancelled and a standby programme of Sir John Barbirolli conducting the Halle Orchestra substituted. The rest of the companies on the commercial network followed suit. It was a decision that meant the loss of something like £60,000 in advertising revenue. Oddly enough, the BBC, who had in the first place made the right decision by taking off their regular programmes, saw that Rediffusion was still transmitting *Emergency Ward 10* and decided to return to their normal schedule.

This meant that while ITV was displaying an appropriate sense of tragic decorum, the BBC was insensitively showing a Harry Worth comedy at a time when the nation was in no mood for laughter. The next day the Press gave the Corporation a bad time over its bad taste. ITV was praised. Nor did the companies lose any revenue, because they were given permission to recoup the lost advertising minutes on subsequent days.

In the meantime it had been decided to mount a special programme in which some attempt would be made to assess the implications of Kennedy's murder. Who had done it and why? Was it a signal for a right-wing take-over of the American government? Was it a left-wing plot? What sort of a man was the new President, Lyndon Baynes Johnson? How would America react? What did it mean to Britain and Europe?

Under Jeremy Isaacs, an experienced current affairs producer, every secretary and programme executive available was rushed to take telephones to contact as many appropriate Americans and authoritative figures as could be assembled in Rediffusion's studios as quickly as possible. Every former ambassador to Russia or America was called without success. Politicians like R. A. Butler, Selwyn Lloyd, Peter Thorneycroft, Edward Heath, Jo Grimond and Patrick Gordon Walker were telephoned and were unavailable. In the course of these frantic proceedings we were told that both the Prime Minister, Sir Alec Douglas-Home, and the Opposition leader, Harold Wilson, would be making national TV statements. Neither was in London. It was a Friday night and London was denuded of both politicians and experts.

Through sheer persistence, however, some appropriate figures were finally located and tracked down. Professor Sir Dennis Brogan, an expert on American history, was available. John Crosby of the *New York Herald Tribune* was approached during the interval of a ballet at Covent Garden and persuaded to come to the studios. Two other Americans, the film producer, Carl Foreman, and the actor, Eli Wallach, also agreed to appear. George Brown, as Labour's Deputy Leader, was at a Mayor's dinner at Shoreditch, which he agreed to leave in order to make his contribution to the programme. To all of us, Brown's availability was most gratifying, not only because of the weight his presence would give to our hurriedly-assembled programme, but because he had only recently returned from a trip to America where he had met both President Kennedy and Vice-President Johnson.

Jeremy Isaacs had planned the shape of the programme. It would include a short account, illustrated by as much film as was available, of the controversial issues facing Kennedy when he was gunned down. Such issues causing great bitterness were right-wing animosity in the South, segregation of schools, race riots and others. Then the three Americans – Foreman, Wallach and Crosby – would be asked to give their reactions to the assassination. This would be followed by interviews with Professor Brogan and George Brown.

The participants assembled in the company's hospitality room and I briefed them about what was wanted while Isaacs sorted out the technical problems of production. Although there tends to be a good deal of easy chit-chat and cynical banter during the behind-the-scenes preparation of a current affairs programme, on this occasion the mood was intense and sombre. Kennedy's death had seemed to touch something deep and personal in those assembled in this room and few were inclined to talk very much.

George Brown, however, was as talkative and communicative as ever. It was obvious that he had enjoyed some generous liquid hospitality at the Mayor's dinner in Shoreditch, but there was no real evidence that drink had affected him in any serious way. Having first expressed his views that the assassination was a great tragedy for both Britain and America, he was positive the presidency would be in safe and sure hands. To this optimistic assessment, Professor Brogan slightly demurred. Brown brushed aside the professor's misgivings.

During the pre-programme briefing I gave to Professor Brogan and Brown, I said that I would like the professor to confine his remarks to an assessment of the constitutional and political implications of the new regime, while we hoped that Brown's contribution would be in the nature of a tribute to Kennedy. Something I said suddenly raised Brown's suspicions.

'It this going to be one of those fifteen-second statements on the air?' he asked me. 'If so I'm leaving the building now.' I assured him he would have reasonable time to make a statement and, mollified, he went off to discuss with Kenneth Harris, who was going to conduct the interview, the general drift it was to take.

At about this time, Eli Wallach, the American actor arrived. He was clearly upset about the news and was in no mood for small talk. He was introduced to George Brown, who immediately told him how much he admired the actor's work. Wallach accepted Brown's compliments with good grace but was not anxious to chat about himself.

Brown, however, persisted in trying to steer the conversation in that direction and when Wallach did not respond, Brown asked in a loud tone of voice, why actors were so conceited. Someone like Wallach always carried a newspaper in his pocket with his name in prominent headlines, said Brown, determined to taunt Wallach. On the contrary, Wallach was finally stung to reply, he was always meeting people who said they recognized his face but could not place his name. It was all meant to be light-hearted banter but Wallach, emotionally upset by Kennedy's death, clearly wanted none of it.

'Have you ever been in a play by Ted Willis?' asked Brown, out of the blue.

'No,' said Wallach. 'Who's Ted Willis?'

'You've never heard of Ted Willis?' said Brown, feigning incredulity.

Ted Willis was created a life peer in 1963, not long after this incident. An ardent supporter of the Labour Party, he had written such plays as *Woman In A Dressing Gown* and was probably best known for his police television series, *Dixon of Dock Green*.

Wallach's curt denial of any knowledge of Ted Willis evidently annoyed Brown. In an effort to break off this pointless conversation, Wallach walked over to the drinks cupboard and poured himself a whisky. This did not stop George Brown. The American actor returned to his seat and said nothing while Brown continued to mutter loudly about the ego of American actors in general and Wallach in particular. Suddenly Wallach lost his temper. He rose from the sofa, pointed at the Labour Deputy Leader and shouted, 'I didn't come here to be insulted. Is this bastard interviewing me on the programme? If so, I'm leaving now.'

Brown muttered something deprecating which infuriated Wallach even more. He began to strip off his jacket. 'Come outside!' he said to Brown, who was sitting on a low chair looking up at him. 'Come outside and I'll knock you off your can!'

Undeterred, Brown shrugged the threat away and told Wallach to shut up and sit down. The American rushed forward as if to hit him and I leapt between them and pushed Wallach back on to his sofa. At that moment the American film producer, Carl Foreman, arrived to see me wrestling with Wallach. Foreman told me afterwards that his first reaction to this startling sight of Wallach and myself locked together in this violent manner was to assume that Wallach was trying to hit me because of something I may have said about him in some film or theatre review.

Although he had no idea what it was all about, Foreman joined me in restraining Wallach and trying to pacify him.

'He's not going to interview you on the programme,' I hissed to Wallach. 'He's one of the guests.'

'Well, who *is* he? Who *is* he?' Wallach kept asking. Although there had been formal introductions when he arrived, Wallach had obviously not worked out who everyone was.

'He's George Brown! Deputy Leader of the Labour Party!' I whispered, trying to prevent my voice from carrying across the room to where Brown was imperturbably watching the tussle.

'That's right,' confirmed Carl Foreman, becoming aware of what was going on. 'Don't be a fool. Sit down! He's an important man in the Labour Party.'

'I don't care who he is,' said Wallach, still trying to break loose from our restraining efforts. 'I'll still knock the shit out of him.'

By now George Brown was reduced to silence. Wallach, realizing that his anger had been directed at an important politician and not some aggressive interviewer, allowed himself to be pacified. It was quickly decided that the best course was to cool the temperature by getting Wallach and Brown as far apart as possible.

The three Americans – Wallach, Foreman and Crosby – were asked to go downstairs to the studio where the programme would be on the air in about fifteen minutes' time. As they rose to leave, Brown got up from his chair and extended his hand to Eli Wallach. 'Brother, brother,' he said, 'I don't think we should go into the same studio feeling this way. Let's shake hands.'

In subsequent comments on the incident some columnists implied that Rediffusion was at fault for allowing Brown to appear before the cameras in that condition. But Kenneth Harris and I, having had experiences of a similar kind with Brown on other programmes, did not think that his behaviour, until the Wallach affair, was so unusual as to assume he would not be able to acquit himself reasonably well on the box. He had displayed the goodwill and good grace to ask Wallach to patch up their understanding. And I was always aware of the libel implications if we had prohibited him from appearing in such a vital programme so late. What defence could we have put up if he accused us of charging him with drunkenness and being unfit to carry out his duties as a significant Labour politician?

Wallach shook Brown's hand, they exchanged a few terse words, and I thought that was the end of the matter. I was wrong. Just as Wallach was leaving the room, in the wake of Foreman and Crosby who had preceded him, Brown could not resist one final word. 'And now you'll know who Ted Willis is!' he shouted after the retreating figure of the American actor.

I spent the next fifteen minutes trying to make light of the whole incident by explaining to George Brown that Wallach had obviously not known who he was and had not realized that the banter was not unkindly meant. By the time he turned up in front of the cameras the intensity of this fracas, the emotion of the occasion, the wait under the hot studio lights, not to mention the alcohol he had consumed, inevitably had their combined effect.

His talk with Kenneth Harris was a disaster. His enthusiasm for Johnson, based upon a short meeting between them which he described in some detail, struck a jarring note of complacency and optimism. His rambling, inconclusive remarks indicated a remarkable insensitivity to the mood of the moment.

It was not until over a week later that the storm over Brown's appearance blew up into a first-class political row. According to Walter Terry of the *Daily Mail*, it was members of the Labour Party, rather than the general public, who reacted 'with horror at the effect it might have on party prestige'. It was their concern that caused Harold Wilson to ask George Brown for an explanation of what had happened that evening and the Deputy Leader, on the Thursday following the broadcast, made a brief personal statement about it to the Parliamentary Labour Party.

But things really began to simmer when the *New York Herald Tribune*, on the front page on 30 November 1963, reported that 'there was trouble at the studio even before the programme began. Mr Brown got into a verbal row with Mr Wallach and friends had to intervene to stop it from coming to blows. Neither of the men had met previously.'

Wrote Derek Marks in the *Evening Standard* of 2 December 1963: 'Now it should be said at once that Mr Brown made an ass of himself in his television appearance on the night of President Kennedy's death – at least, to be more accurate, he did in the view of every single person I have met who saw the programme. But he is not the first, and certainly will not be the last, politician to make an ass of himself on television.'

George Brown's value as propagandizer, energizer and catalyst was too great for an incident like this to exclude him from the higher councils of the Labour Party. When Labour took office in 1964, Harold Wilson gave him the formidable posts of Secretary of State for

Economic Affairs and Foreign Secretary in 1966. But the night Kennedy was shot also riddled George Brown's career with the poisoned darts of doubt about his reliability and stability. His reputation never recovered from that disastrous night.

(iii) Every Home Should Have One
It was seeing *What's New Pussycat?* at a local cinema in 1965 that tempt-ed me into trying my hand at writing a film. Written by Woody Allen, who was in it along with Peter Sellers and Peter O'Toole, it was dis-missed by most critics as a zany sex comedy that was not as enjoyably dirty as it ought to have been. It concerned a fashion editor distracted by beautiful girls like Romy Schneider, Ursula Andress and Capucine and, as directed by Clive Donner, had that quality of anarchic, fast-mov-ing irreverence and irrelevance that was symbolic of the wildly swing-ing sixties. I thought this was a film I'd like to make.

The idea must have already sunk deeply into my subconscious when a friend of mine, Herbert Kretzmer, then theatre critic of the *Daily Express* and later to become very rich as the lyricist of *Les Misérables*, casually told me over lunch that he thought there was a good film idea in a modern version of the Goldilocks nursery tale.

'The theme would basically investigate what might happen to an average middle-class home confronted with the intrusion of a sex sym-bol like Goldilocks,' mused Herbie. 'Goldilocks could be a series of au pair girls each having something to do with the fable – Who's broken my chair? Who's eaten my porridge? Who's been sleeping in my bed? How would an English family react? You can see the funny side of it, can't you?'

I didn't see. I made polite noises and said I would give it some thought. I few days later in my bath, where inspiration often hits me, the conversation returned to me, as did the sexual anarchy of *What's New Pussycat?*, and I gleaned the genesis of a plot.

Almost like Archimedes shouting Eureka!, I leapt out of the bath and phoned Herbie. I spoke very deliberately and slowly as I groped my way through the new-born story. 'Suppose the wife finds her ten-year-old son collecting knickers and pressing them in his stamp album between Malta and Madagascar. She is naturally upset when her son explains he got the hobby watching a programme called *Great Fetishes of Our Time*. Horrified at the unhealthy thoughts polluting her son's mind she joins a puritan pressure group called Keep Britain Clean. She spends so much time going out to see dirty films and TV shows that they have to hire an au pair girl.

'Each au pair is sexier than the last and Teddy, the husband, who is a sort of Walter Mitty fantasist, not only imagines himself in all the filthy situations that he often watches with his wife, but he also acquires creative techniques about how to make passes at the au pairs.

'Complicating matters is the fact that Teddy is an advertising copywriter whose personal account is McLaughlin's Highland Porridge. Who's been eating my porridge? His boss tells him that porridge sales are going down against other cereal competition and the client now insists that his product must be given a sexual image, perhaps even be made into a bed-time food. That's as far as I got, Herbie. While the wife is trying to keep sex out of people's living rooms, Teddy has the job of pumping it in through the commercials. I haven't the faintest idea of how to end it.'

Herbie was mildly enthusiastic about this development. After meeting a few times refining it, we agreed to invite John van Eyssen, Columbia Picture's representative in London, to lunch and put it up to him. He knew both of us as friends and came along little knowing what he was in for. To our delight he joined us in laughing as we outlined the story and asked us to submit a short synopsis in writing. Our agent was then sent a letter offering us £1,000 for the first treatment to be submitted by 24 April 1966, another £2,000 for a second, more detailed treatment, to be written by the end of the year and a final £2,000 if Columbia decided to make the picture. We called it *Goldilocks* or *Who's Been Sleeping In My Bed?*

It was always understood that other writers would be brought in for the final script, particularly to write parodies of the films that filled Teddy's sex-obsessed mind. While watching television Teddy became a Walter Mitty character imagining himself as a ravenous Dracula lunging for the necks of blonde beauties, or a nudist romping in a Swedish nudist camp, or a lusty Hell's Angel riding off on his souped-up Harley-Davidson with a girl from the local Labour Exchange on his pillion seat.

When we presented our 100-page screenplay to Columbia on time in April 1966, wild cries of enthusiasm emanated from the company. A well-known theatrical agency in America caught sight of it and suggested that two such promising young writers would have 'a fine future in films here in America'. When they were informed that we were not promising writers but two ageing theatre critics, their next memos from

America referred to us as 'talented gentlemen' whom they would 'like to expose to a number of producers in the United States.' In the event, either as a team or singly, we were never 'exposed' to anyone.

I had collaborated with another writer once before, when Stephen Watts and I wrote the never-to-be-produced *Man of Decision*. That experience had taught me that the partner in control of the typewriter or word processor would have most influence over the finished product. When we tussled over a line of dialogue that we thought was appropriate Herbie, pacing up and down my living room, would usually settle for the compromise word that I had already put on paper.

Our second treatment, involving another £2,000, was accepted early in 1967 and now that Columbia had a viable film story, they seemed a little uncertain about what to do with it. Herbie and I suggested that some TV gag writers be brought in for the parodies and put up the name of Ned Sherrin, who had been responsible for the much-admired BBC satire show, *That Was The Week That Was*, as a possible producer. To our surprise, because he had never made a cinema film before, Ned was contracted by Columbia to produce our film.

We were also told, now that Columbia had paid us the final £2,000, that Marty Feldman and Barry Took would be re-writing our script. To make us feel better about this cavalier approach to our efforts, Columbia assured our agent that they still wanted our advice about the final product, that Feldman and Took had expressed 'respect, understanding and enthusiasm' about our ideas, and that they were anxious we should not feel that 'our brainchild would be unnecessarily tampered with or held up.' In true film-making tradition neither of us was ever consulted about the film again.

Ned Sherrin spent the next three years trying to get together the various talents needed to collaborate on such a quirky, odd-ball film. For his shooting script he had contacted John Bird, John Mortimer, Clive Exton, Donald Cammel and Johnny Speight, all of whom, for one reason or another, said it was not for them. After Feldman and Took had agreed to write it and produced their script, Ned Sherrin had to hawk the story around to players suitable for the roles. He offered the part of Teddy to Peter Sellers, Tom Courtenay, Albert Finney, Alan Bates, Michael Caine, Michael Crawford, Anthony Newley, Topol, Dick van Dyke and Jack Lemmon. All of them turned it down.

The years slipped by. Ned Sherrin became involved in producing *The Virgin Soldiers* for Columbia. The project looked dead. Then a surprising thing happened. Marty Feldman, our scriptwriter, had suddenly become a comic find on television. With his curious, pop-up eyes and his zany, way-out humour, he was acquiring a large, devoted following, particularly among the young. Late in 1968, Sherrin tried to revive Columbia's flagging interest in the film by suggesting that Feldman be given the leading role of Teddy. They thought about it but in December 1968 – three years after we had first broached the idea to John van Eyssen – they wrote telling us that they had abandoned the project.

Sherrin, however, was undaunted. He went to the Boulting Brothers at British Lion and reminded them that they had just made a packet out of *Till Death Us Do Part* based on a fiercely popular satirical series starring Warren Mitchell, a telly star. Surely they could do it again with a rising, comic personality like Marty Feldman in *Goldilocks*?

Feldman himself, with a TV series beckoning him, was now rather reluctant to go ahead. But when he heard that Dennis Norden, a most successful TV writer, had agreed to work revising the script, and a new director, Jim Clark with magnificent credits as an imaginative film editor, was eager to take part, Feldman decided to take the role of Teddy. A contract was signed with British Lion and the film was made for a relatively modest budget of £330,000.

Another year had to elapse before Herbie's and my idea was finally finished and shown to the Press. Its gestation period had been almost five years. When it appeared in March 1970, its title had been changed to *Every Home Should Have One*. Joining Marty as its co-star was the American comedian, Shelley Berman, and in it was the startlingly beautiful former Miss Norway, Julie Ege, as a Swedish au pair who was described by one critic as 'the nearest thing to Raquel Welch since Raquel Welch.' Other well-known performers whom Sherrin recognized for their comic timing ability were Patrick Cargill, Judy Cornwell, Dinsdale Landen and Penelope Keith.

Trade reports before the press show were enthusiastic. The film censor, John Trevelyan, said it was the funniest British film for twenty years and he was planning to give it the first AA certificate, which would enable it to be seen by unaccompanied fourteen-year-olds. Yet despite this official badge of relative purity, I was shocked to learn how deep was the Puritan, shockable instinct in many professional film critics. The *Financial Times* thought it 'sickeningly vulgar'. The *Guardian* found that the 'persistent harping on the phallic left me with a decidedly nasty taste in my mouth.' The *People* was apoplectic about its vulgarity and the rest of the Sunday papers were divided between those who thought it 'filthy' and those who found it 'funny.'

I found the professed innocence of Penelope Mortimer, in her review in the *Observer*, very refreshing. 'It is sometimes a grave disadvantage not to have a dirty mind,' she wrote. 'One misses so much. A girl eating a chocolate bar, for instance, is to me just a girl eating a chocolate bar; peeled bananas, chlorophyll toothpaste, hair spray, don't mean a thing to me. *Every Home Should Have One* therefore puts me in a bit of a quandary. I'm sure I've overlooked something riotously filthy, but don't know what it can be.'

It came as a decided relief, however, that a reasonable number of critics were not remotely shocked by a film that by today's standards is about as lascivious as a toffee apple. John Russell Taylor in *The Times* came to our rescue with comments like 'sheer fantasy', 'a tone of sustained farce carried off with astonishingly good grace' and 'a genuine triumph'. And if the review in the *Birmingham Post* by Michael Ellington is any guide, they enjoyed it as much in the provinces. 'It has an audacious wit and unquenchable vitality,' he wrote. 'It is a film with a winning intelligence and brio and is likely to give native screen comedy a much-needed nudge into the seventies.' Marjorie Bilbow in the trade paper, *Today's Cinema*, said 'A sure-fire success everywhere except with the minority unable to laugh at themselves or incapable of finding sex funny.'

In the first two weeks of its release in London it looked as if it were going to be the biggest box-office hit in British Lion's history. Then financial disaster struck. The nation was overwhelmed by the longest and hottest heat wave for many years. Practically no one wanted to venture into a non air-conditioned cinema. Because of the rigid distribution system in practice those days pictures had to be seen in certain geographical locations whatever the weather or circumstances. The expected revenue was drastically cut and its balance sheet never recovered from this loss, even though in time it came into profit.

While waiting for the picture to be released, Herbie and I had been contracted to write a paperback of *Every Home*, which was published in March 1970 to coincide with the film's appearance. In the tiny snippets of space masquerading as reviews of paperbacks, the critics echoed words like 'zany' and 'hilarious' that had been applied to the film. Describing the humour of *Every Home* as 'very English', the critic in the *Evening Standard* said, 'I don't propose to see the film. I found the book

Marty Feldman and Shelley Berman with their hands full in
Every Home Should Have One.

highly amusing in its own right. The fact that its Englishness is provided by Milton Shulman, who was born in Canada, and Herbert
Kretzmer, who was born in South Africa, merely proves that something
very catching started with Beowulf.'

Hodders printed 90,000 copies in total. The film did not prove to be
the box-office smash the early returns had indicated. Indeed its small
capital sum took almost eight years to recoup. Although we had been
warned that a box-office percentage would have to be 'gross' rather than
'net' to mean anything to our bank managers, we still settled for 'net'
because Columbia stuck stubbornly to their position. Since 'net' meant
the money left after all expenses associated with the picture had been
met – advertising, promotion, film prints, entertainment, travel – it was
well recognized in the industry that creative accounting would almost
always leave little over for those expecting to share some profit from a
successful picture.

It was about 1985 when Herbie and I were sent our first cheques for
our contractual share. They were for £13.15 each. Since then, although

290 MARILYN, HITLER AND ME

there is now a video of it and from time to time it is transmitted on British television, we receive annual cheques of this order. Fortunately, neither of us need the money

8

NO STATUE HAS EVER BEEN PUT UP FOR A CRITIC

I receive a menacing phone call and consider my enemies . . . A roasting by David Hare in the New Statesman *. . . The good, the great and the angry . . . Simone Signoret and Alec Guinness do Macbeth no good . . . A debate with William Gaskill at the Oxford Union . . . I am shocked by the wholesomeness of* Hair *. . . I make a wager with Lloyd Webber*

(i) *Who loves a critic?*

It was late on a Friday evening in the mid-1980s when a sepulchral, menacing voice said, 'You'll be dead tonight' and hung up. Stunned, I stood with the receiver uselessly in my hand.

I had occasionally received letters threatening me with physical violence for a less than complimentary notice, but never a death threat. My first inclination was to forget about it, but then I thought it would be only fair for me to tell Drusilla. Any serious violent act would obviously affect her as well. Since there was a police station less than 300 yards away, we agreed that I should report it.

The constable behind the station counter looked about nineteen years old. When I told him I wanted to report a death threat, he brought out a huge black book which registered information and complaints that might need police action.

After writing down my name, address and the exact words of the anonymous caller, he asked 'Have you any enemies?' 'Legion,' I answered, taken aback by that first question. I told him I was a theatre critic and that there were no doubt many people who would have a grudge against me because of what I had written. But the list would be too long. Couldn't I get police surveillance of my residence for at least that night? Relieved that he didn't have to write anything more, he said the local patrol would keep a special eye open and we left it at that. Nothing happened and there were no more threatening calls.

Knowing how bitterly adverse criticism is felt by most creative people, in bed that night I stretched my memory back to dig up the names of playwrights, actors, directors I might have hurt in my decades of theatre criticism but mercifully, like counting sheep, the exercise soon put me to sleep.

I have acquired a reputation for being harder to please than most of my colleagues, some of whom have spent their entire careers enwrapped in the glories and the trivia of the theatre. Seeking out plays in suburban pubs and provincial cellars, they find nuggets of writing and acting which they assure their readers are masterpieces of the genre, but unfortunately these rarely reach the heart of London's theatreland where the harsh light of competitiveness can be shone upon them.

But whether they are theatre mad or theatre sane, they are treated with the same suspicion, distrust and apprehension as all critics of any art form. If a critic is rash enough to believe he is in an exalted profession, he can agree with Anatole France who believed our task was to relate the adventures of our souls among masterpieces. However amongst contemporary playwrights, no doubt still stung by a painful critical barb, the function of criticism is not held in such esteem.

Peter Ustinov chides critics with the observation that 'they search for ages for the wrong word which, to give them credit, they eventually find.'

Somerset Maugham brooded over certain caustic remarks made by a critic over an early work of his. On re-reading the work some time later, he realized the man had been right: it was a shallow and badly constructed effort. Nonetheless he never forgot the hurt he had felt and when, several years later, the Luftwaffe were bombing London, he shone a light in the black-out on the critic's house to provide a target for the enemy planes.

Noel Coward, writing to a critic who had savaged one of his plays, said: 'I am sitting in the smallest room of my house. Your notice is before me. It will shortly be behind me.'

And in his own vituperative style, John Osborne has said: 'My own attitude to critics is clear and entirely reasonable. It is one of distrust and dislike based on predictability and historical fact. I regard them as something like kinky policemen on the cultural protectionist make, rent collectors, screws, insurance men, Customs officers and Fairy Snowmen. One should simply not open one's door to them.'

It is understandable that when people have been hurt in either their egos or their pockets they should lash out at the nearest symbol of their failure. Critics perform a very useful therapeutic function for those who have to find an outlet for their angry frustrations. They make ideal wax images for sticking pins into and for explaining away the real reasons for a flop. There is no plausible meaning in the phrases 'the critics killed it' or 'the critics didn't understand it'. Which critics? It is a collective noun that is as amorphous and slippery as 'the people'.

We are not a cabal of faceless men meeting in the gents' lavatory during the interval to plan a unanimous campaign against a dramatist's work. I am just as shocked, flabbergasted, surprised and irritated by some of my colleagues' judgements as anyone else. We are a motley group of tall, short, young, old, liberal, conservative, silent, garrulous, anxious, confident, religious, agnostic, married, homosexual, orthodox, radical, vegetarian, meat-eating, ascetic, hedonistic, clever, idiotic, naive, complex, amusing and boring individuals. The one thing that we have in common is that we don't think alike.

I never particularly wanted to be a critic. Until 1948 I took very little interest in the craft and if it hadn't been for Lord Beaverbrook's instinct that my writing flair, demonstrated in *Defeat in the West* and a number of interviews in the *Evening Standard*, could be adapted to film criticism, I probably would have tried to be a military, political or investigative journalist.

Since then a large part of my vocation has been devoted to criticism of one kind or another. Having filled the post of film, theatre, book and television critic for British publications for over forty years, I have tried in my role as an omnibus critic to join no cliques, to cultivate few prejudices, to recognize genius and decry pretension, to take no malicious delight in being hurtful, to be aware of my limitations and ignorance, to respect the art form I am trying to judge and, above all, to be readable.

But it has been the theatre that has run through my professional career like a silver ribbon, captivating me by its luminosity and always threatening, but never managing, to monopolize my interest and concern above all the other cultural disciplines in which I have been involved. Theatre, I have always felt, should not be judged only by its own particular values. Because of its seniority in the arts, going back over 2000 years to the classics of Euripides and Sophocles, it has been treated by the literary and critical establishment with the awe owed to venerability, and the assumption is that it need not compete with such upstart art forms as the cinema and television on an equal level.

My own approach is more pedestrian. A play is now in the market place competing with a film, a television programme, a book or a sporting event for the time, the attention and the money of audiences. No stage version of Shakespeare's *Henry V* will ever be as enthralling as Olivier's film adaptation. Watching a revival of *Casablanca* on the telly, for free, would be a more rewarding way of spending an evening even for cultivated sophisticates, than spending £50 to £100 for a meal and two tickets to see eighty per cent of the plays on offer in London's West End.

I long ago realized how painful my opinions could be when I noticed that actors, producers or directors that I happened to know socially would, after I had been unenthusiastic about one of their ventures, tactfully cross the street if they saw me approaching from an opposite direction. I have calculated that it takes at least three months before they can bear to be civil to me again. I was only recently reminded of the havoc one can unintentionally cause by a bad review when the *Sunday Telegraph*, on 23 March 1997, reported the coming auction of some of Margaret Lockwood's private letters. In the 1940s and '50s she was Britain's most popular and highest paid film star. When she died in 1990, at the age of seventy-three, she had been a recluse for a long time, seeing only her closest friends.

Writing in one of those letters in 1982 she revealed how devastated she had felt about a notice of mine when she appeared as the consort of Edward VII in a play called *Motherdear* by Royce Ryton. She said, 'I haven't really wanted to do anything since that disastrous *Motherdear*. I know it didn't deserve a good press, but I cannot understand Milton Shulman's paranoic dislike of me. Our stage director asked me if I knew him, as his criticism was so personal. I told him I had never met the man.'

Having forgotten all about the play, I dug up my notice. 'Miss Lockwood is not one of nature's royal consorts,' I wrote. 'The petulance of a wicked lady is not precisely the tone needed for the arrogance of a princess. As Alix, a Danish princess who had to suffer the infidelities of the British heir to the throne, Miss Lockwood is called upon to be sweet, beautiful, playful, charming, delightful, gay and kind. She also has to manipulate a limp and a slight foreign accent. But the only regal emotion she manages to convey is imperturbability ... Knowing nothing about Alix before I entered the theatre, I knew nothing much on leaving it.'

The play folded in less than a month and I was not entirely to blame. My colleagues were just as negative as I was. I never knew that Miss Lockwood regarded me with such venom. Fortunately actors do forgive us if we say something complimentary about a later performance which cancels out their resentment about what we had said on another occasion. But they tend to fight shy of kind words about a critic, only relenting when the critic has either retired or died. When I had given up being the *Standard*'s regular critic, Dame Judi Dench, approached me at a cocktail party to tell me how she had been encouraged by my review of her first appearance in October 1960, as Juliet at the Old Vic. 'I have always appreciated that notice,' she said.

The words she had apparently kept, cherished, in some scrap-book were: 'Her every word rang clear, her every phrase meant something, her every gesture was alive with the rapture of passion or the totality of despair. Here is a fresh and lovely Juliet.'

'But that was almost thirty years ago,' I replied. 'Why has it taken you so long to let me know?'

'Oh, I was too frightened to tell you before you had given up writing about us. Sucking up, you know,' she said, smiling as she skipped away. No wonder Sibelius was right when he observed that no statue had ever been put up for a critic.

What is the essence of a dramatic work, aside from the fact that it is presented in an area, usually a stage, where an audience can watch it taking place? First and foremost, a play is a receptacle for language. Whether banal or glorious, words are the bloodstream and the backbone of a dramatic event. They may be sung in opera or written in a novel or poem, but in a play they must be spoken. Mime merely simulates words. A predictable tale of teenage lovers torn apart for a family feud, can become the most poignant love story of all time through Shakespeare's wondrous poetry. The loss of a feckless woman's estate has made generations weep through Chekhov's gracious words in *The Cherry Orchard*.

A play is structured on characters. Their fate as they strut their few hours on the stage is what holds and intrigues an audience. A successful play has language that justifies the characters, makes them credible or fantastic, gives them the capacity to make us believe in them when they make us laugh or cry. Lady Bracknell says little in *The Importance of Being Earnest*, but the few words she utters makes her one of the great comic creations of the English theatre. Hamlet, on the other hand, says a great deal but each soliloquy, each aside, each quip fuses the tormented prince into one of the most noble figures in drama.

The third element a play requires is a circumstance. My dictionary defines a circumstance as a condition, detail or attribute with respect to time, place and manner that accompanies, determines or modifies a fact or event. Traditionally, most plays are held together by a plot. This implies a beginning that leads inexorably or implausibly to an end. But many modern dramatists no longer feel harnessed to the logical or reasonable demands of a plot. Winnie, up to her waist in a sandhill, could start or end anywhere in her incessant chatter that makes Beckett's *Happy Days*. Characters in many of Pinter's plays end in a limbo with nowhere, apparently, to go. It is the circumstance in which a playwright places his characters, rather than a plot, that is enough to justify a play if the language is right.

And finally, it is the immediacy of the theatre that distinguishes it from any other art form. Language, character and circumstance can be moulded into a cinema or television event but they then become fixed and immutable. A play in the living theatre is as vulnerable as a firefly, with every moment never being exactly like the last and the danger of disaster – a forgotten line, a misplaced prop, a sullen or hectoring audience – heightening the expectation of the event.

I have regarded my function as a critic to assess these four ingredients and, in the light of my experience, judge whether they have come together successfully or fatally in the work I have come to review. I have on my shelves dozens of books providing theories about which kind of drama should be admired or encouraged. There is the drama of ideas, the absurd, alienation, political dogma, the avant-garde, the Method, paradox, enlightenment, Impressionism, comedy, social realism, the abstract, kitchen sink, drawing-room and whatever concoction of human behaviour can be imagined.

These theories or schools have their fierce adherents who, while their passions last, are intolerant of any new play that does not conform to their particular mould. It is under the banner of the avant-garde that most of them march to justify their derision of any ideas or methods of the past they hope to revolutionize. George E. Wellwarth in his book, *The Theatre of Protest and Paradox*, convincingly claims that the term 'avant-garde' means 'out in front of everybody else'. He then asserts that a person who is out in front of everybody else is fully exposed to the fire of the enemy. 'Such intrepidity,' he goes on, 'whether fearless or merely foolhardy, is shocking to the timid, the cautious, and the prudent who comprise the majority; all the more so because the majority – instinctively and in all innocence – always consider its position sacred and inviolate. The power to *shock* is, then, the chief characteristic of avant-garde drama and at the same time its chief source of strength.'

But, in the long run, shock is a wasting asset. In 1914 Liza's words 'not bloody likely' in *Pygmalion* brought scandalized notoriety to the play, but when it was converted into the musical, *My Fair Lady*, fifty years later, the word 'bloody' had to be replaced by an expletive more shocking to modern ears.

When in 1969 *Oh! Calcutta!*, with its sketches involving nudity and masturbation, opened in London, there were ominous omens that it might be prosecuted for obscenity and not allowed to open. In his auto-biography, *Empty Seats*, its producer, Michael White, records his fears on the opening night.

'It was Milton Shulman of the *Evening Standard* and Harold Hobson (of the *Sunday Times*) who mattered. If they together had said that *Calcutta* was a filthy show and should have been stopped, then I believe a way would have been found. But Shulman wrote: "*Oh Calcutta!* will certain-ly shock some people – it will corrupt and deprave nobody." Hobson even tried to be kind...His conclusion was that despite the deplorable taste of the show, it was not harmful.'

When Michael White attempted a similar formula in 1996 with a musi-cal revue highlighting lesbianism, *Voyeurz*, public taste had become so blasé about sexual display that it folded in a few months.

Some critics reinforced their reputations as liberal observers by sup-porting any form of explicit sexual activity on the stage as a dramatic advance. *Shopping and Fucking*, a first play by Mark Ravenhill, re-enacts without inhibitions the sado-masochistic tastes of violence and buggery of teenage characters who exist at about the lowest level of morality to which it is possible for a civilized society to sink. It is accompanied by language matching their behaviour. Discussing the play on TV in 1996 with two other critics, I described it as a psychotic babble written by someone with an anal fetish who sees life through an arse-hole darkly. Did I want to protect audiences from the existence of such a subter-ranean life-style? I was asked. Wasn't shock ultimately a therapeutic experience? The debate was only a few minutes long, but what I primarily objected to in a play like this was its being hailed as revolutionary when it is ultimately a reactionary drama reducing motivations to the instincts of apes and, more importantly, substituting human communication and language with expletives and grunts. This is not a cultural advance but a dramatic retreat.

To sum up, my philosophy about the theatre as a critic is to judge whether language and character are so fused that, whether the words are exalted or vulgar and the characters are realistic or fantastic, the play engages my interest, my concern, my admiration, my repulsion, my awe, my wonder or my sense of comedy. Or whether it provokes my ridicule or leaves me indifferent. And do the circumstances in which such characters are placed offer them a credible arena in which they can explain or exploit the event, the situation or dilemma in a manner consistent with their personalities?

I should add that the designer of the set and the clothes, and occasionally the music, can do much to lift or diminish the impact of a production by magically enhancing its ambience or disastrously ridiculing it.

I follow no theory, no movement, no fad, no popular or ideological causes to vindicate my feelings about a play once the curtain has fallen. I record as best I can the sensations of exhilaration or discomfort that I have felt in those few hours in the stalls. I am distrustful of grand theories about the theatre – political, social or technical – since, like Shaw's plays of ideas, Brecht's concept of alienation, Tynan's promotion of sexual freedom, they are too soon ravaged by time. I am suspicious, too, of movements dedicated to undermining structures of the past and, although I am allergic to categorical labels, I expect these views will associate me with the postmodernist approach.

This refusal to cling to the slipstream of some novel theatrical comet has brought me opprobrium from those who believe a responsible critic should nail his colours to some cultural position variously called avant-garde, progressive, experimental or radical. It is not good enough merely to assess a play's qualities, for one is expected to treat it with charity and respect if it aspires to an ideological fad no matter how inept, shallow or thunderingly boring it is.

Since almost my entire output as a theatre critic has been confined to the pages of the *Evening Standard*, which is not a national paper and with a readership largely resident in London and its suburbs, my views have not been as widely disseminated as those of critics for *The Times*, the *Daily Telegraph*, the *Guardian*, the *Sunday Times* or the *Observer*. Whenever my work is discussed – not often – in books assessing Britain's post-war theatre, my reputation, according to my detractors, is based primarily on the reading of less than one per cent of my reviews – except, of course, by my fellow critics – and within that tiny volume, their resentment of my statements about Bertolt Brecht, Pinter's *The Birthday Party*, Osborne's *Look Back in Anger* and my generally negative approach to a coterie of left-wing playwrights – Bond, Brenton, Barker – who were the darlings of the fringe theatre in the 1970s and '80s. This small cache of opinions has been regurgitated *ad nauseam*, with little evidence to support their disparagement except that they have picked it up from other books who, in their turn, have picked it up from other books.

Typical of this kind of raising of me as a bogey against progressive theatre only to knock me down as of little significance was a long article by David Hare in the *New Statesman* of 14 March 1997. It bemoaned the absence of good new plays in the West End and, by implication, singled me out as someone who 'has never liked plays not set in Eaton Square' and 'gloated openly about the failure of the Royal Court to change the face of British theatre'. Admitting that the theatre for him 'existed for mainly political purposes, to try to dramatize what we took to be the irrevocable decline of our culture,' he blamed the 'forces of reaction' for negating such a noble cause. He was gracious enough to admit that the article I had written 'did point to some greater truth: if you examine the current repertory, it seems remarkably little changed from the middle-brow selection that attracted so much contempt forty years ago.'

But what stung me into writing a letter in my defence, which the *New Statesman* published a fortnight later, was that Hare implied that I had conducted a disparaging vendetta against John Osborne and that I thought his plays were of little moment.

'It is sad to see so distinguished a playwright as David Hare having so little regard for the truth in his mournful account of the state of the British theatre,' read my letter. 'He has implied that I have played some major part in bringing about this state of affairs and particularly has attacked me for not appreciating the work of John Osborne. Typical of his loose language and thinking is his glib comment that I have never "much liked plays not set in Eaton Square." I have written over 4000 first night notices and been a theatre critic for the *Evening Standard* for thirty-eight years – the longest tenure of any critic for a responsible newspaper in this country. How many notices of mine has Hare actually read? Not many I would guess. Indeed, I praised *A Man of the World*, *Pravda* and other works by Hare, none of which were set anywhere near London's Eaton Square or West End.

'But it is his assessment of my views on Osborne's plays that displays a particular prejudiced ignorance. It is true that I thought *Look Back In Anger* an over-rated play, but even in that early review I predicted that Osborne would one day write a very good play.

'I called *Inadmissible Evidence* "a great play". *The Entertainer* I praised as "vital, contentious and contemporary". Of *The Hotel in Amsterdam* I wrote that the dialogue had that "virile, provocative quality that makes the mind quiver with expectation". I was practically alone in finding Osborne's last play *Déjà Vu*, brilliantly waspish and a better play than *Look Back in Anger*. Of *Time Present* in 1968 I said "he wields invective like the whiplash of an angel".

'About that review I received a postcard from John Osborne, the first few lines of which read: "It seems craven to say thank you. I've never done so before. Perhaps one should. I don't know. Anyway, generosity is very welcome, apart from insight and all ..."

'When he died I protested that it was a national disgrace and a snub to one of our "great men" that he had not been knighted.'

A similar approach to my career was adopted by the author of a book published in 1994 who, amongst a series of personal attacks, dismissed me as a critic for 'my howlers and blazoned, unapologetic ignorance', which is fair enough abuse against a critic, but when he went on to claim that I had 'failed to recognize the worth' and gave no serious attention to 'every major post-war theatrical talent', I decided that such lying assertions reflected on my professional reputation and had to be withdrawn.

Since it is an unseemly sight for a critic to protest about being attacked, I did my best by telephone calls and long letters to have the publisher and author acknowledge their libel, even if only by with-drawing the statements by an inserted memorandum. In my letters I set out the encouraging, enthusiastic, complimentary, favourable, laudatory notices I had written for precisely those playwrights for whom the author said that I had never had a kind word. They insisted on doing nothing. But when at last I sought legal advice – being a lawyer myself I knew what his view would be – he made one telephone call and their stubborn maintenance of a mendacious position collapsed. The author made a full apology. The book was withdrawn by the publisher from every library and bookstore in the land. I was paid a sum in damages. A public apology was printed in the trade press publication, the *Bookseller*. When the publisher wrote to me saying he could not afford to pay the full costs of that withdrawal, I contributed some of my damages money to help him out.

While I have discovered merit in almost all the renowned dramatists I had once dismissed in their first plays, I have consistently been affront-ed and dismayed by the adulation and reverence of some of my col-leagues for the work of Bertolt Brecht. I am convinced that his reputa-tion as someone on the same level as Chekhov or Shakespeare was acidulously fostered by the propaganda machine of communism, which duped many responsible academics and critics to parrot these outra-geous claims. Now that Marxism is dead, can Brecht be far behind? It was in a notice about *Galileo* that I summed up my position about this much-hyped German playwright.

'The story deserves mature analysis rather than condescending simplifi-cation,' I wrote about a National Theatre production on 13 August 1980. 'Michael Gambon, as Galileo, starts off like a hectoring physics master with a very dull class on his hands, and then dawdles without much rea-son into an abject gourmet, preferring delicacies to ideals ... To be on Bertolt Brecht's dramatic wavelength one has to lower one's perception and expectations to the level of someone who stopped reading at the age of fourteen.

'It is precisely the view that culture must never be far out of step with the lowest common denominator of mass receptivity that accounts for Brecht's appeal to Marxists and intellectuals. In the East, Brecht fits in perfectly with the ossification of Marxist art ... In the West, his banal prose and ponderous over-simplification of complex issues is hailed by liberals as a significant step towards egalitarian drama ... When I first saw it twenty years ago, it put me in mind of those Hollywood historical films starring Don Ameche with lines like "Hiya, Newton. Watcha doing under that apple tree?"'

As for the other black marks awarded to me by the school of self-styled progressive commentators on the theatre, my mystification about what *The Birthday Party* by Harold Pinter was about was shared by almost every professional critic who saw it on 19 May 1958. Harold Hobson alone tried to save it in the *Sunday Times*, but by then the management had already decided to take it off.

My opening lines were: 'Sitting through *The Birthday Party* by Harold Pinter is like trying to solve a crossword puzzle where every vertical clue is designed to put you off the horizontal. It will be best enjoyed by those who believe that obscurity is its own reward.' Whether audiences are more intelligent than we were thirty-nine years ago, or whether the play's complexities are now explained to students when they take their pre-university examinations, there is no doubt there has been a revival of its popularity in recent years. But I should remind those who take some pleasure in ridiculing the crop of critics who were baffled by Pinter's play, that their icon of the liberal theatre, Kenneth Tynan, was just as dismissive about its merits as the rest of us. He called it 'a clever fragment grown dropsical with symbolic content ... full of those familiar paranoid overtones that seem to be inseparable from much of avant-garde drama.' Tynan was also unimpressed by Pinter's next play *The Caretaker* and wrote: 'It occurred to me, as the curtain fell, that what I had been watching was nothing more than an old-fashioned avant-garde exercise, galvanized into a semblance of novelty by the author's miraculous ear for colloquial eccentricities. Instead of The Brother, The Other Brother and Everyman, the characters were called Aston, Mick and Davies; instead of declaiming, they chatted.'

Look Back In Anger has also provoked derision amongst those who enjoy belonging to the beat-the-critic brigade. Again most first-night critics – myself amongst them – did not think much of Osborne's play and it would have ended ignominiously had not Tynan and Hobson rushed to its rescue on the following Sunday. Because it has been nurtured as a watershed in the history of British post-war drama, I have examined its significance at some length later in this chapter.

As for those in the 1970s and '80s who thought the theatre could be used to bring about the collapse of capitalism, ridicule Britain's historical past, mock authority, utilize violence as an ideological tool and ignite Fringe audiences with the prospect of a socialist millennium, they have become the cowering victims of the political and social blasts that have reduced Marxism to ideological rubble because of the tyranny, cruelty and inefficiency inherent in its cultural imperative. The enthusiasts for Bond, Barker and Brenton are no doubt still waiting for some fresh dimension in their forthcoming plays that could vindicate their initial adulation.

A theatre critic has to recognize that every play he sees need not be judged in the light of past comparative works in the same genre. Most people go to the theatre for entertainment rather than enlightenment and for them the most crass farce or the most inept production starring some personality they adore, is enough to justify the price of the ticket. Even familiar classics, which critics assess by some historical yardstick, have never been seen by most audiences. I remember once at Stratford-on-Avon giving my second seat to a young woman who was in the standing-room only section of the theatre. The production was *Othello*, and at the interval I invited her to join me in the critics' reception room for a drink. Discussing the play with two of my colleagues, we speculated on what method the producer would use to murder Desdemona. Strangulation? A suffocating kiss? A smothering pillow? 'Oh, please,' interrupted my guest who had been listening to us, 'don't spoil it for me. I don't want to know how it ends. I've never seen it before.'

Any critic who is not insanely hooked on the theatre, is aware that he has to survive waves of mediocrity washing over him in order to carry out his duty to his paper and his readers. Some become resistant to trash, lower their standards, and live easily with their consciences, consoling themselves that they are supporting the art form in which Britain is pre-eminent. Others stoically bear the pain of the failures in order to be excited by some different or unusual or imaginative or moving or hilarious play, and in their relief, more often than not, over-praise it. Bernard Levin, in his typical trenchant and hyperbolic manner, divulged in *The Times* of 30 January 1991, his reflections based upon ten years as a professional theatre critic:

> The critics (a meaningless phrase, since no two of them have the same attitudes, beliefs and responses) over-praise almost everything put before them because the quality of practically everything they see is so low that it inevitably corrodes the standards with which they have to judge.
>
> I will go further, and blunter. *At least* nineteen plays out of twenty in the London theatre at any given time should, and in a perfect world, would, be classified as rubbish. Not as 'unsuccessful', 'disappointing', 'lacking theatricality', 'implausible' or 'forgettable', all of which (I blush

to own it) I have, along with my colleagues, pressed into service, but *rubbish*, not to say garbage, offal, trash, bilge and Not Wanted on Voyage.

★ ★ ★

When I retired as a full-time theatre critic on the *Evening Standard* to take on a weekly arts and social column in November 1991, the paper published a long interview – profile by Angus McGill – about my life and career. One of the casual remarks I made in that interview was that in thirty-eight years of reviewing I had not seen a new great play. I defined 'great' in this context as a play that, fifty years after the dramatist's death, would still be revived and revered by audiences throughout the world. An example of such plays, which I did not list in the interview, would be *Hamlet*, *Tamburlaine*, *A Doll's House*, *The Cherry Orchard*, *The Importance of Being Earnest*, *Tartuffe*, *Volpone*, *Electra*, *Long Day's Journey Into Night*, *St. Joan* and, of course, many others. I also claimed that in the entire history of Western drama from Aeschylus to Tennessee Williams, there had not been more than sixty playwrights who warranted the accolade of 'great'.

I realize now that my concept of 'greatness' was too confining. Plays ought to be accorded such a distinction even though their impact is not eternal. If they reflect the longings, yearnings, fears, expectations, laughter of audiences at a particular time and in a particular place, even though the years may eventually reduce their status to that of a quaint relic, a topical antique, a forgotten experience, their greatness should be measured by the impact they made on the theatre of their time and their superiority to the efforts of their contemporaries. It is probably justifiable to label as 'great', plays like *Who's Afraid of Virginia Woolf?*, *Death of a Salesman*, *Inadmissible Evidence*, *Rosencrantz and Guildenstern Are Dead*, *Waiting for Godot*, *The Homecoming*, *A Streetcar Named Desire*, *The Norman Conquests*, *Ring Around the Moon*, *Private Lives* – even though it is not likely that many of them will be enthralling audiences in most countries of the world in 2050.

The word I was really groping for when I talked of plays without the quality to defy decades of time was 'masterpieces'. Although some of my colleagues managed to discover a 'great' play once a month and half a dozen 'masterpieces' a year, I was not so lucky. In my long tenure of office I missed the first nights of *A Streetcar Named Desire* and *Death of a*

Salesman, which were produced before I began my job, and they alone display the consummate skill and excellence which I would call the sign of a 'masterpiece'.

Indeed, the number of playwrights that are 'great' in the sense of having written masterpieces that have endured is surprisingly small. Of the thousands and thousands of playwrights who have had their works displayed on a stage to audiences, posterity is keen to revive the plays of only about sixty to seventy of them. Others may add or subtract from my following list. Since my test is fifty years after their death, it is obvious that no contemporary dramatists are named.

Aeschylus, Aristophanes, Barrie, Beaumarchais, Beaumont, Boucicault, Buchner, Calderon, Chekhov, Congreve, Corneille, Coward, Dryden, Euripides, Farquhar, Feydeau, Genet, Gilbert, Giraudoux, Gogol, Goldoni, Granville-Barker, Hauptmann, Hellman, Ibsen, Ionesco, Jarry, Jones, Jonson, Kaufman, Labiche, Marivaux, Moliere, Molnar, O'Casey, O'Neill, Pinero, Pirandello, Plautus, Rattigan, Rostand, Sardou, Schiller, Schnizler, Scribe, Shakespeare, Shaw, Sheridan, Sophocles, Strindberg, Synge, Turgenev, Vanbrugh, Webster, Wedekind, Wilde, Williams. Noel Coward, Tennessee Williams and Terence Rattigan do not precisely accord with the time criterion but they help bring the figure to almost sixty, and I am sure they will make any future list of this kind.

* * *

Back in 1955 it was an extremely novel idea for a newspaper to become a forum for prizegiving in the arts. Because the proprietor of the *Evening Standard*, Lord Beaverbrook, had never been very keen on the activities of the Arts Council or the British Council, it was with considerable trepidation that the then deputy editor of the *Standard*, Charles Wintour (later to become its editor) put up the idea of annual drama awards for the best new play, best actor, best actress and best musical produced in London.

Seeing an opportunity for extra publicity for their shows in London's most influential evening newspaper, the impresarios and the West End managements were naturally enthusiastic and promised every sort of cooperation. Stars of the acting profession – Peter Ustinov, Orson Welles, Margaret Leighton, John Mills – provided quotes warmly approving of the idea.

It was felt that the panel should be balanced between professional critics (because they would have seen everything), representatives of the working theatre and people distinguished in the arts with an interest in the theatre.

The first panel consisted of the conductor, Sir Malcolm Sargent, the film producer, Sir Michael Balcon, the *Sunday Times* theatre critic, Harold Hobson, the Principal of the Royal Academy of Dramatic Art, John Fernald, the novelist, Rosamond Lehmann, and myself, who had only just become the theatre critic of the *Standard*. Since then that blend of professional critics has been the criterion behind the composition of every panel of judges. I have been on every panel since its inception. In its early years there was never any certainty that the awards would continue. Financial stringency and lack of enthusiasm in management circles, concern about the cost of the sumptuous lunch at the Savoy and the elegant prize-winning statuettes by Frank Dobson, resulted in some very economic, frugal and improvised prizegivings.

Occasionally the lunch was confined strictly to the judges and the winners. At other times the congratulatory meal was eliminated altogether, and the statuettes were handed out on the stage where the plays, actors and actresses were still performing. For the past twenty years, the luncheon has been an occasion of culinary splendour and witty speeches, with 300 to 400 prominent people of the theatre in attendance.

But in 1957, the third year of these awards, they were unexpectedly faced with a situation which could have been their *coup de grâce*. When the judges nominated Sir Laurence Olivier as the Best Actor for his portrayal of the desperate, pathetic, failed actor Archie Rice in Osborne's *The Entertainer*, Olivier notified the editor that he had no intention of accepting it.

Given such a rebuff from the man generally acknowledged to be the leading figure of the English stage, how could other actors and playwrights cooperate with the enterprise? It is probable that after such an insult Lord Beaverbrook would have decided that the *Standard* should have nothing more to do with the awards.

It fell to me to try and get him to change his mind. Being relatively new as a critic, I realized that my stature was hardly likely to have much influence on the great man. Falling back on my training as a lawyer, I marshalled as many arguments as I could and put them as deferentially as possible to Olivier in the dressing room of the Palace Theatre between a matinee and evening performance.

I first pointed out that the *Standard* had only initiated these awards on the assurance that managements and the acting profession would support them. Olivier politely pointed out that he had no intention of deterring others from receiving these awards, but that in principle he was against prizes that attempt to acclaim one performance as superior, when roles were so different and people might be hurt in the process of making these impossible choices.

While I agreed that all awards contained an element of unfairness and arbitrariness, nevertheless they were a fact of life. He had accepted a knighthood, which was a form of award, and he had allowed himself to be nominated for an Oscar. I also suggested that if he rejected the accolade, would he not by implication be robbing four of his fellow players – Richard Burton, Siobhan McKenna, Paul Scofield and Peggy Ashcroft – of the lustre of the honour they had received in the two years these awards had been in existence?

There was another consideration he might have overlooked. The award for the Best Actress of the year was being given to Brenda de Banzie who was playing opposite Sir Laurence as his wife in *The Entertainer*. A much admired actress, this would have been the crowning glory of a long career. Could she possibly accept it if her co-player refused it?

I finally said that it was the intention of the *Standard* to declare him the Best Actor whether he accepted the statuette or not. There was a very long pause while Olivier weighed up the arguments. 'All right,' he said. 'I'll have a word with John (Gielgud) and Rafe (Ralph Richardson) and if they tell me I'm a cunt, I'll accept it.' He did and the statuettes have been accepted by every winner since then – with one exception who refused to take the Best Comedy award because he believed he ought to have been given the one for the Best Play.

Meeting in private rooms at the Savoy, the Gay Hussar or The Ivy, the judges – consisting of independent-minded spirits and lubricated by excellent food and wine – have always been articulate, persuasive and passionate in their pursuit of comparative excellence. In the first year *Waiting For Godot* was given an award as The Most Controversial Play of the Year, the first and last occasion for such a category. Because the panel was impressed with Osborne's *Look Back In Anger* but doubtful about making it the best of year, an award for the Most Promising British Playwright was introduced.

If any of these awards have demonstrated the awareness, sensitivity and far-seeing judgement of the panel about theatrical trends, it has been this one. Its talent-spotting has been almost clairvoyant since these prizes were based entirely on a writer's first play. The list includes John Osborne, Robert Bolt, Peter Shaffer, John Arden, Arnold Wesker, J. P. Donleavey, Henry Livings, David Rudkin, David Mercer, Charles Wood, James Saunders, Tom Stoppard, David Storey, David Hare, Mustapha Matura, Stephen Poliakoff, Terry Johnson, Frank McGuiness and Timberlake Wertenbaker, among others.

Although other theatrical awards have since sprung up – the Olivier, the Critics' Circle, the Plays and Players – the *Standard*'s still remain the most respected and most desired accolades amongst those in the the-atrical profession. The sentiment that has been associated with this event was summed up by the late Richard Burton who won the very first Best Actor award for his *Henry V*: 'I truly believe that my performance of Henry V improved vastly after I received that award. I wear it like the victor of Agincourt wore the leek as a memorable honour, good coun-trymen.'

(ii) The myth of Look Back In Anger

Forty years on from the first night of John Osborne's famous play in August 1996, a loud, abusive, heavy-drinking, phenomenally successful pop group, Oasis, were high in the charts with a song that seems to be cashing in on the reputation of Osborne's early work. Titled 'Don't Look Back In Anger', its resonances have no connection with the ver-bal bile in the play but probably unintentionally do reflect the senti-mental debris that is about all that the years have left of Osborne's fer-vour. The word 'revolution' exists in the lyric but only in the context of a bed (and only serves to evoke John Lennon), and the last line, 'We don't look back in anger, I heard you say,' echoes, rather, the regrets of a failed love affair.

But in the summer of 1956 the play was admired by England's young as a splenetic spasm of rage against the class system, the country's impe-rial past, the nuclear bomb and the absence of passionate causes. Jimmy Porter, a university graduate who runs a sweet stall and lives with his girl friend in a dreary flat in a drab Midland town, constantly belabours any-one within earshot of his discontent. 'I suppose people of our genera-tion aren't able to die for good causes any longer,' is a typical tirade. 'We had all that done for us in the Thirties and Forties, when we were still kids. There aren't any good, brave causes left. If the big bang does come,

John Osborne

and we all get killed off, it won't be in aid of the old-fashioned, grand design. It'll just be for the Brave New Nothing-very-much-thank-you. About as pointless as stepping in front of a bus.'

Required reading for recent generations of schoolchildren, the play has been enveloped in more unjustifiable hype than any dramatic work this century. Its stature has been achieved through the promotion of a number of theatrical myths. It has been admired because it was said to have achieved its fame in the face of uniform critical hostility and was rescued from obscurity only by Kenneth Tynan's words in the *Observer*: 'I doubt if I could love anyone who did not wish to see *Look Back In Anger*.'

In fact the majority of critics welcomed the play and used words like 'an important discovery' and 'writes with searing passion' to support their verdicts. My own assessment for the *Standard* on 9 May 1956 claimed that Osborne had a dazzling aptitude for provoking and stimulating dialogue. 'When he stops being angry – when he lets us in on what he is angry about – he may write a very good play,' I concluded.

A second myth about the play was that it marked a watershed in British play-writing, after which the well-made plays of Coward, Rattigan, Priestley and Christopher Fry were converted into fossilized pieces rarely to be seen again, and would be replaced by a fresh breed of dramatists who dared to tackle political, social and controversial issues never before revealed on a British stage. That the Royal Court Theatre had such a success with it – actually, it only ran for a few weeks and had to wait for another nine years before it was given a West End production – provided the impetus, so runs the fable, for playwrights like Arnold Wesker, N. F. Simpson, John Arden and later, Pinter, Stoppard, Ayckbourn, Orton, Bennett and Shaffer to take advantage of the freedom to handle arcane, complex, adventurous themes that had not been open to them.

Totally untrue. Hardly any of these playwrights were inspired by Osborne's values or technique. Not a single play put on at the Royal Court for five years after *Anger*'s first night had any discernible connection with Osborne's ideas or prose style. They would have written their plays and had them produced had Osborne never lived. Osborne himself confirmed that assessment about the impact of his much-hyped play in a conversation with David Hare reported in the *New Statesman* of 14 March 1997. 'At the end of his life,' wrote Hare, 'John told me in despair that he believed it would have made no difference if he had never lived.'

It is no disparagement of his talent and genius to agree with that glum view of *Anger*. Osborne wrote many far better plays, less known and less ridiculously idolized, which will be the true basis of posterity's judgement about him.

It was the changes taking place in Britain following the Second World War, with a society eager to share the experiences of a new, vibrant and confident working class and the need for the middle-class young, deprived of their traditional roles in the armed forces, the colonies, the civil service and the Church, that encouraged them to seek expression in the world of pop music, television, films, painting, literature, advertising and the theatre.

It was Osborne's fortuitous title – and his youth – that excited the headline writers and TV producers to concoct a cultural pattern in which anyone with recognizable talent could be classified as an example of a disgruntled, weary nation. Had it been called *The Ironing Board* or *Squirrels and Bears* it probably would have had a very brief, undistinguished media life.

In 1958 on the second programme of *Monitor*, which was to become the BBC's most respected arts programme under Huw Wheldon, I interviewed a number of writers labelled as Angry Young Men. There was Colin Wilson whose work, *The Outsider*, examined the feelings of alienation of men of genius and appeared in the same week as *Anger*. With him were Kenneth Tynan, dedicated to changing the direction of the theatre, Stuart Holroyd, whose book attacked humanism, and the novelist, John Wain. They were all in their twenties when their first literary efforts appeared and that was all they had in common.

My questioning tried to elicit from them whether they considered themselves a cult or a myth. Certainly no cult, they agreed. Perhaps a myth. Probably just an accident. In the short run it may have encouraged managements to try their luck with young, unknown playwrights, but usually only in Fringe theatres.

Historically the theatre underwent a political phase in the 1970s – Brenton, Barker, Caryl Churchill, Trevor Griffiths. But, as I have already pointed out, with the death of Marxism their clamour for a different Britain has been stilled. Coward, Rattigan, Priestley attract delighted audiences. *The Mousetrap*, *Cats* and *Les Misérables* run forever. A few serious plays about AIDS and feminist frustrations make short-lived appearances.

The stage's ability to shock even in the once-daring fields of nudity and simulated sex has receded. When *Oh! Calcutta!* was presented on 27

July 1970, it caused a sensation. 'A cast of ten stand before us in their full-frontal nudity glory,' I wrote of that famous first night. 'The equipment thus displayed, as well as being a public relations job for circumcision, proves that the cast consists of five men and five women. After that, the swishing and the dangling of private parts becomes as acceptable and routine a part of the evening as the lighting, the music and the usherettes.'

With the cinema and television catering for millions, how can the theatre compete as a social and cultural influence in our society? It rouses no passions any more, as it did when riots broke out at plays by Ibsen, Synge and Coward. A minority art form has shrunk to a minimalist art form. If there were an angry young dramatist today like Osborne, would he not be more likely to try and get his splenetic message conveyed through a film or a TV drama, rather than a Fringe theatre often not much larger than a telephone kiosk?

The young, of course, have always felt it necessary to resent authority, kick against the Establishment and defy their parents. Back in 1956, they could believe that Marxism was more humane than capitalism, that marching against nuclear weapons would save the world from annihilation, that demonstrations could hasten the dawn of real sexual equality. But the years have blunted the sharp edges of these causes. Parades and banners protesting against something have rarely illustrated a mobilization of youthful opposition in this country, as they did in France in the 1960s and in America against the Vietnam war. Only left-wing militants, neo-fascists and extreme feminists took to the streets more recently against such disparate issues as the poll tax, unemployment and the Gulf war. A young man in his thirties told me that he sensed that his generation was chiefly frustrated because they had nothing to be angry about.

Today the young are more interested in themselves than in others. A career in the media, the City or computers is their goal, rather than concern about beggars in the Strand or slaughter in Burundi. The environment, probably because it is seen as affecting them more directly than it affects the old, provokes more visible dissent among tiny activist groups. Through Greenpeace or Amnesty they can protest about the morality of torture, attack national greed or Big Business as they climb trees to protect rural land, or picket the French Embassy about nuclear testing in the Pacific or join pressure groups trying to save the whales or seals or foxes.

On these single issues they are given no encouragement by either of the major parties. Labour under Blair has become the Blur Party, and is keen to disassociate itself from any cause that will send the young to the barricades and thereby frighten away the support of the wavering voter. In such a bland, ambitious, affluent atmosphere, it is not surprising that the theatre is now bereft of angry young dramatists eager to use the stage to shock and outrage their elders.

(iii) The Royal Court wants me banned

From time to time a playwright, an actor or a management becomes so incensed by the harsh, unsympathetic treatment they feel they have received from critics that they announce a ban on either an individual critic or a declaration that all critics are not welcome to their first night or subsequent performances. Since such a ban is legally unenforceable – if I pay for a ticket I have a right to occupy my seat – such a splenetic gesture rarely amounts to more than a public display of outrage and may or may not affect box-office receipts, depending upon how much publicity the ban receives and whether or not the work is good enough to prove the critics wrong-headed and tasteless.

Since no management has yet resorted to placing heavies at theatre doors to bar a journalist from entering – and I have been at the receiving end of at least three of these boycotts – such exclusions are usually effective because critics and their editors rarely believe it is worth defying them. What it actually amounts to is that the two free tickets for openings are not sent to the offending critic and the paper writes indignant leaders about the freedom of the press and the heinous offence of the theatre – usually a subsidized one – for daring to deprive his paper of that fundamental right.

It is often argued that if a critic is not invited, his review is therefore more vulnerable to damages for libel because it has lost the protection of the defence of fair comment. A libel is a libel whether a critic has been invited or not. It might have some bearing upon the amount of damages a victorious litigant might receive, but generally it is a matter of dignity that keeps critics away from managements that don't want them. Usually, too, a ban on one critic brings about a response from all the critics who, through the Critics' Circle, refuse to take up their tickets. The absence of all publicity or news about a play or musical often means quick financial death. In spite of the futility of such ineffective gestures, they still occur from time to time, activated by dramatists or managements hurt beyond endurance.

A minor skirmish in which I was alone involved occurred in November 1956 when H. M. Tennent, the management presenting Noel Coward's *Nude With Violin,* wrote to the *Standard*'s editor that I would not be invited to its first night. The spurious excuse offered for this discriminatory act was the fact that, while I was on holiday, Philip Oakes had been sent to Dublin to review the production of the play in that city.

'Described as a comedy it emerged as farce and ended as a corpse,' wrote Oakes. Fearing somewhat similar sentiments from me, they foolishly put up a Keep Out sign in my direction. The *Standard*'s riposte was to reprint in full the dismissive notice Oakes had written about the Dublin presentation, thus ensuring a top of the page news story headlined 'The show they did NOT want Shulman to review'.

The Royal Court was apparently incorrigible in its hostility to critics. In 1969 I received a letter from the theatre's artistic director, William Gaskill, with a copy to my editor, asking me not to review Edward Bond's *Early Morning* because I had given two other Bond plays bad notices. 'Why not give it a miss and send someone else?' he wrote. 'I don't mind being hit over the head again but knowing in advance makes it worse.'

My reply was trenchant. 'Your function is to produce plays. Mine is to criticize them. If the Royal Court invites the *Evening Standard* to review one of its plays, I'm afraid it is stuck with me. It is certainly naive of you to assume that because a critic dislikes one or two plays of a writer, he is bound to dislike them all ... Incidentally, I think it is about time you stopped trying to manipulate critics. You are not very good at it.'

The most notorious and acrimonious clash over critics took place three years earlier, predictably enough at the Royal Court. The media talk about its production of *Macbeth* was so enthusiastic that all seats for its entire run beginning on 21 October 1966 were sold out before its first night. The obvious attractions were Sir Alec Guinness as Macbeth and Simone Signoret, the much admired French film star, as Lady Macbeth. For most critics, including myself, the first night was a shambles based upon a production notable only for its perversity and cruelty to Shakespeare.

> It is probably a sad reflection on the theatre-going public's taste that they risked their money without caring about what they were going to see. Guinness and Signoret announcing trains at Crewe might have achieved the same audience response.

Relieved, therefore, of the responsibility of harming the box office, a critic feels more light-hearted than usual when he can solemnly announce that this *Macbeth* is the worst *Macbeth* he has ever seen performed in the West End by a responsible theatre company.

The blame for the pretentious shambles must primarily belong to William Gaskill whose direction was so perverse, so insensitive, so precocious and so self-indulgent that it mangles into ludicrous strips one of our greatest plays.

Carrying Brechtian alienation to its most preposterous extremes, Mr Gaskill has bathed the action throughout in an unrelenting, harsh light that refutes all of Shakespeare's stage directions which indicated that about twenty-two of the play's twenty-six scenes should be played in grim gloom or shadowy darkness...

Devoid of the play's aura of supernatural gloom and conflict, Alec Guinness apparently decided to play Macbeth as some sort of senior civil servant determined to embarrass his Cabinet Minister. It was genteel, even prissy, and the baleful Macbeth, steeped in bloody ambition, was nowhere in evidence.

The choice of Simone Signoret as Lady Macbeth was – and I choose my words carefully – unfortunate. Shakespeare's lines are still relatively important, and Mlle Signoret was almost unintelligible. Even worse, she seemed desperately unconcerned about the menfolk's problems – with chin thrust forward she stared ahead of her contemplating, perhaps, some recipe for bouillabaisse – and when she marched off with two knives to Duncan's bedroom, I half expected her to return with a handsome roast.

For those who have bought tickets for this *Macbeth* there is one consolation. It is Shakespeare's shortest play.

Just to prove I was not alone in this blunt assessment, let me quote Alan Brien in the *Sunday Telegraph*:

Simone Signoret's Lady Macbeth, a conical, bell-tented matron who moves on wheels, like a draped Dalek surmounted by a beautiful Medusa head, speaks with a monotonous French rhythm punctuated by Americanized vowels.

Alec Guinness, eyes as blank as contact lenses, his right leg jumping with epilepsy, the other foot insistently tapping the beat of the lines, makes his Macbeth both boyish and senile, with a voice which hops disconcertingly from Shaftesbury Avenue to Sauchiehall Street ...

The rage that followed these reviews was incandescent. A week after the first night, William Gaskill, not only the director of the controversial *Macbeth* but the artistic director of the theatre, wrote a letter to Fleet Street editors contemplating a ban on all newspaper critics.

> 'Our production of *Macbeth* has produced a predictable crop of cheap journalism from the so-called critics of the national dailies,' reads part of a long letter. 'The concept of the First Night with all that it entails – notices hurriedly written to catch a deadline, the need of the critic to make journalistic capital out of his notice – is destructive of serious work ...
>
> 'In the circumstances we are seriously considering whether we should invite your critic to future performances. This would be a grave step for any theatre to take but we feel the present level of criticism is so low as almost to warrant it ...'

The threat was emblazoned all over the front page of the *Evening Standard* under the banner headline 'THEATRE CHIEF ROASTS CRITICS'. I replied the next day in a half-page article.

> This is only the sequel to a number of abusive letters that Mr Gaskill and his Associate Director, Desmond O'Donovan, have been writing to critics personally over the past few months. The gist of their complaints about me is that I am a 'cheap journalist', that I am eager to indulge in my 'destructive power' and that I am 'stupid'. My colleagues have received personal letters along the same lines. The general tone of all these missives is that of overweening arrogance. In none of them is there the slightest suggestion that they might have erred, that their judgement might be questionable ...

Because the Royal Court was receiving £50,000 from the Arts Council and the Greater London Council was providing another £2,500 a year, Gaskill was treading on some very tricky territory in his attempts to deny the Press the usual amenities and freedom to comment on its product. The Board of the English Stage Company, which managed the activities of the Royal Court's creative people, voiced concern at this state of affairs and a hurriedly organized emergency meeting was called. Mr Alfred Easdale, the board's vice-chairman was particularly incensed at Gaskill's letter to the Press, claiming that he had had no right to make such statements and that he was guilty of unpardonable behaviour.

Interviewed in Tunis, where he was on holiday, Gaskill began to backtrack a bit about his wish to ban critics. 'Let's not get it out of proportion,' he said. 'It's in the old tradition of the Court to provide a little controversy ... I just don't understand the criticisms levelled at Simone Signoret. There is a cheap kind of snobbery about verse-speaking as well as a kind of chauvinistic resentment at a foreign accent, but to me Signoret reveals what the woman is. She was extraordinary – the best Lady Macbeth I have ever seen ...'

The row continued to erupt like bursting fireworks on the theatrical scene. Gaskill was flown in from Tunis to take part in a BBC TV debate involving the *Sunday Times* critic, Harold Hobson, the playwright, Arnold Wesker, and myself. Scheduled for fifteen minutes, with Robert Robinson chairing it, it was acrimonious but resolved nothing. 'After all,' said Robinson, 'none of us thought we were going to.'

The theatre's management committee had to face a call for the resignation of Gaskill, but settled for a letter of apology from him, expressing his regret for his letter and agreeing that in future he would consult them about matters concerning the Press.

The furore dragged on in letters to editors, cartoons, leader columns. It culminated in an Oxford Union debate on 17 November 1966 in which William Gaskill and myself were the two main speakers, supported by two undergraduates for both sides. The question to be debated was 'The critic has too much power and not enough responsibility' which Gaskill proposed and I opposed. Since Gaskill was an Oxford graduate, prominent director of a much valued progressive theatre and critics were, on the whole, objects of derision in academic circles, I assumed I would have little chance of winning the debate.

I spoke last after Gaskill, who was extremely modest and conciliatory considering how vehement his letters had been attacking the critical tribe. He argued that the critics had not shown the enthusiasm for drama that once was displayed by Shaw over Ibsen and Tynan over Osborne. It was a line that did not find favour with the reporter of the debate in *Isis*, the University's magazine. 'We do expect to be kept awake in an arts debate,' he complained. 'Thunder and lightening had been expected from Mr William Gaskill; but in fact his soporific gas nearly killed the debate.'

I had decided, with all the odds against me, to appeal to the undergraduates by asking them to support critics as the last bastion of the independent voice in the arts against the Big Battalions of the state and affluent entrepreneurs who could swamp any negative sounds made by the relatively weak corps of critics. Turning the motion on its head, I claimed that critics had too much responsibility and not enough power. It was the publicists of the film industry and the book trade, the monopolies in TV and the subsidized theatre that determined what should or should not be seen in the arts. The critics alone represented an independent opinion and stood up against the vast financial machines behind many of the artistic endeavours of the day.

It clearly appealed to the *Isis* correspondent, 'Milton Shulman revived the debate,' he wrote. 'The proposition would confine criticism to the reliable adulation and punctual praises of a cliquish claque; as it was, critics (a representative cross-section including homosexuals, Socialists and Jews), powerless to affect audiences that flocked to what they damned, shunned what they praised, were yet the last independent and dispassionate voice to hold out against the mind-and-opinion-forming-money-power of Trade and State.'

To my surprise Gaskill's motion was defeated by 244 votes to 108, giving me a handsome majority of 136.

★ ★ ★

On arrival at Heathrow from New York, two American businessmen asked a taxi driver to take them to the St Martin's Theatre where they could see *The Mousetrap*, Britain's longest running play. To get there on time, the driver had to take some chances with the speed limit.

Getting out of the taxi in a hurry, one of the men paid the exact fare on the clock and added no tip. The furious and exasperated driver shouted after them as they entered the theatre, 'The policeman did it!'

Revealing the surprise ending of any play is an acknowledged critical offence. It is particularly heinous if the play happens to be a thriller with a puzzle element that constitutes its sole appeal. The wrath of my readers fell upon me mercilessly when, early in my career, I revealed who-done-it in an Agatha Christie mystery called *Towards Zero*.

'Either Agatha Christie is losing her touch or I have been seeing too many of her plays,' I wrote about this typical, genteel Christie-land where Lady Tresilian gets her brains beaten out by a niblick. 'No one is more hopeless than I am at solving the most infantile of puzzles and yet, before the second act curtain had dropped, I had already identified the murderer in *Towards Zero* at the St James's. This could be Miss Christie's lowest hour. The experience, from a critical standpoint, is most revealing. Without the magnetism of suspense to hold it together, this Agatha Christie play stands revealed in its almost embarrassing emptiness. It is like X-raying a bustle. The characters are so many clay pigeons waiting to be shot down by a blunderbuss. They speak in starched, formalized phrases devoid of anything but clues and paralyzing small talk. They are only interesting when they are dead.'

I ended my notice with the comment, 'A recent cartoon showed a disgruntled figure picketing a theatre with a sign that read "The butler did it." I now know exactly how he felt. Nevile did it.'

Infuriated readers took me to task. In a footnote to a letter, I offered this defence of my action: 'Agatha Christie, with three plays now running and a fourth just off, is rapidly turning the West End into her own personal puzzle corner. When a person of her reputation produces a play as bad as *Towards Zero*, it is time something drastic was done about warning the public. Miss Christie is apparently immune from ordinary criticism. Revealing the name of the murderer is the critic's ultimate weapon – used rarely and only in desperation. It is done, with all due modesty, for the ultimate good of the theatre.'

I never used the device again. On reflection, I decided that while it may have been part of my function as a critic to discourage people from patronizing trash, I had no responsibility for preventing them from spending their money on bad plays if that was what pleased them. Actually, I was tempted once again to reveal the assassin in another Agatha Christie thriller called *Go Back For Murder*. In my last paragraph I said: 'If I could possibly discourage you from going to see *Go Back For Murder* by revealing the murderer's name, I would gladly do so. But honestly, I can't remember who it was.'

* * *

When *My Fair Lady* opened in New York in 1957, it was the hottest ticket in town. It was said that people were pawning heirlooms to get themselves a seat. It was therefore surprising that only three weeks after its premier, a woman in the stalls had an empty seat beside her. At the interval, she was asked by those in the row behind, how it was possible such a seat would be unoccupied.

'I know it's strange,' explained the woman, 'but it was bought for my husband. We booked the seats months in advance and since then he has unfortunately died.'

'But surely you could have given it to one of your relatives or friends. They'd have loved it.'

'Oh, I couldn't do that,' said the woman. 'They're all at the funeral.'

I have some sympathy with her predicament because I have seen the musical several times and it still is, in my opinion, the best musical ever produced.

When it came to London in 1958 I wrote that 'what makes it a triumphant occasion is that it is unique where a musical should be unique. Its contribution to its genre is in its homogeneity, its fusion of language, lilt, and looks, its blend of action and music so that the songs are not irritating interruptions to the plot and the dialogue is not an embarrassing hiatus between the songs. An even more impressive feat is the disciplining of Shaw's intellectual high spirits so that they appear neither uncomfortable nor pretentious in this highly artificial medium ...'

The fact that *West Side Story* was voted the Best Musical of 1958 by a narrow margin over *My Fair Lady* has always appeared to me to be one of the few errors committed by the usually perceptive panel of judges of the *Evening Standard* Drama Awards.

Assessing the merits of a musical has always been one of the trickier problems facing a theatre critic. Bernard Shaw, after years of theatregoing admitted, 'I cannot pretend to be an expert in the criticism of musical farce.' Another redoubtable critic, James Agate, asked about fifty years ago, 'What is expected of me when I am invited to criticize a musical play? Am I expected to say whether the play will run? In that case my answer must be that I am not a prophet.'

Since the genesis of the musical has always been entertainment rather than enlightenment, the pre-war critic was never concerned with the book of a musical, and just as rarely with its lyrics. The tunes, the dancing, the decor, spectacular stage effects, the comics, the popularity of the stars, the vivacity and the winsomeness of the amalgam had to be tested and compared with similar blends of the same ingredients to justify a critic's judgement. From the 1920s to the early 1950s the British musical concentrated on glamour and innocence with Ivor Novello's *Glamorous Night* and *King's Rhapsody* as well as Julian Slade's *Salad Days* setting the box offices tingling. But the American musical, even though just as silly as the British product with *No, No Nanette*, was becoming more committed to plausible and integrated story lines with *Showboat* in 1928, and then to conquering this melodic world with the Rodgers and Hammerstein and Rodgers and Hart era of *Oklahoma!*, *The King and I*,

South Pacific. The dominance of the American musical from 1958 to 1978, was solidified with the triumphs of *My Fair Lady* and *West Side Story.* It was not until the astonishing topic of the career of a charismatic Argentine woman, told through the music of Andrew Lloyd Webber and the lyrics of Tim Rice in *Evita,* that America's ascendancy in this sphere was threatened and eventually overtaken by Europe.

One of the inhibiting factors that plagued the development of topical, irreverent and satirical subjects being an important aspect of British musicals was the severe and, at times, idiotic censorship powers of the Lord Chamberlain. For instance, the prohibition of the depiction of heads of state on the stage in an unflattering or realistic manner would have smothered the idea of *Evita* at its inception. But in 1967 common sense was at last beginning to break through this restrictive bureaucratic barrier. A Joint Committee on Censorship in the Theatre recommended that the pre-censorship and licensing of plays should cease. It was taken for granted that the government would accept the recommendation.

My comments on this welcome development were contained in a long article in the *Evening Standard,* 21 June 1967. Here are some extracts.

He objected to the suggestive angle at which a wooden plank was carried in the musical, *Fings Ain't Wot They Used T'Be.* In *End Game* by Samuel Beckett, he objected to God being called 'a bastard' but did not mind him being called 'a swine'.

He protested against a revue skit showing Winston Churchill opening a public lavatory. He was distressed by a scene in Roger Vitrac's play, *Victor,* in which a beautiful, statuesque woman breaks wind on the stage. 'It is not only once but continuous,' said one of his assistants, explaining the policy, 'and we would feel that this would be undesirable.'

It has been decisions such as these – coupled with more serious ones like the banning of John Osborne's *A Patriot For Me* for public showing – which have made the Lord Chamberlain one of the longest running gags on the English social scene. Ever since 1727, when the Lord Chamberlain was first granted the power to prohibit public performance because Sir Robert Walpole was eager to suppress a play ridiculing his government, ludicrous censorship decisions have added enormously to the gaiety of the nation.

But at last the joke is over. At least it will be over if the Government accepts the recommendations of the Joint Committee on Censorship of the Theatre whose report has just been issued today… And the ghosts of all those eminent men who fought to extinguish him over the centuries – Lord Chesterfield, Dr Johnson, George Bernard Shaw, John Galsworthy, James Barrie, Arnold Bennett, H. G. Wells – will no doubt be chuckling with satisfaction …

Waiting for the demise of the Lord Chamberlain was the American pop musical, *Hair*, a great success in its home market but its nudity, expletives and drug-taking made it impossible for a showing in Britain. Precisely on the same day as the censorship power of the Lord Chamberlain was buried forever, *Hair*, amidst a hurricane of media attention, turned up at the Shaftesbury Theatre on 30 September 1968.

'It is relevant to judge a protest musical like *Hair* by the nature and quality of its protest,' I wrote in a distinctly unfriendly notice in the *Evening Standard*. 'To judge from the critical reception from some of my colleagues, its electrifying beat, its anarchic frenzy, its youthful exuberance, its plotless abandon, its taboo-breaking defiance have more than compensated for the general level of mediocrity, verging on amateurism, that is shared by most of these performers.

'Strung together tenuously on a no-plot about a boy who burns his draft card for the Vietnam war, the pounding, quirky music of Galt MacDermot, the wild dance routines of Julie Arenal and the uninhibited direction by Tom O'Horgan which clobbers the audience with confetti, pamphlets and rope-swinging bodies, sweeps every individual presence into a rhythmic maelstrom where professionalism takes a bad second place to youth …

'Their frenzy is directed chiefly at middle-class American values and their protest is against a society that has given them affluence and education without meaning. They prefer filth and long hair to West Point crewcuts and armpit deodorants. They blaspheme to shock their parents and shout sexual expletives to affirm their freedom. They take dope to find a prohibited road to escape.

'And what secret urge of man does all this marijuana and free love and four-letter words unlock? Why love, man, perfect love! Better than ethics or Marxism or Christianity or all that jazz!

'It is not the blasphemy or the obscenity or the nakedness that shocks. The much-publicised mixed nudity scene was displayed in such shadowed lighting and was of such a short duration that I almost missed it entirely leaning over to pick up a dropped programme.

'What was much more shocking to me was the wholesomeness, the suffocating worthiness, the relentless naivety of it all. The effect at times was like being a voyeur at an orgy of Boy Scouts and Girl Guides. After the lessons of the Inquisition, de Sade, Buchenwald and Stalin, I find it difficult to tune in sympathy with this Pollyanna fantasy, this tot's eye view of life in which all evil will evaporate after a trip on the Good Ship Lollipot.'

Hair ran for many years in London and New York. When an attempt to revive it was made in London about twenty-five years later, it flopped.

★ ★ ★

Statistical evidence of the mass appeal of musicals is provided by their numbers in London's West End in the early months of 1997. Of the almost sixty theatrical productions available, no less than twenty-two could be described as musicals or revues. And to show how far the American musical had fallen behind those written by British or European talent, only seven could claim to have an American origin. The successes filling theatres for years were those produced, managed, written or directed by Andrew Lloyd Webber, Cameron Mackintosh, Trevor Nunn, Tim Rice, Alain Boubill, Claude-Michel Schonberg and others – *Cats, Les Misérables, Sunset Boulevard, Miss Saigon, Phantom of the Opera, Starlight Express, Jesus Christ Superstar, Martin Guerre.*

But even the multi-millionaire instinct of Andrew Lloyd Webber for finding successful musicals occasionally falls flat on its financial face. In November 1984 he backed, as the producer, an adaptation of a novel by Melvyn Bragg about the hard, jobless times in the fens and coal mines of Cumbria at the turn of the century. A dour, humourless story, even with music by Howard Goodall that verged on the operatic, it defied the entertainment criteria of the conventional musical and it took an act of faith and considerable courage on the part of Lloyd Webber to put his money into it. My review of *The Hired Man* indicated that I thought he was bound to lose his investment.

Andrew Lloyd Webber has become a very rich man by accurately assessing the box office appeal of such unlikely subjects as Argentine politics,

rhyming cats and amorous locomotives. I suspect, however, that his ability to make a profitable musical out of almost anything will be facing its
most severe test with *The Hired Man*.

The Hired Man is, strictly speaking, not a musical. The use of music to
integrate the action in a continuous flow gives it the flavour of an opera
– which is an art form, as someone once said of poetry, that can disperse
an English crowd faster than a fire hose. And, as its title implies, it is also
concerned with work, or more precisely the working class, whose drawing power at the box-office at this precise moment would be about on a
par with a lantern slide lecture on the early days of the grocer's co-op.

To my surprise, this mild attack on his financial judgement struck a sensitive nerve in Andrew Lloyd Webber. He wrote a letter to the *Standard*
saying that he would be eternally glad, financially and commercially, to
be associated with the composer, Howard Goodall. I contacted his press
agent to affirm that, in my opinion, no one could make a box-office hit
of the trade union movement and that *The Hired Man* was bound to
have a short life.

A bet seemed to be the only way of resolving the matter. Asked to
predict how long I thought it would run, I said less than three months.
The resultant wager was that if *The Hired Man* folded before 24
February 1984, Andrew Lloyd Webber would fly me to New York for
the première in a Manhattan church of his new Requiem Mass and pay
my expenses for two days in a luxury hotel. If it lasted beyond 24
February, I would pay for a three-star lunch at a famous restaurant. The
odds were a little lop-sided but considering the comparative wealth of
the protagonists, it seemed fair enough.

Early in February, because audiences had been so sparse, Lloyd
Webber announced he would no longer be backing *The Hired Man*.
Morally, since I had made my bet with him, I had won it. But instead of
folding, the show went on. This was because the theatre's owner, Laurie
Marsh, and Melvyn Bragg thought that business would pick up over
Easter and, without Lloyd Webber's money, decided to keep it afloat
until after the vital date of our wager, 24 February. It went on for a few
more weeks, enough to make me technically a loser. There was therefore some uncertainty as to how the bet should be settled.

I told Lloyd Webber that I would take him to a grand lunch whenever he would set a date, but his press agent said that a more amicable
way of resolving the matter would be for me to have lunch at his flat in

Grosvenor Square and that I should provide the champagne. A date was agreed and other interested people joined the party – Andrew's wife, Sarah Brightman, Melvyn Bragg, the *Standard* editor, Louis Kirby and two or three others. I contributed three bottles of Dom Perignon and a most sumptuous meal was provided by our host.

In the chit-chat that accompanied the lunch, I asked Andrew what was in his mind for his next project. 'I've been reading Gaston Leroux's novel, *The Phantom of the Opera*,' he said. 'I'm trying to make up my mind whether it could be turned into a musical.'

I don't often wax enthusiastic about other people's ideas, but this time I gripped his arm and said, 'That's a brilliant story for you. You can write the interior opera and there are all those dramatic effects that would make an exciting impact on the stage. I wouldn't hesitate another second. Go for it!'

Whether my eager approval had anything to do with his decision to produce it, I would never know. But in a small way, it has offered me some solace for all those other failed projects in my life, because it showed I could recognize a gold mine when I saw it, even if it was only to help make Andrew Lloyd Webber one of the richest men in the world.

* * *

Towards the end of 1991, a new editor of the *Standard,* Paul Dacre, my seventh, called me into his office to tell me that he thought I had had enough of the gruelling business of attending first nights and that he wanted me to take on a weekly column on the arts. It was a column I wrote for six years which spread out from the arts to politics to social affairs to everything.

The paper devoted a full page to my going with a large, behatted picture of me smiling at my new fate. Angus McGill wrote the premature obituary on 7 November 1991 under the headline 'A Legend Takes A Bow'.

'Mr Milton Shulman would like to know why he is not in the *Guinness Book of Records*,' wrote McGill. 'John Iles of Salisbury is there for going to the theatre 3,687 times. Milton has been far more often than that. Seven thousand times he reckons, though I make it 5,084, and every single time he has let the world know exactly what he thought of it.

'Milton Shulman has been theatre critic of the *Evening Standard* since 1953. He is by far the longest-serving theatre critic in London, often the most critical, always the most readable, a rock-solid judge of a play and a performance, unbudgeable and usually right. After thirty-eight years of reviewing comedy, tragedy, history, pastoral, musical, tragical-comical, pastoral-musical-historical, for the *Standard*, London's senior theatre critic is about to become London's newest columnist.'

9

THE HALF-TRUTH MACHINE

An analysis of the effects of television on society ... The Soap Opera Syndrome ... I predict the impact of TV on the Royal Family ... Mary Whitehouse confuses sex with violence ... Who killed the Saturday Evening Post? ... I did!

(i) Even if you put the truth in, it lies

Awards are always welcome. For a few days they give you the illusion that you are important. Your telephone is busy with friends and relatives telling you how pleased they are for you. And in the very fickle field of newspapers, they constitute some sort of insurance that you are not likely to be fired for some time yet.

The Hannen Swaffer Awards, named after Fleet Street's best known popular journalist and gossip columnist, were annually presented to those toiling in the medium's vineyard in the fields of foreign affairs, news, features, sports, provincial reporting, women's problems and criticism. The name has since been changed to that of the International Press Awards and they are the most coveted in the profession. I was named the best Critic of 1966 (previous winners had been in the fields of theatre, film, literature) and my commendation read 'Though a forceful critic, Mr Shulman is not content with comment on current TV programmes. He enters into the intricacies of production, finance and motive. Both viewer and technician are likely to be stimulated by his well-argued case for reforms and re-appraisals.'

When I began writing a regular weekly column about television in the *Evening Standard* on 27 May 1964 I was acclaimed as someone with 'a unique view from the inside' who had returned to full-time journalism. There was a certain amount of scepticism about how I would be able to manage attending three or four first-nights in the theatre, and also keep a comprehensive eye on the full range of TV programmes. In those days there were few facilities for seeing previews of peak-time

327

shows, something which has now become almost the universal practice for TV critics and journalists. I honestly didn't know the answer to that query, but since I wasn't expected to write immediate notices of individual programmes I thought I could manage my allotted brief, to give my opinions and views about the general direction being taken by the small screen, using isolated programmes to illustrate my arguments or philosophy.

Having served four years with Granada TV and two years with Associated-Rediffusion, for the first time in my critical career I was formally equipped with the experience and know-how to write with considerable authority about this art form from the very beginning of my assignment. Not only did I know how the critical mind operates, because of my decades of film and theatre assessments, but I also had sat in at a fairly high level on the deliberations of managements, producers and advertisers about the creation and financing of network TV. I had also been responsible for supervising the nuts-and-bolts of putting the elements of a programme together in the fields of documentaries, politics, social issues and entertainment.

I functioned as a weekly TV commentator on the *Evening Standard* for eight years, from 1967 to 1974. In a very short time I gained the reputation of being a Savonarola of the Box, demanding a 'bonfire of the vanities' for which television was primarily catering. I realized that when I had been actually involved in the production of programmes, I hadn't paid much attention to the overall output of the BBC and the independent companies, let alone the social consequences of the small screen. Watching TV regularly, with a responsibility to think and write about it, I soon became appalled by the general level of mediocrity offered to viewers and, in some important areas like the proliferation of violent TV, the apparent lack of social concern exercised by those in control.

Because television is less an art form and more a way of life, its impact cannot be dismissed as merely another means of disseminating information or providing entertainment. As far as most children are concerned it has become the most important conditioning factor in their lives – far more pervasive in terms of hours and influence than their parents, their teachers, their community and the Church.

Adults in the TV age are involved in an environment unique in the history of mankind and more important, because of the speed of its development, than the invention of the Guttenberg press and the spread of reading. Never before has the human mind been bombarded by so many facts, ideas, dreams, lies, fantasies in such rapid succession in so compressed a period of time. An ordinary evening's television in Britain and America can be equivalent to seeing a one-act play in the theatre; skimming through a short story; going to the town hall to hear a political or communal debate; being harangued or flattered or frightened or intrigued by fifty salesmen trying to sell their wares; glancing through the main items in a newspaper; sitting in a stadium watching a football game or a cricket match; and watching a discussion about social or moral problems in a university lecture room.

Before television, some individuals might have experienced one or two of these activities perhaps once a week; some, once or twice a year; some hardly at all. Now it happens to most people almost every day of the year. The average Briton or American devotes more hours to television than the average person before him devoted to radio, books, theatre, cinema and newspapers *combined*. Does the individual psyche remain immune to this unique battering by visual and aural stimuli? Can any society, deeply immersed in the telly environment, remain unaffected by its influence and pressures? Does it matter?

Because reviewing television was almost like trying to judge and appraise all human activity, there has never been any acceptable set of standards or criteria for its performance. It would be an unrewarding and impossible task. The last debate that seriously tried to lay down social and moral principles for the governance of TV took place in 1954, when a Conservative Government introduced TV financed by advertising to compete with the monopoly of the BBC.

The paternalistic Lord Reith, who dominated the early days of radio and TV, did his utmost to found a tradition of public service rather than private exploitation. However the ranks of competition, enterprise and investment capital were too powerful a force for change. In the debate in the Lords, Reith thundered, 'Somebody introduced Christianity into England and somebody introduced smallpox, bubonic plague and the Black Death. Somebody is minded now to introduce sponsored broadcasting ... Need we be ashamed of moral values, or of intellectual and ethical objectives? It is these that are here and now at stake!'

But the Reithian concept of broadcasting as a structure for good in any society has always been an impossible dream. Its hypnotic power has just been too great for any government to allow it total freedom. Where democracy does not exist – China, Libya, Iraq – TV is an instrument of state domination. In Western democracies TV freedom is limited by state regulations or the need for private enterprises – American networks like NBC or CBS, ITV's independent companies, the Internet – to be profitable.

In my early years as a TV commentator, I naively thought that castigating or ridiculing the product being offered by the commercial TV companies, with the BBC soon to follow in their footsteps, might shame their programme executives into aspiring for something on a slightly higher level of talent and imagination. The kind of article that made me unpopular with the TV establishment, written in November 1964, six months after I took on the job, was provoked by the publication of the annual report of the Independent Television Authority, chaired by Lord Hill.

Judging from the ITA annual report,' I wrote, 'commercial TV is an Elysium of good taste, public service, responsibility, reflective documentaries, religious discussions, classical concerts and art programmes concerned with such heart-warming matters as Japanese Art and Portuguese Fado.

'Most of us, of course, have a different image of commercial TV. It's the place where couples in boiler suits can win refrigerators if they smash enough balloons with the needles pinned to their noses. It's the channel where bedroom suites are given away if you happen to know that Shakespeare wrote *Hamlet*. It's the visual mausoleum for old films that the cinema has discarded. It's the haven for the tired Western, fatuous adventure thrillers and moronic panel shows. It's the enclosed fortress determined to keep out any adventurous or new ideas and the gilded treasure trove where the Great Ratings God TAM reigns supreme.'

It is awesome that the relevance of those strictures are still valid almost thirty-five years later. The soap opera has spread from ITV to the BBC and Channel Four like a contagious disease. In the week of 13 April 1997 the BBC's soap flagship, *EastEnders*, accompanied by the Australian fictional detergent, *Neighbours*, watched by between 18 to 10 million for each of three episodes weekly, monopolized the top twelve programme slots, which this particular week had as its cultural competition the Grand National steeplechase and the National Lottery. On the commercial channel, 17 to 18 million viewers for doses of three to five episodes weekly were gripped by *Coronation Street, Emmerdale Farm* and *Home and Away*. Between them they occupied almost half of the thirty top rating programmes of ITV. Channel Four – the controversial, supposedly different channel – has *Brookside* in its top five slots, mesmerizing between 7 and 6 million viewers every day of the week. No other offering on Channel Four comes close to these ratings.

This deterioration of value and choice had become so evident that the usually tolerant, soft-spoken, supportive watchdog of the commercial companies – the Independent Television Commission – was finally moved to protest. In its annual report issued on 23 April 1997, the ITC insisted that ITV was screening too many soaps at the expense of documentaries, arts and children's programmes at peak times. 'The rot has got to stop and it's got to move in the other direction,' said Peter Rogers, its chief executive.

The reaction of those who control ITV companies to these strictures was predictable. One of the chief executives claimed that Mr Rogers was talking rot, justifying his stand with the fact that 35 million drama viewers watched his schedule of cheap soap and trivia – and they couldn't be wrong. Using the argument that popularity was the chief criterion for judging what should be offered to the public for their excitement and entertainment, a case could be made out for bringing back public hangings, for encouraging cigarette smoking and for lifting the laws against marijuana and heroin.

My many years observing television have convinced me that nothing practical can be done about changing the essential superficiality and triviality of the medium. There may be a minority clamouring for more mature drama, more cerebral social and political discussions, more serious attention to science, medicine, literature, philosophy and the arts, more awareness of the deleterious impact of violence-sodden programmes on the behaviour and values of children. But it is a derisive minority, whose influence is not enough to change the practices of profit-motivated companies or popularity-seeking politicians.

The truth is that there is not enough talent in any society to produce a meaningful ration of enlightenment or entertainment that will satisfy those living in a dream-land of Reithian expectations. With the proliferation of cable and satellite channels to join the five terrestrial channels in Britain, there will be a maw of voracious TV hours demanding to be filled by almost anything. Not the highest. More likely the lowest. The villain in the piece, conditioned by decades of pap, is the public which wants more and more of the same. My moaning about this state of affairs as a TV critic, joining the enfeebled voice of those insisting that something should be done about it, had as little effect as the relentlessly dashing waves have had on the cliffs of Dover.

Although television has always denied that its function or purpose or goal is to change anything in society, claiming that it is only a mirror or neutral communicator of what the people are up to, by its very existence it has been, in Western industrial societies, the most powerful agency for change the world has ever known. No other technological revolution – the printing press, the electric light, the railway, the motor car, the aeroplane, the telephone, the radio, the computer, the newspaper – has brought about such significant changes in people's lifestyles in such a relatively short period of time. Every medium has had to adjust to its existence. Books, magazines, the cinema, the theatre, the press have all been stifled or altered by its competition or have had to enlist its aid for survival. It has transformed the nature of democratic politics. No product can be mass-marketed without its assistance. Ceremonials and sports events have had to be shaped to conform to its scheduled demands. It produces instant heroes, idols and icons and just as quickly demolishes them. It has stultified conversation in the home and become the most influential factor in the socializing of children.

There is nothing inherently evil or demonic about television. Most people would contend that their personal experience with television has been benign and harmless. It provides relaxation for tired workers. It is a constant joy and companion to the sick, the lonely and the elderly. It broadens the horizons of the young, brings them into contact with lands and sights they could never possibly have seen before, encourages them to take up interests, hobbies, adventures that might never have inspired them had it not been for something seen on the small screen. It brings to millions the cultural heritage of the past – plays, concerts, opera, ballet – that were denied their forefathers.

But as a critic, I came to believe it was my responsibility not merely to commend its positive virtues but to comment on those programmes which, in my opinion, could have a deleterious impact not only on those watching it but on the institutions its presence might effect. For example, what have the cameras done to the images of the monarchy or Parliament? Has their authority and prestige been enhanced or diminished by their exposure to the public gaze? Will the admission of cameras into the law courts ensure worse or better justice for litigants or the accused? Some of these issues with which I concerned myself as a TV commentator are discussed within this chapter.

* * *

'The medium is bound to deceive,' said Malcolm Muggeridge, informed and waspish journalist and broadcaster. 'Even if you put the truth into it, it comes out a deception.'

While the verbal lie is as old as man's ability to speak or write, the visual lie is something that still runs counter to most people's conception of the natural order of things. The stage magician earns his livelihood because the audience clings to its notion that there is something awesome about the fact that the eye can be fooled. The eye-witness in our law courts is accepted as more reliable evidence of the truth of a happening than the touch, hear or smell witness. This readiness to believe in the veracity of TV pictures, as compared with the printed or spoken words of other media, has repeatedly been confirmed by numerous sociological surveys which show that almost double the public name TV as 'the most trustworthy and reliable of media' on political news, compared to the press or radio.

Yet the distortion of the visual image has become one of the commonplace techniques of the cameraman and the film editor. The faked photograph is already a familiar ingredient of espionage and blackmail. How far away are we from the faked newsreel, the faked reconstruction of a past event (the routine component of historical films), the faked documentary?

In the hands of someone like Peter Watkins who provided compelling, realistic visions of the Hungarian uprising and the after-effects of a nuclear war, the technique can be used to provide a fresh insight into a historical event. But in less scrupulous hands, what are its potentialities?

We take for granted verbal and printed propaganda, since the use of words and drawings to produce distortions of the truth has always been with us. We have therefore developed a natural scepticism about facts and views conveyed in this way. The more educated and sophisticated we are, the more refined is our ability to sift the true from the implausible, the logical from the illogical. But most people have not yet cultivated the same wariness about such relatively new communications phenomena as the photograph and the moving picture. While ignorance persists about the ease with which celluloid and electronic tape can be tampered with and counterfeited, the television medium is likely to be believed even when it distorts and misrepresents – intentionally or not.

Every serious journalist who has worked in TV news or current affairs recognizes that there is inherent in the medium – even when it is used with no intention to misrepresent – a basic dishonesty.

Philip Whitehead, a Labour MP, who was editor of ITV's *This Week* and had worked on BBC's *Panorama* said: 'Television is the only profession in which the word "cheat" is an inseparable part of the vocabulary. I think it's alarming that so often, in order to preserve a smooth visual flow and in order to re-create an assumed sequence of events or to prepare a visual montage which approximates to an idea, you do dishonest things.'

There are a number of ways in which the quality of truth is reshaped and restructured when it is subjected to the attentions of the camera. The mere presence of the cameraman and the paraphernalia of his art divides an occasion into performers and audience. What the viewer sees, selected for him by the cameraman and the producer, is often significantly different from the atmosphere and mood being experienced by those actually on the spot. The camera eye transmits a contrived image of the event, not its reality.

The propaganda uses to which cameras can be put, especially if there is live coverage, have not been lost on the organizers of demonstrations and protest marches. Not only are the banners most vigorously flaunted and slogans most loudly chanted where TV cameras are known to be taking pictures, but it has also not been unknown for police to be deliberately provoked into retaliatory reaction in the hope that some nasty piece of police brutality will catch the camera's eye.

Like so much else in our approach to television, war, too, has become an aspect of entertainment. If it's a dull war – nobody much being killed – the viewer will get bored and the executives back home will be tempted to cut costs and bring the crews out of the war zone. To justify their existence, TV newsmen will be tempted to find something exciting or dramatic to film. Thus an isolated bit of action, caught by some enterprising reporter, can give millions of viewers an impression of widespread bloody fighting when in reality the front is relatively quiet and uneventful.

'With a typical TV crew at work,' reflected Murray Sayle, 'with lamps and clapper boards no one would any longer doubt that this is at least in part show business, with a powerful effect on the audience. When massacres are staged, and hostages coached for the media, the convention that our presence does not make some of these things happen is getting impossible to swallow.'

In spite of the medium's predisposition towards superficiality and misrepresentation, it is one of television's fondest boasts that its cumulative effect has been to create a society that is better informed about the wide social and political issues of the day than ever before. It is an assumption not only accepted by politicians and broadcasters, but the public itself believes that it gets more reliable information from the box than from other media such as newspapers, journals or radio.

Every survey shows that, for most people, television has become not only their primary source of information but also their most trustworthy source. Because it is believed, it is also influential. A survey conducted by *The Times* amongst important people listed in *Who's Who* showed that the majority of a representative sample thought that the BBC was more influential in Britain than Parliament, the Press, trade unions, the civil service, the monarchy and the Church. A similar survey about ITV would probably have shown a similar result.

The impetus to turn every serious issue – industrial disputes, foreign affairs, capital punishment, Europe, housing, unemployment, education, sexual deviation, causes of crime, drugs – into a 'good show' means that programmes are planned to ensure a dramatic confrontation between extreme points of view. Conflict television holds viewers: consensus television loses them. A true reflection of how problems are treated and absorbed in a democratic society would reveal that most of them are resolved by a slow osmosis of like opinions. This process is rarely shown on the small screen. Instead, the polarized opposites are invited to take up belligerent stances in public, vowing to stand by their positions at all costs and making retreat from them even more difficult. By constantly reflecting social, political and industrial disputes in the guise of intransigent and stubborn conflicts, television too often distorts and misrepresents reality. It also encourages the protagonists to be more abrasive and uncompromising in their public relations postures than is either wise or profitable. The public are rarely offered more than half-truths about these important situations.

* * *

Early in November, 1966, there occurred on the chat show, *BBC-3*, a follow-up series to the BBC's notorious and controversial satire programmes beginning with *That Was The Week That Was*, a cataclysmic linguistic event. The TV critic, Kenneth Tynan, deliberately uttered the work 'fuck'. My column that week was devoted to the social implications of that media breakthrough which caused papers like the *Express* to headline their news story with the words THE BLOODIEST OUTRAGE OF ALL.

I wondered in my reflections on the matter how many viewers were so appalled or disgusted by hearing this verbal affront near midnight that they immediately turned off their TV set? Or how many had telephoned the BBC to register their indignant protests? Or how many had kept their sets on waiting to see what further shocks the programme had in store for them?

Since the BBC no longer issued statistics about the volume of viewer reaction, we never really found out whether Tynan was right or wrong when he blandly proclaimed, 'I doubt if there are any rational people to whom the word "fuck" would be particularly diabolical, revolting or totally forbidden.' In spite of Tynan's liberal optimism on this matter, the *Evening Standard* dared not affront its readers and in my column the euphemistic ★★★★ had to be used for any taboo expletive I talked about.

I claimed, however, that in spite of the spate of hysterical articles in the Press and four Motions of Protest to be raised in the Commons, Tynan's assessment was more right than wrong.

But even if most rational people – and even the majority of adults – remained unperturbed by a four-letter word, the question remained as to how far broadcasting authorities had a responsibility towards protecting the irrational and the minority from the shock of hearing their deeply-held prejudices and values being ridiculed on TV, or shielding them from being confronted with the breaches of the conventions governing standards of conversation in middle-class homes.

Judging by the threats of some MPs, there seemed to be a widely-held view that in some way Ken Tynan and the BBC had broken the law. Fortunately the law is far more liberal and tolerant about four-letter words than these critics. To establish an obscene libel it would be necessary for the Crown to convince a jury that the word 'fuck' spoken in such circumstances would tend to deprave and corrupt those who heard it.

I had been involved with the question of the illegality of the word 'fuck' on a different occasion. During the preparations for the case against the publication of the unexpurgated version of D. H. Lawrence's *Lady Chatterley's Lover*, the solicitors for the defence asked me to talk to them about my views on the dangers of taboo words on the stage. I felt that my expertise as an authority on English literature did not equip me adequately for facing cross-examination in the subject in the witness box.

However, I did make one contribution to the defence. I suggested to the solicitors for Penguin Books that if the word 'fuck' was deemed to corrupt then the British Army, who in my experience used it as a universal adjective and adverb, was corrupt beyond redemption. Mr Gerald Gardner in summing up for the defence in his address to the jury, picked up my contention but, being judicious about such an overall generalization, said, 'if the word is deemed to corrupt then ninety per cent of the British armed services are corrupt beyond redemption.'

By dismissing the Crown's prosecution, the jury by implication agreed that a word good enough for its heroes was not likely to lower the moral standards of those who read it in a serious novel.

But if it can be agreed that no crime was even remotely committed, what responsibility did the BBC or any broadcasting authority have for not affronting its viewers with what, for want of a better phrase, one can only call bad manners?

Here we edge into a very tricky area of speculation. Who can possibly arbitrate about manners and please everyone? What is bad manners to some is a necessary gesture of protest, progress, liberalization and freedom to others.

There are those who insist that TV should always behave with the propriety of a guest in their living room. But if in that household it is considered bad manners to discuss homosexuality, abortion, birth control, AIDS, incest or the existence of God, surely no one could seriously argue that such significant social issues should be banned from the small screen.

A word that is shocking today may become bland and innocuous tomorrow. It is hard to credit that in 1913 a similar indignant row broke over Bernard Shaw's use of the words 'not bloody likely' in *Pygmalion*. When I first began to write in the *Evening Standard* in 1948, my articles were pitted with euphemisms for taboo words. A prostitute had to be called a lady of the street or of easy virtue. Adultery was referred to as a marital offence. Homosexuals were men of unnatural habits or vices. But with the passage of time I became free to use words like whore, queer, tart, lesbian, gay, shit, cunnilingus, masturbation, fornication, without compromising the *Standard*'s reputation as a family newspaper. But even in the late 1990s I still had to use asterisks for prohibited expletives. This is an astonishingly prim approach when television revels nightly in every form of expletive, often spoken by schoolchildren, and the most explicit and pornographic displays of sexual behaviour.

That something like Tynan's candid outburst was bound to happen was recognized by those who produced TV in the 1950s and 60s. Malcolm Muggeridge has written about an interview he was about to conduct with the constantly inebriated playwright, Brendan Behan. Recognizing the possibility of Behan's colourful language on the box and the impossibility of censoring it in a live programme, the anxious producer took Muggeridge aside and said, 'If he says "fuck", for God's sake, don't laugh!'

Robert Robinson, who was chairing *BBC-3* when Tynan shocked the TV establishment, recalls that at the programme's end, when the credits were rolling, the American novelist, Mary McCarthy, who had been on the discussion panel, commented, 'I suppose it's a historic moment,' to which Robinson reports he rather spinsterishly said, 'Then history's made very easily.'

'But if I implied the event had no historical status, I was wrong,' Robinson goes on to reflect in his Memoirs, *Skip All That*, 'for it was a taboo, and a universal one, and if you defy such a magic prohibition you release the power it conceals which is then free to take on other shapes; one of these turned out to be an even more irritating ju-ju, in which "fuck" was now to be used as often as possible as an emblem of sincerity. If a historic event is something after which nothing is ever the same, then this one counts – however callowly contrived.'

Robert Robinson also has another pertinent anecdote about the occasion. In the King's Road in Chelsea a week later, he was approached by an 'elderly lady with a red face and wearing a ginger fur coat'. She introduced herself as the wife of Lord Normanbrook who was then Chairman of the BBC governors. After some polite exchanges, she said, 'You know that word Mr Tynan used?' Robinson said he was afraid he did. 'Well,' she said, 'it doesn't form part of *my* vocabulary. But ever since I heard Mr Tynan say it, I use it all the time.'

(ii)   Trial by television
It was with mixed feelings of regret and exhilaration that I switched off my set after watching the *Frost Programme* on 3 February 1967. I suspect

it was somewhat similar to the feelings of millions of viewers through-out the world when the jury finally brought in a verdict of Not Guilty in the O. J. Simpson murder trial almost thirty years later in Los Angeles. What had the cameras done to the concept of justice? Whether one agreed with the Simpson jury or not, it was clear that the apparatus and procedures of an objective trial had undergone a drastic change because of the dominating presence of TV in the judicial process.

The court-room drama has always been one of the most popular forms of dramatic entertainment. Few things are more intriguing than seeing how an accused person convinces a court or a jury that he or she is telling the truth. Whether the issue is one of murder or fraud, the legal game that is taking place is always fascinating. That is why I regretted that the efforts of Dr Savundra, manager of the Fire, Auto and Marine Insurance Co, who had caused drastic losses to its policyholders, to prove his innocence was over as a TV programme. I was exhilarated because I had just witnessed a dramatic confrontation in which right seemed to have triumphed over wrong.

'Well done, Frostie! ... Good old Frostie! ...' were approving cries coming from the studio audience as David Frost, breathing heavily with indignation, verbally demolished the imperturbable Dr Savundra. It was clear that under Frost's ruthless questioning Savundra's dubious man-agement, had been exposed.

But away from the emotionally charged influence of the TV screen, my initial approbation was being undermined by doubts about the ethics of using TV in such an enterprise.

Having been trained as a lawyer, I was aware of the safeguards that the English legal system provides for any person in conflict with the law. The most obvious is that one is presumed innocent until proved guilty. And the other is that one has the right to be represented by trained counsel. There are other supplementary conditions which ensure a fair hearing from any defendant. The jury is chosen from objective, unin-volved citizens. The defendant has the right to put his case in direct examination without being harried by the prosecution's questions and he has the right to cross-examine witnesses testifying against him. Finally, the dull, dispassionate, antiseptic quality of a British courtroom is another guarantee that the facts will be sifted in a calm atmosphere free from anger, hate or prejudice.

'This paraphernalia of objectivity may seem cumbersome and tedious to the impatient who demand instant justice,' I wrote, 'but they are the rocks upon which the right of an Englishman's freedom from oppression and tyranny have been established for centuries.'

Now there is no doubt that in the context of the Frost programme, Dr Savundra was being asked to defend himself against accusations which, had they been proved, could have resulted in criminal charges. Foolishly and conceitedly, he allowed himself to take part in a mini-trial under conditions which would have horrified any British judge.

He was not represented by counsel. He was not given an opportunity to present his full case. His jurors, the studio audience, not only indicated their lack of impartiality by heckling him right from the start, but included a large number of victims of the collapse of Fire, Auto and Marine Insurance.

Even worse, his inquisitor, David Frost, unskilled in legal technicalities, asked questions which would have been disallowed in any courtroom as either prejudicial or irrelevant. Thus after a quick summary of previous shady enterprises with which Dr Savundra's name had been connected (not admissible in a British court), one of Frost's early comments was: 'You said you're a secret agent for the Pope, I believe.' Hardly likely to endear him to Catholics on the jury.

> 'What happened to Savundra,' I wrote, 'is in essence little but lynch TV – a phrase which implies that the rule of the mob has overruled the guarantees of the law. Someday someone with a more sympathetic case than Savundra's, as well as being innocent, will be forced by pressure of public opinion to undergo a similar trial by TV and will similarly be deprived of his inherent rights as a Briton. Both the ITA and the BBC should consider seriously the dangerous implications of the Frost-Savundra confrontation and decide whether or not such trials are the proper function of television.'

Later that year Dr Savundra was tried and found guilty of fraud. He appealed and in his judgement dismissing the appeal, Lord Justice Salmon referred to the *Frost Programme*. 'This court hopes that no interview of this kind will ever again be televised,' he said. 'Trial by television cannot be tolerated in a civilized country.' Much to my satisfaction, he then went on to quote, with approval, after outlining the safeguards of the English legal system, my exact words: 'They are the rocks on which freedom from oppression and tyranny have been established in this country for centuries.'

The *Frost Programme* highlighted the issue of the impact of TV on justice which has now been rumbling through media and legal circles for decades. The argument is whether the values and techniques of TV should dominate or influence every important and major institution in the land, or whether they should be excluded from venues where their presence, on balance, can only do harm.

The monarchy has suffered grievously for allowing itself to be a willing participant in the electronic circus. Newspapers, books and magazines have popularized the personalities and contents of top programmes and as a result have been financially diminished by having to compete with them. Parliament, after a long rearguard struggle, has finally permitted cameras to transmit its proceedings and been rewarded by taking part in the lowest ratings programmes to be seen on the box. State ceremonials and sporting events have had to accommodate their procedure and displays to the location and timing of TV cameras and schedules. In this country, although there is a continuous swell of opinion for it, the law courts have not yet succumbed to the blandishments of the electronic media.

The *Frost Programme*, although not analogous to the proceedings in a law court, revealed some of the dangers inherent in linking showbiz values with a quest for justice. The O. J. Simpson trial, in 1996, with the humiliating spectacle of big money and sharp lawyers hypnotizing millions by the devious antics of the participants, disclosed the perils of turning a law court into an entertainment extravaganza, by returning a verdict of manifest injustice. The repugnance felt in Britain, and even in America, by this demonstration of what cameras can do to the judicial process, has dimmed, for the moment, the ardour of those pressing for the televising of British courts or trials.

★ ★ ★

'1992 is not a year I shall look back on with undiluted pleasure. In the words of one of my more sympathetic correspondents, it has turned out to be an *annus horribilis*.' So spoke Queen Elizabeth in a hoarse, tired voice on 24 November 1992 to 730 people, at a lunch in the Guildhall in the City of London commemorating her fortieth year as Queen.

Kenneth Harris in his impressive biography of Her Majesty, *Queen*, assessing her words, believed that she had made a speech 'which may rank with the Abdication speech of the Duke of Windsor as the most emotional made by a member of the Royal Family in the twentieth century.'

In trying to calculate what the exposure of the Royal Family had done to its image ever since the Queen had allowed herself to be the star of a documentary called *Royal Family*, directed by Richard Cawston, Harris compared the shift in public opinion about the Royals between 1969 and 1992.

> As in 1969, in 1992 also, the Royal Family was unhappy about its stand-ing in the public perception. But there was a difference. In 1969, the Royal Family had been perceived as remote, formal and out of touch with the modern world. The film made then demystified them, made them seem more contemporary, presented them to the viewers as 'real' and 'human'. The problem for the Royal Family in 1992, it could be said, was too much de-mystification. The members of the Royal Family had become all too 'real', their every movement scrutinised and sometimes censored by the press. In 1969 the Royal Family had benefited greatly from the Cawston film and from the televising of the investiture of the Prince of Wales ten days later. They had continued to make good use of television in the seventies and early eighties, through such events as royal weddings and the Silver Jubilee. But in so doing they changed from being masters of the situation, controlling access, to servants of it. What Milton Shulman had warned them about had come to pass.

The warning which Kenneth Harris was referring to was contained in my column in the *Evening Standard* of 25 June 1969 under the headline 'Will The Royal Family Live To Regret Making That Film?' Andrew Duncan in his book, *The Reality of Monarchy*, reporting that the Cawston film was seen by twenty-three million people on its first showing and was greeted by most critics with reverential praise also claimed that cer-tain doubts about its wisdom were making themselves heard. To sub-stantiate that observation he quoted extensively from the same article of mine that Kenneth Harris had used. Its content could still have some relevance. I wrote:

> The making and showing of such a film, with the monarch's cooperation, may have constitutional and historical consequences which go well beyond its current interest as a piece of TV entertainment... Before tak-ing sides about the value to both the Crown and the nation, one must

first of all ask oneself what this small film has really done. What has actually happened is that an old image has been replaced by a fresh one. The emphasis on authority and remoteness, which was the essence of the previous image, has ever since George VI has been giving way to a friendlier image of homeliness, industry and relaxation. But just as it was untrue that the Royal Family sat down to breakfast wearing coronets as they munched their corn flakes so is it untrue that they now behave in their private moments like a middle-class family in Surbiton or Croydon.

Yet is it, in the long run, wise of the Queen's advisers to set as a precedent this right of the TV camera to act as the image-making apparatus for the monarchy? Every institution that has so far attempted to use TV to popularize or aggrandize itself has been diminished and trivialized by it. Having succumbed to the blandishments of the electronic box, there is a danger that the monarchy, too, will lose its essential mystique and distance that has been the bulwark of its survival.

From the monarch's standpoint the use of TV must be looked at and judged as a long-term proposition. If a precedent is established to reveal the intimate lives of future Kings and Queens, what will be the consequences when one day a member sitting on the Throne has a physical or mental persona that is clearly in serious divergence from the image that has to be projected on the box? A mad George III, a sadistic, misshapen Richard III, a libidinous Henry VIII?

Discretion and rarity would now seem to be the best course that the Queen's advisers could give the Royal Family in planning their future relationship with television.

It is reported that in a forthcoming interview with David Frost, Prince Charles answering the question: 'How would you describe yourself?' has said 'Sometimes a bit of a twit.' Heard once, such frankness is endearing. If he repeats it too often, his subjects might start believing him.

(iii) TV violence as a social pollutant

As a pollutant, television has done much more harm to Western industrial societies like America, Britain, Australia and Canada than nicotine, thalidomide, petrol fumes, asbestos, nuclear radiation or mad cow disease. The evidence that the emission of violence from TV screens has been a major contributor to the violence in those societies, particularly amongst the young, has been conclusively established by hundreds of authoritative studies and surveys. There has not been a *single* properly conducted scientific investigation, as far as I know, that proves that there have been no harmful effects caused by the thousands of hours annually depicting violence on television.

The remarkable thing about this state of affairs is that while the public is constantly agitated and concerned about various pollutants, sentiments whipped up by pressure groups like Greenpeace or anti-smoking lobbies, TV viewers numbering almost ninety per cent of the population, reveal no similar concern about the box in their living room that has helped to make many of their children anti-social and their streets relatively unsafe.

It was the assassinations in quick succession in 1967 and '68 of John F. Kennedy, Martin Luther King and Robert Kennedy that alerted politicians and sociologists to the possibility that TV programmes may have had something to do with the environmental climate that was being created, by the proliferation of violence being routinely beamed into the homes in democratic societies. It was the murder of the President's younger brother, Senator Robert Kennedy, that provoked me into filling my column in June, 1968, with my first serious reflections about what impact a regular dosage of mayhem and murder might have as a conditioning factor on the psyche of the young subjected to it.

Spurred by this latest act of insane horror, President Johnson has set up a Commission to investigate violence in America and to suggest solutions. If it does its job properly, it must gather what facts are available so that they can be examined to determine what baleful influence, if any, they might have on Western societies. In the routine Westerns and police and espionage dramas that make up the bulk of American TV, such moral issues as they occasionally raise are nearly always settled by some form of violence.

The sheriff only prevails over the outlaw because in the long run he can shoot faster than his adversary. The plain clothes officer has more physical courage and is better with a revolver than the drug pusher. The men from U.N.C.L.E. have more ingenious electronic ways of committing mayhem than their international opponents in Russia or the Middle East.

From the moment he can first perceive anything – the box becomes an electronic nipple from about the age of three – the American child is subjected to this scale of moral values. You don't have to be persuasive, to argue, to be logical, to be compassionate, to be ethical to achieve your goals in this world. You just have to be fitter, faster, stronger. The best way to defeat evil is to beat it to the ground or obliterate it. There is no more convincing persuader on the side of morality than a quick draw.

Through its infancy and adolescence, the American child watching TV is brainwashed to think in terms of violence as a righteous, socially approved form of conduct. And this gospel of moral behaviour is preached to the child for more hours every day than any contrary message conveyed by the teachers, the parents and the priests of that child *all put together.*

My article prompted a question in the Commons from Mr Eric Lubbock, the Liberal Chief Whip and MP for Orpington. He said he had been impressed by my arguments and asked Labour's Secretary for Education, Mr Edward Short, to request the Social Science Research Council to sponsor an inquiry into the effects of TV violence in Britain. Nothing came of it.

* * *

In the decades that followed my first alarm note about this possible baleful consequence of the contents of television, there has been a slow corrosion of the resistance to the idea that the small screen was a major accomplice in the growth of violence amongst the young in our society. Almost every year I wrote an up-date warning about TV's involvement in the creation of a violent society, and with time a minority of parents became aware of what was being done to the psyche of their children, followed by pious words of concern from leading members of the Establishment.

Because of the stance I had taken about the proliferation of mayhem TV, I was inevitably derided by the so-called liberal elements in the media. In order to ridicule my suspicions, they bracketed me with Mrs Mary Whitehouse, General Secretary of the self-organized National Viewers and Listeners Association. This group treated the need to deplore the excess transmission of violence as if it were the same problem as the excess depiction of sex. The lumping of these anti-life and pro-life aspects of human behaviour in the same abhorred category offered an easy opportunity for the anti-Whitehouse TV executives and producers to make her a laughing stock amongst commentators and leader writers in the Press. Occasionally I was invited to take part in a studio discussion on these troublesome aspects of programming and I would often find myself seated next to Mrs Whitehouse, so that the Chairman could conveniently link both of us as objects of derision from a baying audience. In August 1969 I attempted in my TV column to set the record straight about where I differed from Mary Whitehouse:

> Unfortunately when one expresses concern for the possibilities of TV's baleful influence in the spread of violence, one is immediately bracketed with Mrs Mary Whitehouse and her pressure group. I say 'unfortunately' because in principle I am opposed to most of what Mrs Whitehouse stands for. I am suspicious of her claim that only she and her followers know what offends against 'good taste and decency'.
>
> I detect beneath this assertion of moral infallibility a yearning for some control apparatus over the world of artists, writers and producers which is only a short step away from the censorship of anything that does not conform to her views of 'Christian values and the character of the nation'.
>
> I am against her and her organization because they are relatively unconcerned about the blandness, the trivia, the frivolity, the nonsense that occupies most of the hours of TV and which, in my opinion, are more potentially harmful to society than the permissive, liberal, controversial programmes she so often rails against.
>
> I am also totally opposed to her constant practice of lumping together sex and violence as if they both had the same deleterious effect on viewers. Unlike Mrs Whitehouse, I believe that programmes that deal forthrightly, frankly and wittily about sex can do this nation very little harm and might actually do it some good. Mrs Whitehouse, for example, finds four-letter words corrupting. The British Army, on a diet of them, saved this country from Nazi enslavement. If that is corruption perhaps the nation needs more of it.
>
> Even on the question of violence on TV, we have very little in common. She is concerned about the imitative consequences of seeing gore, bashings and slashings. I don't think that it matters how many times a razor is seen cutting a face or a groin is kicked. What matters is the glorification of violence as a way to achieve moral ends and the constant depiction of it in a medium which has no concern about its responsibility to negate or dissipate that message.

To this disavowal of any mutual interest between myself and Mrs Whitehouse about the proper goals of television, the *Evening Standard* received a letter from her a few days after my article.

'No critic has done more than Milton Shulman to alert the public to the dangers of violence on the television screen,' was her opening, complimentary sentence. It did not continue in that vein. 'It is a pity, therefore, that he suffers from the compulsion to ensure that no one will associate him with us.'

Asserting her organization's right to speak openly and forthrightly about what offends them on TV, she denied that she constantly lumps sex and violence as if they had the same deleterious effect on society.

'Sex is essential for the perpetuation of mankind,' she wrote, 'violence could destroy it. But any serious student of the violent society will know that permissiveness in sex has gone hand in hand with increased violence.'

I thought I could not let this final massive generalization go by without reminding her of a bit of recent history. 'Mrs Whitehouse has a very short and convenient memory,' I wrote in a footnote to her letter. 'The two nations in our time with the more repressive views on sex were Stalin's Russia and Hitler's Germany. Their non-permissive regimes went hand-in-hand with the cruellest and most violent societies mankind has ever known.'

Violent crimes against the person had risen to almost 240,000 by 1996. It is pathetic to watch Home Secretaries being badgered for more police, heavier prison sentences, measures to curtail recidivism, more investment and TV cameras in the city centres, penalties for parents of persistent young offenders, tighter drug control, and hardly ever being asked to take seriously the major role that TV violence might be playing in this national scourge.

After another polemic I wrote in 1970 about the possible effects of TV violence, I was asked by the Labour Home Secretary, James Callaghan, to meet him at the Home Office. In a large, high–ceiling ministerial room, seated behind a large desk with a secretary at his side taking notes of our conversation, he told me he was having lunch that day with the Chairmen of the BBC and ITV. He had been impressed by the case I had been putting about TV violence and wanted to hear what these TV executives had to say about it. What should he tell them?

I had suspected that something of that nature would be asked of me and marshalled my argument very carefully. I pointed out that a research team at Leicester University had reported that no less than 63 per cent of all programmes on British television in 1969 contained violence, that there was an average of five violent incidents an hour (compared to nine in America) and that children saw more violence before 9 p.m. than after that threshold hour.

Having spent one-fifth of their waking hours in an atmosphere of media violence, was it surprising that children so conditioned would be more prone to aggressive behaviour than those generations brought up to believe that violence was rare and abnormal? I reminded him that when commercial TV came to Britain in 1955, which was the beginning of mass viewing, crimes of violence against the person were 7,884. Only fifteen years later, they had risen to 41,088, with the main escalation having taken place amongst the under-twenty-ones. This increase of 7 to 10 per cent a year had been relentless and had occurred in every kind of economic environment. The most telling rebuttal against the view that a prosperous nation would solve the problem was the worrying rise from almost nil offences to many thousands of recorded violent incidents amongst the *under-tens*. Could the reason for such children turning to antisocial behaviour be attributed to poverty, unemployment, unfulfilled expectations?

Having brought my statement to an end, I waited while the Home Secretary looked at the notes his secretary had handed to him. 'That is a very impressive argument and I think there is a great deal in it,' said Mr Callaghan. 'What should I tell the TV chairmen at my lunch to do about it?'

I answered that there was no immediate solution to the problem. The children who had been infected by their massive dose of violence – perhaps two or three per cent without proper parental or educational constraints – would not be changed by a serious reduction in current violent programmes. Since the whole question was a conditioning one, there were no short-term solutions. Only a shift in the acceptance of violence as a norm would change the cultural climate polluting the young. If schedules were to reduce their violent programmes drastically we could expect some beneficial results about ten to fifteen years from now.

I saw a glazed look come into his eye. I offered him nothing which he could use on the hustings in the coming General Election. I realized then that politicians were, at best, short term merchants. There were no votes in social remedies that would take a decade to prove themselves. I met James Callaghan at a social gathering about twelve years later. He told me that he had pressed my point of view on the broadcasting authorities at that lunch. Not surprisingly, nothing was done about it then or since.

I nevertheless continued with my campaign, using any abnormal violent outbreak or any new survey or research finding as a topical peg to justify old and fresh reflections on the topic. At first it was instinct and common sense which formed the main props of my case about the consequences of TV violence. But the issue was becoming so ugly and dominant that governments and institutions began to finance independent investigations about the matter. It was President Johnson's Commission on Violence, massively funded and provoked by the concern over the Kennedy assassinations, that pointed directly at the link between TV images and a frightening increase in American domestic violence.

Having unequivocally declared their belief in a cause and effect relationship, the Commissioners said in their Report on 23 September 1969 'Television entertainment based on violence may be effective merchandising, but it is an appalling way to serve a civilization – an appalling way to fulfil the requirements of the law that broadcasting serve "the public interest, convenience and security."'

A supplementary investigation for the commission was based on detailed studies of violence in the seventeen largest American cities. Its report, issued a short time later, envisaged that if crime continued to rise in the way that it had in the decade 1960-70, the central cities of the United States would in a few years time become 'fortresses' in which the wealthy would live in privately guarded compounds; people would travel on high-speed patrolled expressways connecting safe areas; private automobiles, taxi-cabs and commercial vehicles would be routinely equipped with unbreakable glass and light armour; armed guards would ride shot-gun on all forms of public transportation; and the ghetto and slum neighbourhoods would be places of terror with widespread crime, perhaps out of police control at night time.

All these dire predictions have now been realized. Nothing much has been changed about the volume of violent TV in America, except that there is more of it.

In 1975 I was contacted by Dr William Belsen, an Australian sociobiologist, who was being financed by the American Columbia Broadcasting Corporation to conduct a massive research study into the question of TV violence and the behaviour of London adolescents. He led a team of researchers who selected 1,565 London boys – the largest statistical sample ever assembled for such a work – aged thirteen to sixteen who represented a meticulous cross-section of the community. We met on a number of occasions to discuss the progress of the project. It was my intention to get as much publicity as I could for Belsen's findings when they appeared.

Part of the stonewalling tactics used by TV executives to discredit any adverse findings about TV violence was the claim that there was no satisfactory methodology yet devised by social scientists to accurately measure its impact. Dr Belsen in his book *Television Violence and the Adolescent Boy* published in 1972, using graphs, charts and mathematical equations provided a precise methodology to support all his conclusions. The ultimate findings, contained in three huge volumes, were the most definitive yet published.

'This is one of the most massive child sampling exercises ever done,' Dr Belsen told me, 'and the quality of the evidence linking TV violence with violence among certain adolescents is at least as accurate, probably more so, than the evidence connecting lung cancer with cigarette smoking.'

Following loosely on the heels of Dr Belsen's impressive findings came the book *Sex, Violence and the Media* by Professor H. J. Eysenck and Dr D. K. B. Nias. Because there had been so much literature on the subject, and because there was so much controversy about the validity of many of these studies, it was the aim of Eysenck and Nias to make an objective assessment about the quality of this research. They concluded that the evidence was fairly unanimous that aggressive acts can be evoked by violent scenes on TV and film and that there was ample evidence that media violence increases viewer aggression. Their final conclusion was that TV was a 'powerful and omnipresent' influence on the stimulation of social violence.

The defensive reaction of the broadcasting authorities to these authoritative, damning judgements was predictable. 'The evidence does not exist by which broadcasters can draw up hard and fast rules about the showing of violence,' said Sir Charles Curran, the BBC's Director General. 'The Belsen report appears to suggest that in some cases there is an intensification of the likelihood of violent action among some people who would be prone to it. There is other evidence coming along which will suggest that there is no such causality.' As far as I know, twenty years later the evidence promised by Sir Charles Curran has not yet appeared.

When Dr Belsen's report was issued, the leader writers of most British newspapers commented that its findings were just 'common sense'. That recognition of the obvious has now been accepted by almost all governmental agencies and important politicians in Britain and America. The Annan Committee on Broadcasting, the American Medical Association, the American Association of Advertising Agencies, a ten-year study by the American National Institution of National Health and most recently in 1996 an investigation concluded by a US Senate Committee under Senator Simon, which said that the evidence connecting TV violence with national violence was 'just overwhelming'.

Individuals who have voiced disquiet about this matter include Prince Charles, Chief Justice Lane, Labour Home Secretaries James Callaghan and Merlyn Rees, Tory Home Secretary Kenneth Clark, Dame Shirley Williams, Liberal Party leaders David Owen and David Steel, Prime Ministers Margaret Thatcher and John Major as well as dozens of prominent MPs and social scientists.

When Margaret Thatcher in 1985 made the throw-away remark 'I find it difficult to believe that the effect of seeing so much violence on television is not damaging to our people,' the media took up its entrenched positions on the issue. The BBC made its usual placating noises to prime ministers by promising less mayhem in their Christmas schedule, and arranged a top level meeting of its executives to once again pore over its guidelines about the portrayal of violence.

Predictably, the *Guardian* wearing its anti-censorship heart on its leader page sneered derisively at Mrs Thatcher's tentative initiative. 'The substance of the debate is dismaying and ephemeral,' it pontificated. 'It is devoid of valid research.'

Commenting about this particularly obtuse sentiment in a column I wrote at the time, I said 'One wonders if *Guardian* leader writers read anything but their own ephemera. Devoid of valid research? There have been no less than 700 studies done in a number of countries which either positively or cautiously support the view that violence on TV does have adverse effects on children. I do not know of one single piece of serious research that proves such an influence does not exist.'

In that article of December, 1985, I reiterated my previous arguments and added a few more supplementary reflections.

> The most common and easily the most stupid and uninformed rejection
> of the claim that TV violence is a major contributor to youthful violence
> comes from those who say they are TV addicts and that they do not bash

people over the heads or from those who proudly claim their children regularly watched TV violence and are now non-aggressive responsible citizens.

But it is a minority we are talking about. A minority. A minority. I repeat the word three times in order to get some much-needed logic into the debate. Yet if the reassurance that it is only a minority in our society which is affected makes anyone complacent, they should be reminded that our criminal element is a minority, our prisons are filled with a minority. In other words if only three per cent of the under-twenty-ones were encouraged to be anti-socially aggressive, they would be enough *alone* to fill our prisons four times over ...

One day someone who has been raped or assaulted will claim that their assailant was the victim of TV viewing. His lawyers could claim that he behaved as he did because of the hours of violent conditioning produced by the TV authorities who were negligent in their transmission of pollutant material.

If a judge, sharing the misgivings recently expressed by Chief Justice Lane, ever allowed such an issue to go to a jury, I suspect that the resultant massive damages would do more to diminish the present volume of TV violence than all the appeals of Prime Ministers, social scientists, pressure groups or common sense.

In an attempt to do something practical about the issue I posted a copy of that column, recognizing that my words in the *Evening Standard* were not essential reading for those in authority, to about 100 individuals who I felt were influential in the body politics. The response was most gratifying. Some of the most senior members of the Cabinet and the Shadow Cabinet indicated they agreed with my argument. Others also supported my view but asked that their letters be kept private.

Peter Walker, the Energy Minister, wrote: 'I very much agree with your article, I will certainly do all I can to influence matters in this sphere.'

The Liberal Leader, David Steel, said: 'I have never doubted the validity of your conclusions. My impression is that there is too much gratuitous violence on TV, and I say so whenever I meet the IBA or the BBC.'

Dr Jeremy Bray, Labour spokesman for Science and Technology, had no doubts. 'I understand and share your concern,' he wrote. 'While I think it is important to ensure freedom of speech in the media I cannot condone the use of violence simply to boost the number of viewers.'

Dr David Owen, the SDP leader, not only backed my views but gave a wide-ranging speech on the subject. He realized what was needed was an anti-violence culture in Britain. He rightly recognized that it was not individual programmes or isolated acts of violence that were the evil, but the polluting effect of a menu of violence night after night. He thought the broadcasting authorities should get together and reduce violence across the board by at least fifty per cent. He also understood that there were no short-term quick fixes that would help and that a new generation would have to be conditioned to reject violence as a norm and that would probably take fifteen years. 'But it is worth a try,' he claimed.

None of this hand-wringing, none of the sickening crimes reported on the front pages, none of the terrifying escalation in the statistics about rising crime, moved the broadcasting authorities to do more than promise more committees to look into their guidelines, and to contemplate whether anything was being achieved by their complacency and negative gestures.

I plugged on with my campaign, using each fresh horrific crime committed by children or fatuous statement by an authoritative figure about the harmlessness of TV violence to inspire articles in publications like the *Observer*, *Television Today*, *World Medicine* and, of course, the *Evening Standard*. A survey conducted by the Broadcasting Standards Council of 227 programmes transmitted in a single week in 1992 recorded no less than 308 scenes of violence. My own observations would categorize that week as a particularly pacific one. Back in 1987 a similar mayhem count by BBC researchers found over 900 violent scenes in one week.

Almost coincidental with these reports, the BBC's newly appointed programme controller, Alan Yentob, issued a statement saying that his study of the available research left him unconvinced about any direct causal link between TV violence and the rise in youthful mayhem. Such a breathtakingly obtuse vision of his responsibilities caused me to ask in an article in the *Standard* in March, 1993, 'which of the now 800 studies on the subject Mr Yentob has actually read.' He never revealed which particular research had convinced him that almost all the serious studies were wrong.

There was, however, a new dimension to the problem that had grown since I first voiced concern about it a quarter of a century ago. 'With the video now available for children to watch the most horrific films on their own,' I wrote, 'and their ability to record any violent programme that they fancy without their parents knowing about it and watch it in their own time, makes nonsense of the nine o'clock threshold and the ability of the BBC and other channels to stem the immoral pollution they blithely transmit. It may well be that technology has made future attempts to curb the menace almost impossible.'

The climate of violence suffusing the nation caused headlines to fill front pages and the public to wring its hands when two teenage girls murdered an old lady, when two ten-year-olds killed Jamie Bulger, when almost every week some fresh report of horrendous mayhem or rape by teenagers was splashed across the TV news bulletins. Was there any attempt to investigate the viewing habits of these incarcerated children? Were they heavy or light viewers? Did they watch such programmes on their own? What were their favourite programmes and who were the characters they most admired? Did their parents ever make any attempt to explain the contents of such films and point out to them the difference between reality and the cinematic fiction that occupied one quarter of their waking hours? As far as I know no attempt was ever made by the police or educational authorities to study in any depth the part violent TV may have had in encouraging these children to commit such evil offences.

What was becoming increasingly evident in the late 1990s was that public opinion was becoming really frightened about what was happening to British society while the broadcasters, practically alone, continued to stonewall, delay and prevaricate about the part they might have played in this moral decline. After the killing of Jamie Bulger and the murder of a headmaster, Philip Lawrence, by a schoolboy, the passion and eloquence of Frances Lawrence, pleading for a new moral agenda, galvanized the media for a few months into paying some serious attention to the manner in which violent TV corrupted any such moral agenda.

No credence was placed in the promises, futile as they have proved over the decades, that the broadcasters would do their utmost to clean up their schedules. However, there emerged a technical innovation that might, if governments would cooperate, put some ability back into the hands of parents to supervise their children's viewing, an ability largely taken away from them by the video and satellite broadcasting. The device, called the V-chip, built into TV sets could be programmed to blot out any drama parents considered unsuitable viewing for their children.

Studying the advance schedules in the TV press, the publicity attending the programmes would reveal the likelihood of unacceptable violent scenes or stories which could be the target for a united boycott by parents with V-chip sets. President Clinton, enthusiastic about the V-chip, promised in his Inaugural Presidential address in 1996 that legislation would be introduced requiring all new TV sets manufactured on America to contain the chip.

Writing about this development in the *Daily Mail*, I said:

President Clinton's promise was undoubtedly influenced by the findings in 1993 of a Congressional Committee headed by Senator Simon. Speaking to the heads of the major TV companies, Simon said: 'Since 1961 there has been a perception that violence on the screen added to violence in our society. Today we know that is a fact. The research is just overwhelming. There is no question that it is a causal factor.' None of his listeners dared contradict him.

The V-chip will offer hope to parents. The mass boycott of particularly violent programmes, organized by conscientious adults, could seriously affect the ratings and profits of the companies. Advertisers would not be keen to have their products blackened by such a protest and pressure on them to find alternative entertainment would be irresistible.

It is perhaps symptomatic of the low priority the issue still is given in Britain that the Conservative Heritage Secretary, Virginia Bottomley, in the last months of the Tory regime in 1996 considered the advisability of ordering TV manufacturers to include V-chips in their new sets, and concluded it was either unnecessary or impractical. No doubt there were representations from the TV manufacturers, claiming it would add an undesirable cost to their fresh products, and protests from the broadcasters that their hopeless guidelines and thresholds were all that was necessary.

In the 1997 General Election the question of law and order was a major political issue. All parties claimed they knew what had to be done and advocated either lower unemployment, banning of handguns, drug control, more severe prison sentences, more police, TV cameras in city centres, teaching of morals and Christian values in schools, penalties on parents of criminal adolescents or other nostrums which had already been tried and singularly failed in stemming the tide of growing violence. I did not read in a single manifesto any recognition that TV violence might have been a major, or even a minor, contributor to the problem. In no forum, debate or discussion in the media did I hear anyone from any party even raise the matter.

So alarmed have our political guardians become of daring to interfere in any way with what has become the nation's favourite leisure activity that its harmful effects are hardly ever tackled by any serious politicians. I'm afraid that the new Labour Government shows no sign of worrying about TV violence any more than did the Tories.

On 26 May 1997, just three weeks after Labour's electoral victory, a survey for the International Crime Victimization Survey gave England and Wales the top spot in their crime league for Western nations. Based on interviews with 20,000 people, it claimed that victims of crime and fear of crime in Great Britain recorded the highest rates in the industrialized world – more than the United States, Canada, France, Sweden, Netherlands, Finland and Austria. Italy and Germany were not included in the survey. The reaction of Jack Straw, the Labour Home Secretary, was predictable. He blamed the incompetent Tory administration, high unemployment and lack of sufficient police on the beat. He said not a word about television.

I predict that in a few years time under Labour, unless something meaningful is done about the pollutant in our living rooms, crimes of violence against the person will have risen to 300,000 from the 5,400 in 1956. Schools will be patrolled by security police. Individual homes will have their windows and doors padlocked like prisons. Women and elderly persons will not walk the streets at night unattended. City centres will be rife with clashes between rampant hooligans and serried ranks of police. The country will be at virtual war between its mature and elderly citizens and the young indulging in their taste for violence cultivated in them by the pollutant of TV violence. It will be a high price to pay for the joys of the box.

★ ★ ★

In 1971 I was paid a reasonable advance by Cassell's to write a book about the history and the social consequences of British television. The commissioning editor thought it should contain somewhere between 120,000 to 140,000 words. I called it *The Ravenous Eye* with the subtitle *The Impact of the Fifth Factor*. Explaining my thesis I wrote:

In terms of sheer volume alone there is no medium in man's history that has taken up so much of his time. Although there is no mathematical formula that equates the importance of an environmental factor with the number of hours spent in it, it is obvious that time is a significant aspect of the influence of environment. Home, neighbourhood, school and church are generally accepted as the most powerful environmental factors in a child's life simply because, between the four of them, they occupy practically all his time.

If that is so, then television in terms of time has ample justification to be listed as the Fifth Factor. Do any of the other influences in a child's life command full attention for three to four hours a day?

Nor can it be convincingly argued that what comes out of the box is merely an echo, a reflection, a synthesis of the four other factors...If the overall image of our civilization as reflected on the small screen is trivial, frivolous and violent, will it not set up, particularly amongst the young, patterns of imitative acceptance, on the one hand, and spasms of violent rejection, on the other? Can the countervailing influences of formal education, home environment, parental control, religious teaching, conventional mores, reduce the conditioning power of television to negligible proportions? Lastly, is there any danger that the electronic jester in our midst is slowly becoming a beaming cyclops, devouring with its ravenous eye, old attitudes, values and assumptions and leaving in their place little but an illusory euphoria and an increased demand for consumer goods?

Pushing my luck as far as the book's wordage was concerned, I included a short history of the BBC and commercial TV as well as comparative figures about violence, particularly in countries with controlled TV like Russia or non-commercial TV like Holland. To acquire the necessary statistics for this global view of TV I employed an exceptionally bright researcher, Ann Casement, who while avoiding the amorous attentions of various diplomats in East European embassies, managed to acquire hitherto unpublished evidence of TV's impact in those highly secretive communist countries. Since those days Ann Casement has displayed similar perceptive prowess in her ascent to the top echelons of the Jungian world, where she is held in high regard as an analyst, author and administrator.

When I finally submitted my manuscript, it had become a bulky 250,000 words. The original commissioning editor had left Cassell's and the executive who had taken his place viewed my voluminous offering with horror.

'We can't possibly publish a book that size about television,' he said. 'You were contracted to write around 125,000 words.'

'But you haven't read it,' I said. 'Maybe you'll change your mind when you see what's in it.'

'I'm sorry, Mr Shulman,' he said, 'It doesn't matter what's in it. We simply haven't scheduled for a book that long.'

Trying to cajole him into, at least, reading this version, I said face-tiously and unsuccessfully, 'Are you telling me that if Count Tolstoy had offered you a huge novel called *War and Peace*, you might have said, looking at its size, "I'm afraid, Count Tolstoy, we might be able to print a novel called *Peace* or one called *War* but War *and* Peace! That's impossible."?'

He did not see the joke. Fortunately I could see an immediate solution to the impasse. The volume had been written in three sections with the middle one, called Book Two, confined to an account of how the BBC and the commercial companies had come into being and their historical development. It stood out completely independently from the first and last sections with their concern about the social consequences of the medium. I removed Book Two and handed the truncated volume back to him.

He took it with a sigh of relief and it was published in 1973. I took the severed section to Christopher MacLehose, the young editorial director of Barrie and Jenkins whom I had met at Elizabeth's Bistro and who had on a number of occassions told me his firm would be interested in a book about television. I called the rump pages – about 100,000 words – *The Least Worst Television in the World*. I received a second advance for the material from this supplementary publisher and it too was published in 1973. The reviews for both books were generous, although the experience taught me that television was not a subject that was ever likely to make the best-seller lists.

There were two pleasing consequences of writing *The Least Worst Television in the World*. It received a rave two-page notice by Simon Raven in the *Spectator*, together with a monstrous caricature of myself on its cover showing me devouring TV tubes like chicken bones and looking like a horrendous human gorilla. The title has also acquired a certain prominent coinage amongst writers keen to discredit the BBC's claim that it produces the Best Television in the World. I have also been acknowledged as the begetter of the phrase in several respectable books of quotations.

The cover of The Spectator, *1973*

My career as an author has about it the same sort of haphazard, arbitrary feel as the rest of my professional activities. *Who's Who* lists ten volumes to my credit and from each one of them I have enjoyed the mixed blessings of the almost erotic pleasure of running one's hands over the first bound, finished copy the publisher sends you, the disappointment of not seeing it in the shops on its publication day, the anxiety of rustling through papers and journals for reviews, the trawling through bookshops for a sight of it and surreptitiously placing it in a more conspicuous place on a table or shelf, the hasty reading of an unfavourable review and the re-reading three or four times of generous ones, the joyous news that Americans or Germans or Danes are going to publish it, the elation surrounding a film option with the corresponding dejection when it is not taken up, the royalty statements that bring welcome relief to your overdraft or make you resolve never to write another book again.

My adventures over *Defeat in the West, How To Be A Celebrity, The Ravenous Eye* and *The Least Worst Television in the World* have already been recounted. It was almost predictable that the writing of my first novel, *Kill Three*, would come about by sheer accident. Its genesis, unusually, was a TV play.

In a TV interview with Malcolm Muggeridge, P. G. Wodehouse confessed that he had no idea about how to get one of his plays on television. 'You can't just send one in,' he asked, plaintively.

Had I been contemplating writing a TV play, I would probably have not known what to do with it. Fortunately, luck took a hand and I did not have to face the dilemma. Indeed my first, and only, TV drama would never have been born had it not been for my Portuguese cook. But before her fine Latin hand entered the affair, I had received in early November 1964, a phone call from Peter Luke, a playwright friend of mine who was now a BBC drama producer.

Mr Luke explained that he was preparing a series of plays for the new television channel, BBC2, which was to see the light of day in April 1964, and these were going to be its first TV dramas. The stories were all to take place in London, the programme would probably be called *The Londoners*, each work was to be seventy-five minutes long and did I have any ideas? I was flattered by the invitation, but why me, who had never been involved with such an enterprise? Peter Luke replied that he'd been reading me for years and just thought I might come up with something different. He had been contacting friends of his – writers with no TV dramatic experience like John Betjeman, Dan Farson, Frank

Norman, Hugh Whitemore – and he had received some positive responses.

Drawing a deep breath, I let out a long 'Well …' and said that I had been thinking about an idea for a thriller, but it had little or nothing to do with London. Peter Luke was polite. He was going to New York in a few weeks' time and would contact me when he got back. Almost three months went by and I had heard nothing more.

This is where my Portuguese cook comes in. Having limited English, she has developed into a mystic art the trick of converting all my telephone messages into a kind of cabalistic code. It was clear that the BBC had called me, but the name and the extension number could have been anything. I telephoned five or six people at the TV Centre but they didn't want me. I thought of Peter Luke. No, he hadn't telephoned me either. But now that he had me on the phone, what about that idea for *The Londoners*? We arranged a lunch.

Over the canneloni, I outlined my idea to Peter and his story editor, Harry Moore. I prefaced my remarks by explaining that there was nothing adventurous, avant garde, experimental or even particularly televisual about my plot. They stared non-committally into their pasta.

The idea was based upon a kidnapping in the French town of Poitiers. The local council, composed of the town's most affluent citizens, had been asked to pay the ransom money demanded by the kidnappers of three children of a poor family. I thought we could set the same situation in Acton or Ealing and have some municipal or borough council confronted with this dilemma. The real crunch in the story would come when the body of one of the children is deposited on the steps of the town hall with a note demanding a larger sum for the remaining two. What would the councillors do to save them? At this point Mr Luke and Mr Moore brightened up.

Yes, decided possibilities, they agreed. We bounced it around over the entrecote and the peach melba, and then Harry Moore suggested a firm of London solicitors as the victims of the blackmailers. Not only would this give it a true London setting, but the moral dilemma would be even more acute. With my knowledge of legal practices I thought this was a plot development I could handle.

And so I was commissioned. Not a line had been written; not a word had been put on paper. Could I write it in four weeks? Agreed.

Terrified of what I'd undertaken, I did nothing for a fortnight except talk to a few lawyers and read a few books on legal procedures and cus-

toms. The arrival of a cheque for £325, the first half of the fee, galvanized me into action. Working at weekends and evenings when I wasn't
at the theatre, often with a wet towel around my head, I finished it in
four weeks. Precisely on the deadline day I took it to the TV Centre,
frantically reading it for the first time as an entity in the taxi.

Four days later it was accepted. There were a few minor rewrites and
some pertinent suggestions from Peter Luke and Harry Moore – all of
which helped the play – and a few more small tinkerings to suit the
ideas of the appointed director, Peter Sasdy, when he took over.

The casting – some twenty speaking parts – was done in a weekend.
I attended three rehearsals and on 11 May 1965 – less than three months
after I started to write it – the whole thing was tape-recorded, over and
waiting for transmission.

The promotion people for the new channel did their best to drum
up interest. Since few TV sets had yet been converted to receiving
BBC2, we were all resigned to a minuscule rating for my play which I
had first called *What Price Blood?* but changed to *Kill Three* when it was
produced. Amongst the publicity bits that involved me in its promotion
were a five minute film about Chelsea during which I sat on a wet
bench in the King's Road for an entire afternoon, and another short
piece about what it felt like to be a critic contemplating criticism of
one's own work. 'I'm looking forward to it,' I said, jauntily. 'I expect the
critics will be judicious, wise and perceptive. I'm sure I'll learn something from them.' As far as I know, not a living soul in Britain saw either
of these items.

I raced home from a first night in time to catch the last half of *Kill
Three*. Hardly had the final captions come up when the telephone rang.
It was a well-known actress telling me how much she had enjoyed it.
'But I'm going to ring off quickly,' she said, 'because dozens of people
will no doubt be phoning you.' Five minutes later the phone rang. It was
my agent. Five minutes later there was another call. It was the producer. After that, silence. So much for the exhilarating thrill of being a TV
playwright!

Naturally I awaited the critical notices with trepidation. Most of the
morning papers found something better to criticise. There were only
two reviews and they cancelled each other out. The *Daily Express* found
it 'a moving realistic study with an exciting and plausible climax.' The
Guardian disagreed. It complained that I had 'constructed almost too
clever a play … the pieces well designed and the moves cunningly

made.' The critic disapproved of all this and, while grudgingly acknowledging that it had tension and suspense, was nevertheless unmoved by the play.

A friend of mine who had caught *Kill Three* suggested I convert it into a novel. To my surprise, Robert Knittel, a senior Collins executive, had seen my play and asked me if I was prepared to re-write it as an orthodox thriller to be published under his aegis. We met and I was impressed to discover he was the husband of the captivating actress Luise Rainer whose roles in *The Good Earth* and *The Great Ziegfeld* had won her two Oscars.

The book was duly published in February 1967, and translation rights in Sweden, Italy, Holland and Brazil were sold before it appeared, with Random House picking it up for the American market. The snippets from the reviews that Collins selected for their advertisements could hardly have been more enthusiastic. 'Stirs up pity, terror and indignation, *New Statesman*... Diabolically ingenious, *Daily Telegraph* ... Seekers-out of really compulsive reads are going to curl up with it in their thousands, *Smith's Trade News* ... A novel of tension, gripping on every page, *Church Times*.'

I was particularly gratified that the moral dimension of the story – the exploitation of a human dilemma by individuals and institutions – impressed most reviewers, sometimes not to my advantage. Frederic Raphael, with a long review in the *Sunday Times* was particularly biting.

'When a television programme makes much of a juicy case, does it glamorize and cash in on what it affects to expose? Milton Shulman marches boldly into this territory for his first novel,' he wrote. 'Three small children of a poor widow are kidnapped and held to ransom. A hundred and fifty thousand pounds is demanded of a starchy firm of solicitors who have no connection with the victims. How far does private humanity demand that they save the children? ...What matters to the pious jackals of the Press and TV is less the fate of three snotty kids than the advantage that can be taken of it.

'What a magnificent comedy, one cannot help thinking, an Evelyn Waugh might have made of this sickening inversion of proper sentiment! What dark depths a Dostoievsky might have plumbed! Mr Shulman, alas, reaches for his cliches like a traffic warden slapping a ticket on an ambulance.'

Smarting from this derisive last sentence, I sent a brief letter to the *Sunday Times* which they printed a week later. 'Frederic Raphael, in reviewing my first novel, *Kill Three*, regrets that I cannot write a novel as well as Dostoievsky or Evelyn Waugh. So do I.'

But my most pleasing reward was that it had been bought for serialization by the *Saturday Evening Post* for a substantial sum. Back in Canada, when I first dreamed up my short stories, my ultimate goal was one day to see my name in that much admired journal which was founded in 1728 and had become an American literary institution. The book ran for twenty pages in the issue of 21 November 1967, in its 240th year and took up a similar amount of space in the following issue.

Unable to match the competitive menace of American television, its catastrophic loss of readers and advertisers forced the *Post* to close shortly after my novel appeared. I believe *Kill Three* was the last substantial novel it serialized. Being grateful for this accolade, I have always hoped that the generous treatment my book was given in the magazine's death throes did not hasten its demise.

10

COLUMNIST AND PANELLIST

I join the starry ranks of columnists... I get involved with a nice class of demo... I acquire British citizenship... Campaigns I have known...

(i) The fight for authors' rights

Having a column of one's own used to be one of the most cherished achievements of a professional journalist. 'A regular feature in a newspaper or magazine having a readily identifiable heading and the by-line of the writer or editor that reports or comments upon a particular field of interest such as politics, theatre or etiquette' is how my dictionary defines a column. Some of the greatest essayists and social commentators in English literature – Hazlitt, Steele, Chesterton, Belloc, Dickens, Priestley, Orwell, Samuel Johnson – were given the freedom of a columnist in a paper or journal.

Amongst contemporary journalists the provocative and readable opinions of Paul Johnson, Bernard Levin, Peregrine Worsthorne, William Rees-Mogg, John Junor, Lynda Lee-Potter, Mary Kenny, Matthew Parris, Auberon Waugh, Harold Nicolson, acquired the status of independence, regularity and typographical consistency to justify being labelled a columnist. In the United States Walter Lippman, Walter Winchell, Art Buchwald and Stewart Alsop were writers of politics, humour and gossip and were identified by their readers as columnists. Sometimes newspapers will resurrect the names of popular journalists of the past and columns like Beachcomber, William Hickey, Ephraim Hardcastle will be written by a variety of scribblers in the office.

Just how protective a journalist can be about a threat to his column was made evident to me when Lord Beaverbrook asked me to take over the regular weekly slot that was usually filled on the *Sunday Express* by its former long-time editor, John Gordon. It was a virile, pugnacious, assertive feature in which Gordon attempted to set the land aright by his standards. I cannot say I agreed with many of his views.

'Mr Gordon has gone on holiday to Norway for four weeks,' said Beaverbrook. 'I never take a holiday but Mr Gordon does. We cannot drop his column, so will you take it over until he comes back?'

Thinking to myself that Beaverbrook never took official holidays because he was on holiday all the time, I muttered something about not being on the same wavelength as John Gordon and wondered whether the readers would like my views, which were so far apart from Gordon's.

'Oh, you write what you like,' said Beaverbrook. 'Goodbye.'

Although the six items I wrote – one was which ten great people of all time would you invite as guests to the same dinner party – were vastly different in tone and subject-matter to Gordon's, it would take a very discerning reader to realize the column had not been written by its usual begetter. The column was laid out in its same spot, the typeface of the heading the same and my name, replacing Gordon's, was set in precisely the same fount.

A few days after my column appeared, Lord Beaverbrook's secretary called to tell me that I didn't have to write any more Gordon columns because he would be doing them from wherever he was. Gordon never again took a holiday or allowed anyone to encroach on his space. I believe he was banging out his required words on his death-bed.

But the notion of a column has been considerably devalued in most British newspapers. Longevity can be measured in weeks. Columnists give the life-span of a firefly respectability. Their provenance in previous journalism is practically nil. If someone opens a shop, wins the lottery, does a short session on a chat show, leads a pop group, dances with Prince Edward, some newspaper will splash a pretty face at the top of a page proclaiming them as their newest columnist. Readers, on the whole, dismiss their contributions as space filler to be read on a tube where skipping chunks of words doesn't matter. Some editors, bizarrely enough, believe they sell newspapers.

Although I had been a film and theatre critic for many years, a feature writer, book reviewer and weekly TV commentator from 1964 to 1972, it wasn't until 1972 that I received my first column, entitling me to express my views freely about any topic that amused, intrigued, stimulated or angered me. Writing about my new status, I told the *Evening Standard* readers that I intended to comment, 'as the mood takes me, on politics, finance, the arts, the media and other matters that appear to excite or amuse the town. I do not expect to raise by more than a few decibels the general hubbub. But it will be fun trying to make oneself heard.'

Two years later I was offered a generous increase in salary to transfer my column to the *Daily Express* – in the same ownership as the *Standard* – where everything conspired to make my column unappealing to Sir Max Aitken, Lord Beaverbrook's son and the *Express* editor. I was cut to half the size I was used to; my political views didn't match those of the editorial hierarchy; they didn't share my sense of humour. After a year we agreed to part and I was given a handsome pay-off.

When I stopped being the regular theatre critic of the *Evening Standard* in 1991, I appeared every week in that paper, taking up cudgels on behalf of any issue that seemed to need some newspaper support as well as commenting generally on anything to do with the arts. Judging from my letters, I had acquired quite a respectable following when Max Hastings, the latest editor – I had survived eight editors – fired me in 1996. My crime was, apparently, that I had been around too long.

Although I cannot say that the column from 1991 to 1996 had any particular bias, there were occasional issues like TV violence, British war crime trials, the plans for closing and rebuilding the Covent Garden Opera House, honours for playwrights, that I would turn to more than once, no doubt to the annoyance and irritation of those I was castigating. Praise, too, was also showered on individuals and projects that, in my opinion, warranted it.

In this penultimate chapter of my memoirs, details of some of these indicate what occupied my thoughts and interests, aside from my hours spent as a theatre and film critic. They are certainly evidence of a very higgledy-piggledy mind – the essential equipment of a true columnist.

* * *

In 1982 a British government finally passed a bill righting a massive wrong. Authors were at last to be given some pecuniary compensation for the lending of their books to the public. Song writers and lyricists had long ago acquired performing rights to their works so that the transmission of any song anywhere would mean a negotiated reward for those that had brought it into being. The campaign for lending rights began in the early 1950s and took over thirty years before victory was finally achieved. In May 1975, I wrote a column in the *Evening Standard* joining the fray. It was an author's demonstration which received some amused publicity in the Press, that provoked my piece.

' "I must say, sir, this is a very nice class of demo," said a police constable to Kingsley Amis, one of the authors protesting about the delay in bringing in a Public Lending Rights Bill.

And certainly this group of mainly middle-aged writers – Angus Wilson, Dilys Powell, Frank Muir, Lady Antonia Fraser, Brigid Brophy – discreetly waving banners outside the Ministry of the Arts in the stately environs of Belgrave Square must have been a decided change from the usual shouting, belligerent demonstrations which London police often have to control. Indeed, instead of facing a forest of brandished fists, Hugh Jenkins, the Labour Minister of Arts, was presented with two dozen roses and a plea to save English literature.

But where has all this civilized, hand-shaking discourse and discreet pressurizing got the writers of this country? Exactly nowhere.

The writers and actors who are now asking for a minimal hand-out of state money belong to the poorest section of workers in the land. It is shocking that the country that owes its reputation for civilization and humanity to the written word should complacently stand by while those who practise the art of Shakespeare, Dickens, Shaw, the Brontes, Byron, Orwell, Austen, Wilde and Boswell should be reduced to living in penury.

More than half of the professional authors living in Britain in the 1970s earn about £10 per week. That is between a third and a quarter of the average national wage. Librarians, who owe their existence to authors and who are paid from communal funds six or seven times the annual earnings of most writers, only last week reiterated their opposition to public lending rights.

If they can't make a living as writers or actors why don't they do something else, is the argument most often deployed against state help for professional artists. Yet if the same argument were used to deny subsidies or state funds to over-manned shipyards, motor car factories, local councils or steel works, the nation would probably have a general strike on its hands. It is obvious that nosegays for Ministers, smiling petitioners, appeals to save our cultural heritage, are going to make no impact on a Government that is only moved by direct action or muscle-power. These polite campaigns by writers for lending rights over the past twenty-five years have rewarded them only with a mountain of shamefully broken promises and evasions by politicians.

The Swedish writers achieved their object of proving their importance to society by marching into libraries and removing their books from the library shelves. British writers must now think of doing something similar. Libraries have for decades illegally handled the works of writers in the name of a free library service. They bind books in covers which give them an extra longevity than their original covers; they hand out photostatted copies of pages without compensating writers; they purchase books from reviewers at cheap rates and deny writers a royalty on them; they charge fees for reservations and late returns which help subsidise librarians but not authors. Some of these activities infringe the copyright laws; all of them are a moral exploitation by the state of possibly the poorest workers in the land.

If British writers in large numbers removed their books from library shelves and threatened to keep them until lending rights were granted, there would be a sudden dawning in Government circles about the justice of these causes. Writers unite! You have nothing to lose. Who, these days, can afford chains?'

The first reaction to this call to arms was a pamphlet distributed in Brighton by a group of authors inviting all writers to remove their work from local libraries and contribute them to a book-burning in a prominent square. Unfortunately, the organizers muddled up the time of the event by giving the wrong day of the week with the date of the month, so that potential book arsonists didn't know when to go. There was no address or phone number to contact to check the information and as a result the demonstration petered out.

A somewhat bizarre consequence of my involvement with PLR played an amusing part in my acquisition of British citizenship. Having a Canadian passport and always having considered myself a British citizen, I never thought it necessary to apply for British nationalization papers. I was reluctant, too, to renounce my Canadian citizenship since at that time dual citizenship was not possible. When registration for Public Lending Rights finally began in 1982, I filled in the necessary form listing ten books that ought to come under the scheme. To my chagrin and surprise, I was told I was not eligible for these payments because I was a Canadian. Although Dutch and German writers, being members of the European Union, would receive these allowances, Commonwealth countries were out. I was naturally outraged by such an exclusion and wrote a letter to *The Times* pointing out that as a resident of Britain who had paid taxes here for over forty years, I was entitled to every privilege enjoyed by my fellow countrymen. Not only did I pay the same taxes but I could vote, run for Parliament, even become Prime Minister. The only privilege denied me was Public Lending Rights. Since Canada and Britain were also ruled by the same monarch, was it not an affront to natural justice that such an arbitrary discrimination should prevail? Other Commonwealth writers like the Australian author and TV personality, Clive James, also took up the cudgel, without much immediately being done about it.

This bureaucratic stalemate remained until 1983 when the Canadians passed a bill enabling dual citizenship to be accorded to people like myself. We could become British citizens and still retain our Canadian passports and identity. That opened the door for me for lending rights and I filled in the appropriate nationalization form and the required cheque. I had already missed the first distribution and was hoping that if my papers were in order I would be registered in time for payments due in 1984. Eight months went by and I had heard nothing from the Home Office. Impatient with the delay I telephoned the citizenship section at Acorn House and miraculously got through very early in the morning. I gave the details of my situation and wondered how long I would have to wait for these papers since I had the necessary residential and language qualifications. Hearing that I had already been waiting about eight months, she told me that it would probably take another year for them to come through.

What was the reason for such a delay? I asked.

'I'm afraid the queue is desperately long,' I was told, and it had been aggravated by the priority that was being given to a large number of East Africans due for citizenship.

'Can the queue be by-passed for compassionate reasons?' I said, trying to argue for some shortening of my waiting period.

'What compassionate grounds?'

'I need a British citizenship, although I am a Canadian, to get public lending rights on ten books I have written. Dual citizenship is now available to me. I have already missed the first distribution and unless I can get my papers before February, I will miss a second round of fees. It is money I would like to have.'

She said she would make some enquiries. After about ten minutes, she returned.

'I'm afraid that's not compassionate enough to move you up the queue. I'm sorry,' she said.

Suspecting that she would like to help if I only gave her something substantial to justify my being given priority, I tried a long-shot.

'I understand that Roy Thomson, the Canadian newspaper proprietor, had his citizenship application expedited when he was offered a peerage. If I were offered a peerage do you think I would also have a reasonable chance of being moved up the queue?'

'What did you say?' she asked, not sure that she had heard me right.

'I was only wondering if I could accept a peerage in this year's Honours list in June if I were offered one. Or would I have to reject it because I was not a British citizen yet.'

I never for a moment thought that anything I had just said would be taken seriously. I was not claiming that there was a peerage in the offing for me. I was only posing the question out of a sense of curiosity and mischief. Was a prospective peerage more important than my loss of lending rights?

She told me that she would put my query to her superior. About fifteen minutes later she returned.

'We rarely make exceptions about people in waiting lists, but in your case it has been agreed that we will. I can't say precisely when your papers should come through, but I don't think it will be too long.' Three weeks later I received my certificate of registration as a British citizen and I was able to receive my first small cheque for public lending rights to my books. I trust the authorities have not been scanning every Honours list since then to see if my name is on it. I had never intended to deceive them and I feel no guilt for a speculative, innocent query that brought me British citizenship and a few extra pounds a few months earlier than I would have received it anyway.

(ii) The knighthood scandal

In the last few years of my *Standard* column I would at the year's end provide a balance sheet listing the major causes I had championed and which had been lost, which won, and which were still unresolved. Always on the debit side was my argument that in a country that owes so much of its cultural fame to Shakespeare, dramatists were consistently neglected for honours compared to those showered on actors. I thought this was a shameful imbalance of priorities.

Commenting on the 1992 Honours list I noted that amongst the heap of awards given to politicians, civil servants, academics and businessmen were scattered one knighthood to literature – the author,

Peter Quennell – and one to broadcasting – the BBC's Michael Checkland.

Actors were, as usual, very generously treated with Brian Rix of the maniacal Whitehall farces and Dirk Bogarde receiving a knighthood each. But why, I asked, was there such reticence on the part of the committee recommending such accolades to granting dramatists a peerage or a knighthood, instead of such less notable honours as a CBE, OBE or MBE? Why is the handle which goes with a knighthood or makes a woman a Dame, and which gets you a good table in restaurants and probably more generous accommodation from your creditors, so rarely given to a dramatist?

At the end of the war Laurence Olivier became the first Baron of the British stage. Amongst the Knights who had bowed their knee to the Queen by 1992 there had been John Gielgud, Alec Guinness, Ralph Richardson, Michael Redgrave, Rex Harrison, Charles Chaplin, Anthony Quayle, John Clements, Michael Hordern, Harry Secombe, Ian McKellan and Dirk Bogarde. Amongst the actresses who have become Dames since 1945 were Flora Robson, Celia Johnson, Anna Neagle, Peggy Ashcroft, Gwen Ffrancon-Davies, Maggie Smith, Margaret Rutherford and Judi Dench.

But actors would be the first to agree that they are at best merely the messengers and interpreters of other people's imagination and words. Without playwrights how could they display and project their talents to excite, stimulate and entertain audiences? Yet what is the status of the dramatist in the Honours list compared to that of the performers?

Since 1945, there have been only two dramatists who have received knighthoods – Noel Coward and Terence Rattigan. Both at the time were on their death beds. Not another playwright has been so honoured since 1945 compared to the twenty-four performers who are now Knights and Dames.

Although many of these artists have gained their reputations in the classics – Shakespeare, Chekhov, Shaw, Ibsen – they have also wrenched our hearts and cheered our spirits through the dialogue and speeches of contemporary dramatists. Olivier, Guinness, Richardson, Hordern, Maggie Smith, Judi Dench, Ian McKellan have all lived out on the stage the characters created by John Osborne, Alan Bennett, Harold Pinter, Peter Shaffer, Tom Stoppard, Robert Bolt, Simon Gray and Alan Ayckbourn.

Among this cornucopia of dramatists whose work is admired and performed throughout the world, is it not a scandal that not one of them has been deemed worthy of the same honours and accolades as those whose fame has been achieved only through their talents?

As Honours list after Honours list – two a year – followed on after that, it was quite evident that my fulminations about this state of affairs had not made the slightest impact on those curious beings who were responsible for deciding which of our artists should be acclaimed by the nation and which should not. Performers continued to pepper the lists – Diana Rigg, Derek Jacobi, Robert Stephens, but no playwrights.

The death of John Osborne early in 1995 gave me an opportunity to attack, once again, the anonymous custodians of the Honours system.

The Times devoted three full pages to his death and it was the main news on the front page of the Daily Mail. Every national paper and TV and radio bulletins considered it to be amongst the most important news event of the day. Not since the death of Noel Coward and Bernard Shaw has so much media attention been focused on a British playwright.

His writings were acclaimed as 'breaking the mould,' 'a blazing comet whose fall leaves us all poorer,' 'a new force who caught the rebellious spirit of his age.' But where in this consensus was there any evidence that either the cultural establishment or the state shared such admiration? Had Osborne, by dying unexpectedly, foiled the honours system of its churlish practice of knighting dramatists only when they were suffering from some terminal illness as in the case of Noel Coward and Terence Rattigan?

In 1994 when Derek Jacobi had been knighted and Diana Rigg made a Dame, I listed once again the eminent playwrights, including Osborne, who had been insulted by establishment neglect. The scandal of Osborne going to his grave without being honoured by his country had provoked some support for my campaign.

'A less modest man might have been more puzzled by the complete absence of any official recognition of his contribution to the English language and the British theatre in particular,' commented the Spectator, for which journal Osborne had been a frequent contributor. 'John Osborne through his writing enriched the lives of others. That is a far greater achievement and is a far greater honour than any which the state can bestow.'

But the most ironic aspect of the following honours list was that, while no playwrights were on it, another actor had been added to the twenty-five thespians so ennobled since the war. He was Robert Stephens, who in 1958 was acclaimed in his first leading role in a play called *Epitaph for George Dillon*. Its author? John Osborne.

In 1996 it seemed a glimmer of light had at last broken through the opaque minds of those responsible for artists' honours. Alan Ayckbourn was knighted. And in 1997, with a fresh Labour government, it seems that at last the insensate prejudice against dramatists has been lifted. Tom Stoppard was knighted.

* * *

Having interrogated many of Germany's senior war commanders, some of whom were tried and convicted of war crimes, and having been born a Jew, it was natural that I would take a close interest in the many war crimes trials that took place in Israel, Canada, France and other bolt-holes in which guilty military men tried to live out their days in secrecy and disguise.

My first contact with the atmosphere of irrational hate that would envelop any trial of a suspected war criminal carried out in Britain took place in a studio discussion at Central TV's studio in Birmingham in May 1991. The subject was whether the Commons had been right in passing a war crimes bill designed to prosecute suspected Nazi murderers living in Britain. The atmosphere was highly charged and very emotional.

In the audience were relatives of Jews murdered in concentration camps and they were in no mood to listen to my contention that such a trial fifty years after the event smacked more of a desire for vengeance than a plea for justice. There were only three of us, in a packed audience of almost 100, who argued that such a piece of retrospective legislation – which was trying non-British citizens for crimes committed against non-British people which had taken place outside of Britain – was totally alien to our courts. We also insisted that finding geriatric witnesses to identify defendants over eighty-years-old would probably result in an expensive, futile fiasco.

We were only reiterating the case put more elegantly in the House of Lords by almost every senior law lord who spoke. But the Lords, opposed by Mrs Thatcher in the Commons using its power under the

Parliament Act to chuck out their devastating logic, could not prevail.

That Birmingham studio audience howled with derision when I pointed out that even in Israel they could not convict John Demjanjuk, imprisoned for seven years and then released because of mistaken identity, and that the same unreliability of such dated evidence would almost certainly result in acquittals in a British court. At that moment reason was certainly in short supply in that debate.

But then an elderly, white-haired man in the front row spoke up. He said he was one of those under investigation and his only offence was that he was an ordinary soldier in a unit listed as having been involved in atrocities. He knew nothing of such crimes and was completely innocent.

His words changed the entire atmosphere. One could feel a chill of uneasiness in the audience. There was no longer such certainty that mistakes would not occur. It was this demonstration of how quickly a British crowd could shift from certainty to doubt that convinced me that the chances of getting a conviction in any future war crimes trial in this country, because of the unreliability of the evidence and a jury's sense of fair play, would be almost nil.

But in pursuance of this aberrant Act, a war crimes unit of fourteen police officers and seven civilians was set up. In three years these investigators had visited almost a dozen countries at the cost of 5 million pounds by February 1994, without discovering enough evidence to make a single charge. At first it was claimed 363 cases were being reviewed, which swiftly dwindled to sixty-seven, with death and lack of evidence shrinking the list almost daily.

At last the labours of such a mighty mountain brought forth one tiny mouse in the shape of Szymon Serafinowicz, an eighty-four-year-old retired carpenter living in Banstead, Surrey, who stoutly maintained his innocence. The mere charge showed the Press at its most arrogant exhibiting contempt for British justice by displaying his photograph under screaming headlines which, by implication, branded him a mass murderer even before a trial had begun. When suspicion first alighted on Britain's first alleged war criminal, there were veiled allegations that he would be charged with murdering thousands of men, women and children in Byelorussia in 1941. By the time he was actually indicted, the figure had been reduced to less than five. Serafinowicz died on 12 August 1997.

The men convicted at Nuremberg in 1946 were intimately connected with decisions that led to murders of millions in an immoral war. With the passage of time most of the top echelon of Nazi monsters have either been captured or executed like Eichmann, while Klaus Barbie died in prison and Martin Bormann successfully escaped his pursuers and probably died in Paraguay. John Demjanjuk in Israel, Ivan Polynkhovich in Australia, Imre Pinta in Canada were all charged with horrendous atrocities and found not guilty after lengthy and costly trials.

'Britain's entrance into the war crimes exercise marks a deterioration in the stature and authority of those still being pursued,' I wrote in my column in July, 1995. 'Serafinowicz was the commandant of a village police force in Byelorussia when he allegedly murdered four unknown Jews between 1941 and 1942. His rank was probably equivalent to that of a lieutenant and it is depressing to realize that the same awesome paraphernalia of justice that was deployed at Nuremberg is now being set in motion in Britain fifty years on to put on trial pygmy figures like junior officers.

'Most senior judges during the Lords debate argued strenuously against the morality of the War Crimes Act. By giving our courts the right to try a non-Briton for a crime against another non-Briton in a foreign land over which we have no jurisdiction is equivalent to justifying the right of the Iranian courts to carry out a death sentence against a non-Iranian, Salman Rushdie, who committed no crime in Iran or against any Iranian subject.

'Should Serafinowicz appear for trial there are a number of defences he might rely on, such as mistaken identity or that he was obeying the orders of a superior officer. Photographs of the young Serafinowicz in uniform in 1941, which I have seen, bear little resemblance to the puny, bent eighty-four-year-old figure we see now, nor does the description of him as "a tall man with an imposing presence" match up with the frail figure recently arrested. No doubt, however, the prosecution believes it has the right man.

'The defence of "obeying orders" has been deemed not good enough even if death was a certain consequence of not doing what was demanded. Yet when the playwright William Douglas Home took a moral stand against the bombing of Le Havre by our planes in 1944 because it would kill innocent French civilians, he was told by the British that his first duty was to obey orders and not his conscience.'

As was evident to anyone not blinded by prejudice, the case of Szymon Serafinowicz eventually collapsed. In January 1996, just before his trial was to begin, the prosecuting authorities claimed he was not physically fit to face the ardours of a long trial. It was said he was suffering from Alzheimer's disease. He died on 12 August 1997. Something like six or seven million pounds of taxpayers' money was lost pursuing a fond hope by anti-Nazi pressure groups that Britain would come up with at least one war criminal, no matter how petty and how much British justice had to be bent to achieve it.

One might think that the humiliation of this fiasco would see the abolition of the War Crimes Unit which the Scots had done, many months before. But no. On 1 June 1997, the *Sunday Times* reported that a second alleged war criminal, Andrzej Sawoniuk, aged seventy-seven, now living in East London, has been questioned about the mass murder of Jews in Byelorussia. Considerable costs have already been involved since the Crown Prosecution has had lawyers in Byelorussia for some time, hunting for witnesses. Sawoniuk obviously denies the allegations. And it could well be that the taxpayers are going to be burdened with a few more million pounds of wasted money pursuing vengeance instead of justice. Can one hope that Mr Blair's government will see the light and abandon this bureaucratic farce?

★ ★ ★

When I finally ended my days as a critic and columnist on the *Evening Standard* after almost fifty years, I found it difficult selecting the right words and stance to accompany the ending of my column and my final appearance as a regular contributor. I made an attempt to make a graceful exit through humour on 16 February 1996:

> Journalists' goodbyes are always in peril of being sentimental or pompous. I have therefore decided to go out on a jaunty note with my hat at a rakish angle, a cigarette dangling loosely from my lips, refusing a blindfold and, with a cynical smile, telling three of my favourite jokes.
>
> A sense of humour was one of the weapons we used to defend ourselves against the Axis powers in the Second World War. We fought the early years of the struggle with songs like 'We're going to Hang Out Our Washing on the Siegfried Line' and, to the tune of Colonel Bogey: 'Hitler has only got one ball, Goering has two but very small ... Himmler has something similar, and poor old Goebbels has no balls at all.'

But while we melodiously ridiculed the Wehrmacht, we knew in our hearts that the Germans were a formidable enemy. The Italians, on the other hand, were never taken seriously by us as an impressive military nation. It was reported recently that a jumpy Italian pilot had baled out too early and wrecked a £20 million Tornado. Angry RAF chiefs want to bar Italian aircrews from an exchange scheme because, it is claimed, they are too temperamental and their performance leaves much to be desired. That nothing much has changed about our assessment of Italian airmen is illustrated by the story we used to pass around in 1943. The Italians possessed a newly designed plane for airborne operations and parachute drops. It had a crew of sixteen. They were a pilot, a co-pilot, a navigator, a gunner, a parachutist – and eleven men to push him out.

. The reputation of English tailoring is not as pre-eminent as it once was but there are still many foreigners who look upon a Savile Row suit as the epitome of taste and social success. Last week there appeared two advertisements discreetly announcing sales of suits with the English look and clothing proclaimed to be the essential British kit. When Goldberg met the rabbi in Piccadilly, it was evident that the rabbi would have been intrigued by such advertisements.

'Goldberg,' said the rabbi, 'I have never failed to be impressed by how you always look like an Englishman. I, too, have wanted to be taken for an Englishman. What is your secret? How do you do it?

'It's all a matter of clothes,' said Goldberg. 'If you buy the right material from the right places, you, too, could look like an Englishman.'

'Which shops, Goldberg? Which people? Tell me. I have a pencil and paper and I will write them down.'

Goldberg explained. 'First of all, of course, you must shave off your long beard and give up the black suit and hat you are wearing. You then buy your suits at Huntsman, hats at Herbert Johnson, shoes at Lobb's, shirts at New & Lingwood, ties at Turnbull & Asser, slippers at Fortnum's, socks at Harrods, and umbrellas in the Burlington Arcade. If you follow those instructions you'll be taken for an Englishman anywhere.

Six months later Goldberg sees the rabbi in Piccadilly again. The rabbi is transformed. He is wearing a bowler hat, a pin-striped suit, an impeccable shirt and tie and carries a furled umbrella.

'I hardly recognised you,' says Goldberg, astonished at the figure before him. 'You are the rabbi, aren't you? You look exactly like an Englishman.'

'Thank you, Goldberg. It is all due to your advice. I owe you a deep debt of gratitude.'

'But, rabbi,' says Goldberg, peering at him. 'You have a tear in your eye. You're crying. Why are you crying, rabbi?'

'I'm crying because we lost India.'

I must end on a much told and much appreciated Jewish joke. Mrs Goldberg takes her grandson, Irving, to the seaside. Playing at the water's edge, a huge wave sweeps over five-year-old Irving and carries him out to sea. Grandmother, distraught and unable to rescue him, falls to her knees and cries to God for help. 'Please, please bring him back. He is the most precious part of his mother's life. She will probably die if he is lost. She worships You and is worthy of Your mercy. I, too, pray to You daily. Please, please God, bring him back.

At that moment another giant wave sweeps on to the beach and drops the dripping wet Irving at her feet. She looks down at the living, exhausted child and then, raising an arm to the sky, she shouts, 'He had a hat!'

(iii) Stop The Week

When in 1974 I was first invited to take part in the first of a new series of chat shows called Stop The Week on BBC Radio 4, I assumed I would make two or three appearances in such a conversational jamboree and gratefully pocket a modest participation fee for a programme likely to disappear in a year, at most two. Eighteen years later I was still burbling regularly many Saturday evenings on this peculiar media exercise whose purpose, except listenability, no one has even been able to define.

My only qualification for the invitation was the fact that I was a personal friend of its chairman, Robert (Bob) Robinson, with whom I had had many noisy, amiable, loquacious sessions at dinner tables and in pubs. There were four speakers on the panel and they were usually chosen because Robinson liked them as individuals or its producer, Michael Ember, thought there was some amusing topicality about the issue which we could discuss without committing ourselves to any conclusion about it.

On one of the last programmes we gave our views about Australians and the problem of getting rid of people who didn't want to go. Celia Hadden said she admired Australians because of their tall bronzed bodies and the tiny white socks they wore, while Professor Laurie Taylor suggested that if Jehovah's Witnesses arrived at your door, you should invite them in and introduce yourself as a double-glazing salesman. The irrelevance of these observations demonstrated how little the programme had matured in almost two decades. As one of its first guests I talked about gambling and the pity I felt for anyone who had never acquired the addiction. Other topics in whose insignificance I became embroiled over the years were the nostalgia of custard, the excitement of chocolate, the scarcity of famous Belgians and the ethics of cutting one's nails in a bathtub.

Ember and Robinson dreamed up the topics each week and then tried them out on the selected panel to make sure we all didn't have the same prejudices about it, and to alert us about the kind of reminiscences or anecdotes we might be able to contribute to the mêlée. In about its tenth year I would let Ember know, when he was briefing me, that I wanted to tell a story that I had told before. 'But many years ago. Nobody will remember it. Even you.'

'Tell it to me,' Ember would insist, because he was allergic to stories or jokes he could remember.

I would tell my anecdote, stopping at the concluding observation or punch-line. 'Well, you see,' I would argue, 'you don't know how it ends, do you? Neither will the listeners.'

'Finish it,' Ember would insist, refusing to concede my point. 'I want to hear it all.'

I would then reluctantly tell him the punch-line. 'I've heard it before,' he would snap. 'Don't use it.'

'The conversations were artificial because they were designed to be overheard,' wrote Bob in his Memoirs, *Skip All That*, trying to explain this elusive phenomenon, 'and this may have given us all our fine competitive edge; but I think our main impulse was to entertain each other. Conversation is *ex tempore* at the point of delivery, but you can't simply turn up and hope to think of something. Ember and I spent our lives on the telephone, finding out if the topics we were drumming up were part of a conversational route which would reveal itself as we talked, or were cul-de-sacs leading nowhere. Then Ember would feed it out to the others, acting as a sort of placenta.

'You had to stare hard until you recognized the subjects. Are they the same seagulls all the way across the Channel from Dover: at what point are English seagulls joined by French seagulls? Is it possible to name six famous people called Stan? Why put a shelf up, since someone is sure to fill it with things they didn't know they had? Why is it easy to imagine the pubs in Ilford to be the sort where a man with a sawn-off shotgun rushes in and shoots an old friend? The subjects were almost invisible to the naked eye, the very viruses of conversation.'

The regulars over the years included Laurie Taylor, Ann Leslie, Dr Michael O'Donnell, Nicholas Tucker, Anthony Clare, Sarah Harrison and myself – a *mélange* of academics, psychiatrists, doctors, novelists and journalists. Others who made frequent appearances were Matthew Parris, Tessa Blackstone, Celia Hadden, Edward Blishen, Gillian Reynolds and Stephen Oliver. Dozens of others, recruited from the same milieu of universities and the media, failed to pass the Ember-Robinson suitability test and were heard only once or twice. Politicians were notable by their absence.

There was something paradoxical about the fact that while the programme was derided as élitist and monopolized by a coterie of garrulous eggheads, the subjects it discussed were the essence of triviality.

Occasionally a serious subject was tackled, like coming to terms with one's own mortality or the media coverage of the Gulf War, but neither Bob nor Michael Ember encouraged such descents into profundity. Its essential tone was mocking, which earned it a reputation for being smug, patronizing and infuriatingly clever.

Bob's fluency never allowed him to be at a loss for a riposte and his erudition made him sound like an exhibitionist don fond of intellectual slumming. Bob was well aware of his reputation for non-stop garrulousness. 'It was claimed I talked too much,' he acknowledged in his memoirs. '"How unkind of your guests to spoil your attempt to speak uninterrupted for thirty minutes," someone wrote . . . The thing became a bit of a cult and we got letters saying "We never get conversation like yours at our dinner parties," and I'd write back and tell them how lucky they were . . . And being something of a cult, it was passionately disliked by many who never missed it. "Dear Sir," wrote a listener from Willesden, "I have listened to your programme for the last five years. It's crap. All best wishes."'

In March 1992, I received a letter from Caroline Millington, Radio 4's Head of Magazine Programmes, telling me that *Stop The Week* was in its death throes, and that in a few months time it would be dispatched to that media graveyard in the sky from whence no aphorism or apophthegm ever makes itself heard. The gist of Miss Millington's reasons for giving this veteran programme the *coup de grâce* was that it was in danger of growing stale, although she acknowledged the fact that substantial audiences were still enjoying it.

Its listening figures – about a quarter of a million – were about the same as they had always been. They were higher than audiences on Radio 1, 2 and 3 at the same time on Saturday evenings. One takes some mild sadistic pleasure in knowing that the programmes that replaced it have rarely matched our ratings. Most years they have been much lower. But new executives in almost every aspect of the media – papers, radio, television – feel they have to justify their existence by making changes in what is handed to them, whether or not the alternative offering is a success or a disaster. In some BBC establishment circles, where *Stop The Week* was considered too middle-class and too middle-aged, there was probably relief and joy that the pallbearers had finally been called in.

With its demise went the last of a series of conversational programmes that did not rely on politics, pomposity, controversy, slapstick humour and solemnity for their appeal. Its targets were simply the obvious, the banal and the pretentious. There was always champagne to help lubricate the conversation and the regulars had acquired the knack of opening bottles away from the mikes so that the explosive sound of a popped cork would not perplex our listeners.

I suspect my mild Canadian accent was one of the reasons for my eighteen-year association with this unique programme. On radio it had a distinctive sound which helped sort out my interventions from those of the mainly refined, cultivated Oxbridge-educated voices that distinguished most of the other guests.

This is also where I acquired my wide reputation for telling Jewish jokes – a reputation that helped me to make that light-hearted exit from the *Evening Standard*. There are only about twenty-five very good Jewish jokes and I had to be discriminating in their use or occasionally very lucky in hearing a fresh one. I tried to slide them into a discussion only when I thought some light and apposite relief was needed to prevent a topic from dwindling into desperation.

My central character was always referred to as Mr or Mrs Goldberg and the mere mention of the surname often became the excuse for some good-natured barracking from the rest of the panel as I ploughed my way to a punch-line. The telling of this particular kind of anecdote, with its roots in Yiddish values and manners, needed a specific type of sing-song cadences to bring out its alien roots. Bob tried to tell a couple but never got it right. The others never tried and left me alone to monopolize this specialized brand of humour.

Because the stock of genuine Jewish stories was easily exhaustible –

most Jews acquired an ear for them with their mother's milk – I often converted an Irish or Polish joke by re-naming the traditional Kelly to Goldberg. They were always politically incorrect because they exploited the conventional mockery of popular anti-racial characteristics.

Goldberg tells his doctor that he is extremely worried about his sex life. He can no longer perform adequately and his wife is beginning to complain. 'What you need is more exercise,' advises the doctor. 'I want you to run ten miles a day – no more, no less – for seven consecutive days. When you have done that get in touch with me. I'm sure it will help your sex life.'

Seven days later Goldberg phones his doctor. 'I have done exactly what you prescribed,' he says. 'I have run ten miles – no more no less – every day for seven days.'

'And how is your sex life?' asks the doctor.

'How should I know?' replies Goldberg. 'I'm seventy miles from home.'

This was probably originally told as a joke about Kelly or Stanislaus, but those seeking more of this genre never seem to be bothered by false attribution.

A less dubious joke, as far as its racial attributions are concerned, were the actions of Mrs Goldberg on the death of her husband. At *The Times* Personal Column Department for the announcement of bereavements, she handed in a brief notice saying 'Goldberg dead.' She was told by the clerk in charge that there was a minimum fee of ten pounds for five words and didn't she want to use up her allowance by adding another three words to her announcement? She returned with five words which read 'Goldberg dead. Volvo for sale.'

11

JUST PEOPLE

An embarrassing evening with Peter Sellers and some scrambled eggs ... My daughter arrives in time for a deadline ... Nicola and Jason follow ... Lord Rothermere's yak ... Conversations overheard ... My brother and his medical advances ... Life, Love and laughter

(i) Princess Margaret is not amused

It had been a typical noisy, garrulous, champagne-lubricated party given by Quentin Crewe, the popular journalist and raconteur, for his many friends in the aristocracy, Fleet Street, the theatre and cinema. It was after midnight and the guests were starting to leave his Belgravia flat when Tony Snowdon, Princess Margaret's husband, whispered in my ear, 'Peter Sellers wants us to come to the Oliver Messel Suite at the Dorchester for scrambled eggs. Will you and Drusilla join us?'

Taken by surprise at such a late invitation, I muttered something about not having any transport, to which Tony replied, airily, 'Oh, Margaret will take you. There's room in her car.'

It was 1967 and there were rumours that the marriage was going through an unhappy patch. 'Are you sure she won't mind?' I asked, anxiously. 'Of course not. She's in her car waiting for you,' he said, disappearing.

As a writer for the *Sunday Times*, Drusilla had often worked with Tony when he was on a photographic assignment for its magazine. The Earl of Snowdon, one of the country's leading photographers, was determined to carry on with his work despite being the husband of the Queen's sister, but there were occasions when the proper protocol became a very tricky matter. Suspecting that the princess would not be too keen on extending the evening, Dru was reluctant to come but on my urging we approached the chauffeur-driven limousine in which Princess Margaret was sitting. Through the open car window I said, as deferentially as I could, that Tony had suggested she wouldn't mind giving us a lift to the Dorchester. It was evident she wasn't too pleased about the idea, but we were invited to join her.

At the entrance to the hotel, we were met with an awkward sight. There were two women cleaners on their knees washing the floor of the lobby. To do their job they had flooded the entire entrance with about two inches of water and there was no discernible way of getting to the hotel lifts, even on tiptoes, without getting one's shoes extremely wet. The princess waited for me or someone else in our party – there were about ten of us – to guide her through this minor indoor flood. Fortunately there were about two inches of dry space against one of the walls which had not yet been watered. Since none of the men was ready to, Raleigh-like, throw their coat in front of the princess for her to tread on, we all had to squeeze ourselves against the wall and thread our way through the narrow dry passage to the lifts. If Princess Margaret had been resentful about the enterprise in the first place, this rather undignified beginning to Peter Sellers's scrambled eggs treat added visibly to her misgivings.

The penthouse Oliver Messel suite had been designed by Tony's uncle with all the elegance and panache Messel had lavished on his theatre sets. The furniture was luxurious and the view over Park Lane and Hyde Park at one in the morning was a velvety dark spectacle. Peter Sellers busied himself offering us more champagne and drinks and then went to the phone trying to order his scrambled eggs. He had taken the suite because he was awaiting the birth by his wife, Britt Eckland, of their first child. She was in a maternity hospital and Peter had been told she was not likely to deliver for at least another twenty-four hours.

Under these conditions, it was perhaps natural that Sellers would not be displaying the comic personality of one of the funniest men in the world. As we waited for the eggs to arrive, it was clear that something had gone wrong. The hotel kitchen had shut up and there was no one available to fill Sellers's order.

Instead of announcing it to us with a few quips and a light-hearted apology for the inefficiency of the hotel, and ushering us out after we'd finished our drinks, Sellers was determined at all costs that his culinary demands would be met by the Dorchester. Offering a huge sum of money, he got the chef and an under-chef out of their beds to do their duty in the kitchen.

The bonhomie or his genius as a comic were nowhere in evidence as Sellers either kept rushing to the phone to discover what was happening or sat morosely in a large chair slumped in silence. The atmosphere of frustration and hysteria communicated itself to all of us and conversation was forced and limited. Princess Margaret, tapping her feet with obvious annoyance, waited like a dark cloud hovering over a Wimbledon final. It was after three o'clock when the eggs finally arrived. Never has food been so quickly bolted down and exits so hurriedly made. I recall it as one of the most awkward occasions of my social life. After that, whenever I saw a Peter Sellers film, I reflected how sad it was that a man who could bring so much laughter and joy into millions of lives could find so little for himself when he was not in front of the cameras.

★ ★ ★

I must not give the impression from this episode that I was now moving in the higher reaches of British society. After my marriage in 1956, the parties that Drusilla and I gave, as well as those we went to, had a predominantly left-wing guest list whose appetite for wine and politics seemed insatiable. But after the crushing of the Hungarian and Czechoslovakian uprisings, and the revelations of the Soviet gulags after the death of Stalin in 1953, my ardour for Marxism as a bulwark against capitalism had distinctly cooled. Having recognized that communism was responsible for more mass murders than Hitler, and that tyranny was its inevitable fruit, I became suspicious of all my previous political beliefs and convictions.

I clung to socialism for a number of more years but the unscrupulous use of trade union power and the influence that militants had in the Labour Party in the 1960s and '70s convinced me that democratic socialism was a contradiction in terms, and that repression and inefficiency inevitably followed in the wake of socialism. The incident that turned me off the British Left forever took place during the notorious winter of discontent of 1979, when the unions refused to allow the dead to be buried, and where the streets of the country's major cities were heaped high with mounds of uncollected rubbish in which rats and vermin flourished.

Even in the hospitals small groups of militant cleaners and male nurses formed themselves into committees, taking over the administration and determining what goods or persons should be permitted to break the picket lines surrounding the buildings. A friend of mine had a small import business specializing in canned fruit which would be suitable for hospital meals. His van containing peaches, treated so that they were sugar-free and thus suitable for diabetic patients, had been stopped by the pickets. My friend had to face questioning by one of these workers' councils, was made to sound like a capitalist boss, and then was told that they saw no need for special privileges for diabetic sufferers and had his van turned away. To me this was the petty, tyrannical pass the Labour Party had come to and I never voted for them again.

I began to write columns with a distinctly anti-socialist flavour, such as protests against secondary picketing and the Envy Tax which was driving high-earning authors, performers and pop stars out of Britain. The consequence was that my invitations to left-wing social gatherings became fewer and fewer, eventually drying up altogether.

Drusilla gave birth to our first child, Alexandra, in November 1957. In those days husbands were not expected to be present during the delivery and as I left her she called after me from her bed in Queen Charlotte's Hospital, 'Remember! Roses, jewellery, champagne and foie gras!'

When I arrived the next day, having been told the welcome news at six in the morning, laden with these rewards, I found her sitting up in bed with a cradled Alexandra beside her and a portable typewriter in her lap. She was going to meet a deadline even in these hectic circumstances.

My reactions to fatherhood so relatively late in life were summed up in a light-hearted piece about having a six-week-old daughter at Christmas.

Drusilla has always felt there was an unfair division of labour in the business of child-bearing. Why should father get so much sympathy when all he had to do was hand round cigars? To equalize matters, she decided there must be a fairer distribution of pain. And what more effective way to make me realize the glories of fatherhood than to make me suffer through my wallet?

After paying for a private hospital room, a gynaecologist, an anaesthetist, baby's clothes, a pram, a nursing sister at home and a weekly nappy service, you will understand why my wine merchant, my grocer, my butcher and my bank manager are in for such a haggard Christmas. Even my bookmaker is suffering.

But what Alexandra has done to me financially is comparative bliss to what havoc she has wreaked upon me conversationally. I view with mounting horror the approaching round of cocktail parties where I will be made the butt for baby talk – easily the most boring and repetitive conversation ever indulged in by man.

At first I was most touched by the obvious joy with which everyone greeted my new domestic status. But I now suspect there was method in their gladness. A whole underworld of parents has suddenly surfaced, eager only to chat about their own offspring. To my astonishment, everywhere around me people were tearing off disguises as in some Victorian melodrama and revealing themselves as fathers. Their delight at your child is merely a measure of their sense of relief that they can now talk to you about the subject closest to their hearts. Welcome to the club, brother, and listen.

'How is it getting along?' they ask, and the use of the neuter pronoun indicates they've forgotten its sex already. Before you can gulp a reply they are telling you about the wonders of their child – its weight, its speech, its hair, its wind.

Unfortunately it needs considerable discipline to prevent this conversational rot spreading to oneself. Only a few days ago I caught myself seriously telling someone that Alexandra's right eyeball now seemed to be moving in roughly the same direction as her left eyeball. Is there no cure?

Nicola was born a year and a half afterwards and Jason, my son, two years later. With my increasing scepticism about the efficiency of socialist institutions, I decided that, as far as my family was concerned, I would pay privately for their health and educational needs. I reconciled this action with the remnants of my left-wing beliefs by assuaging my conscience with the argument that by opting out of the state system while still contributing to it with my taxes, I was contributing double, while not using them, to the overall resources of the Welfare State. Why should anyone complain?

The girls' education at small, private primary schools like Lady Eden's was good enough to gain them admittance to St Paul's Girls' School, a secondary school with high educational standards. Nicola, in spite of acquiring an unparalleled record for late attendances and complaints by some of her teachers as a disruptive element, settled down in her final year to study for Oxford and was accepted as one of the first women admitted to Corpus Christi. Her other distinction was that

The family in a happy mood

Alexandra and Nicola as teenagers

during the holidays she was taken on as a cat-walk model for Jean Muir, and as a photographer's model for the agency Models One.

Alexandra, not particularly keen on striving for a higher education, was talked into going to Sussex University where she acquired a degree in anthropology. Jason revealed not the remotest interest in pursuit of 'O' or 'A' levels but displayed exceptional talent in the fields of art and design. His work was good enough to get him a three-year course and an honours degree at the London College of Printing.

When Alexandra was fourteen she told me that none of them wanted to be journalists like her parents because it was 'too much hard work and not enough money'. They are all, more or less, journalists now. Alexandra is the editor of British *Vogue*, has a son and is married to an American writer, Paul Spike, who was given the job, as editor, of keeping the magazine, *Punch*, from extinction. Nicola married Constantine, the Earl of Mulgrave, and when his father died in 1994 she became the Marchioness of Normanby. Nicola is much in demand as a perceptive book reviewer and ironic essayist and pursues her writing career in spite of the demands of three small children and a large Yorkshire estate. Constantine, too, has written two well-received novels.

Jason quickly moved up the ladder of magazine art design and has been Art Director of *Harpers & Queen* and the *Sunday Telegraph* magazine. For a short spell in 1997 he became art director of a new fashion and art magazine called *Frank*. He is married to Susan Aurora Irvine who is also a journalist, specializing in the mores and history of beauty and cosmetics. We have naturally been dubbed as a Media Mafia but, like everything important in my life, there was never any plan, purpose or pressure that brought about this familial state of affairs. It's all been an Accident.

(ii) Preep

Since as a theatre critic I had to be ensconced in my stalls seat before 7 pm most nights, I had few opportunities to spend much time with my children before they went to bed, when they were small. On week-ends, however, I either read them bedtime stories or made them up.

The tale that they took an inordinate delight in listening to night after night was one of many I had invented myself. Preep lived with his family on the top of Nelson's Column in Trafalgar Square. When Papa Pigeon first saw him coming out of an egg, he was so startled by the ungainly, long beaked, oddly-coloured look of his latest offspring that he

Journalist and book critic, Nicola.

Jason, designer and art director

shouted 'Preposterous!' The long word stuck to him but was shortened to 'Preep' which all his family called him.

Preep turned out to be the sunniest and merriest pigeon in the Square and gave much delight to children who wanted to be photographed with him. He could flutter his wings while standing on their fingertips or fly up and down while landing gently on their heads. He was the most popular bird in the Square and the photographer's pet, because the pictures they took with Preep were always sold.

One day an unemployed chef kidnapped Preep, planning to fatten him up to be turned into pigeon pie. Papa Pigeon, desperate to get his son back, decided to do what he had often seen humans do in the Square. He assembled all the pigeons in London and made a speech to them from the foot of Nelson's Column, calling upon them to stop playing with any children until Preep was returned. The newspapers ran the story about the disappearance of London's pigeons on their front pages and the photographers complained bitterly about the situation because they were not able to earn any money. Inevitably there was a happy ending when Preep was returned by the chef to Trafalgar Square.

I paid a young illustrator to do me four drawings about Preep, which were promising although she didn't capture the distinctive physical qualities of a pigeon. Four publishers turned it down. They all agreed it had a good story line but they balked at the idea of a strike, which they felt was too arcane a concept for small children to grasp.

I had more or less given it up when I met an agent who had represented some very successful children's authors. He was trying to sell me a series of TV cartoons based on one of his client's books. Buying that sort of material was one of my jobs at Granada TV. I suspect he was trying to ingratiate himself as part of his salesman's pitch when I mentioned my attempts to sell Preep. Skimming through the story in my office, he said he thought he could sell it in America.

The head of children's books at Random House, who later became its chairman, was enchanted by Preep, bought it and commissioned one of their most popular children's artists, Dale Maxey, to illustrate it. Collins, who had originally rejected it because it was unsuitable, then took it up and William Collins, its chairman, became one of its greatest promoters. It was selected by the Junior Literary Guild in America as its Christmas choice for 1964.

Margaret Drabble, the distinguished novelist, reviewed it when it came out in Britain and wrote: 'The narrative is very powerful and was almost too much for my tender-hearted small boy.' Kenneth Tynan, the theatre critic, complained to me that he had been cajoled into re-reading it night after night by his young daughter, who apparently could never get enough of it. Its combined sales in one year in Britain and America was almost 80,000 copies in hardback.

In the next four years I followed it up with two more Preep stories – *Preep in Paris* and *Preep and the Queen*. The formula was basically the same. They told an incident-packed story with illustrations that showed children various architectural delights and amusing places for children – the Louvre in Paris and the Round Pond in Hyde Park. They sold reasonably well but when I found myself being described in the Press as a 'children's author', I decided to give it a rest for a while.

A few decades later Preep was, at last, out of print. Because I was still getting enthusiastic letters from America, often signed by an entire class of twenty-five children who were devoted to my lovable pigeon, I thought I'd try to revive my publisher's interest in reprinting it.

I had not counted upon an unpleasant, censorious development that had changed the cultural environment for the pursuit of any artistic endeavour in Britain and America. It was called 'political correctness'. Beginning with the admirable idea that the denigration of racial and religious stereotypes must be discouraged, because it cultivates bigotry and intolerance in democratic societies, it was taken over by precisely the repressive minds they were denouncing.

These media censors seemed unaware that when the differences between races, religions, or genders cannot be probed, imagination is blighted, laughter is threatened and culture becomes a wasteland.

But for over a decade – and it has not been extirpated yet – these semi-fascist regiments of the 'politically correct' and the 'ecologically pure' have pressurized authors and publishers of children's books to eliminate anything from their stories that might upset the ultra-sensitive.

Of course, it is not a new problem. Back in 1972 Helen Bannerman's charming *Little Black Sambo*, written in 1899, was attacked as racist by a teachers' pressure group. They complained that the story patronized Sambo as a clownish, irresponsible plantation 'nigger' whose greed was demonstrated by the fact that he ate 169 pancakes.

The tales that have delighted and excited children for generations would have no chance of being published today, when Three Little Pigs are excommunicated for annoying Moslem sensibilities and wicked witches are taboo for having satanic implications. Little Red Riding-

Hood cannot possibly be devoured by a wolf, nor Little Miss Muffet be frightened by a spider, without some animal lovers' cabal picketing the publishers for giving un-human creatures a bad name.

The backlash against this do-gooding nonsense seems to have started at last with PEN, the international writers' society, asking its members in August 1992, to send its executive details of censorship and unjustified editing of their stories so that some retaliatory action can be taken. I doubt, however, if much will be done to save my Preep from extinction, because some pious busybodies have declared that pigeons, as a species, are no longer ecologically acceptable.

When I put the suggestion of a reprint for Preep, the children's book director at Collins rejected the idea with the following letter: 'So much has changed since these books were written. The pigeon population of London has increased enormously, and now many people see pigeons as a nuisance and a health hazard. Indeed if all the pigeons disappeared today (as they did in the first Preep book) many people would be delighted.'

I was tempted to reply personally to this letter but took it up, instead, in my *Evening Standard* column in August 1992. 'But if pigeons have become victims of the politically correct bigots,' I said, 'what about the other animals in children's classics that might similarly be doomed because some people thought they were "a nuisance or a health hazard"? What about the rats and moles in *Wind in the Willows*? Because rabbits carry myxomatosis does that mean that Peter Rabbit is to be exterminated? And because many people are terrified of wolves, should Mowgli's adventures with wolves in Kipling's *Jungle Books* be banned?'

To reduce the themes of children's books to bland conformity that will please every timorous crank in the land would be to shrink still further the power of the printed word to compete effectively with TV and the cinema for influence over the minds of children.

* * *

The lifestyle of a theatre critic also meant that I needed some cafe or restaurant that would provide me with a meal after 11 p.m. I became involved with Elizabeth Furse, whose small bistro near Sloane Square offered passable food, mediocre wine and argumentative conversation until the early hours of the morning. Elizabeth, a dark, bustling, middle-aged woman with anecdotes about her days in France as a courier for the Resistance and a manner that cowed anyone she thought inferior, ran her place as something between a shouting *soirée* and an exclusive club whose admittance card depended entirely upon the bizarre and arbitrary whim of the proprietress.

Amongst those who could be found in off-and-on attendance were David Owen, Peter Jenkins, brilliant political columnist for the *Guardian*, the Earl of Snowdon, Eartha Kitt, Prince Merid Beyene, Grandson of Haile Selassie of Ethiopia, Simon Jenkins – former editor of *The Times* and a renowned social columnist, Richard Casement of *The Economist*, his wife Ann Casement who became one of the country's leading Jungian analysts, Kenneth Tynan, David Frost, the novelist Alan Williams, Terry Kilmartin, literary editor of the *Observer* and translator of Proust, George Melly and the horror actor Christopher Lee.

'The prices were what I thought people could afford,' wrote Elizabeth in her autobiography, *Dream Weaver*. 'If they were rich, they paid extra for steak and salad. If they were broke, I gave them spaghetti for nothing. Girls on their own didn't pay. I used an old tea-caddy as a money-box. There was no cover charge and no corkage and certainly no tips. I could not be a restaurateur: I was the hostess and they were the guests.

'People had to sit where I told them, and they were allowed to stay as long as they were talking intelligently – until two or three in the morning, if the discussion was good. But if they were just drinking and silly I sent them home. I made sure the car owners gave the footers a lift.

'The leader of the late people was Milton Shulman, drama critic of the *Evening Standard*, who came in half an hour before midnight after he had seen the play and written his review at the *Standard*. He was much respected for his solid presence and big wise head, his Canadian common sense and dry wit...'

It was through Elizabeth that I met Hugh Millais, the great-grandson of the famous Victorian painter, Sir John Everest Millais. With three small children, the school holidays were always a problem for us because we had no second cottage where they could play during the summer. A series of rented houses in the British countryside was usually the solution, although we had taken them to a house rented from friends in Gassin, a Saracen village near St Tropez, a few times. Elizabeth, who fancied herself as a Mrs Fixit, heard that Hugh's father, the painter Raoul Millais, was looking for someone to rent the small dower house adjacent to his gracious house in the Cotswolds. It turned out to be ideal for us, having a pleasant village nearby with local children for ours to play with.

We were there for five years each winter, Easter and summer holiday when Raoul came to us with an exciting proposition. His son, Hesketh, had been left a large, rambling house by a spinster friend of Raoul's who had just died. But Hesketh was only eleven years old. Raoul thought it would be an ungrateful act to sell the house which was such a personal and generous gesture. There would also be large inheritance and gift taxes to be met should the house be disposed of. Would Dru and I like to take it over until Hesketh, after a spell in the army, was mature enough to decide what he wanted to do with it?

Dippersmoor was located in the village of Kilpeck in Herefordshire. To approach it one drove up an avenue of Dutch elms. It was a three-storey country house, stately and forbidding in its isolation, with an adjacent huge barn whose brick wall was punctuated with parallel rows of crosses for the wind to sweep through. A small section had been built in the 16th century and other additions had been made to it over the years. Inside it was furnished with a well-stocked library, four-poster beds, large fireplaces and paintings of horses and doves by Raoul Millais in every room. We all fell in love with this curious edifice immediately.

An especial *frisson* of excitement about Dippersmoor was the conviction in the village that it was haunted. This rumour probably came about because the mother of the owner, Jane McBride, had been a friend of M. R. James, the Cambridge don and medievalist, some of whose tales of supernatural horror, collected in his famous *Ghost Stories of an Antiquary*, were written at Dippersmoor. I believe it was a collective disappointment that, although we occupied this unusual house for eleven years, we never ever saw a roaming spirit. The closest I came was hearing some eerie sounds that sent chills down my spine and tracing them at four o'clock in the morning to the flapping of the wings of two birds caught in one of the large chimneys. The children were more imaginative about speculative apparitions. One night Nicola, aged about ten, burst into our bedroom, wakening me from a deep sleep with the exciting words, 'Come quick, Daddy! There's a ghost flushing our loo!'

A great friend of Jane McBride had been Lady Mary Clive, whose large, stately home, Whitfield, with its swimming pool, tennis court and gracious grounds became a paradise for our children, whom Lady Mary would generously invite to play there. Through Lady Mary and her son

George, we entertained and were entertained by many of their friends and formed some very close friendships over the years. Because of my reputation as a tennis player – modest but good enough for country house standards – I was occasionally asked to make up a four by Lord Rothermere, who in his seventies was still a keen devotee of the game. Esmond, the father of Vere, the present proprietor of the *Daily Mail* newspaper group, had as his usual participants the journalist Godfrey Winn and two or three other elderly men who had played at Wimbledon before the war. After an enthusiastic session of two or three sets we would be invited to have tea in the grand drawing room at Daylesford, the Rothermere home.

Daylesford was historically renowned for having been the ancestral home of Warren Hastings, the controversial Governor General of India. The elegant house with its spacious grounds had been tastefully furnished with memorabilia of India under the Raj – furniture covered in rich Asian hues, sedan chairs, Eastern carpets and landscape paintings. As I munched on my cucumber sandwiches while chatting to Mary Murchison, the third wife – an American – of Lord Rothermere, I asked her about the long-horned, shaggy-haired animal that was browsing in the meadow beyond the house.

'It's a yak,' she said, and seeing my look of surprise at siting a yak in the Cotswolds, she went on, 'We were at our wits' end trying to find something different for Esmond's seventieth birthday – you see, he has everything – someone thought of a yak, which would be appropriate for Daylesford with its Indian connections. We got a licence to import it months ago.'

On the wall near the window we were standing at, was a painting by Stubbs of a yak. It was a magnificent work up to the best standards of this great 18th century animal painter.

'If you're looking for something for his next birthday why don't you commission someone to paint a companion piece of your yak, to accompany the one you have by Stubbs?' I suggested, not believing she would take the idea seriously.

'What a splendid thought,' she said, enthusiastically. 'Have you any idea who might be willing to do it? A very good painter.'

'The best painter of horses and bulls and similar creatures that I know is Raoul Millais,' I said. 'I'm having dinner with him tonight – we stay in their dower house – and I could ask him.'

Lady Rothermere knew the Millais and asked me to sound out

Raoul about the project. Knowing that Raoul was not keen on any financial transactions involving his work and his friends, I decided that a light-hearted, round-about approach would be best in dealing with him.

Towards the end of the dinner, I told him that I had been playing tennis at Daylesford and over tea afterwards, Mary Murchison had wondered if he would be interested in painting an animal for her. 'I'll give you twenty guesses to name the animal,' I said. Everyone joined in with bulls, goats, doves, peacocks, wolfhounds, sheepdogs, gorillas and no one came close.

'A yak!' I shouted triumphantly when the game was over. I then explained about the Stubbs yak and the plan to have a companion yak painted for Esmond's next birthday. Would Raoul be interested?

There was a long, thoughtful pause.

'I'll do it for a lifetime's fishing rights on the stream that runs through Daylesford,' he said.

'Oh, I'm sure they'll be only too happy to accept those terms,' I said. 'I'm going back to London in the morning. You can talk to her about it, can't you, Kay?' I said to Raoul's wife.

I left it at that and a year later I was again invited for tennis at Daylesford and tea and cucumber sandwiches to follow.

'I wonder what happened to that project about the yak painting by Raoul Millais,' I said to Mary. 'It doesn't seem to be on the grounds any more.'

'Oh, that was a disaster,' she said. 'You see, the yak began to molest the cows on the estate. In order to temper his inordinate physical appetite, we had to have him gelded. But after the operation, it died even before we were able to arrange anything with Raoul.'

'That was a sad end,' I commiserated, and we both agreed that where sex raised its ravenous head, art was unlikely to survive.

★ ★ ★

As in most families with children, animals inevitably became part of the household. A beautiful King Charles spaniel was our companion for nine years until it died. We knew that Nicola would not be receiving a prize at the end of term at Lady Eden's because, at seven, her punctuality was suspect. When she came home from the ceremony on the verge of tears, she was given the King Charles puppy called Rufus to prove that we loved her even if she didn't win a prize. It more than made up for the humiliation of being prize-less.

We were also bound together as a family by our concern for the two goldfish who had been sharing a small tank in our kitchen for over two years. Seeing that they were properly fed was a task that was shared by all of us. We had named them Goldfinger and Goldilocks. One morning we found Goldfinger, the larger of the pair, floating in the *rigor mortis* position of a dead goldfish. There were a few tears and gulped throats and the children indignantly protested when I indicated I was about to throw him into our dustbin. They insisted that Goldfinger be properly buried with full family honours. A small matchbox was large enough to take him and I bound it in black tape so that it resembled a coffin. At a ceremony in Eaton Square gardens, attended by my wife and three children suitably dressed for mourning, I made a brief address recalling the pleasures this gilded creature had given us, and laid it to rest in a shallow grave.

That evening I noticed that Goldilocks, alone in the tank, was behaving in an unusually frantic manner. She kept nosing around the tank, clinging to her own image reflected in the glass. If I turned off the light in the kitchen so that there was no reflection to follow, Goldilocks stopped her circular peregrinations and occupied herself in the centre of the tank. When I turned the kitchen light on, she began cuddling up to her image again.

It needed no fish psychiatrist to tell me that Goldilocks was suffering from the deprivation of losing her companion. She was developing acute paranoic symptoms and it was clear, unless we were to be left with a mentally disturbed goldfish, that we would have to get a companion goldfish as soon as possible. Sex, we assumed, was irrelevant. Unfortunately it was Saturday evening and no shop selling goldfish would be open until Monday.

Working on the premise that goldfish are not particularly intelligent, I decided to carry out an experiment. Taking a carrot, I carved a shape vaguely resembling that of the deceased Goldfinger. Placing a thin piece of wood across the centre of the tank, I hung a thread on to it which was tied to my sculpted carrot. The carrot twisted slowly and serenely in the water in much the same manner as a leisurely goldfish. That did the trick. Goldilocks ceased her desperate infatuation with her reflection in the glass and contentedly returned to her former, non-troubled swimming ways until we were able to replace the carrot with a true goldfish. Whether or not my analysis and treatment of Goldilocks's trauma was correct I do not know, but I suspect on issues like loneliness and deprivation there is not much to choose between the behaviour of goldfish and humans.

★ ★ ★

Although I would resent being categorized as a Peeping Tom, I am plagued with curiosity about what is happening across the road or on the other side of the hill. I will join the crowd of on-lookers at any accident or fire that is anywhere in my vicinity. I was once visited by the police, who warned me I had been acting illegally when I reported on the exchange of police calls that I had overheard on the radio following an IRA bomb explosion. On another occasion I joined in the chase for a suspected robber, whom I had seen flash by me, followed by three panting constables. A police car asked me to hop in and we drove around Sloane Square for half an hour trying to spot him without any luck.

Since I often dined on my own late at night after writing a theatre notice, my ear was occasionally caught by the conversation of diners at nearby tables, and if it was unusual enough I would take surreptitious notes which I thought might come in handy for a short story or novel I intended to write. Elizabeth's Bistro was, of course, a fruitful source for bizarre chit-chat and gossip. There was also the Pickwick Club near Leicester Square, which was a very convenient late dining hole because it was so close to the theatres in Shaftesbury Avenue. The Club folded a long time ago.

Sitting a few yards from my table were two middle-aged couples. The older pair were Americans and it appeared that the other man and his wife did not know them very well but were entertaining them because of some joint business enterprise. While the English woman was animatedly trying to make conversation, her husband was slumped face down on the table, oblivious to what was going on because he had drunk too much.

The woman signalled a waiter. 'Would you please get me a jug of iced water,' she said and continued her light-hearted chatter. When it arrived, she tipped its entire contents over the head of her sleeping spouse.

He shot up as if he had been electrocuted. There was a crown of ice cubes in his hair which dripped tricklets of water down his astonished face.

'Why did you do that?' he shouted at his wife when he realized what she had done. 'Why?' He was doing his best to mop up his wet suit with a soggy napkin.

'You were asleep and I had to wake you up,' she answered, imperturbably.

'Don't ever do that again!' he spluttered menacingly. 'Never again!'

'Well,' she began, 'if you fall asleep ...' Before she could finish the sentence, he slapped her vigorously across the face.

She took the blow impassively and called over the head waiter. The other diners in the restaurant, typically English, kept their heads concentrated on their food, pretending they weren't aware of the undignified raucous going on.

'Luigi,' she said to the head waiter, whom apparently she knew. 'What would you have done in my place? He was fast asleep.'

'Madame,' replied Luigi, bowing slightly and trying to be diplomatic. 'I think there are other ways of waking a man without spilling a jug of water over him.' Luigi then bowed away. His comment not only eased the tension but united the table.

'Cheeky,' said the husband, still wiping his dripping jacket. 'What a nerve!'

'They've no manners these days. They don't know their place, servants,' said the wife. The Americans, who until then had been watching in frozen silence, joined in the condemnation of Luigi and agreed that his remark had been impertinent. They spent the rest of the meal agreeing with each other that the decline of service in London was deplorable. It could have been something out of a comedy by Alan Ayckbourn or Harold Pinter.

* * *

Another conversation overheard at the Pickwick Club had all the ingredients of a short story from the American *New Yorker* magazine. He was plump, round-faced and in his middle thirties. An American obviously involved with some aspect of the film business. She was a baby-faced blonde about nineteen. They were sharing a banquette. He had his arm around her shoulder although she was sitting up straight, not reciprocating his amorous gesture. It was just after midnight and they seemed oblivious to my table within easy earshot.

'Come on, honey,' he was saying, trying to be as persuasive as possible. 'I've got two tickets booked for a late flight to Paris tonight and a room reserved at the Ritz. You've never been to Paris and you'll love it. We'll be back in two days.'

She suddenly untangled herself from his arm and stood up.

'Where you going, hon?' he asked.

'To use the telephone.'

He kept sipping his champagne until she came back in a few minutes.

'Who you been phoning, honey?' he asked when she had sat down.

'My mother,' she replied, impassively.

'Your mother? What about?'

'I've asked her if it's alright for me to go to Paris with you tonight.'

'And what did she say?'

'She's coming here to meet you.'

I've rarely seen a man so taken aback and at a loss for words. 'Coming here to meet me? What for?'

'She just wants to know if it's safe for me to go. That's all.'

'But it's after midnight! How long will it take her?'

'Not long. She'll first put the cat out and get a taxi. About half an hour, I would guess.'

Never having been faced with such a situation, it was clear he had no idea of how to escape from the prospect of meeting her mother.

'What's your mother like?' he said and trying to be casual, added, 'Maybe I'll take her to Paris.'

'Don't be silly. She won't bite you.'

He fondled his drink in silence and then said, 'Did you tell her I was Jewish? I'm Brooklyn born, Brooklyn bred. She hasn't any prejudices, has she?'

'Of course not,' she said, as he continued to babble on, obviously trying to discover whether the mother was genuine or he was being set up for some confidence trick.

There were only a few people left at the bar, but I couldn't resist the prospect of watching what would happen when mother arrived and I stayed on over another glass of wine.

It wasn't long before the mother appeared. She was a short, stout, genial looking woman with a neighbourly smile. She took a chair next to the American, after being introduced, while he converted himself from the Casanova-like seducer to a wholesome, respectable American boy. He was all polite conversation about the joys of London and how wonderful the people were.

'Would you like a drink?' he asked. 'Some grapefruit juice or maybe a sherry?'

'No, I'd like a gin and tonic.'

'A small one?'

'No. A large one.'

They had not yet discussed the trip to Paris when one of the people at the bar wandered over to his table. She was April Ashley, a striking, handsome creature whose sex change from being a merchant sailor had made her a popular presence in tabloid gossip columns. She obviously knew him. Standing at the head of their table, a few yards away, she said, 'How about a late-night drink?'

The American pretended he hadn't heard her or seen her and busied himself with innocuous conversation with the mother, clearly trying to establish his respectability. April repeated her request, a little more urgently. He refused to acknowledge her.

'What the fuck's going on?' said an exasperated April. 'How about a fucking drink?'

The American now realized she wasn't going to go away. Trying to retain his credentials as a trustworthy escort for her daughter, who was saying nothing during all this, he snapped at April, 'Is that the only word you know? Mind your language.'

'Fuck off,' said April, refusing to go away.

'Alright,' said the American, realizing he was defeated. 'Have a glass of champagne.' He poured it out for her and she sat down to join in the conversation. The mother did not seem remotely upset and started to chat to April with a big smile on her face.

It was now well past two. The waiters had placed upturned chairs on most of the tables. I had surreptitiously taken notes of all the exchanges but I realized there would be no resolution to the situation for some time yet. Whether eventually she went with him to Paris or went home with mother, I do not know. I had to leave to get some sleep. I suspect from his deferential and paralyzed demeanour that the American thought better about the consequences of his invitation, and slept alone at the Paris Ritz that night.

★ ★ ★

Contrary to my own professional career which has zig-zagged erratically from activity to activity, my younger brother, Alexander, had never swerved from one determined goal all his adult life. At fourteen he decided to become a doctor, and although he occupied himself with different branches of medicine, he never indicated any disillusionment with his chosen vocation or wanted to become anything else.

Alexander Shulman

My mother managed to scrimp enough money to pay for his fees at the University of Toronto from where he graduated just before the war. He immediately took a bus to Los Angeles, having been robbed of his wallet on the way, and survived on peanuts for three days until he reached the Cedars of Lebanon hospital where they had already accepted him as an intern.

By the time the Americans entered the war, he had become an American citizen and in 1942 enlisted in their medical corps as a neurosurgeon. Studs Terkel, who used the method of interviews and tape recordings of people living through the Great Depression or the Jazz Age to produce some very popular books, had also done one called *The Good War – An Oral History of World War Two*. The interview my brother gave Terkel provides a moving, brief record of a doctor's experiences in battle. He was twenty-six at the time. Here are some extracts from that account.

I was in Belgium at the time of the Bulge. Winter '44. I was doing neurosurgery, head surgery. This German youngster was brought in. He was fourteen, fifteen. Looked like a lost little boy. Hitler was taking the kids and the old men: this kid was cut off from his outfit several weeks before, and he hid in a barn. He was a sad, dirty-looking kid, with a terrible gash in his head. It was actually a hole through his scalp and his skull.

When I first saw him, he was covered with old straw and manure and blood, and it was all caked together. I didn't know what to do with him. What was his injury? We always pictured Germans as having short-cropped hair. It was the GIs who had short-cropped hair. The German boys had long hair, long before our boys did. So did this kid, and his hair was matted together.

As I took him to the operating room, he began to cry. I said, 'Stop crying.' I could speak a little German, and a little bit of Yiddish helped. All I did was get a basin of hot water and some soap and washed his hair. Here was a captain in the United States Army washing the hair of a little German boy. I finally cleaned him up and looked at the wound. It wasn't bad. Nature had done quite a job healing it.

Then he really started to cry. I said, 'What are you crying about?' He said, 'They told me I'd be killed. And here you are, an American officer, washing my hands and my face and my hair.' I reminded him that I was a Jewish doctor, so he would get the full impact of it …

By the time I got to Normandy, several villages had already been captured. We'd just set up a tent hospital. It was unbelievable. I was the admitting officer. We were on the highway to Cherbourg, which had just been captured. There were supposed to be several evac hospitals to pick up the wounded. But something went screwy that day. A sergeant came in and said, 'Captain, you better come out and take a look at this.'

I went out, and as far as the eye could see, for miles up the highway, there were ambulances waiting to get in. We had a four hundred-bed hospital and we were already filled. Then he said, 'I want you to look out there, too.' I looked around and there lying in the field are several hundred wounded. I said, 'My God, what do we do? This is incredible. Sergeant, get me twenty syringes and twenty shots of morphine and we're going out for a walk.' It was a bright, beautiful summer day. The two of us wandered from group to group. Wherever I went, I said 'Are you fellas okay?' They always pointed to some other guy. Even though they were wounded, they were pretty well off compared to the other guy. I did this for several hours around the field.

I had to get in that war. I had a compulsion. Maybe it's because I'm Jewish. I knew how horrible it was. There was nothing more horrible than to see youngsters with heads partly blown off ... I'm glad I participated. My job was to save lives. I was asked, how could you take care of those Germans? Doesn't that bother you? Oh, I started looking at them at first as Germans and Nazis. Then I started looking at them as victims. Especially at the end, when I saw the kids and the old men. Could I blame that kid for what his parents or the Nazi leaders did? It was a terrible, mixed feeling. Why shouldn't I take care of a sixteen-year-old kid that's been shot to pieces?

We only met twice in Europe – in Normandy and in Germany. We patted each other on the back, laughed and exchanged family reminiscences. When he got back to Los Angeles, he took up abdominal surgery. He tried brain surgery for a while but the inevitable high death rate, and having to explain to relatives why their loved one had died after an operation, depressed him too much. He married a vivacious, ambitious girl, Constance Stone, who a few years later became head of one of the major public relations businesses in America. They had two children – a girl and a boy.

I first became aware of Alex's roving medical mind when he sent me a cutting from *Time* magazine October 1961, which had this to say about his cold water treatment for burns:

Los Angeles Doctor Alexander Shulman is a good surgeon but a poor chef. Nine years ago, trying his hand at cooking, he only succeeded in burning it badly with boiling grease. Ignoring medical training which calls for wrapping the burn in a bandage, he plunged the burned hand into a sinkful of cold water. The pain stopped. He kept his hand in cold water for an hour, permanently killing the pain, and his hand healed quickly.

Since then Surgeon Shulman has treated almost two hundred cases of burns the same way. Medical text books ignore the cold water treatment for burns. Shulman found that it was a remedy in frontier America and it is the traditional treatment in Iceland.

Time's account did not mention that my brother had also noticed that airmen in the Second World War that had to ditch or were shot down over the Channel, and were immersed in the water for hours, did not suffer from the intensity of burn damage that was expected. At first this was attributed to the salt water in the Channel, but it is now accepted that it was the water alone, not the salt, that did the trick. The treatment is now prescribed, conventional first aid for minor burns.

After a couple of trips to China Alex became fascinated by their methods of surgery and the theory of acupuncture. He had drafted out a book on the subject but never had it published.

Having suffered a heart-attack in his early seventies, necessitating a by-pass operation, he became an advocate of the use of low-dose heparin – an animal extract – which, if properly administered, achieved exceptional results in limiting certain forms of heart attack. He was a frequent correspondent in learned medical journals in America and Britain, as well as the author of investigative articles about all these subjects.

He continued pursuing his main source of practice, abdominal surgery, until in the late '80s he joined the Lichtenstein Hernia Institute in Los Angeles. He travelled to many major cities in America and Europe demonstrating and lecturing on the mesh system for hernia operations, which has had an unprecedented non-recurrence record – not far off 100 per cent. The method, now commonly practised in most major medical centres, usually means that the patient can return to his home shortly after the operation and need not require a three or four day stay in hospital.

In a letter to the *British Medical Journal* of 28 July 1994, my brother and his associates queried the advice given by the Royal College of Surgeons in a patient information booklet: 'Patients should take it easy after a hernia operation... no heavy lifting for four weeks ... resume full activity by eight weeks.' Were such lengthy periods of convalescence absolutely necessary? My brother thought not. He believed that after some initial soreness, patients receiving a correctly performed mesh operation could be back at their jobs in two or three days. Among 3,125 patients observed over a ten year period, most desk workers were back at work in less than a week. Manual workers averaged seven to ten days. The recurrence rate was under 0.2 per cent.

The importance of these findings for the finances of the NHS are obvious. Instead of the conventional eight weeks occupation of hospital beds, as were recommended at that time, less than half that time would be needed for recovery, with the consequent freeing of beds for more urgent cases and a reduction in disability costs for industry. When that letter was written the NHS performed an average of 100,000 hernia operations in a year. In 1996 my brother was demonstrating this alternative operation, with its savings of millions for the NHS, to large conventions of doctors in London and on the Continent. Early that year he was also still playing tennis – a passion he shared with me.

With little warning, he developed liver cancer and died on 7 July 1996. On his death bed, he was correcting proofs of a book setting out the precise details of the Lichtenstein hernia operation. He insisted that the pages be spiral bound, so that surgeons could have it open in front of them to make sure they were getting the technique exactly right. Three days before he died word was received that he had been made an Honorary Fellow of the Royal College of Surgeons, a most unusual accolade for a non-British doctor. He was buried in a coffin made out of the deep-red wood of Canada's maple tree.

(iii) Finis

Reflecting on my life with its accidents, its detours, its cul-de-sacs, its bumpy patches, I realize that it has had a circular momentum of its own, landing me back, after some four million words, not very far away from where I began. The metaphor that most aptly comes to mind is whirling on a roundabout, occasionally snatching a brass ring if one is alert and eager enough. I am still peddling ideas, causes, reminiscences and absurdities to editors.

'What is the answer?' asked Gertrude Stein on her death-bed, seeking help about the purpose of mortality. Receiving no reply, she said, 'Well, then, what is the question?' I have no intention of probing so profoundly into the secret or the purpose of existence. I leave that to priests and philosophers. After all, that is their business.

It is banal to dismiss oneself as a speck of dust. Nor is it realistic to claim much more. Would a ledger sheet of debits and credits prove any more revealing than a tombstone? 'Here he lies. Spiked at last' seems a fitting epitaph for a journalist who started work when unused copy was pierced and then stacked on a steel needle.

Each year in my column I attempted an assessment of the fortunes of hobby horses I had ridden. Perhaps something similar is appropriate for the end of these memoirs. Let's try. I have written ten books of which two – *Defeat in the West* and *The Ravenous Eye* – deserve to be in print for some years yet. My decades of criticisms about the theatre, films, television and books have provided some amusement and some pain, but I doubt if the shape of any of these art forms would have changed very much had these criticisms never been written. Others may be more objective judges of that.

Has my campaign against violence on TV done much to reduce this pollutant in our society? Perhaps a little. Have my efforts to gain proper honours for British playwrights achieved anything? Maybe a trifle, because Alan Ayckbourn and Tom Stoppard have recently been knighted. Have my vituperative complaints about the holding of expensive, futile, vengeful war crimes trials in Britain, helped bring them to an end? I hope that my voice, supporting the humane position of the House of Lords, may have embarrassed those who are still pursuing low-level, Nazi geriatrics to call a halt. What, if anything, have my columns against the current plans to re-furbish an Elastoplast Opera House in Covent Garden done to encourage the government to do something about this cultural shambles?

And what has gone on in between? People I have loved. Ideas that have enriched me. Friends galore. Places I have cherished. Talk embedded in my memory forever. Surprises innumerable. Drusilla and my children, who have always supported me no matter how daft some of my activities may have seemed to them. Tennis and champagne and bookmakers. Regrets: not speaking French fluently, never knowing how to cook properly, never learning how to play the piano. Despair, but fortunately not too much. And laughs and laughs and laughs.

INDEX

Extracts included with kind permission:
G is for God Almighty: An Autobiography, David Farrer, Weidenfeld &
     Nicolson 1996
Dream Weaver, Elizabeth Furse & Ann Barr, Chapmans 1993
Marilyn, Norman Mailer, Hodder & Stoughton 1973
Skip All That, Robert Robinson, Arrow 1997
All Authors are Equal, Frederic Warburg, Hutchinson Books 1973
Tricks of the Memory, Peregrine Worsthorne, Weidenfeld & Nicolson 1993